Employment Litigation Handbook

Jon W. Green
John W. Robinson IV

Editors

SECTION OF LITIGATION
AMERICAN BAR ASSOCIATION

Cover design by Richard Laurent.

Printed in the United States of America.
02 01 00 99 98   5 4 3 2 1

Employment litigation deskbook / Jon W. Green, John W. Robinson, IV, editors.
        p.   cm.
    ISBN 1-57073-578-6
    1. Discrimination in employment—Law and legislation—United States.
    2. Actions and defenses—United States.   I. Green, Jon W., 1954–   .
    II. Robinson, John W., 1950–   .
    KF3464.E46   1998
    344.7301'133—dc21
                                                                98-23325
                                                                CIP

Discounts are available for books ordered in bulk. Special consideration is given to state bars, CLE programs, and other bar-related organizations. Inquire at Book Publishing, ABA Publishing, American Bar Association, 750 North Lake Shore Drive, Chicago, Illinois 60611.

www.abanet.org/abapubs

Acknowledgments

We dedicate this book to our colleagues who practice labor and employment law. This book evolved from continuing dialogues among the lawyers who practice in this area. These lawyers have assembled their collective thoughts, suggestions, and wisdom.

A hearty thanks to the Employment and Labor Relations Litigation Committee, Section of Litigation of the ABA. This Committee conceived, sponsored, encouraged, and contributed to this publication. The success of the Committee's predecessor book, *Model Jury Instructions: Employment Litigation*, suggested this publication. Recent Committee chairs have included Wayne Positan, Carol Mager, Vicci Stratman, John Robinson, Barbara Evans, and Herb Gerson. All made significant contributions to this publication.

Thanks also to our chapter authors and editors. Input from the management and plaintiff's perspectives, minority employment litigators, in-house counsel, mediators, and others helped provide balance. We express our deep appreciation to all of those listed below for their contributions:

Commencing the Lawsuit
Author—Carla D. Barboza
Editor—Jon W. Green

Responding to the Lawsuit
Authors—Catherine Novack (Mediator) and James R. Erwin, II
    (Management)
Editor—Domenick Carmagnola and Herbert E. Gerson

Discovery
Authors—William C. Martucci (Management) and Charles G.
    Douglas III (Employee)
Editor—Jon W. Green

Experts
Authors—Herbert E. Gerson, Nancy Erika Smith, and Christopher P.
    Lenzo
Editor—Maureen Rayborn

Summary Judgment Motions
Authors—Kenneth Bello, Bruce S. Harrison, and Jon W. Green
Editor—Herbert E. Gerson

Pretrial Motions
Authors—Anne K. Millham and Burton Kainen (Management)
Editor—Wayne Outten

Special Evidentiary Concerns
Authors—Kyle Francis, Nancy Erika Smith, Domenick Carmagnola, and Wayne J. Positan
Editor—Maureen Rayborn

Trial Preparation
Authors—Barbara Ryniker Evans and Jon W. Green
Editor—Jeffrey I. Kohn

Juries
Authors—Daniel C. Emerson (Management) and Samuel Matchett (Management)
Editor—Barbara Ryniker Evans

Trial
Authors—Douglas Dexter (Management), Victoria D. Stratman, and Christine Masters (Employee)
Editor—Barbara Ryniker Evans

Posttrial Motions
Authors—Carol A. Mager and Maureen M. Rayborn
Editor—Barbara Ryniker Evans

Appeals
Authors—Bless Stritar Young (Management) and Calvin House
Editor—Barbara Ryniker Evans

Professionalism and Ethics
Authors—John W. Robinson, IV and Robert J. Truhlar (Employee)
Editor—Barbara Ryniker Evans

Settlement and Alternative Dispute Resolution
Authors—Jody Forchheimer, Christopher P. Lenzo, and Nancy Erika Smith
Editor—Jon W. Green

A book of this nature ultimately requires one or two "push" contributions from lawyers and their law firms. This book is no different. Herb Gerson and McKnight Hudson/Ford & Harrison graciously hosted our editorial board in Washington, D.C. From those hands-on sessions emerged computer drafts of all chapters for final editing. Fowler, White, Gillen, Boggs, Villareal & Banker, in Tampa, took the lead for the next step. Fowler White completed the drafts, revisions, and edits and coordinated publication with the ABA. Deutsch, Resnick, Green & Kiernan provided final invaluable editing and proofreading.

A special thanks to those law firms and their personnel who "pushed" this publication to the end. We single out Pam Mosley and Mayra Martinez, of McKnight Hudson/Ford & Harrison, for their help. Likewise, Margaret Brader, of Deutsch, Resnick, Green & Kiernan, helped immensely. Special thanks to Denise Diana and Glenda Walker, of Fowler White, for their cheerful contributions.

JON W. GREEN
JOHN W. ROBINSON IV
Co-Editors

Contents

CHAPTER 3 **Discovery**

G. CHARLES DOUGLAS II
WILLIAM C. MARTUCCI

CHAPTER 4 **Experts**

HERBERT E. GERSON
CHRISTOPHER P. LENZO
MAUREEN M. RAYBORN
NANCY ERIKA SMITH

CHAPTER 5 Summary Judgment

KENNETH BELLO
JON W. GREEN
BRUCE S. HARRISON

CHAPTER 6 **Pretrial Motions**

BURTON KAINEN
ANNE K. MILLHAM

CHAPTER 7 **Special Evidentiary Concerns**

DOMENICK CARMAGNOLA
WAYNE J. POSITAN
KYLE FRANCIS
NANCY ERIKA SMITH

CHAPTER 8 **Trial Preparation**

JON W. GREEN
BARBARA RYNIKER EVANS

CHAPTER 9 **Juries**

DANIEL C. EMERSON
SAMUEL M. MATCHETT

CHAPTER 10 **The Trial**

DOUGLAS DEXTER
CHRISTINE MASTERS
VICTORIA D. STRATMAN

CHAPTER 11 **Posttrial Motions**

CAROL A. MAGER
MAUREEN M. RAYBURN

CHAPTER 12 **Appeals**

BLESS STRITAR YOUNG
CALVIN HOUSE

CHAPTER 13 **Professionalism and Ethics**

JOHN W. ROBINSON, IV
ROBERT J. TRUHLAR

CHAPTER 14 **Arbitration and Mediation**

JODY E. FORCHHEIMER

Introduction

This is a handbook for employment litigators whatever your experience level. This book is not a textbook about or survey of employment law. Rather, this book deals with the practical aspects of assessing, settling, litigating, and appealing employment cases.

Good lawyers differ on how to handle all cases, especially employment cases. We have welcomed the views of lawyers who represent both management and plaintiffs. We have included various views and suggestions and have provided legal authority supporting those contrasting approaches.

There is no standard recipe for employment litigation. We have, however, explained common litigation ingredients and approaches. You need to customize your cases, using this handbook as a starting point. Bear in mind that just during the years of drafting this handbook, the law of employment litigation has evolved. Our law will continue to evolve. This book cannot replace your ingenuity and resourcefulness, nor can it substitute for your independent research.

JON W. GREEN
JOHN W. ROBINSON IV
Co-Editors

CHAPTER 1

Commencing the Lawsuit

CARLA BARBOZA*

* Barboza & Associates; Los Angeles, California.

I. Case Evaluation: "To Take or Not to Take"*

A successful plaintiff's employment litigation practice requires patience, skill, courage, tenacity, and meticulous planning. Each phase of the litigation process, from the initial client interview to posttrial appellate argument, offers opportunities for success but also risk of failure. No aspect of the litigation process, however, has as much long-term impact on the probability of success as the initial case evaluation.

Counsel can reduce the element of surprise and the possibility of failure by a thorough and effective case selection process. Given the substantial risk and expense involved in litigation, especially for the solo practitioner, counsel must carefully select only those cases that have a high probability of surviving the rigors and pitfalls of litigation. Investing a substantial amount of time and effort in case evaluation can make a critical difference.

A. How Strong Is the Plaintiff's Case?

The case evaluation process begins with the initial interview. Counsel should create an environment that will encourage open and honest communication without fear of judgment. It is best to meet with the prospective client in a quiet, private place and to allow no interruptions. No third parties, including spouses, significant others, family members, friends, or friendly witnesses should be present. Regardless of how supportive third parties may be, they make it more difficult for a prospective client to be forthright, and they put confidential attorney-client communications at risk of disclosure. This is especially true for the prospective sexual harassment plaintiff, who usually suffers from an overwhelming sense of shame and self-blame. Afraid of losing love and being judged, the prospective client may withhold critical information that might otherwise be disclosed in the absence of loved ones. Therefore, the security of a private, confidential interview is essential.

Before conducting the initial interview, counsel should ask the prospective plaintiff to prepare a written chronology of events and to submit it in advance of the interview. This simple request will enable counsel to conduct a more thorough and focused interview and to assess the prospective plaintiff's ability to tell his or her story clearly and succinctly. A rambling, poorly written chronology may indicate a prospective plaintiff who does not possess the communication skills necessary for litigation. It also may be a sign that the prospective client is suffering from debilitating symptoms that affect his or her cognitive skills. However, the fact that a prospective plaintiff may not be able to

---

*See also Preliminary Investigation, chapter 13, "Professionalism and Ethics."

communicate effectively in writing should not deter counsel from considering the case for litigation. Rather, counsel should proceed with the interview and pinpoint the underlying cause before making a final decision. The written chronology also serves the purpose of documenting events for future use in the litigation. Counsel should instruct the client to address the chronology "to my attorney" and to not disclose it to anyone other than counsel to preserve the attorney-client privilege.

During the initial interview, counsel must explore facts relating to both liability and damages. In all cases counsel should obtain the following information regarding the prospective plaintiff's employment with the company in question:

1. date and circumstances of hire;
2. documentation regarding hiring, including any employment agreement, offer and acceptance letters, job descriptions, resumes, and applications;
3. salary and salary increases;
4. a history of positions held, including promotions, demotions, transfers, and so on;
5. representations made by the employer;
6. witnesses to the employer's representations and other material events;
7. employee handbooks, personnel policy manuals, and affirmative action plans;
8. performance-related documents, including evaluations, disciplinary memos, awards, and commendations;
9. facts relating to discharge, failure to hire, failure to promote, or other potential unlawful act, including dates, identity of decision makers, reason(s) given, content of conversations, and persons present;
10. complaints to higher management;
11. grievances;
12. whether administrative complaints and/or claims, such as Equal Employment Opportunity Commission (EEOC) charges and unemployment benefits, disability, and workers' compensation claims have been filed;
13. client's postemployment job-seeking activities or mitigation of damages; and
14. journals, calendars, and/or diaries.

If state or federal law provides the prospective plaintiff with the right to review his or her personnel file, counsel should insist that the file be reviewed. Even if not legally required to provide review, an employer may allow review upon request. If copies cannot be made, then counsel should instruct the prospective plaintiff to create a written inventory of the documents, if possible, contained in the personnel file at the time of review. Reviewing the employee's personnel file before litigation is filed enables counsel to determine whether any relevant documents that were not provided directly to the employee have been included in his or her personnel file. It also allows counsel to create a record of the contents of the personnel file, as of a certain date, which can be helpful if additional documents mysteriously show up in the file or disappear from it.

Counsel should take special care when advising a prospective client who is still employed by the prospective defendant. An employee must still perform lawful and appropriate tasks. An administrative charge of discrimination or a demand letter may make the prospective client vulnerable to retaliatory or whistle-blower discharge. Therefore, counsel must explain the possible consequences of claims or litigation in the workplace. Counsel can reassure prospective clients how to behave properly in their workplaces.

Counsel must also explore the prospective plaintiff's prior employment history, including prior job applications and resumes. The defense typically conducts a thorough investigation of plaintiff's employment record, searching for evidence of a history of dismissals or performance-related problems or evidence of resume fraud that could trigger an after-acquired evidence defense. (See chapter 7, "Special Evidentiary Concerns.") Preparing in advance for these types of defenses by obtaining this information during the initial interview will facilitate early identification of potential vulnerabilities.

Any prior history of complaints of discrimination or other unlawful conduct should also be examined given that the defense also typically uses this type of evidence to prove that the plaintiff engages in a pattern of bringing unfounded complaints or to establish other alternative sources of emotional distress. This type of information almost always becomes the subject of discovery disputes and motions in limine and therefore its potential impact should be considered and evaluated before litigation is filed.

All prior litigation involving the prospective client must also be identified. Routine pretrial investigations by defense counsel include a search of court files to locate other past or pending litigation with the prospective client as a party. If the prospective plaintiff has been a party to a lawsuit, counsel should inquire as to the nature of the litigation, the time period during which the litigation was active, the manner in which the litigation was resolved, and the availability of any court records related to the litigation. Counsel should be sure to identify other litigation similar to that being contemplated, as well as any litigation that involved the disclosure of private information, such as a marital dissolution or bankruptcy proceedings. Again, by taking these precautionary measures, counsel can assess whether any evidence is available to support a defense portrayal of the plaintiff as litigious and experienced in abusing the legal system.

Once all such documents and information within the client's possession have been obtained, counsel should identify those documents that are not in the client's possession that will corroborate plaintiff's claims, as well as those that the defense will likely obtain during discovery. These records may include files of an administrative agency, that is the Equal Employment Opportunity Commission or state equivalent; union grievances; unemployment benefits claim records; disability benefits applications and supporting records; and workers' compensation files, including depositions and mental examination records. If available, counsel should obtain copies of these documents and review them before making a final decision.

In cases with potential claims for emotional distress damages, it is critical that counsel obtain copies of the prospective client's medical and psychological records. At the very least, get all such records for treatment received during and after the prospective plaintiff's employment. Given the frequency with which defense counsel seek medical and psychological records for substantial periods of time before the prospective plaintiff's employment began, the time frame should be expanded to include preemployment treatment records as well. By seeing these records before deciding to take a case, counsel can assess what impact they may have on the case. Medical and psychological records often contain references to the prospective client's employment experiences that could be helpful to his or her case. They also typically include private, personal information that the defense will inevitably use to attempt to establish alternative sources of emotional distress. Obtaining these documents before the defense subpoenas them will also permit counsel to take all necessary precautions to protect from disclosure any privileged or private information that is outside the scope of permissible discovery.

Once all potentially relevant documents have been identified, counsel should focus on identifying potential third-party witnesses. It is not enough to rely on the prospective plaintiff's hope that third-party witnesses, especially those who remain employed by the potential defendant employer, will provide useful information. Due to the fear and risk of retaliation, third-party witnesses are usually reluctant to become involved. Therefore, counsel should make efforts to contact all potential third-party witnesses and interview them as early as possible. When conducting prelitigation interviews of third-party witnesses, counsel should carefully consider the ethical rules regarding ex parte contacts with witnesses such as current and former employees of opposing parties. (See Witness Interviews/Ex Parte Contacts, chapter 13, "Professionalism and Ethics.")

The prospective plaintiff should not be the one to interview or speak to the prospective witnesses other than to obtain their permission to provide their names and phone numbers to counsel. It is best for counsel, a private investigator, or a paralegal to conduct the interviews. Once counsel has interviewed a third-party witness who has provided useful information, counsel should attempt to obtain a sworn declaration or signed statement.

Finally, counsel must review the applicable law and assess the probability of success. One easy way to analyze and test the legal theories of a potential new case is to review jury instructions. If jury instructions are not available on a particular theory, then counsel should review the lead cases that discuss the elements of proof and possible defenses. Once all available information and documents have been obtained and reviewed and all applicable theories considered, counsel is ready to decide whether to **file** a lawsuit.

B. What Are the Plaintiff's Damages?

Given the ever-rising costs and inherent risks of litigation, only those cases with the potential for substantial recovery of damages should be the subject of a lawsuit. Assessing the potential value of a case is one of the most difficult and challenging tasks of the case evaluation process. It involves both objective, quantifiable methods and subjective intangible elements.

1. Economic Damages

The logical starting place for any damages evaluation in an employment case is lost earnings. Tangible hard-dollar economic damages such as past and future lost earnings and benefits offer one method of objective quantification of the plaintiff's damages. However, even this seemingly objective method also has its subjective elements. Counsel should begin by exploring all possible sources of lost earnings and benefits, including salary/wages, periodic raises, car allowances, merit increases, stock options, pension contributions, and medical, disability, and life insurance. Ordinarily the amount plaintiff earned and the benefits received are not disputed. The controversial and more difficult questions are (1) the length of time before the plaintiff becomes reemployed at a comparable salary and (2) how far out courts will be willing to allow future or front pay.[1]

The client will be able to provide much of the information necessary to assist counsel in making a sound and reasonable estimate of the future lost earnings at stake. The client's work history is one of the key factors to be considered. The length of employment at each job, the financial health of the industry, and the economic climate will all have an impact on a prospective plaintiff's ability to find new employment.

Each case must be valued on its own particular facts, taking into account age, education, experience, and the state of the industry and the economy. If finances permit, an economist can assist in evaluating the past and future lost earnings and benefits. By investing in a lost earnings analysis early on, counsel can take the guesswork out of the process.

To assist in defending against a claim that the plaintiff failed to mitigate his or her damages, it is a good idea to instruct the client early on to be meticulous in his or her record keeping of efforts at reemployment. All classified newspaper advertisements and correspondence sent to or received from prospective employers should be maintained. Juries are often suspicious of plaintiffs who remain unemployed for any significant period of time; any doubts or suspicions about the plaintiff's diligence may be confirmed if the plaintiff has no written record of efforts to find work. A journal or diary of leads and contacts made will go a long way in substantiating the plaintiff's testimony regarding his or her diligence in pursuing other employment.

2. Emotional and/or Compensatory Damages

Once past and future lost earnings have been estimated, counsel must determine whether the client is legally entitled to emotional distress damages and the preliminary value of such damages. Although no formula exists for assigning a value to this elusive component of damages, counsel should not underestimate its potential worth. A number of factors must be considered when determining whether a prospective plaintiff has a viable claim for emotional distress damages. First, counsel must evaluate the incidents giving rise to the claim for emotional distress to determine whether they are of the type that one would ordinarily expect to cause substantial emotional and mental suffering. For example, no one would dispute the fact that a rape causes substantial emotional distress. Similarly, if a sexual harassment case involves physical touching of intimate body parts, then it is highly likely that mental suffering resulted.

On the other hand, if the alleged incidents of sexual conduct involve only comments over a short period of time, it will be much more difficult to persuade a trier of fact that such conduct caused severe emotional distress. In another context, if a prospective client is a long-term employee who invested a substantial portion of his or her work life in a company only to be fired for discriminatory reasons, one would expect that client to suffer substantial pain and suffering. Conversely, a short-term employee may not have as strong a claim, depending on the circumstances of the termination.

After obtaining this information, counsel should consult experienced lawyers in the local jurisdiction as to the value of the emotional damage claim. While some practitioners prefer to use a percentage of the potential lost earnings as a guide, this approach may result in underestimating the value of the claim, especially for a low wage earner. Thus, scanning employment jury verdict reporters and reviewing published posttrial and appellate decisions will also be helpful in determining the value of the client's emotional damage claims.

Assuming the facts lend themselves to developing a substantial emotional distress claim, then counsel must determine what evidence is available to prove the claim. One obvious and material consideration is the plaintiff. Often employees who have suffered deep emotional trauma are not able to articulate their painful experiences, particularly in a public forum. It is critical to carefully assess a prospective client's ability and willingness to be vulnerable and to expose his or her wounds. The ability to express such pain must be evident at the initial interview. A tight-lipped plaintiff will usually undercut counsel's ability to recover substantial damages for emotional distress.

Third-party witnesses, particularly family, friends, and coworkers who were close to the prospective plaintiff before and after the precipitating trauma, should be interviewed. They often can be quite helpful in corroborating the plaintiff's experiences and emotional suffering. Often it is more effective to have third-party witnesses testify regarding a plaintiff's emotional distress than to have a forensic mental health expert do so. Given a jury's inherent suspicion of mental health professionals, third-party lay witnesses who can effectively describe a plaintiff's suffering are invaluable.

Additionally, a plaintiff who sought psychological treatment lends necessary credibility to an emotional distress claim. Opposing counsel, judges, and juries all expect that a person will seek treatment if the psychological injury is portrayed as a serious one. If a prospective plaintiff has received psychological counseling, counsel should obtain all treatment records and speak directly to the treating therapist to explore any possible alternative sources of emotional distress. It is best to evaluate as soon as possible what possible sources of alternative distress may arise during discovery.

It is critical that counsel advise and emotionally prepare the prospective plaintiff for the inevitable intrusion into his or her private life during discovery. Few employees anticipate that their medical and psychological histories will be the subject of discovery during litigation.

Finally, it is always difficult at the case selection phase to make a judgment on the potential for a punitive damage award in a case. Given the heavy burden that plaintiffs must bear to be entitled to a punitive damage award, counsel should carefully review the applicable law in the area and refrain from making any early judgments about the value of any potential punitive damage claim.

C. Does the Plaintiff Make a Good, Appealing Witness?

Determining how good a witness a prospective plaintiff will make is one of the most critical assessments counsel must make when evaluating a potential new case for litigation. Counsel must assess whether a prospective client will make an appealing witness based on a limited amount of face-to-face interaction. Strong facts alone will not ensure that a prospective client will be effective. Nor does the fact that a prospective client is highly educated and sophisticated necessarily mean that he or she will make an appealing witness.

Given that counsel must evaluate a client's appeal and character for honesty early on in the attorney-client relationship, it is essential to pay close attention to gut feelings and instincts. Often counsel's first impressions prove to be one of the most accurate measures of a client's appeal. A judge or a jury may have the very same first impressions of the prospective client, which will inevitably affect the outcome of the case.

1. Is the Plaintiff a Good Storyteller?

Regardless of the type of case or damages sought, a plaintiff must possess the basic qualities of a good storyteller. Ideally, those qualities include a likeable personality, an ability to fully describe events, thoughts, and feelings in an intelligent and emotionally compelling fashion, and the capacity to maintain a sense of humor, regardless of the circumstances. Given the primary role of the plaintiff in the litigation process and the substantial amount of information that must be digested by the trier of fact in a relatively short period of time, a good plaintiff must also be able to tell his or her story with sufficient detail without being long-winded.

2. Is the Plaintiff Capable of Demonstrating His or Her Emotional Damages?

As made clear above in the discussion of emotional distress damages, the qualities of a good storyteller must be coupled with a willingness and capacity to be emotionally vulnerable in a public forum. Regardless of whether damages for pain and suffering are sought, presenting a vulnerable and emotionally expressive plaintiff will contribute to greater understanding, compassion, and empathy by the trier of fact.

If damages for pain and suffering are sought, then it becomes absolutely critical that a plaintiff possess the ability to fully describe his or her emotional trauma. This is a particularly difficult task when any of the alleged wrongdoers are present. Therefore, if the plaintiff has difficulty showing emotion in the privacy of counsel's office, then it is highly unlikely, although not impossible, that he or she could do so in a public forum in the presence of the alleged wrongdoers. Without compelling testimony from the plaintiff concerning the emotional and psychological harm he or she has suffered, it is virtually impossible to obtain a significant emotional distress award.

3. Is the Plaintiff Intelligent?

The plaintiff also must be intelligent enough to understand legal theories and to withstand a vigorous cross-examination. Educational level is not necessarily indicative of intelligence. An intelligent, well-spoken, uneducated plaintiff may make as good, and sometimes a better, witness than the highly educated, sophisticated plaintiff, who may appear arrogant or distant. As long as the plaintiff is intelligent enough to understand the basic theories of the case and counsel's instructions, that will suffice.

4. Does the Plaintiff Have an Appealing Demeanor?

An appealing plaintiff is one who appears honest, reliable, confident, and open. Plaintiffs who are prone to express anger, bitterness, and hostility will rarely make a good impression in any context. Confidence and assertiveness are qualities that must be assessed along with the plaintiff's other personality characteristics. If the plaintiff's confidence is coupled with arrogance and a sense of entitlement, then it is not likely that a trier of fact will empathize or be willing to award substantial damages. On the other hand, a plaintiff who is not assertive and confident enough to hold his or her own during cross-examination will not make a good witness and will be easily manipulated by opposing counsel.

D. Is the Employer Financially Solvent?

No matter how strong a case may appear on its merits, counsel must assess the financial solvency of the employer. Only if it is probable that plaintiff can collect on a judgment should litigation be considered. During the initial client interview, counsel should attempt to obtain all financial information within the knowledge or possession of the prospective client. Often clients have copies of annual financial reports compiled by the company or knowledge regarding the current financial status of the company. (If the client possesses financial documents, counsel should carefully assess the applicability of the after-acquired evidence doctrine. Counsel for the employer will more likely than not claim that the prospective client had no right to remove such confidential documents and would have been summarily fired for such conduct. See chapter 6, "Pretrial Motions," and chapter 7, "Special Evidentiary Concerns," regarding after-acquired evidence.)

In addition to finding out what the client knows, counsel should obtain any financial information that is a matter of public record. Private investigators usually offer basic financial histories on a company at a reasonable cost. In addition, other services are available that offer this type of public information at a minimal cost. Counsel should always be sure to explore any hint of a potential bankruptcy filing. A visit to the public library or an online search to review any articles regarding the company in question may also reveal useful information. News of layoffs, restructuring, profit margin, expansion, or other such developments will help counsel determine the question of solvency.

II. Drafting the Complaint:
The Theme of the Case

Once counsel has completed the prelitigation investigation and decided to take a case, the complaint must be drafted. The complaint should be much more than simply a recitation of the necessary elements of each applicable theory. It should be based on a theme and include as much detail as necessary to tell a compelling story and to successfully defeat any responsive pleadings, such as motions to strike, motions for judgment on the pleadings, and motions to dismiss.

The theme of the case should be developed as early as the initial interview. Often, upon hearing a story for the very first time, several possible themes arise. It is a good idea to capture these possible themes early on and develop one or more of them as discovery proceeds in a case. The drafting of the complaint offers a good starting point for the development of a theme. The theme is the thread that weaves together each of the pieces of the story that will ultimately be presented to the trier of fact. A compelling theme will fortify the chances of success on the merits and contribute to a substantial verdict.

During the initial interview, counsel should have calculated the applicable statute of limitations. All timely theories of liability should be considered; counsel should analyze, however, whether pleading all potential causes of action is necessary to prevail, keeping in mind the discovery demands and motion practice that multiple causes of action will generate, and whether a shotgun approach is advisable. In addition, all viable defendants should be named, including individual wrongdoers and supervisors when appropriate if the law allows for personal liability.

III. Venue and Forum

Prior to making any decision regarding the appropriate forum and venue for a case, counsel should thoroughly investigate all possible theories and remedies under both federal and state law. Any procedural differences between federal and state law should also be considered, including the right to a jury trial, the right to reasonable discovery, and trial-setting schedules. (See chapter 14, "Arbitration and Mediation.") To determine proper venue, jurisdiction, parties, and applicable theories, counsel must obtain the following information regarding the employer: name, address, state of incorporation, principal place of business, number of employees, type of business, and organizational structure.

When deciding whether to file in state or federal court, counsel should consider the following factors:

1. the applicable burden of proof under each legal theory;
2. the availability of emotional distress and punitive damages and attorneys' fees;
3. the right to a jury trial;
4. the requirement of a unanimous verdict;
5. the community from which the potential jurors are selected;
6. the trial judges available and their attitudes towards employment cases;
7. procedural differences, including the code of civil procedure and the local rules of court;
8. counsel's familiarity and experience with the court system; and
9. the state and federal appellate courts' judicial philosophies towards employment cases.

If counsel decides to file in state court, any possibility of removal to federal court by the defendants should be considered.

If counsel has a choice of venue, careful consideration should be given to the community from which the jury will be selected and the available trial judges. The prospective client's race, gender, profession, and class should also be considered when determining the appropriate venue.

IV. Relief

All possible forms of relief should be requested in the complaint, including past and future lost earnings, emotional distress and punitive damages, prejudgment interest, attorneys' fees, and costs. The appropriate standard for each form of relief requested should be properly pled in the body of the complaint. Injunctive relief should also be requested, particularly where the plaintiff remains employed by the defendant employer. For example, in a sexual harassment or retaliation case, counsel may wish to seek an injunction prohibiting the employer from engaging in further unlawful acts.

Reinstatement is also typically an available form of injunctive relief that should be considered if the plaintiff is willing to return. If the plaintiff has not obtained other comparable employment and is emotionally prepared to return to work, reinstatement should be requested when available. The practical reality, however, is that few employees choose to return because of fear of retaliation.

V. Appendixes*

Employment discrimination questionnaire
Checklist of Claims
Sample complaints:
- General Allegations
- Sexual Harassment and Retaliation
- Disability Discrimination
- National Origin Discrimination
- Battery
- Assault
- Age Discrimination
- Failure to Prevent Sexual Harassment

A. Employment Discrimination Questionnaire[†‡]

Today's Date: _____ Referred by: _____
Name: _____
Address: _____
_____

Date of Birth: _____ Social Security No.: _____
Country of Birth: _____
Telephone No.: Home: _____ Work: _____

TYPE OF DISCRIMINATION:

___ Age   ___ National Origin   ___ Retaliation
___ Sex   ___ Race   ___ Sexual Harassment
___ Pregnancy   ___ Handicap   ___ Reverse Discrimination
___ Whistleblower ___ Failure to Promote ___ Terminated
___ Not Terminated

EMPLOYMENT INFORMATION

Name of Employer: _____
Address: _____
_____

Phone No.: _____
No. of Employees in Your Department: _____ In Company: _____
Date of Hire: _____ Date of Termination: _____

---

*See also the following forms at the end of chapter 13, "Professionalism and Ethics": Potential Client Cover Sheet, Initial Consultation Confirmation Letter, Consultation Follow-up Letter with Fee Agreement, Disclosure Statement, Contingent Fee Agreement, and Hourly Rate Fee Agreement.

[†]See also Possible Case Intake Questionnaire, chapter 3, "Discovery," and Telephone Inquiry Form, chapter 13, "Professionalism and Ethics."

[‡] Thanks to the firm of Deutsch, Resnick, Green & Kiernan, Springfield, New Jersey, for the use of this questionnaire.

Date and Amount of Last Paycheck: _____

Full Time: ___ Part Time: ___ Title in Last Position: _____

Job Duties and Description of Position: _____

_____

_____

_____

_____

_____

_____

_____

All Other Positions Held: _____

_____

Date of: Last Promotion: _____ Last Salary Increase: _____

Name of Supervisor in Last Position Held: _____

Title of Supervisor(s): _____

Name and Title of Supervisor's Supervisor: _____

DISCRIMINATORY TREATMENT

Nature of Discrimination and Disciminatory Comments/Actions
Towards You: _____

_____

_____

_____

_____

_____

_____

_____

_____

MANNER OF TERMINATION/TERMINATION MEETING

Name and Title of Person Who Notified You of Your Termination:

_____

Date of Notice: _____

Names and Titles of All Other Persons Present: _____

_____

_____

Reason Given For Your Termination: _____

_____

_____

_____

Detailed Description of What Was Stated to You: _____

_____

_____

_____

_____

_____

_____

_____

_____

Did You Receive a Termination Letter? _____

Did You Have an "Exit" Interview? _____ If Yes, Date and With Whom: _____

_____

_____

REDUCTION IN FORCE

Was There a Reduction in Force? _____ If So, When and How
Many Employees? _____

_____

What Departments Were Included in the Reduction in Force: _____

_____

Was Someone Hired for Your Position? Yes ___ No ___ If Yes, Name, Address,
Age and National Origin: _____

_____

_____

SALARY & BENEFIT INFORMATION

Salary on Date Terminated or At Time of Discrimination: $ _____

Description of Benefits Given: _____

_____

_____

_____

Holidays and Vacation Entitled to: _____

_____

_____

Severance Given: $ _____ Did You Sign Any Release or Other Documents?

_____

PROMISE OF EMPLOYMENT

Was There an "Employment Manual"? Yes _____ No _____

Were You Given a Copy? Yes _____ No _____ If Yes, When? _____

Were Any Promises Made to You Regarding Future Employment? _____

If So, Set Forth: 1) Name and Title of Person Making Such Representations; 2) Date They Were Made; and 3) Exact Statements Which Were Made to You:

_____

_____

_____

_____

_____

_____

_____

_____

CHARGE OF DISCRIMINATION

Did You File a Charge of Discrimination With the Equal Employment Opportunity Commission or Other Agency?
Yes _____ No _____ If Yes, Date of Charge and Where Filed: _____

_____

_____

WITNESSES

Names, Addresses and Titles of Persons Who Have Knowledge of, or Who Have Witnessed Acts of Discrimination: _____

_____

_____

_____

_____

_____

_____

Other Persons Discriminated Against: _____

_____

_____

_____

_____

PERFORMANCE EVALUATION/APPRAISALS

Was There an Appraisal System? Yes _____ No _____ If So, Was It Oral or Written, How Often Were You Appraised, and With Whom: _____

_____

_____

Dates of Last 3 Appraisals: _____
Do You Have Copies of Your Appraisals? Yes _____ No _____
Which Appraisals Do You Have? _____

B. Checklist of Claims

1. Statutory
   (a) Discrimination: sex; pregnancy; age; race; color; national origin; religion; sexual orientation; veteran's status; marital status; physical, mental, or perceived handicap
   (b) Illegal retaliation claims under antireprisal statutes
   (c) Whistle-blower claims
   (d) Equal pay claims
   (e) Jury duty
   (f) Filing worker's compensation claims
   (g) Wage and hour claims
   (h) Union organizing
   (i) Worker Adjustment Retraining and Notification Act (plant closing law)
   (j) Employee Retirement Income Security Act (ERISA) benefit claims
   (k) Family leave (state and/or federal)
2. Common law claims
   (a) Employer handbooks and/or implied contracts
   (b) Employment agreements
   (c) Oral promises and/or promissory estoppel
   (d) Covenant of good faith and fair dealing
   (e) Intentional infliction of emotional distress
   (f) Public policy and retaliatory discharge
   (g) Intentional interference with current or prospective contractual relationship
   (h) Defamation (libel and slander)
3. Federal constitutional claims (42 U.S.C. § 1983 and/or *Bivens* claims)
   (a) First Amendment (public employment only)
   (b) Due process
   (c) Equal protection
4. State constitutional claims

C. Cause of Action (General Allegations)

_____ COURT OF THE [STATE] OF _____
FOR THE [COUNTY] OF _____

)	CASE NO.
)	
Plaintiff,)	
)	
v.)	
)	
)	
Defendants.)	
)	

GENERAL ALLEGATIONS

1. _____ (hereinafter "Ms. or Mr. _____" or "Plaintiff") is an individual who is and at all times relevant herein was, a resident of the County of _____, State of _____.

2. Plaintiff is informed and believes, and based thereon alleges, that defendant _____ (hereinafter "_____") was and is a corporation doing business in _____ County, State of _____. Defendant _____ employs [more than _____ employees] [and is engaged in interstate commerce/is an employer within the meaning of _____ (statute).]

3. Plaintiff is informed and believes, and based thereon alleges, that defendant _____ (hereinafter "_____") was and is an individual residing in _____ County. At all times relevant herein, _____ was a supervisor, managerial employee or agent of defendant _____.

4. Plaintiff does not know the true names and capacities of the defendants sued herein as Does 1 through 10, inclusive, and will amend this Complaint to state the true names and capacities of such fictitiously named defendants when such information is ascertained.

5. Plaintiff is informed and believes, and based thereon alleges, that each defendant is the agent, servant, employee, successor in interest, co-conspirator, and/or *alter ego* of every other defendant, and that, in doing the acts alleged herein, each defendant acted as the agent of and with the consent, knowledge, authorization and/or ratification of every other defendant herein.

6. Plaintiff is informed and believes and based thereon alleges that each defendant was in some manner intentionally and/or negligently and legally responsible for the events and happenings alleged in this Complaint and for plaintiff's injuries and damages.

Date: _____   [FIRM]

By: _____
[Name]
Attorneys for Plaintiff,

D. Cause of Action (Sexual Harassment and Retaliation, against All Defendants)

1. Plaintiff repeats and realleges the allegations contained in paragraphs 1 through _____, inclusive, and incorporates the same by reference as though set forth fully herein.

2. Defendants, including defendant _____ through its agent or supervisor, _____ engaged in a pattern and practice of unlawful sexual harassment by subjecting plaintiff to unwelcome sexual harassment, including but not limited to, requests for sexual favors, sexual advances, and physical sexual harassment, in violation of [California Government Code § 12940.]

3. The above-described unwelcome sexual harassment created an intimidating, oppressive, hostile and offensive work environment which interfered with plaintiff's emotional well-being [his or her] ability to perform [his or her] work.

4. Defendant _____ at all times relevant hereto had actual and constructive knowledge of the conduct described in paragraph .

5. Defendant _____ failed to take all reasonable steps to prevent sexual harassment from occurring, and to protect plaintiff from sexual harassment and retaliation.

6. Defendant _____ violated [California Government Code § 12940] by failing to adequately supervise, control or discipline and/or otherwise penalize the conduct, acts and failures to act of defendant _____ as described in paragraph _____.

7. Defendant _____ engaged in unlawful retaliation against plaintiff [by terminating plaintiff] because [he/she] [opposed practices forbidden by California Government Code § 12940.]

8. As a result of the hostile and offensive work environment maintained by defendant _____ and defendant _____'s failure to protect plaintiff from further harassment and retaliation, plaintiff was forced to resign [his/her] employment.

9. Plaintiff is informed and believes, and based thereon alleges, that in addition to the practices enumerated above, defendants, and each of them, have engaged in discriminatory practices against [him/her] which are not yet fully known. At such time as said discriminatory practices become known to [him/her] plaintiff will seek leave of court to amend this Complaint in that regard.

10. Plaintiff has filed charges of discrimination with [the California Department of Fair Employment and Housing ("DFEH"),] a true and correct copy of which is attached hereto as Exhibit _____ and incorporated herein by reference. Within one year of the filing of this Complaint, [the DFEH] has issued a Right to Sue Notice authorizing this lawsuit, a true and correct copy of which is attached hereto as Exhibit _____, and incorporated herein by reference. Plaintiff has exhausted [his/her] administrative remedies.

11. As a direct and proximate result of defendants' actions, plaintiff has suffered and will continue to suffer emotional distress, consisting of outrage, shock and humiliation, reasonably occurring and likely to occur based on sexual harassment and retaliation [he/she] experienced and the employer's failure to take prompt and appropriate remedial action; and [he/she] has suffered and will continue to suffer a loss of earnings and other employment benefits and job opportunities. Plaintiff is thereby entitled to general and compensatory damages in amounts to be proven at trial.

12. Plaintiff is informed and believes, and based thereon alleges, that the outrageous conduct of defendant _____ described above was malicious and oppressive, and done with a conscious disregard of plaintiff's rights, and with the intent to injure plaintiff. Because defendant _____ acted in [his/her] capacity as the managing agent of defendant _____ and because defendant _____ ratified defendant _____'s conduct by doing nothing despite

its knowledge of defendant _____'s unlawful conduct, plaintiff is entitled to punitive damages from defendants _____, _____ and Does 1 through _____.

13. As a further direct and proximate result of defendants' actions, [violation of California Government Code § 12900-12996, as heretofore described,] plaintiff has been compelled to retain the services of counsel in an effort to enforce the terms and conditions of the employment relationship with defendants and has thereby incurred, and will continue to incur, legal fees and costs. Plaintiff requests that attorney's fees be awarded pursuant to [California Government Code § 12965.]

WHEREFORE, Plaintiff demands judgment as follows:

1. For compensatory damages and general damages according to proof at trial;
2. For attorney's fees pursuant to statute and costs of suit;
3. Prejudgment interest on all amounts claimed; and
4. Such other and further relief as the Court deems just and proper.

Date: _____   [FIRM]

By: _____
                          [Name]
                          Attorneys for Plaintiff

E. Cause of Action (Discrimination on the Basis of Disability, against All Defendants)

1. Plaintiff repeats and realleges the allegations of paragraphs 1 through _____, inclusive, and incorporates the same by reference as though set forth fully herein.

2. Plaintiff was terminated as of _____, 199___ on the basis of [his or her] disability, _____, in violation of [Government Code § 12940.]

3. Plaintiff's termination constituted a failure to accommodate [his or her] disability as required by [the Fair Employment and Housing Act,] insofar as [he/she] is able to perform all of the essential functions of [his/her] job with reasonable accommodation. Reasonable accommodation would require the company only to _____.

4. Plaintiff is informed and believes, and based thereon alleges, that in addition to the practices enumerated above, defendants, and each of them, have engaged in discriminatory practices against [his/her] which are not yet fully known. At such time as said discriminatory practices become known to [him/her] plaintiff will seek leave of court to amend this Complaint in that regard.

5. Plaintiff has filed charges of discrimination with [the California Department of Fair Employment and Housing ("DFEH"),] a true and correct copy of which is attached hereto as Exhibit _____ and incorporated herein by reference. Within one year of the filing of this Complaint, [the DFEH] has issued

a Right to Sue Notice authorizing this lawsuit, a true and correct copy of which is attached hereto as Exhibit _____, and incorporated herein by reference. Plaintiff has exhausted [his/her] administrative remedies.

6. As a direct and proximate result of defendant's actions, plaintiff has suffered and will continue to suffer pain and suffering, and extreme and severe mental anguish and emotional distress; [he/she] has incurred and will continue to incur medical expenses for treatment by psychotherapists and other health professionals and for other incidental expenses; and [he/she] has suffered and will continue to suffer a loss of earnings and other employment benefits and job opportunities. Plaintiff is thereby entitled to general and compensatory damages in amounts to be proven at trial.

7. Plaintiff is informed and believes, and based thereon alleges, that the outrageous conduct of defendant _____, as described above, was malicious and oppressive, and done with a conscious disregard of plaintiff's rights and with the intent to injure plaintiff. Because defendant _____ acted in [his/her] capacity as the managing agent of defendant _____ and because defendant _____ ratified defendant _____'s conduct by doing nothing despite their knowledge of defendant _____'s unlawful conduct, plaintiff is entitled to punitive damages from defendants _____, _____ and Does 1 through _____, individually.

8. As a further direct and proximate result of defendant's [violation of Government Code § 12900-12996, as heretofore described,] plaintiff has been compelled to retain the services of counsel in an effort to enforce the terms and conditions of the employment relationship with defendants and has thereby incurred, and will continue to incur, legal fees and costs. Plaintiff requests that attorney's fees be awarded pursuant to [California Government Code § 12965.]

F. Cause of Action (Discrimination Based on Race or National Origin, against All Defendants)

1. Plaintiff repeats and realleges the allegations of paragraphs 1 through _____, inclusive, and incorporates the same by reference as though set forth fully herein.

2. Defendants, and each of them, including defendant _____ through its agent or supervisor, defendant _____, engaged in a pattern and practice of unlawful discrimination on the basis of race or national origin by denying plaintiff promotions, fair salary increases and subjecting [him/her] to an arbitrary lay off and discharge, on the basis of [his/her] race and/or national origin in violation [of California Government Code § 12940(a).]

3. Defendant _____ at all times relevant hereto had actual and constructive knowledge of the conduct described in paragraph _____.

4. Defendant _____ failed to take all reasonable steps to prevent the discrimination based on race or national origin from occurring.

5. Defendant _____ violated [California Government Code § 12940(a)] by failing to adequately supervise, control, or discipline and/or otherwise penalize the conduct, acts, and failures to act of defendant _____ as described in paragraph _____.

6. Plaintiff has filed a charge of discrimination on the basis of race or national origin in employment with [the California Department of Fair Employment and Housing,] a true and correct copy of which is attached hereto as Exhibit _____ and incorporated herein by reference. Within one year of the filing of this Complaint, [the California Department of Fair Employment and Housing] issued a Right to Sue Notice authorizing this lawsuit, a true and correct copy of which is attached hereto as Exhibit _____, and incorporated herein by reference. Plaintiff has exhausted [his/her] administrative remedies.

7. As a direct and proximate result of defendant's actions, plaintiff has suffered and will continue to suffer pain and suffering, and extreme and severe mental anguish and emotional distress; [he or she] has incurred and will continue to incur medical expenses for treatment by psychotherapists and other health [he or she] has professionals and for other incidental expenses; and [he or she] has suffered and will continue to suffer a loss of earnings and other employment benefits and job opportunities. Plaintiff is thereby entitled to general and compensatory damages in amounts to be proven at trial.

8. As a further direct and proximate result of defendant's, [violation of California Government Code § 12900, *et seq.*, as heretofore described,] plaintiff has been compelled to retain the services of counsel in an effort to enforce the terms and conditions of the employment relationship with defendants and has thereby incurred, and will continue to incur, legal fees and costs. Plaintiff requests that attorney's fees be awarded pursuant to [California Government Code § 12965.]

9. Plaintiff is informed and believes, and based thereon alleges, that the outrageous conduct of defendant _____ described above was malicious and oppressive, and done with a conscious disregard of plaintiff's rights, and with the intent to injure plaintiff. Because defendant _____ acted in [his/her] capacity as the managing agent of defendant _____ and because defendant _____ ratified defendant _____'s conduct by doing nothing despite its knowledge of defendant _____'s unlawful conduct, plaintiff is entitled to punitive damages from defendants _____, _____, and Does 1 through _____, individually.

G. Cause of Action (Battery against All Defendants)

1. Plaintiff repeats and realleges the allegations contained in paragraphs 1 through _____, inclusive, and incorporates the same by reference as though set forth fully herein.

2. As described more fully above, defendant _____ subjected plaintiff to repeated, nonconsensual and intentional invasions of [his/her] right to be free from offensive and harmful physical contact.

3. As a direct and proximate result of defendants' actions, plaintiff has suffered and will continue to suffer pain and suffering, and extreme and severe

mental anguish and emotional distress; [he/she] has incurred and will continue to incur medical expenses for treatment by psychotherapists and other health professionals and for other incidental expenses; and [he/she] has suffered and will continue to suffer a loss of earnings and other employment benefits and job opportunities. Plaintiff is thereby entitled to general and compensatory damages in amounts to be proven at trial.

4. Plaintiff is informed and believes, and based thereon alleges, that the outrageous conduct of defendant _____, as described above, was malicious and oppressive, and done with a conscious disregard of plaintiff's rights and with the intent to injure plaintiff. Because defendant _____ acted in [his/her] capacity as the managing agent of defendant _____ and because defendant _____ ratified defendant _____'s conduct by doing nothing despite their knowledge of defendant _____'s unlawful conduct, plaintiff is entitled to punitive damages from defendants _____, _____, and Does 1 through _____, individually.

H. Cause of Action (Assault against All Defendants)

1. Plaintiff repeats and realleges the allegations contained in Paragraphs 1 through _____, inclusive, and incorporates the same by reference as though set forth fully herein.

2. Defendant _____'s conduct as described above, caused plaintiff to constantly be apprehensive that defendant _____ would subject [him/her] to intentional invasions of [his/her] right to be free from offensive and harmful conduct and demonstrated that at all times material herein, defendant had a present ability to subject [him/her] to an intentional offensive and harmful touching.

3. As a direct and proximate result of defendants' actions, plaintiff has suffered and will continue to suffer pain and suffering, and extreme and severe mental anguish and emotional distress; [he/she] has incurred and will continue to incur medical expenses for treatment by psychotherapists and other health professionals and for other incidental expenses; and [he/she] has suffered and will continue to suffer a loss of earnings and other employment benefits and job opportunities. Plaintiff is thereby entitled to general and compensatory damages in amounts to be proven at trial.

4. Plaintiff is informed and believes, and based thereon alleges, that the outrageous conduct of defendant _____ as described above was malicious and oppressive, and done with a conscious disregard of plaintiff's rights, and with the intent to injure plaintiff. Because defendant _____ acted in [his/her] capacity as the managing agent of defendant _____ and because defendant _____ ratified defendant _____'s conduct by doing nothing despite its knowledge of defendant _____'s unlawful conduct, plaintiff is entitled to punitive damages from defendants _____, _____, and Does 1 through _____, individually.

I. Cause of Action (Age Discrimination in Employment, against All Defendants)

1. Plaintiff repeats and realleges the allegations contained in paragraphs 1 through _____, inclusive, and incorporates the same by reference as though set forth fully herein.

2. Plaintiff was subjected to discrimination in the terms and conditions of employment because of [his or her] age as described above.

3. The above-described age discrimination against plaintiff violates plaintiff's right to be free from age discrimination in employment guaranteed to [him or her] [by California Government Code § 12900-12996.]

4. Defendant _____ at all times relevant hereto had actual and constructive knowledge of the conduct described in paragraph _____.

5. Defendant _____ failed to take all reasonable steps to prevent the discrimination based on age from occurring.

6. Defendant _____ violated [California Government Code § 12940(a)] by failing to adequately supervise, control, or discipline and/or otherwise penalize the conduct, acts, and failures to act of defendant _____ as described in paragraph _____.

7. Plaintiff has obtained from [the California Department of Fair Employment and Housing ("DFEH"),] a true and correct copy of which is attached hereto as Exhibit _____ and incorporated herein by reference. Within one year of the filing of this Complaint, [the DFEH] has issued a Right to Sue Notice authorizing this lawsuit, a true and correct copy of which is attached hereto as Exhibit _____, and incorporated herein by reference. Plaintiff has exhausted [his or her] administrative remedies.

8. As a direct and proximate result of defendants' actions, plaintiff has suffered and will continue to suffer pain and suffering, and extreme and severe mental anguish and emotional distress; [he or she] has incurred and will continue to incur medical expenses for treatment by psychotherapists and other health professionals and for other incidental expenses; and [he or she] has suffered and will continue to suffer a loss of earnings and other employment benefits and job opportunities. Plaintiff is thereby entitled to general and compensatory damages in amounts to be proven at trial.

9. Plaintiff is informed and believes, and based thereon alleges, that the outrageous conduct of defendant _____ described above was malicious and oppressive, and done with a conscious disregard of plaintiff's rights, and with the intent to injure plaintiff. Because defendant _____ acted in [his or her] capacity as the managing agent of defendant _____ and because defendant _____ ratified defendant _____'s conduct by doing nothing despite its knowledge of defendant _____'s unlawful conduct, plaintiff is entitled to punitive damages from defendants _____, _____ and Does 1 through _____, individually.

10. As a further direct and proximate result of defendants' violation [of California Government Code § 12900, *et seq.*, as heretofore described,] plaintiff

has been compelled to retain the services of counsel in an effort to enforce the terms and conditions of the employment relationship with defendants and has thereby incurred, and will continue to incur, legal fees and costs. Plaintiff requests that attorney's fees be awarded pursuant to [California Government Code § 12965.]

J. Cause of Action (Failure to Prevent Sexual Harassment)

1. Plaintiff repeats and realleges the allegations contained in paragraphs 1 through _____, inclusive, and incorporates the same by reference as though set forth fully herein.

2. Defendant _____ [violated California Government Code § 12940(i)] by failing to take all reasonable steps necessary to prevent discrimination and harassment from occurring.

3. As a direct and proximate result of defendant's failure to act, plaintiff has suffered and will continue to suffer emotional distress, consisting of outrage, shock and humiliation, reasonably occurring and likely to occur based on defendant _____'s failure to take all reasonable steps necessary to prevent discrimination and harassment from occurring, and [he or she] has suffered and will continue to suffer a loss of earnings and other employment benefits and job opportunities. Plaintiff is thereby entitled to general and compensatory damages in amounts to be proven at trial.

4. Plaintiff is informed and believes and based thereon alleges that the outrageous conduct of defendant _____ described above was malicious and oppressive, and done with a conscious disregard of plaintiff's rights, and with the intent to injure plaintiff. Plaintiff is entitled to punitive damages from defendant _____.

5. As a further direct and proximate result of defendant's [violation of Government Code § 12900-12996, as heretofore described,] plaintiff has been compelled to retain the services of counsel in an effort to enforce the terms and conditions of the employment relationship with defendants and has thereby incurred, and will continue to incur, legal fees and costs. Plaintiff requests that attorney's fees be awarded pursuant to [California Government Code § 12965.]

Note

1. *Compare* Diggs v. Pepsi-Cola Metro. Bottling Co., 742 F.2d 916 (6th Cir. 1988) (46-year-old awarded front pay until retirement age) with Williams v. Pharmacia Ophthalmics, Inc., 926 F. Supp. 791, 797 (N.D. Ind. 1996) (17 years of front pay held to be excessive).

CHAPTER 2

Responding to the Lawsuit

JAMES R. ERWIN[*]
CATHERINE NOVACK[†]

I. Introduction

    This chapter discusses the first steps corporate counsel and outside counsel should take in responding to an employment lawsuit. The pur-

---

[*] *Pierce, Atwood, Scribner, Allen, Smith & Lancaster; Portland, Maine.*

[†] *Mediator; Tampa, Florida.*

pose of the chapter is to focus the practitioner on some key tactical decisions at the beginning of the litigation, when action will have the greatest benefit for the employer.

II. Selection and Retention of Outside Counsel

Several routes exist for selection of outside counsel. When selecting counsel in specialized areas such as employment litigation, it is critical to engage counsel with a thorough understanding of the substantive area of the law. A good source is either an employment/labor law department within a large firm or an employment law boutique. Research in Martindale-Hubbell, combined with inquiry of in-house colleagues, should allow corporate counsel to develop a list of three to five prospective lawyers. The initial response to corporate counsel is frequently key in the evaluation of potential outside counsel. Corporate counsel should note who answers his or her initial call, how promptly, and in what manner. This evaluation should include the receptionist and secretarial/support staff. The reason is simple—these are the people with whom corporate counsel has the most routine contacts.

During the first telephone call with the prospective outside counsel, it is critical to resolve any potential conflicts of interest. For example, if the outside firm handles insurance coverage matters for insurers and the case has a possible coverage issue, you may need a waiver. If so, determine what format will be adequate to protect the client's needs. Sometimes insurance companies are a bit slow in responding to waiver issues. This delay could affect the ultimate selection of outside counsel.

Fee arrangements, hourly rates, and case billing procedures are often competitive. Therefore, expect a case budget at the outset of the case. A budget in stages (such as responsive pleadings, discovery, dispositive motions, trial preparation, experts, and trial) gives the client an idea of the costs of defense. Such a budget breakdown forces outside counsel to evaluate the potential work and expenses. To avoid misunderstanding, it is important that everyone understands at the outset the purpose and use of the budget. Clients do not usually complain if a case is under budget. Problems arise as to who pays and how much if the case exceeds the budget.

This chapter is not a discourse on fee options. Everyone should be aware of the variety of fee agreements, including the flat or case fee. Fee arrangements and budgets lead right into discussions of how to prepare bills, how often, and so on. Budgets often include an initial evaluation of case handling strategy with regular updates.

Strategy discussions should include whether corporate or outside counsel will interview corporate witnesses, what depositions are likely, and expert issues. Outside counsel usually evaluate liability in percentages of risk. However, "all or nothing" and 50/50 estimations rarely help. All lawyers know that guarantees are impossible and that juries can do anything, but counsel should attempt to give some meaningful assessments, however qualified or subject to revision. An employer wants outside counsel who is familiar with the local court system, judges, and jury pool, as well as the law, so that outside counsel can handle the defense most effectively and efficiently.

Corporate counsel will want to know about the outside firm. Usually one designated outside lawyer will handle or be responsible for the case. Other identified lawyers and staff will work on the case at approved rates. Because corporate counsel and outside counsel constitute the defense, a key question is how team oriented the outside firm is. This can be critical if corporate counsel intends to be an active manager of the case.

The selection of outside counsel can be quite a difficult process, especially if there are several good choices. Therefore, corporate counsel should be prepared to conduct personal interviews. Corporate counsel, corporate managers, and outside counsel must all work together productively and cooperatively. Upon selection, an engagement letter is a good practice. (See sample retention letters at the end of this chapter and at the end of chapter 13, "Professionalism and Ethics.")

After selecting outside counsel, it is important to establish procedures for working together on an ongoing basis. In this regard, it is advisable that corporate counsel set an initial meeting with all corporate managers and outside counsel. Corporate managers want to meet the corporate or outside counsel who will be trying the case. This meeting will provide responsible counsel an opportunity to conduct an on-site investigation. Corporate counsel may want to contact corporate managers directly. A status report schedule should also be established. Although written monthly status reports are sometimes overkill, monthly telephone discussions will likely keep the case moving on track. If a client requests a written status report, outside counsel should send it to corporate counsel rather than operations personnel. Corporate counsel should also keep the right to approve the retention of experts, other expenses, and the filing of motions.

III. Conflicts of Interest

Apart from the conflicts that arise in the ordinary course of practicing law, counsel should be aware of two principal areas where conflicts can arise in employment litigation: the representation of multiple defendants and insurance companies.

A. Representing Multiple Defendants*

When a complaint names multiple defendants including, in particular, individuals who work for the employer defendant, counsel must confront the question of whether it is possible, or desirable, to represent any individuals in addition to the employer. Joint representation can have significant benefits: greatly reduced cost, a united front for the jury, some control over the individuals, and relative peace of mind for the individuals. However, serious risks are also involved. Do not make the tactical choice to present a united front in a vacuum; you need knowledge of the facts and of the credibility of the individuals involved. You may not be able to make this choice at the beginning when sorting out representation. In addition, you may find that a hasty assessment harms the parties' interests: Facts may come to light that cause you to change your initial decision to represent multiple defendants. Also, a direct conflict of interest may arise, requiring you to withdraw from representing one or more of the parties. Worst of all, the conflict may be such that you cannot represent anyone. This situation will cause hardship for everyone and possible prejudice to the employer.

Generally, if the employee is clearly not managerial and the alleged behavior is contrary to established corporate policy (for example, sexual harassment), it may be in the best interest of the corporate defendant *not* to provide counsel for the employee. When the employee clearly is a manager and agent of the corporation, most likely the corporate defendant expects to defend the individual. You still need a prior conflict waiver from the individual manager, which allows the corporation to keep its counsel should later facts reveal that the manager acted outside his or her authority or against corporate policy. Without a waiver at the outset, when a conflict arises, the corporate defendant would likely need to obtain new counsel. (See the sample letter at the end of this chapter and samples at the end of chapter 13, "Professionalism and Ethics," and the text of that chapter.)

B. Insurance Situations

As noted later in this chapter, insurance presents its own set of potential conflicts. These most frequently arise in three situations: reservations of rights, multiple claims for which there is only partial coverage, and excess exposure. (See chapter 13, "Professionalism and Ethics," on this topic.)

---

* See also Joint Representation, chapter 13, "Professionalism and Ethics."

1. Reservation of Rights

When an insurer agrees to defend a lawsuit under a reservation of rights, it is reserving the right to deny coverage in the event there is an adverse judgment. This reservation influences the insurer's conduct of the litigation and its motivation to settle. If the insurer is correct about the lack of coverage, then all it has at risk is the cost of defense. In most states, counsel retained by an insurer nevertheless represents the insured and not the insurer. Yet, if counsel is selected by the insurer, he or she probably has a business relationship with the insurer to protect. In these circumstances, a conflict can arise in the context of settlement. Although counsel can attempt to limit the scope of the representation to exclude any advice or advocacy regarding coverage or settlement, this limitation itself is detrimental to the insured. The lawyer most familiar with the case is unable to participate in the settlement analysis. Whatever the resolution, the lawyer must be sure the client fully understands the scope of representation.

2. Multiple Claims

When coverage is possible for some, but not all, of the counts in a complaint, the insurer usually has a duty to defend the whole case. However, the insurer still has a motivation to concentrate the defense on the covered claims, shaping the case in a way that pushes the liability over to the uncovered ones. At the same time, the insured has every desire for its attorney to do the opposite, so that the insurance will pay for any judgment. Counsel faces the same kind of pressure here as with the reservation of rights situation: the conflict may not rise to the level of an actual conflict of interest, but the client may fear divided loyalties.

3. Excess Exposure

For the same reason—possible divided loyalties—exposure beyond policy limits can create a conflict for the insurance lawyer. Although the motivation for the insurer is weaker than in the case of a reservation of rights, it arises from the same fact: the relative risk for the insurer is less than for the insured. Assume a case of questionable liability but substantial damages. It may cost over $100,000 to defend a claim, the policy limits are $500,000, and the exposure is several million dollars. The insurer may be willing to assume the risk of litigation when the insured would not. In these cases, the insured is protected by the insurer's duty to settle, but counsel nevertheless can be caught between insurer and insured.

In any case involving insurance, the lawyer must know how the law of the jurisdiction determines who is the client and how the applicable bar's rules and interpretive decisions address these issues.

IV. Evaluating Liability

The first task is to understand what your client is facing. This task has two parts: first, *understanding* the claim, and second, *evaluating* the claim. Both are essential at the beginning of a lawsuit so that the client can make early, well-informed judgments about the effect of the litigation on its overall business mission, settlement, costs of defense, and key tactical issues such as joint representation of individually named defendants and discipline of wrongdoers.

A. Threshold Issues

In understanding and evaluating a claim, counsel should analyze numerous threshold issues. The first is whether service of process was proper. Counsel should examine all documents relating to service of process immediately. If the service of process was not according to statute, a motion to quash will likely succeed. Even if the plaintiff still has time to seek proper service after the motion to quash, while the plaintiff is doing so, the defendant will have the time to thoroughly investigate the case.

The second threshold issue is whether personal jurisdiction is proper. This determination involves an analysis of the following issues.

1. Was the employer entity properly named in the complaint? (See, for example, 42 U.S.C. § 2000e-5(f)(1) defining an employer.)
2. If there are multiple parties, does the complaint properly identify each one?

If the answer to either of the above is no, counsel should carefully research local procedural laws to determine whether a defense based on lack of personal jurisdiction can be asserted.

The third threshold issue is subject matter jurisdiction. If a case is filed in state court, analyze subject matter jurisdiction to determine whether there are any exclusively federal claims. If so, consider by a motion to dismiss for lack of subject matter jurisdiction. Also, determine whether to remove the case to federal court (for example, on grounds of diversity jurisdiction). At this point, counsel need not evaluate whether it is a good tactical choice to remove, but rather whether he or she can do so. Evaluate the number of employees required to trigger coverage under various federal, state, and local laws.

The fourth threshold issue is venue. Is venue proper in the jurisdiction? Can the court transfer the case to a better venue, where better law applies for the defendant? If so, consider a motion for a transfer based on forum nonconveniens.[1]

The fifth threshold issue is to consider certain defenses that recur in employment litigation. Today most complaints plead the same essential facts to fit into a variety of statutory and common law causes of action. Analyze potential defenses in the same fashion. Review statutory counts under all the requirements for making a claim. In this regard, counsel must determine:

1. Whether the statute of limitation bars any or all claims. (See, for example, 42 U.S.C. § 2000e-5; 29 U.S.C. § 626(e).)
2. Whether failure to exhaust administrative remedies bars any claims. (See, for example, 29 U.S.C. § 626(d); 42 U.S.C. § 2000e-5(e).)
3. Whether each count states a valid statutory or common law claim.
4. Whether possible workers' compensation preemption of any claim exists.
5. Whether there is possible Employee Retirement Income Security Act (ERISA) preemption of any of the claims. (See, for example, 29 U.S.C. § 1001, *et seq.*)
6. Whether any Title VII, or federal age or disability discrimination claims have been brought against *individuals* employed by a corporate client. Although such claims against individuals may well not survive a motion to dismiss under Fed. R. Civ. P. 12(b)(6),[2] it may not be in the employer's interest to dismiss such claims. For example, the allegations may involve serious misconduct by a supervisor. Under these circumstances, however, there may be an immediate conflict that precludes you from advising the individual defendant in any respect.
7. Whether wrongful discharge is recognized under applicable state law.
8. Whether emotional distress torts are recognized in the jurisdiction, properly pled, and/or barred by a workers' compensation exclusivity provision.

The sixth threshold issue is whether any conflicts exist among defendants. Counsel must first determine the extent to which all claims against all defendants are viable. Although some claims may not survive a motion to dismiss for failure to state a claim, others may be likely to survive at least until summary judgment. Still others, such as disparate treatment claims, may be very difficult to eliminate short of trial. Quickly categorize claims now, although the ensuing investigation may alter this initial analysis. Counsel must then determine whether he or she can defend all of the defendants. This question may not be answerable at this point, but as noted above, sometimes the conflicts will be clear enough to rule out joint representation. In that case, consider informing clients you cannot represent so that no prejudice results from any delay. Otherwise, you should come back to this question no later than when you give your initial case evaluation to the client after the investigation. (See Conflicts of Interest, chapter 13, "Professionalism and Ethics.")

The seventh threshold issue involves determining what damages, if any, are recoverable. A thorough analysis of all damages requested in the complaint should be made to determine whether they are recoverable under relevant statutes. In this regard, the following questions should be contemplated:

1. Are there any damage caps under an applicable statute based on employer size? (See, for example, 42 U.S.C. § 1981a(b)(3).)
2. Are punitive damages sought? Available? (See, for ecample, 42 U.S.C. § 1981(a)(1) and (3).)
3. Are any claims equitable in nature, based on the relief sought?

The eighth threshold issue is whether the relevant statute of limitations has expired. In employment litigation, there are limitation periods both for filing claims with administrative agencies and for filing judicial actions. With respect to filing claims with administrative agencies, some employment claims have short limitation periods. (See, for example, 42 U.S.C. § 2000e-5(e)(1).) Review the complaint for allegations respecting filings at the state or federal level to be sure the plaintiff has properly pled compliance with all such requirements. At the federal level, failure to do so may deprive the court of jurisdiction altogether. In some states, failure to file a timely charge does not bar the claim, but it eliminates a claim for attorneys' fees or certain damages.

With respect to statutes of limitations for judicial complaints, because limitation periods will likely vary for multiple claims based on a variety of state and federal statutes and common law rules, you should look at each claim's limitations period with care. Note that federal claims often "borrow" their limitation periods from analogous state claims, and it is not always clear which state claim will "lend" its statue of limitations.

B. Investigation of the Claim*

You should quickly investigate the facts. No analysis of value to the client can proceed without a thorough investigation. Although the depth of this investigation will vary widely depending on the specific nature of the case, it is important to inform the client at the beginning

---

* See Internal Investigation—the Employer's Perspective, chapter 3, "Discovery."

of the need to do your own investigation. It may be difficult to complete the investigation before the answer is due. Even if you answer before completing your initial evaluation process, you should press on to complete the investigation and evaluation as soon as practicable. You can amend answers, but you must make certain tactical choices early on. Your choices must be informed ones. When a client has already done an internal investigation, such as when the case has already been before an administrative agency, you still need to investigate. You may be able to rely on some or all of what has already been done. But experience teaches that internal investigations are often compromised by a variety of factors, including internal politics, time constraints, lack of resources, and lack of expertise to investigate for a lawsuit.

When clients have inside counsel, the quality of the investigation probably improves, depending on counsel's experience in employment matters. Even so, certain things simply cannot be transmitted through the written word, such as the credibility of key witnesses. If you are ultimately going to be responsible for trying the case, you must be able to make your own judgment on this sort of subjective issue.

The point is that at the end of the investigation, you should have the information that you need in order to give the client the evaluation it will need to decide how to handle the case. If others have gathered information, of course you will want to use it. But your evaluation depends on your own judgment and experience. So, insist on being able to decide what you need to do to give a proper evaluation. The key steps in an investigation of an employment suit are as follows:

1. Obtain and Review All Relevant Documents from the Client

The first step involves gathering and reviewing all relevant documents from the client. In this regard, counsel should obtain the plaintiff's *entire* employment record. Although virtually all employers keep personnel files, these files are usually limited, by design, and do not constitute the entire employment record. Often line supervisors create and retain their own records, such as notes of counseling sessions, minor discipline, evaluations, complaints, performance appraisals, and the like. Moreover, these records are often kept haphazardly: Some supervisors keep them, some do not, and in neither case is the decision based on a document retention policy.

In addition to these informal records, files may be separately kept on harassment investigations and other aspects of employment. Some files are within the purview of human resources and some are outside. Given the variability of record-keeping practices, it is critical to look beyond the employer's first inclination to provide only the personnel file. Otherwise, there is a real risk of finding a document that either undermines your defense (such as by destroying the credibility of a key witness) or would have been much more helpful to you if you had known about it from the beginning.

Counsel should also obtain the entire employment record of other involved employees. In sexual harassment cases and cases involving allegations of misconduct by other employees, get each employee's entire record. Any prior history of relevant misconduct is particularly important in evaluating the employer's response to a harassment claim.

Further, counsel should obtain certain documents relevant to disparate impact claims. Disparate impact claims, particularly those arising out of corporate downsizings, present special problems for the initial evaluation. To properly investigate and analyze such claims, obtain documents relating to the following:

1. A statistical breakdown of the pre-event and postevent workforce
2. The employer's plan for carrying out the downsizing, including any legal and validity analysis
3. The selection criteria used for both the plaintiff(s) and others in the company
4. The employment records of employees who competed with the plaintiff(s) for the positions that survived the downsizing

Counsel should also obtain any applicable collective bargaining agreement. Some or all claims may be arbitrable. Evaluate whether the union contract requires the plaintiff to first submit his or her claims to arbitration prior to filing a judicial complaint. If so, consider moving to compel the plaintiff to arbitrate, rather than litigate, his or her claims.

Likewise, counsel should obtain all employment policies, procedures, and handbooks. Any evaluation of a wrongful discharge claim must begin with an assessment of the legal nature of the employment relationship. In a discrimination or harassment case, the promulgation and dissemination of a proper policy against such conduct is an important element of the defense. Many employers have a written procedure for responding to harassment claims. Following procedure is important to a successful defense. It is also important to know if the employer followed any other relevant written policies and procedures in its dealings with the plaintiff(s); failure to do so can have direct legal consequences in harassment cases (failure to take prompt, effective remedial action) and can create bad "atmospherics" in front of a jury even without having a direct effect on liability. For these and many other reasons, you should insist on unfettered access to all employment policies. You can expect plaintiff's counsel to seek policies in discovery, and your initial evaluation requires that you consider them as well.

Moreover, counsel should obtain copies of any relevant employment agreements. Many employers have entered into confidentiality agreements or employment agreements or have added provisions to employee handbooks that limit access to the judicial system or control the jurisdiction forum. Therefore, it is important to determine if such agreements or provisions exist and to determine the enforceability of them. In the securities industry, for example, an employee may have signed a form U-4, requiring arbitration. Your first course of action would be to stay or dismiss the suit pending arbitration before the National Association of Securities Dealers. (Note that this group and other arbitration organizations have proposed changes to exclude discrimination claims.)

In appropriate cases, counsel should obtain copies of relevant training materials. If the case involves a harassment claim, a key defense may be the employer's preventive measures against harassment. Any records relating to training supervisors or any other segment of the workforce may affect the claim. If possible, you will use these records to show, for example, that the plaintiff was trained to recognize harassment and report it through a variety of channels and that the accused supervisor understood harassment, as well as the consequences for engaging in it. Similarly, the plaintiff will want to show that the employer failed to train in these respects. If that is true, your evaluation must take that failing into account.

Counsel should also obtain all records relating to any administrative proceeding. If the case has gone through an administrative proceeding before the Equal Employment Opportunity Commission or an analogous state body, get anything relating to that proceeding, including the following:

1. The charge, usually signed by the plaintiff under oath
2. Documents created by the employer in the course of any investigation of the charge, including witness interviews, summaries, and so on
3. The employer's written response to the agency
4. The transcript or notes of any fact-finding
5. The agency's investigative report
6. Any additional written submissions by either party
7. The agency's written decision, which may be admissible under an exception to the hearsay rule

2. Check on Insurance

Counsel should further obtain copies of any applicable insurance policies. Clients often overlook insurance coverage for the claim, or at least the cost of defense, under the employer's existing insurance policies. Despite assurances that there is no insurance coverage, counsel should insist on a search to see whether employment practices liabilities insurance policies, workers' compensation policies, or comprehensive general liability policies are in effect.

Growing in popularity, employment practices liability (EPL) policies are a relatively recent addition to the insurance market. These policies provide coverage for discrimination, wrongful discharge, and other kinds of employment claims. These products vary significantly. Some provide coverage for costs of defense only. Some permit the insured to choose its counsel. Many exclude coverage for "intentional" acts or claims for punitive damages, which may narrow coverage beyond the employer's expectations. If an employer has EPL coverage, however, it will likely provide for the cost of a defense. Regular outside counsel who may not be retained by the carrier to handle the litigation can help the insured client realize all the benefits to which it is entitled under the insurance contract.

Workers' compensation policies cover whatever claims are compensable under the applicable state workers' compensation act. If, for example, a claim for emotional injury arising out of and in the course of employment is compensable, then the workers' compensation act may preempt any other claims. Because some states exclude emotional injuries from workers' compensation, there is no general rule here. However, review the policy and current applicable state law. Furthermore, consider a defense of the exclusivity of workers' compensation.

Comprehensive general liability (CGL) policies have spawned the most litigation on coverage issues. The core coverage of a CGL is "bodily injury" from or by an "occurrence." Courts are split on whether this insurance covers typical employment claims.

"Bodily injury" usually means "bodily injury, sickness, or disease." An emotional distress claim may or may not include allegations of physical manifestations that could meet this definition. Some courts have held that emotional distress falls within the meaning of "bodily injury."[3] Other courts take the contrary view.[4]

An "occurrence" under CGL policies is an "accident" that results in bodily injury or property damage that was "neither expected nor intended" from the standpoint of the insured. Coverage litigation regarding this language splits into two camps. The majority view holds that if the *conduct* was intentional, then there is no coverage for claims arising out of the resulting injury.[5] Under this view, harassment may be intentional, thereby precluding coverage under a CGL policy.[6] The minority view holds that as long as the *injury* itself was neither expected nor intended, there is coverage.[7]

The distinction between the two views is crucial for discrimination cases in particular. Under the majority view, there can never be coverage for disparate treatment discrimination, or most other employment claims, since the actions—hiring, firing, and so on—are by necessity intentional acts, no matter how well intentioned. There is a possible coverage distinction between the corporate employer and its agents. If an employer was unaware of, and did not condone, the improper conduct giving rise to liability, the corporate employer could argue that although its agents may not be entitled to coverage or a defense, the employer should be.

Consistent with the majority view, most courts hold that disparate treatment claims are not covered, and there is no duty of defense. The same is not necessarily the case for disparate impact claims, however. The Seventh Circuit has held that because disparate impact claims do not require proof of discriminatory motive, standard CGL language means the insurer owes at least a duty of defense.[8]

Counsel analyzing possible insurance coverage for an employment lawsuit must be aware that there is a distinction between the duty to defend and the duty to indemnify. The duty to defend is a broader duty. A duty to defend arises if, from a reading of the complaint and the policy, there is *any possibility* that a covered claim may be proved. Most courts have held that if not all the counts in a complaint trigger a duty to defend, the insurer nevertheless owes a duty to defend all claims, including those where there is no possibility of coverage. Counsel should also be aware that some CGL policies simply exclude any claims relating to employment.

A host of other issues relate to insurance in the employment litigation context, as discussed above in connection with conflicts. The first issue involves choice of counsel. Under most CGL policies, the insurer retains the right to select counsel. Your client may have a great interest in pushing an issue that results in obtaining separate counsel if the insurer selects counsel who is inexperienced in employment litigation.

The second issue to consider involves the denial of insurance coverage under a reservation of rights. If the insurer offers a defense but denies coverage under a reservation of rights, the insurer creates a potential conflict for the attorney who represents the insured.

The third issue involves an insured's possible exposure to damages above policy limits and the insurer's duty to settle. An insurer has a duty to the insured to try to settle within policy limits if the claim may exceed those limits. However, the insured and the insurer have conflicting interests regarding settlement: While the insured will want settlement at the limits, in a big enough case, the insurer may have a financial incentive to roll the dice, since its ultimate exposure, unlike the insured's, is limited by its policy. One of the important aspects of an early thorough evaluation of an employment suit is to consider the availability of any insurance proceeds for settlement.

The final issue involves determining whether to bring a declaratory judgment action to determine coverage. In rare cases, it may be necessary to bring an action against an insurer to determine the client's right to indemnification or defense. Determining the insurance issue may decisively affect how the employer wants to handle the underlying litigation. In some cases, the insurer will save the employer the trouble by suing first.

3. Interview Key Witnesses

The third step in investigating an employment suit involves conducting interviews of key witnesses. Once counsel has obtained all relevant files, counsel should determine whom to interview, when, and where. In corporations where the corporate or staff counsel will directly handle the case, interviews can proceed without outside counsel. Where the corporate counsel will manage rather than litigate the case, it is usually most efficient to postpone personal interviews until outside counsel is selected.

Even if others have interviewed key witnesses, outside counsel should personally interview witnesses early on for at least three reasons. First, there is no substitute for experienced counsel's assessment of credibility. Second, as the strategy for possible dispositive motions evolves, it is the right time to learn if the witnesses can provide specific, necessary facts for that purpose. Third, counsel needs someone to represent—to personify—the employer at trial. This witness should be someone who will defend the decision at issue. You may want to lock in key witnesses through statements—signed, if appropriate—so that as memories fade or motivations change, you have preserved the facts. With the interviews and signed statements, counsel will both understand the facts better for purposes of taking discovery and provide a better case evaluation.

At least two schools of thought exist on how to record such interviews. One approach is to try to get an accurate, complete statement through a recording, the witness's own hand, or notes, which are later put into a statement for review and signing. Another approach is to talk to the witness and take notes or dictate notes immediately after the interview. The first approach has little or no protection from discovery. Your notes, particularly if they include impressions, are more likely to be work product. A full exploration of how to conduct an investigation is beyond the scope of this book, but the handling of written material generated in an investigation merits close attention. (See the discussion of work product and investigative privileges in chapter 13, "Professionalism and Ethics.")

You should interview key witnesses as soon as possible. Start with all persons involved in making a decision regarding the plaintiff's employment status. Also contact any human resources officer early to get an overview and helpful background information.

Second, interview all accused wrongdoers, such as a harasser, or persons accused of discrimination. At this stage, since it is probably too early to determine whether to represent both the employer and any individually named defendants, counsel should take care to inform the accused that there is no attorney-client relationship between the accused and counsel. Clarify that counsel represents the employer. The employee should be allowed to obtain counsel and/or refrain from participating at this point. This step has the dual virtue of playing fair with the accused and protecting against the disclosure of confidential information that might disqualify counsel from continuing to represent the employer. (See Conflicts of Interest, chapter 13, "Professionalism and Ethics.")

Also, you might attempt to interview all potential victims before a lawsuit. Consider asking the victims, through counsel if necessary, for a meeting where you can ask about the allegations. If there is a new allegation of harassment, the employer has a duty to take prompt, effective remedial action. Interviews with the victims are a necessary part of this obligation. If a policy or procedure exists for this investigation, you should stick to it in the face of plaintiff's attempts to set unacceptable ground rules for the interview. Second, send a letter to opposing counsel detailing the employer's obligation to investigate. Document the plaintiff's or potential victims' refusal to assist. On the other hand, if there is no requirement to conduct an interview, it may pay to be flexible with the ground rules for such a meeting. You may want to look at the plaintiff(s) and hear as much as possible of the story that will drive the case. Of course, approach any "off-the-record" meeting with the plaintiff(s) with care. The timing should not betray a sense of desperation on the part of the employer to settle the case. You must not let the meeting become a discovery opportunity for the other side.

A final interview group are all fact witnesses. Especially in harassment cases, these witnesses may be the key to the defense. Determine their potential impact on the case, and preserve their statements in some fashion.

V. Preparing the Initial Evaluation

At this point, you are ready to give the client an initial evaluation of the case. Your evaluation should touch on at least the following points:

1. The legal nature of the claims
2. The significant facts known to date
3. The most likely line of defense
4. The employer's exposure

5. The likelihood of prevailing, claim by claim, via
    a) A motion to dismiss that concludes all or a significant part of the case
    b) Summary judgment
    c) Trial
6. The approximate cost of getting to each stage at which something dispositive can happen, tailored to the employer's standard budgeting requirements. (A word of caution is advisable here. Corporate defendants are usually very bottom-line oriented and dislike significant legal fees for a motion practice that provides no meaningful benefits. Therefore, only bring motions that will significantly improve the posture of the case if granted.)
7. A timeline for the case, including a discovery plan and a clear indication of the decisions the employer has to make and when they have to be made, for you to conduct the defense

At this point it is likely too early to put a "value" on the case, unless you expressly qualify to what is not known or sufficiently understood, and how those factors could affect your analysis.

VI. Preparing the Legal Response

The first defensive pleading may come before or after the complete initial evaluation. It is hard to complete a thorough evaluation in the relatively few days before a responsive pleading is due. Several options for your legal response to the suit are available.

A. Removal

The first question is whether to remove a state court action to federal court. You *must* accomplish removal within 30 days of notice or knowledge of the litigation. So you may need to remove even before you need to file responsive pleadings. You generally cannot extend this deadline.[9] Federal jurisdiction requires either diversity and at least $75,000 in controversy, or a federal question. Be sure you are on solid ground in one of these two ways.

Some plaintiffs do not want to be in federal court, depending on the damages available under state law and the relative hospitality of the two forums. If so, the complainant will try to avoid pleading a federal cause of action. The plaintiff may also sue an individual defendant of the same state as the plaintiff to defeat complete diversity.

Look beyond the surface of the complaint for federal jurisdiction if that is your forum of choice. First, look for a federal claim masquerading as a state one. Second, consider the viability of any claims against individuals brought solely to defeat diversity. If you can show they are frivolous in time to survive a motion to remand to state court, you may succeed in keeping your case in federal court.

Before removing to federal court, be sure what is your preferred forum. You may have your own tactical reasons for staying in state court, depending on such factors as the speed of the docket, the judge, and the jury. Federal court tends to be more hospitable to employers than state court, because judges often have the time to give better attention to legal defenses. However, there is obviously no firm rule.

B. Motion to Transfer Venue for Improper Venue

If venue is improper, inconvenient, or legally hostile, consider a change of venue or a motion to dismiss.[10]

C. Motions to Dismiss

By now, the claims typically asserted in employment litigation are well established, as are the rules regarding jurisdiction, parties, and so on. Unless there is a legitimate chance of knocking a claim out altogether because of lack of personal or subject matter jurisdiction or a failure to state a claim, probably no cost justification exists for pursuing a motion to dismiss independently.

Where federal preemption (for example, Employment Retirement Income Security Act) or state preemption (for example workers' compensation) is an issue, raise the issue of subject matter jurisdiction. Assert the preemption defense as a separate defense within the answer. You can brief the issue later in a motion to dismiss or for summary judgment. If the preemption claim is a strong one, you should alert the court early that the case could turn on the issue, such as by a separately filed motion to dismiss. For workers' compensation preemption, however, it is likely that matters outside the pleadings will enter the debate. Your motion will ultimately turn into one for summary judgment. This again raises the question of the cost-effectiveness of pursuing most motions to dismiss at the beginning of your case.

Of course, some theories of liability are legitimately defective (for example, disparate impact under the Age Discrimination in Employment Act). If a complaint is clear enough and an amendment cannot cure the defect, then an early motion to dismiss may be worthwhile. However, you can file the motion while answering. Many judges are reluctant to stay discovery for the consideration of such a motion in any event. (See chapter 7, "Special Evidentiary Concerns," and chapter 6, "Pretrial Motions," regarding pretrial motions.)

D. The Answer

For the reasons cited above, avoid pleading as affirmative defenses matters that are no more than what you have to show under the complex burden-shifting formulas that govern employment law claims. Instead, stick to true, legitimate affirmative defenses such as the following:

1. Statute of limitations
2. Statute of frauds (in wrongful discharge cases alleging something more than an employment-at-will relationship)
3. Failure to exhaust administrative remedies
4. Failure to mitigate damages
5. Equitable defenses where appropriate, such as fraud, laches, estoppel, and waiver
6. Rule 12(b)(6) defenses

E. Offer of Judgment

If, after you have evaluated the case and filed an answer, you believe that some liability exists on the part of your client, you should consider making an "offer of judgment" pursuant to Rule 68 of the Federal Rules of Civil Procedure. An offer of judgment constitutes an offer to allow judgment against the defending party for the amount specified in the offer, with costs then accrued. This offer provides a twofold benefit to the defendant. First, if a plaintiff rejects an offer of judgment, and the judgment is not more favorable than the offer, the plaintiff must pay the costs incurred after the making of the offer. Those costs may include defense attorneys' fees.[11] Second, even if rejected, making an offer of judgment may stimulate further settlement discussions. Counsel should understand that an accepted offer of judgment may trigger additional plaintiff's attorneys' fees if the offer does not mention fees or costs.

F. Corrective Action Such as Unconditional Offer of Reinstatement

In the appropriate case, an employer may recall a laid-off plaintiff or offer reinstatement to a discharged plaintiff. An unconditional offer of reemployment may effectively mitigate damages; unreasonably refusing such an offer can cut off back pay liability.[12]

VII. Conclusion

By properly responding to the lawsuit, defense counsel will significantly improve the likelihood of success at later stages of the proceedings. An investment of as much time as possible in investigating and preparing your defense at this early stage will reap great rewards at later stages in the case. The work at this early stage provides the foundation for everything else that occurs thereafter.

VIII. Appendixes

A. Sample Individual Defendant Engagement Letter*

Re: Case Caption

Dear _____:

As we have discussed, you along with [the company] have been sued or identified in this lawsuit [or claim]. The company has retained our firm to represent it and is willing to have our firm also defend you in the case. As we discussed, at this time our interests are mutual and unopposed. However, facts could develop during the handling of this case that would put us at odds. A conflict of interest in representation could arise. Should such a conflict arise, [the company] would want our firm to continue to represent [the company]. We would give you written notice and a reasonable period of time to hire your own counsel. Our firm would not use against you the adverse information obtained while representing you.

Of course, you have the right to retain your own lawyer at the outset. If you have personal and/or homeowners/renters insurance you should contact your insurance agent or other contact person as soon as possible. You must put your insurance carrier on notice of this litigation. Your insurance carrier may provide you with defense counsel depending on the allegations and the terms of your policy.

Based on our previous discussion, you indicated your understanding of, and agreement to, this waiver of a potential conflict. You also agreed to the payment of your legal fees to our firm by the company.

You hereby consent to any use of any information that you provide to us as lawyers for [the company]. You also specifically consent to our firm continuing to represent the company if a conflict develops. You agree that any exchange or disbursement of any information is not waiver of any privilege and you will protect any privilege.

So that both of our files are complete, I am sending you two signed originals of this letter along with a self-addressed, stamped envelope. Please sign and return one while keeping the other for your files. Should you have any questions, or wish to discuss this further, do not hesitate to call me at the above number.

Very truly yours,

_____

Attorney

---

*See also Defense Counsel Engagement Letter and Consent to Payment of Legal Fees by Another, chapter 13, "Professionalism and Ethics," and Conflicts of Interest, Joint Representation, and Payment of Fees by Nonclient in chapter 13.

Read and Agreed to the _____ day of _____, 19 _____

By: _____

Enclosure   Individual Defendant

B. Defense Litigation Checklist and Timetable

Style of case _____

Type of Case:

    Title VII: Sex ____ Race ____ Religion ____ National origin ____

    Age ____ Disability ____ Equal pay ____ ERISA benefits ____

    State Antidiscrimination act: Sex ____ Race ____ Religion ____

    Other (specify) _____

    Common law tort (specify) _____

    Contract _____

    Other (specify) _____

Attorneys responsible _____

Client contact _____

Local counsel _____

DUE TO PASSAGE OF THE CIVIL JUSTICE REFORM ACT AND THE 1993 AMENDMENTS TO THE FEDERAL RULES OF CIVIL PROCEDURE, IT IS IMPERATIVE THAT WE CHECK LOCAL RULE REQUIREMENTS AS SOON AS WE RECEIVE A NEW CASE.

I. 10 days from service of complaint:

    a. Do the following

        Copy information on plaintiff's firm and assigned judge from Martin-dale-Hubbell and Federal Judiciary Almanac for the information file _____

        Determine multiple representation issues _____

        Obtain written authorization to represent individual defendant(s) _____

        Secure local counsel _____

        Send standard retention letter to local counsel _____

        Obtain copy of local court rules _____

        Obtain preliminary facts from client _____

        Request names, addresses, and phone numbers of key witnesses from client and begin interviewing _____

        Request/obtain all documentary evidence in client's possession _____

        Send Freedom of Information Act letter for agency investigative files _____

        Examine possible insurance coverage _____

        Get extension of time to respond to complaint/check to see if service can/should be waived _____

        File notice of appearance _____

        File motion to admit pro hac vice _____

   b. Determine if complaint is subject to a motion to dismiss or strike
      _____

      Check:
         Jurisdiction _____
         Venue _____
         Proper named defendant(s) _____
         Service _____
         Standing _____
         Statute of limitations _____
         Conditions precedent to suit satisfied _____
         Claim for relief stated _____
         Damages proper _____
         Prejudicial allegations _____
         Preemption _____
         Workers' compensation (or other) exclusive remedy _____

   c. Consider:
      Does Fed. R. Civ. P. 26, as amended, apply for discovery? _____
      (Rule 26, as amended, imposes a stay on discovery until the parties
      have satisfied the Rule 26(f) "meet and confer" requirements. You
      may, however, meet and confer early on and then initiate formal
      discovery.)
      If waiver of service is requested, determine whether to waive service
      _____

      Removal to federal court _____ (note 30-day time limit from
         notice)
      Filing any counterclaims _____

II. 20 days from service of complaint
    File motion/responsive pleading (UNLESS extension obtained OR ser-
       vice is waived) _____
    Return executed waiver of service _____

III. 30 days from service of complaint (or notice or knowledge, if earlier)
     Remove to federal court (no extension allowed) _____
     IF amended Fed. R. Civ. P. 26 stay on discovery DOES NOT apply:
        Serve contention and witness interrogatories (including experts)
        _____

IV. 45 days from service of complaint
    Interview company witnesses _____
    Check local rules for discovery cut-off time and docket on calendar ____
    IF amended Fed. R. Civ. P. 26 stay on discovery DOES NOT apply:
       Notice deposition of plaintiff _____

V. 60 days from "service" of complaint AND service was waived:
   File motion/responsive pleading _____

VI. IF amended Fed. R. Civ. P. 26 discovery APPLIES:
    At least 14 days before scheduling conference, satisfy Rule 26(f) meet and
       confer requirements _____

At least 10 days before scheduling conference, serve/file Rule 26(a)(1) initial disclosures _____

Once meet and confer satisfied, serve discovery and notice deposition of plaintiff _____

VII. 120 days from service of complaint
Deposition of plaintiff's witnesses _____
Summarize all depositions _____
Additional discovery:
    Follow-up interrogatories _____
    Request for production of documents _____
    Medical Records _____
    Income tax returns _____
    Information from other employers _____
    Verification of plaintiff's lost earnings _____
    Consider filing motion for summary judgment _____
    Assess merits of case—write litigation assessment letter to client and discuss settlement with client _____
    Serve request for admissions _____

VIII. Three months prior to trial date
Serve expert report under Amended Rule 26, if necessary _____
File motion for summary judgment (check local rules) _____

IX. Two months prior to trial date
Notify witnesses of trial date _____
Complete:
    Pretrial brief, proposed findings of fact and conclusions of law _____
    Voir dire and jury instructions _____
    All exhibits/witnesses identified _____
    Consider filing offer of judgment (must be served more than 10 days before trial) _____
    Consider motions in limine _____
    Depositions signed and filed with court _____

X. One month prior to trial date:
    Disclose rebuttal experts/reports, if amended Rule 26(a)(2) applies _____
    Disclose witnesses/exhibits if amended Rule 26(a)(3) applies ____

XI. Three weeks prior to trial date
    Initial preparation of witnesses for trial _____
    Preparation of trial book (including all witnesses' expected testimony and exhibits for each allegation at issue) _____
    Subpoena witnesses _____
    Prepare opening statement and closing argument _____
    Brief evidentiary issues _____

Notes

1. 28 U.S.C. § 1404.
2. *See* EEOC v. AIC Secur. Investigations, Ltd., 55 F.3d 1276 (7th Cir. 1995).
3. *See* State Farm Mutual Auto. Ins. Co. v. Ramsey, 297 S.C. 71, 374 S.E.2d 896 (1988) (bodily injury includes emotional distress) and NPS Corp. v. Insurance Co. of N. Am., 213 N.J. Super. 547, 517 A.2d 1211 (App. Div. 1986) (bodily injury includes emotional and psychological consequences allegedly resulting from sexual harassment).
4. *See* St. Paul Fire and Marine Ins. Co. v. Campbell County. Sch. Dist. No. 1, 612 F. Supp. 285 (D. Wyo. 1985) (emotional injury arising out of harassment not bodily injury); Allstate Ins. Co. v. Diamant, 518 N.E.2d 1154 (Mass. 1988) (bodily injury encompasses only physical injuries to the body).
5. *See, e.g.,* St. Paul Fire and Marine Ins. Co. v. Superior Court of Yuba County, 161 Cal. App. 3d 1199, 208 Cal. Rptr. 5 (1984) (policy that covered claims resulting from an "accidental event . . . [which] must be something the insured did not expect or intend to happen," did not cover wrongful termination claim); E-Z Loader Boat Trailers, Inc. v. Travelers Indem. Co., 106 Wash. 2d 901, 726 P.2d 439 (1986) (no coverage for sex and age discrimination wrongful termination claim because discharge was an intentional act).
6. *See* St. Paul Fire and Marine Ins. Co. v. Campbell County Sch. Dist. No. 1, 612 F. Supp. 285 at 287 (D. Wyo. 1985).
7. *See* Maine Bonding & Casualty Co. v. Douglas Dynamics, Inc., 594 A.2d 1079, 1081–82 (Me. 1991) (*discharge* may be intentional but the *harm* covered by the insurance may not be subjectively intended by the employer, requiring insurer to defend claim); *see also* Andover Newton Theological School, Inc. v. Continental Cas. Co., 964 F.2d 1237 (1st Cir. 1992) (in order to avoid indemnification under intentional act exclusion in both educational institution policy and statute, under Massachusetts law insurer has burden of proving that termination was done with knowledge of its illegality under the Age Discrimination in Employment Act).
8. Solo Cup Co. v. Federal Ins. Co., 619 F.2d 1178 (7th Cir. 1980).
9. 28 U.S.C. § 1446 (1998).
10. 28 U.S.C. § 1404 (1998).
11. Marek v. Chesny, 473 U.S. 1, 105A S. Ct. 3012 (1985).
12. Ford Motor Co. v. EEOC, 458 U.S. 218 (1982).

CHAPTER 3

Discovery

G. CHARLES DOUGLAS II*
WILLIAM C. MARTUCCI†

---

* Douglas & Douglas; Concord, New Hampshire.

† Spencer, Fane, Britt & Browne; Kansas City, Missouri.

I. Introduction

The key to effective discovery is to develop a focused discovery plan at the outset of the case and then implement it. To put it simply, an effective discovery plan consists of at least two elements: (1) knowing the information necessary to support plaintiff's claim or the employer's defenses and (2) using the proper and most efficient discovery methods to obtain that information.

II. Plaintiff's Discovery Plan

Typically, employment discrimination cases are difficult to prove. Conducting discovery with a strategic plan in mind will avoid random and mindless time and effort, which will allow the case to be managed efficiently.

By way of illustration, the following discussion is a suggested framework for discovery in an age discrimination case involving a reduction-in-force action by a large company, which employs several thousand employees. Obviously, discovery goals should be modified to fit the specifics of a given case.

The most important step in the development of a discovery plan is to research the law so that you know what evidence you need to prove your case. In the age discrimination context, cases are proven by either direct or circumstantial evidence; in the vast majority of cases, sophisticated employers know that they should not be informing soon-to-be terminated employees that the reason for termination is the employees' age. Consequently, the typical age discrimination cases will require proof by circumstantial evidence. The federal courts have developed evidentiary formulas to enable employees to prove discrimination in a reduction-in-force setting through circumstantial evidence. Typically, state courts follow federal case law when interpreting their jurisdiction's antidiscrimination statutes. Thus, in the reduction-in-force context, an age discrimination victim needs to prove a prima facie case, which is as follows;

1. plaintiff was in the protected class, that is, plaintiff was over 40 years of age;
2. plaintiff suffered an adverse personnel action;
3. plaintiff was qualified for the position or job duties that remained;
4. the circumstances of plaintiff's discharge give rise to an inference of age discrimination.[1]

After the employer expresses its legitimate nondiscriminatory reason for the employee's discharge, then the plaintiff must prove that this ostensible nondiscriminatory reason is not true or is a pretext for age discrimination. Thus, plaintiff's counsel must mold his or her discovery plan to prove these elements.

With the above law in mind, the following is a simplified list of major topics of information that need to be sought in an age discrimination case through a discovery plan.

1. The employer's complete statement of reasons and circumstances for the personnel action taken by the employer and all supporting data regarding the reduction in force or reorganization. The employer should be pinned down on this as early as possible in the case.
2. A complete employment history of plaintiff, including all evaluations, commendations, criticisms, and the plaintiff's entire personnel file.
3. Any data or information on the basis of which the plaintiff can be judged against other employees with similar job assignments.
4. Statistics for retaining and discharging employees in the reduction in force or reorganization, broken down by age groups and positions, of the entire employment force over the relevant period of time.
5. Computations of the monetary value of salary and all fringe benefits from date of discharge to date of trial and the average annual raises of employees in plaintiff's department from date of discharge to time of trial.
6. All policies and procedures of the employer relating to implementing the reduction in force or reorganization and the criteria utilized in selecting the employees to be discharged in the reduction in force or reorganization.
7. Information pertaining to other age discrimination suits or administrative charges brought against the employer.

8. Information on job openings during and after the reduction in force or reorganization and the age of the employees who filled these openings.
9. Salaries and ages of those employees retained compared with those employees were discharged.

Rule 26(a) of the Federal Rules of Civil Procedure sets forth six major methods by which parties may obtain discovery:

1. initial disclosures,
2. depositions upon oral examination or written questions,
3. written interrogatories,
4. production of documents,
5. physical and mental examinations,
6. requests for admission.

The sequence of discovery methods is important in employment discrimination cases. The order of march is important because there is a logical progression in using the discovery methods as each device builds on the previous one.

The following four discovery techniques are the keys to any successful discovery plan in employment litigation:

- Written interrogatories
- Requests for production of documents
- Depositions on oral examination
- Requests for admission

Before these discovery devices are briefly discussed, it should be emphasized how important a plaintiff is as a resource of information. A plaintiff provides the identity of key witnesses and also relevant documentary evidence.

After the initial telephone contact and before deciding to represent a plaintiff in an employment discrimination claim, many plaintiff-oriented firms forward the potential client a detailed questionnaire to be completed. The completed questionnaire provides important information, such as a chronology of events, a list of key witnesses, and a request for key documents.

The plaintiff should obtain in discovery the necessary admissible evidence to defeat the employer's summary judgment motion. In other words, the plaintiff needs to submit admissible evidence that would survive a Rule 50(a) motion to dismiss at the end of the plaintiff's case in chief at trial, a Rule 50(b) motion for judgment at the end of the entire case before the jury retires, and motion for judgment as a matter of law if the plaintiff's evidence survives these tests, then such evidence will survive the employer's summary judgment motion. Thus, the plaintiff must craft discovery requests that will elicit the critical information and documents that often are exclusively in the hands of the defendant. To this end, the plaintiff, like the defendant, is well advised to issue discovery requests as early as possible. Previously the Federal Rules of Civil Procedure allowed for the service of written discovery before the filing of an answer. Under the 1993 amendments, however, and in particular Fed. R. Civ. P. 26(e), the parties may not commence discovery before they confer pursuant to Fed. R. Civ. P. 26(f). This immediately will test a defendant's willingness to invest the resources (for example, management time, legal fees, and the like) necessary to respond to discovery requests and defend the lawsuit. It also is likely to highlight those areas where an employer is vulnerable to attack. It may even reveal areas of concern to the employer that may not be directly related to the claims at issue, but that are nevertheless awkward if exposed. For example, it is not unusual for an interrogatory question or document request in a discrimination case to require disclosure of information that might yield the factual basis for other claims, such as defamation, interference with contractual relations, and wrongful discharge.

In order to enhance the plaintiff's chances of identifying a material issue of fact, the scope of the plaintiff's requests should be as broad as permissible and should include requests for any and all documents that support the underlying claims and defenses. However, careful consideration should be given to the fact that the defendant will object to any requests that are excessively broad or that call for the production of confidential or proprietary information. Focused and specific requests are therefore far more likely to yield meaningful responses than are broad-based requests. They are also more likely to expose facts that will allow the plaintiff to overcome summary judgment.

Unlike the defendant, who in the typical employment case will need to take only a few depositions (and often only the plaintiff), a plaintiff may need to build the case and defeat summary judgment by taking multiple depositions of agents of the defendant. Since the number of depositions may be limited by state or federal rules, careful and strategic decisions must be made. Fed. R. Civ. P. 30(a)(2)(A) provides that each party may take only ten depositions without leave of court.

Of critical importance is the deposition of the key witness in the case—the plaintiff. Assuming that material disputed facts exist that could support a fact-finder ruling in favor of the plaintiff, the plaintiff must be fully prepared to get those facts on the record at the deposition. The plaintiff must be prepared to state clearly facts that will support each element of the claim. The following illustrates a plaintiff who is prepared to respond to the critical questions presented:

Q. You testified that Mr. Smith was your supervisor at the time of your termination, is that correct?

A. Yes.

Q. You also testified that you believed that Mr. Smith made the decision to terminate you, is that right?

A. That's correct.

Q. Now, Mr. Smith never made any statement to you that you considered to reflect a bias or animus based upon your age, isn't that right?

A. That's not correct. On several occasions Mr. Smith wanted to know if I was slowing down, how was I feeling. He once even said it must be tough for me to get going in the morning. He also said to me that his brother had retired at my age and was really enjoying himself. At the time, I never thought much about these statements, but in light of what happened to me later, I believe that Mr. Smith's statements were directly reflective of his age bias.

Presented with that answer, the defendant has no choice but to review in detail each of the identified statements, thus possibly solidifying a record that may preclude summary judgment.

A. Initial Disclosures

On December 1, 1993, the discovery provisions of the Federal Rules of Civil Procedure, Rule 26(a), were radically revised. This change moved the philosophy of the federal rules from a policy of discovery by one party of the other party's documents and information to that of disclosure. Now each party in possession of information or documents has an obligation to disclose that information without a specific request. In federal district court, depending on the particular district, initial disclosures at the beginning of a lawsuit are a critical part of the discovery process. Some district courts have opted out of the amendments, and others have adopted only part of the amended rules. Counsel must understand and know the local rules of the particular district court in which a case is pending.

As a result of the change requiring parties to voluntarily disclose information in their possession, the federal rules now impose critical restrictions on a party's entitlement to ask interrogatories and take depositions without leave of court. Only ten depositions and twenty-five interrogatories, *including* the subparts, may be used absent leave of court.

A plaintiff's lawyer, who is normally at a disadvantage at the start of the case because he or she lacks access to the defendant-employer's records and files, can turn the revised federal rules into a striking tactical advantage. This can be done by sending the defendant a letter before the mandatory Rule 26(f) meeting of counsel. In such a letter, plaintiff's counsel can list what documents he or she believes are relevant to the facts disputed in the pleadings, as well as the identity of witnesses likely to have discoverable information relevant to the disputed facts. In addition, the new federal rules contemplate that the parties will cooperate in framing a discovery plan for presentation to the court, which will be changed only upon a showing of changed circumstances or other good cause.

B. Written Interrogatories

Written interrogatories should be included in the first step of the plaintiff's discovery plan. They are extremely useful for obtaining background information on the company and the identity of persons and documents involved in the decision-making process. The use of interrogatories also helps define and narrow your list of persons you need to depose and focuses your request for production of documents. Ultimately, well-crafted interrogatories will pin down the employer's defense so that you do not have to poke holes in a defense that may become a "moving target." View them as a source for leads and later contradictions.

If counsel attempts to use interrogatories beyond their limitations, discovery disputes are bound to arise in response to the discovery requests. Plaintiff's counsel must be careful to draft the interrogatories to avoid the defendant's objections that they are overbroad and unduly burdensome. This may mean, for example, narrowing an interrogatory to the relevant time period when the employment decisions were made or to the location where the relevant employment decisions were made. Objections based on overbroad interrogatories will only delay obtaining the requested information because these disputes are usually followed by a motion to compel. In the same vein, careful drafting can avoid discovery disputes that involve exceeding the number of interrogatories allowed by Rule 33(a) of the Federal Rules of Civil Procedure or by local federal rules. Because the number of interrogatories one may ask is not limitless, the interrogatories must be very directed and focused. Appendix A provides excerpts by major topics of a first set of interrogatories that were used recently in a reduction-in-force or reorganization case involving a large defendant company. Many of these interrogatories would be applicable in any employment discrimination case.

C. Requests for Production of Documents

Rule 34 of the Federal Rules of Civil Procedure (and state procedural rules) provides that a party may request the production of documents from other parties. As with written interrogatories, a request for the production of documents should be served early in the litigation. A request for the production of documents can be served after interrogatories or in combination with them. It is important to obtain document discovery early in the case because, in addition to identifying persons to depose, the employer's documents will also assist counsel in conducting prepared and efficient depositions. Getting the documents in advance of any depositions will allow you to study them beforehand and avoid wasting time at the deposition.

At a minimum, a request for document production in an age discrimination case should include the following:

- Plaintiff's personnel records, including all evaluations, written warnings, complaints and reprimands. Have it certified as complete.
- All documents regarding the policies, procedures, and standards for implementing the reduction in force.
- All documents, including performance evaluations, regarding other discharged employees.
- All documents, including performance evaluations, regarding retained employees.
- Organizational chart of the company.
- Copies of all fringe benefit plans, personnel handbooks, and policies for reducing the workforce.
- All documents regarding other age discrimination charges.

Keeping in mind that an important part of the discovery plan in an age discrimination case is to elicit all possible reasons for plaintiff's discharge, plaintiff's counsel needs to pay special attention to the request for the personnel file. Simply requesting plaintiff's complete personnel file is insufficient because some companies do not place all warnings, complaints, or reprimands in an employee's personnel file. In fact, some supervisors even maintain separate files under their control that may contain additional documentation regarding a plaintiff's job performance. To avoid being surprised with this documentation at some late stage in the case, it is necessary to request specifically an employee's *entire* personnel file and any files regarding the employee and his or her performance maintained by prior or current supervisors.

D. Depositions by Oral Examination

After the responses to interrogatories and requests for production of documents have been reviewed, the next step in the discovery plan should be depositions. Because depositions are expensive and time consuming, the use of written interrogatories and requests for document production helps narrow the list of persons to be deposed. These two discovery methods will also help determine what areas need to be covered in the deposition.

Depositions are very important in discrimination cases because plaintiff's counsel will need to establish more than a prima facie case to survive a summary judgment motion or to prevail at trial. Deposition testimony may be the most important device to establish discriminatory pretext or even direct evidence of discrimination.

At a minimum, plaintiff's counsel will want initially to depose supervisory employees who were involved in making and implementing the employment decision being challenged. This group may also include other employees who had a role in the adverse action against the plaintiff, such as human resources employees and the plaintiff's current and prior supervisors. Supervisors or decision-making personnel may claim that they relied on allegedly legitimate factors based on information given to them by coemployees or subordinates, customers, and/or vendors. Plaintiff's counsel should then follow up with depositions of these individuals, which in many instances may last no more than five or ten minutes to prove the decision maker was lying.

As stated previously, a plaintiff may initially be at a disadvantage because the company or its employees possess the relevant information. To depose persons with knowledge of the plan to reduce the workforce, under the federal rules plaintiff's counsel may use a Rule 30(b)(6) deposition. This provision allows the plaintiff to depose someone the company identifies as having knowledge on this topic. A Rule 30(b)(6) deposition should be used if the interrogatory method fails to identify such persons.

E. Requests for Admissions

Requests for admissions typically will be the last step of your discovery plan. This discovery method is useful to establish the authenticity of documentary evidence and establish basic facts because such an approach forces the defendant to take a position on these basic facts.

For example, requests for admission are useful in establishing plaintiff's prima facie case. Specifically, the plaintiff should serve requests regarding plaintiff's being a member of the protected class, plaintiff's qualifications (met employer's expectations), and plaintiff's discharge (experienced adverse employment action in workforce reduction). If the employer denies a request for admission, it may be necessary to follow up with another set of interrogatories to determine the basis for the denial.

F. Make That Motion!

Typically, employers will refuse to supply many of the documents or answers to interrogatories that you have requested. After scrutinizing the case law and analyzing how badly the information requested is needed to prove the case, it is absolutely essential that plaintiff's counsel file the appropriate motion to compel, taking care that plaintiff's rights are preserved for appeal. For example, it may be wise to appeal any adverse federal magistrate judge's ruling to preserve the issue on appeal to a federal court of appeals.[2]

In the discovery motion, counsel must take great pains to lay out the law for the motion judge so that he or she understands why this information is sought. Too often plaintiff's counsel files a bare-bones discovery motion without laying out the legal elements of the cause of action that in turn explain why the information sought is needed. As tedious as these motions can be, they are absolutely essential to obtaining critical evidence. Just remember that it is not for nothing that employers refuse to supply this requested information. In a vast majority of incidences, the information that is obtained from a successful discovery motion may be the critical evidence that tips the scales in plaintiff's favor.

III. Discovery from the Employer's Perspective

In an employment case, the bulk of the available information relevant to the case is either in the hands of the employer or in the hands of third parties. Although a plaintiff certainly has one view of the factual circumstances, it is rare that the plaintiff is exclusively in possession of some important piece of information. Thus, from the plaintiff's perspective, discovery is often truly needed to "discover" information. From the defendant's perspective, however, discovery is often focused on pinning the plaintiff down to one story and/or obtaining admissions necessary to support a motion for summary judgment.

Because of the imbalance in possession of information, formal discovery may be accurately characterized as a flow of information from the defendant to the plaintiff. Previously, the flow of information was limited to that actually requested by the plaintiff. With the implementation of the required disclosures of Fed. R. Civ. P. 26(a)(1) in most jurisdictions, defendants are now required to be more forthcoming with information, even if no specific request has been made. Because of this new disclosure requirement, it is more important than ever that a defense attorney move quickly to learn as much from the employer as there is to know about a case before engaging in, or responding to, significant discovery.

A. Internal Investigation—The Employer's Perspective*

The most critical part of the defense of any employment case, and the most often neglected portion, is the internal investigation of the plaintiff's allegations. As mentioned above, the defendant has, or has access to, virtually all of the information there is to know about a case. Defendant's counsel must take steps early on to collect and synthesize available information.

1. Documents

The first search should be for relevant documents. The types of documents relevant in any particular case will necessarily depend on the allegations of the case. Whatever the case, however, it is important to carefully consider the breadth of potentially relevant documents and to seek documents diligently.

Often, defense counsel has a primary contact with the employer through a human resources manager or in-house counsel. This relationship has the benefit of creating a key person to respond to inquiries but also has the potential limitation of restricting the flow of information. One common mistake is to rely too heavily on the knowledge of the key contact person. For example, assume that some computerized transaction data is relevant to a particular employment dispute. A request to the human resources manager may elicit a response such as "We don't have that information beyond six months ago because the system was designed to delete older information." What the human resources manager may not know is that, beginning a few years ago, the data processing manager was dissatisfied with this computer program and began making back-up copies of all transactions. A simple call to the data processing manager would have revealed this information. Failure to inquire beyond the human resources manager may result in the information never coming to light, or the information could come to light only during the data processing manager's deposition or on the eve of trial. Plaintiff's counsel may have a legitimate objection to such late-discovered evidence, and the court may exclude it from trial.

The same concern applies to other types of document searches. For example, employers commonly hand over to their lawyers a master personnel file and report: "This is everything we have on this employee." It is critical for the lawyer to go beyond the master file and seek any other files or notes that may be in the hands of other employ-

---

* See also Investigation of the Claim, chapter 2, "Responding to the Lawsuit."

ees, especially current and former supervisors. In addition, it is important to press these other employees to review their calendars or diaries to determine whether there is any information contained in these sources that may have any bearing on the case. In short, defendant's counsel must be diligent and not take "I don't think so" for an answer.

2. Potential Witnesses

In addition to gathering potentially relevant documents, it is important for defendant's counsel to get out to the workplace, get a feel for the working conditions, and talk with individuals who may have any connection to the case. In some cases, where the issue is relatively narrow, it may be sufficient to focus the interviews on those persons actually involved in the decision-making process. Where there are broader allegations, such as an allegation that the workplace is overrun by sexual harassment, it is important to talk with as many coworkers as possible.

The interviews serve primarily two purposes. First, the interviews are essential to determining what the facts are and to finding who will be able to testify to the facts. Second, the interviews are essential to determining the character of potential witnesses. It is important, even at this early stage, to begin determining who will and who will not make effective witnesses to communicate the defendant's side of the case. Defense counsel must consider that potentially favorable testimony will lose its impact if the witness is not able to present the testimony effectively.

Interviews should also extend to any third parties who may have some information relevant to the case. Care should be taken, however, to distinguish between a management employee who may be deemed "the client" for purposes of attorney-client privilege and those nonmanagement and former employees who may not fall within the attorney-client privilege. To protect the privilege, counsel should be very careful to avoid discussing any trial strategies with nonclient witnesses.

3. Wrapping up the Investigation

Once the internal investigation is complete, it is important to synthesize the information gathered into a usable format. Notes of witness interviews should be legibly transcribed and placed into witness files. Documents should be organized and indexed for ease of access. In addition, two other steps are extremely helpful in organizing and summarizing the internal investigation.

First, counsel should prepare a detailed chronology of events. The chronology should be cross-referenced to the witnesses and documents that will establish the existence of the event. This chronology then becomes an invaluable quick reference in trial preparation and at trial. Second, counsel should prepare a summary of the defendant's legal argument. This can take the form of a draft closing argument or a draft motion for summary judgment. In whatever form, the document should set forth clearly and concisely the key facts and law that support the defendant's position.

Both the chronology and the summary of legal argument should be seen as living documents, to be revised as additional discovery changes the shape of the case. In combination, these two documents serve two enormously useful purposes. First, they force the lawyer to apply critical analysis to the case very early on. Second, they provide a quick reference to enable the lawyer to get back up to speed in the case after those inevitable periods of time in any litigation during which other matters demand attention.

B. Rule 26 Disclosures—As Applied to the Employer's Defense

New Rule 26(a)(1) now requires employers to disclose relevant documents and individuals (along with any applicable insurance agreement) without the necessity of a formal request. If an appropriate internal investigation has been completed and documented, the Rule 26 disclosures will flow easily from the investigation. All the lawyer need do is refer to those relevant documents and individuals that have been identified during the internal investigation. In preparing for the Rule 26 disclosures, counsel should view relevance broadly and be overinclusive. Failure to identify a potential witness or relevant document may preclude counsel from later using that witness or document at trial.

The new rules also require opposing counsel to meet and discuss the case shortly before the Rule 26 disclosures are made. It is best to prepare a draft of the Rule 26 disclosures in advance of the meeting with plaintiff's counsel. If nothing else, preparation of draft disclosures will help counsel focus on the issues of the case and be able to discuss the case knowledgeably during the conference. The draft of disclosures should then be modified by any legitimate inquiries suggested by plaintiff's counsel during the Rule 26 conference.

C. The Employer's Discovery against Plaintiff

Through the Rule 26 process, defense counsel should begin to learn more about the plaintiff's theory or theories of the case. This information should be applied to formulating a discovery plan. Although the plan will vary somewhat from case to case, generally discovery should proceed with a limited round of interrogatories and document requests, followed by the plaintiff's deposition and any expert depositions, and then any wrap up written discovery necessary to tie up any loose ends. In most cases, the defendant does not need to depose third parties unless the third parties are adverse or will not be available for trial.

1. Initial Document Requests and Interrogatories

Written discovery requests to the plaintiff can help, especially in obtaining documents. Because the plaintiff's lawyer will answer your requests, save key issues on which the plaintiff's testimony is critical for depositions. For example, an interrogatory asking the plaintiff all ways in which she believes she has been subjected to discrimination may serve only to force the plaintiff's lawyer to discuss this issue with the plaintiff in detail. That discussion may or may not otherwise have taken place prior to the plaintiff's deposition. In addition, an interrogatory response will likely elicit a more comprehensive response than plaintiff alone would provide in a deposition. Accordingly, typically save ultimate issue questions for the deposition.

Several specific matters are appropriate for written discovery. These matters include requests for documents that plaintiff received during her employment; any journal, diary, or other handwritten notes by the plaintiff; and any documents or other information regarding subsequent employment and efforts at mitigation of damages. Interrogatories about damages and medical treatment and actions are also possible areas of inquiry. It is best to time these initial requests so that responses arrive before the plaintiff's deposition for use in the deposition.

2. Plaintiff's Deposition

The key to an effective plaintiff's deposition is to be prepared strategically, legally, and factually.

Strategically, counsel must know what the goal is in taking the deposition. Is it to obtain admissions to support a motion for summary judgment? Is it to explore all details of the plaintiff's allegations so that there are no surprises at trial? Is it to try various levels of pressure to determine how the plaintiff will respond under the pressure at trial? Most plaintiff's depositions involve, to a greater or lesser extent, more than one of these and other goals. A good starting point is the complaint and its basic chronology of events. Then counsel ordinarily exhausts the plaintiff's memory of those alleged and other events. Other topics are damages, medical treatment, and interim earnings.

Legally, counsel must know what admissions are necessary from the plaintiff to obtain summary judgment or to support a motion in limine. It is critical that counsel have an understanding of the legal objective prior to the deposition.

Factually, counsel must come to the deposition knowing as much as possible about the plaintiff and the plaintiff's claim. A thorough internal investigation will go a long way toward preparing counsel for the deposition. Have the plaintiff identify key documents such as warnings, evaluations, resignations, and her personnel documents. A demonstration early on in the deposition that counsel is well informed should help persuade the plaintiff to recall events accurately to the extent possible. In addition, with a more complete understanding of the factual circumstances, counsel will be better able to understand the plaintiff's testimony and to know the significance of various statements made during the deposition.

If well prepared, counsel will also know where documents will limit plaintiff's testimony. Armed with this knowledge, counsel may confront the plaintiff with any inconsistencies during the deposition in an effort to get favorable admissions. Or, counsel may encourage the plaintiff to embellish testimony, with the intent to save any impeachment for trial.

Defense counsel will usually cover the following topics with the plaintiff: education, criminal background, work history, subsequent employment, similar claims or other litigation, damages, mitigation, witnesses, medical problems and treatment, basic claims and chronology, internal complaints, performance or other problems, basis for discrimination, and any statements from managers that may be direct evidence of discrimination.

3. Follow-up Written Discovery

Any unresolved discovery issues remaining after the deposition may be the subject of follow-up written discovery. These may include requests to admit or produce or interrogatories. If the preliminary investigation and plaintiff's deposition are handled effectively, little if any follow-up discovery should be necessary. Inevitably, however, new issues arise that necessitate further inquiry. If the matter is significant, counsel may consider seeking to reopen the plaintiff's deposition for purposes of inquiry into the issue.

4. Discovery of Experts and Medical Condition*

More and more, plaintiffs are alleging that they have suffered emotional distress as the result of some employment action. Courts are divided on whether a simple allegation of emotional distress is suffi-

---

* See also chapter 4, "Experts," especially Expert Discovery and other portions of this chapter dealing with primary concerns, psychological evaluation, and protective orders, especially from mental examinations.

cient to trigger an obligation on behalf of the plaintiff to submit to a Fed. R. Civ. P. 35 medical examination. (See *Bridges v. Eastman Kodak Co.*, 64 Fair Empl. Prac. Cas. (BNA) 1100 (S.D. N.Y. 1994); *Jansen v. Packaging Corp.*, 66 Fair Empl. Prac. Cas. (BNA) 556 (N.D. Ill. 1994); *Robinson v. Jacksonville Shipyards, Inc.*, 54 Fair Empl. Prac. Cas. (BNA) 83 (M.D. Fla. 1988).) An allegation of emotional distress should at a minimum, however, open the door to inquiry into the plaintiff's personal and medical history.[3]

If a Rule 35 examination is not an option (or before going to the expense of seeking a Rule 35 examination), counsel should first obtain all available medical information regarding the plaintiff. This information may be obtained through an authorization signed by the plaintiff or through subpoenas of pertinent health care providers. Once this information is compiled, it should be reviewed in conjunction with the information from the plaintiff's medical expert (if any) and perhaps with the assistance of a defense expert in the field. This review should help counsel decide whether to insist on a Rule 35 examination to simply cross-examine the plaintiff's expert, or to obtain an expert on behalf of defendant to testify at trial.

D. Responding to Plaintiff's Discovery

Of at least equal importance to discovery initiated by the defendant is the formulation of responses to the plaintiff's discovery. In formulating discovery responses, it is important to understand what the plaintiff is looking for, overtly and covertly. Aside from a general search for information, plaintiff's lawyers are always in search of inconsistencies—inconsistencies between two management witnesses, inconsistencies between what one witness had to say at different times, and inconsistencies between testimony and documentary evidence. Any inconsistencies on important issues will severely undercut the defendant's credibility and may be fatal to the defense. Again, a thorough internal investigation is the best means to avoid inconsistencies in discovery responses.

1. Interrogatories

Unlike defendant's interrogatories, which often focus on ancillary matters, plaintiff's interrogatories often focus on the very heart of the case. There are generally two goals for these inquiries: (1) to identify potential witnesses and (2) to create the opportunity for inconsistencies.

Plaintiffs often serve interrogatories early in the case. On occasion defense counsel formulate answers to the interrogatories after discussion with one or two key individuals involved in the decision in question. This approach often leads to trouble. For example, when asked who made the decision to terminate an employee, a senior manager may respond that the direct supervisor made the decision and that the senior manager simply approved the decision. On the other hand, the direct supervisor may believe that he merely gathered the pertinent information and presented it to the senior manager for decision. It is important, at the interrogatory answer stage, to discuss this matter with the two individuals and to attempt to establish what really happened. If the interrogatory answer is based solely on the senior manager's perception, it is likely that the direct supervisor's testimony in deposition will create an inconsistency that could be used to persuade the jury that the employer is either covering something up or does not know what is going on. For this reason, it is important to involve all potentially relevant parties in the formulation of interrogatory responses and as early in the process as practical.

2. Document Requests

If a thorough internal investigation has been completed, no proper document request should come as a surprise. If there is a new, relevant inquiry, it is important to inquire diligently as to the documents responsive to the request. The inquiry must go beyond counsel's contact person (for example, the human resources manager) to those persons who may actually be in possession of relevant documents. It does not serve the client's best interest for counsel to produce documents late in discovery or on the eve of trial.

3. Scope of Plaintiff's Discovery

Plaintiff's attorneys often serve written discovery requests that are extremely broad and seek discovery of matters without regard to time or geographic scope. For example, an employee discharged from a local branch facility may seek documents on similarly situated employees from all facilities of a nationwide operation. Depending on the court, counsel may be successful in limiting the scope of discovery to the particular facility in which the plaintiff was employed.[4] Many courts will limit discovery to those circumstances arising under a common decision maker.

With respect to the relevant time period of inquiry, most courts will permit discovery beyond the applicable statute of limitations because the evidence may be relevant to establish a pattern or practice of discrimination.[5] Another issue of scope of discovery relates to prior discrimination claims; plaintiffs often request information on all kinds of discrimination claims against the defendant. Courts generally hold that only those prior claims alleging the same protected class as the plaintiff are discoverable.[6]

At least as an initial matter, counsel should object to these types of overly broad discovery. Many times, plaintiff's counsel will accept defendant's response without further comment. Even if plaintiff's counsel pushes for broader discovery, the court may limit the discovery to some relevant scope. The court is more likely to restrict the scope of such discovery if defendant's counsel can establish the burden or expense of undertaking the broader discovery.

4. Depositions of Management Witnesses

Depending on the case, plaintiff's counsel may seek only one or two depositions or may seek ten or more. Regardless of the number of depositions, preparation of witnesses for depositions is critical. The more important the witness is to the case, the more time should be spent with the witness in preparation for the deposition. Witnesses must be prepared for the scope of inquiry that they are likely to face. Witnesses should be advised of any allegations in the complaint directed at them. In addition, each witness should be advised of prior discovery responses (by the plaintiff and from the defendant) relating to the witness. Finally, witnesses should be shown any documents produced in the case that relate to them. The goal should be to give the witness all the information necessary to enable the witness to recall as fully as possible the sequence of relevant events.

With management witnesses, it is also important to discuss the defendant's theory of the case and the manner in which the particular witness fits into the theory. This will help the witness to understand the importance of his or her testimony and to know where it is particularly important to be strong during the deposition.

5. Ex Parte Witness Contact

One common dispute in employment cases revolves around the lawfulness of attempts by plaintiff's counsel to talk with defendant's employees and former employees outside the presence of the defendant's counsel. The general rule has been stated that current supervisory employees are "the client" and may not be contacted ex parte by plaintiff's counsel. Conversely, some courts have held current rank-and-file employees are not "the client" and may be contacted by plaintiff's counsel.[7] Different jurisdictions have applied different tests to determine what employees come within the definition of "client."

For example, *Suggs v. Capital Cities/ABC, Inc.*, 52 Fair Empl. Prac. Cas. (BNA) 1984 (S.D.N.Y. 1990), rejected an outright prohibition of employee contacts as inappropriate. Plaintiff's counsel could interview employees with 72 hours' notice to defense counsel and other protections.

With respect to former employees, defense counsel have generally taken the position that former supervisory employees continue their "client" status, even after leaving employment with the defendant. Recently courts have found that a former employee is not the client and may be contacted by plaintiff's counsel.[8] (See Witness Interviews/Ex Parte Contacts, chapter 13, "Professionalism and Ethics.") It is important to research the case law and ethics decisions in your jurisdiction at the time the issue arises.

E. Discovery regarding Summary Judgment

1. Strategic Discovery Geared toward Summary Judgment*

As discovery in an employment case is the foundation for a motion for summary judgment, defendants should aim to complete discovery as soon as is practical after a complaint has been filed.[9] This allows the defendant, early in the litigation process, to obtain important information and documents and to test the plaintiff's willingness to invest the necessary time, effort, and money to pursue his or her case. It further allows the defendant to begin the process of framing the issues for the summary judgment motion that counsel hopes to file at the end of the discovery process. (As noted above, because summary judgment in employment cases almost always is initiated by a defendant, the presentation here focuses first on various discovery and other strategic issues from a defendant's perspective. The various countervailing considerations that are critical to a plaintiff are better understood in that context).

The timing and strategy of discovery has been, and will continue to be, influenced by the new Federal Rules of Civil Procedure, which are intended to alter substantially the fundamental discovery process. By requiring "automatic disclosure" of relevant information and documents, the 1993 amendments to the Federal Rules of Civil Procedure, which have been adopted by a number of the U. S. district courts, are intended to make many of the traditional preliminary interrogatories and requests for production of documents unnecessary. Fed. R. Civ. P. 26(a)(1) provides that the names of individuals who are likely to have discoverable information, the subjects about which these individuals have knowledge, a copy or description of documents that are relevant to disputed facts alleged with particularity, and a computation of damages should all be furnished no more than ten days after the parties

---

* See also Summary Judgment and the Discovery Process, chapter 5, "Summary Judgment."

confer pursuant to Fed. R. Civ. P. 26(f). In light of the short period of time that the amendments have been in effect, however, it remains to be seen whether this preliminary discovery will merely serve as a precursor to the same traditional forms of written discovery that predated the amendments. (See sample discovery in the appendixes at the end of this chapter.)

The defendant, through its initial requests for production of documents, should seek documents relating to every aspect of the case, ranging from background documents regarding education and employment history to documents that support each factual allegation and legal conclusion. A typical example of the sort of specific, substantive request that is appropriate in the defendant's first set of requests is as follows: "Any and all documents in any way supporting, refuting, or otherwise concerning Plaintiff's allegation, contained in Count 1 of the Complaint, that ABC Company failed to promote plaintiff because of her gender, including, but not limited to, any and all documents concerning the vice-president position identified by Plaintiff in paragraph 26 of the Complaint." Aside from allowing the defendant to review the full range of documents relied upon by the plaintiff, requests for documents also permit the defendant to establish those areas for which the plaintiff has no supporting documents. In cases where there are no documents to support a material issue of fact, the defendant will be in a better position to argue at summary judgment as plaintiff has no tangible evidence for his or her allegation. It should be noted, however, that in most cases much of the documentary evidence is in the possession of the employer-defendant and that the defendant generally is seeking in addition documents created by plaintiff or taken from defendant's offices by plaintiff.

In contrast to the requests for production of documents, the interrogatories should be strategically limited. Remembering that interrogatories typically are written by or with the assistance of counsel, the defense counsel aiming for summary judgment should avoid propounding detailed fact interrogatories. Such interrogatories often force a plaintiff and his or her lawyer to evaluate the case in far greater detail and from perspectives that might not occur otherwise during the early stages of the litigation. This makes it far more likely that the plaintiff will be better prepared to respond to those critical deposition questions upon which the motion for summary judgment may turn. Interrogatories are useful for gathering background information, including the names of individuals with discoverable information, a summary of the plaintiff's employment and educational history, and an accounting of each item in his or her prayer for damages. They also are valuable for certain "date, time, and place" facts. For example, interrogatories requesting the names, dates, and so on of any psychiatric or other similar treatment for emotional distress can give a party a head start in evaluating the plaintiff's emotional distress claim and in preparing a suitable line of questioning during the plaintiff's deposition.

For example, the following is a typical interrogatory in an age discrimination case:

> Identify any and all statements made by any manager or supervisor that the Plaintiff believes reflected a bias or animus based on age. Without limitation, include in your answer the following: (i) the name of the person making the statement and any person who heard the statement; (ii) the place where the statement was made; (iii) the substance of the statement; and (iv) the date of the statement.

Such an interrogatory forces both plaintiff and counsel to review carefully any possible age-based statements. Although the plaintiff's initial instincts may be that there are no such statements, after consultation with his or her attorney, the plaintiff's interrogatory answer is likely to contain a variety of statements that he or she will contend are age based. Furthermore, at the deposition to follow, the plaintiff will be fully prepared to answer the inevitable questions concerning the statements.

By contrast, if no such interrogatory is served, it is quite possible that a different picture will emerge that effectively will assist in obtaining summary judgment. At plaintiff's deposition, a defendant is far more likely to elicit testimony that will maximize the opportunity for summary judgment. Consider a typical deposition colloquy:

Q. You testified that Mr. Smith was your supervisor at the time of your termination, is that correct?

A. Yes.

Q. You also testified that you believed that Mr. Smith made the decision to terminate you, is that right?

A. That's correct.

Q. Now, Mr. Smith never made any statement to you that you considered to reflect a bias or animus based upon your age, isn't that right?

A. Well, I'm not sure how you would define bias or animus. I definitely believe that Mr. Smith wanted to get rid of me because of my age.

Q. Sir, please listen to my question. In fact, you are unable to remember a single statement by Mr. Smith where he made a statement directed to you that made reference in any way to your age?

A. I guess that's correct, at least I can't recall any.

Q. In fact, you cannot identify a single statement by Mr. Smith that you considered to reflect a bias or animus based on age directed to any employee of the company, right?

A. Not that I can recall.

The foregoing example, which is reflective of deposition testimony in several actual cases, illustrates how a deposition unencumbered by prior interrogatory answers and presented in a cross-examination format can create a record of a party's immediate perceptions and instinctive reactions. Unlike the plaintiff in this example, the plaintiff who has responded to detailed fact interrogatories will have the benefit of reflection and hindsight, thus increasing the probability that statements previously forgotten or perceived as innocent are presented at the deposition as "smoking guns." Thus, serving fact interrogatories that give a plaintiff the opportunity to reflect upon his or her case can potentially doom summary judgment.

As the deposition of the plaintiff is the key event leading towards a motion for summary judgment, the ideal timing is immediately following the receipt of the plaintiff's responses to written discovery requests. The deposition must be thorough, covering each area of possible factual inquiry that could be "material" to the case. Otherwise, a plaintiff will be able to use an affidavit to address previously unexplored issues and to establish a material issue of disputed fact.

2. Committing the Opposing Party to His or Her Evidence

As mentioned previously, a lawyer who is using discovery to elicit information for a motion for summary judgment must pin down the opposing party to the facts that he or she offers in support of a particular claim. If this is overlooked, then the opposing party has the opportunity to "wiggle out" and submit additional evidence when the motion for summary judgment is filed. Often this freedom may be enough to permit the opposing party to survive summary judgment.

Many jurisdictions prohibit a party from offering affidavits that contradict sworn deposition testimony.[10]

Ordinarily the process of committing a party to a circumscribed set of facts occurs at the party's deposition. There, once the deponent has exhausted those facts upon which he or she relies in support of a claim, the lawyer should make certain to ask if there are any other facts that are being relied upon. If the deponent answers in the negative, then the lawyer has achieved his or her objective. Frequently, however, the deponent will respond by saying that he or she cannot recall any other facts "at the present time." Such a response obviously is intended to preserve the deponent's ability to come forward with additional facts at a later time, be it in an affidavit or at trial. Whatever benefit the deponent gains from such a response can be minimized, however, if the lawyer follows up by asking if there is anything he or she can do to aid the party's recollection. Assuming the deponent answers in the negative, he or she will find it difficult at the time of summary judgment to go beyond the set of facts offered at the deposition. This benefit also can be minimized, if not eliminated altogether, by a few careful questions. Consider the following exchange:

Q. Are you aware of any other facts that lead you to believe that you were terminated because you were pregnant?

A. Well, not at the present time.

Q. Are you aware of any other statements made by anyone in management that you believe reflected a discriminatory motive on the basis of your pregnancy?

A. Again, I can't remember any others as I sit here.

Q. Well, if someone had made a statement regarding your pregnancy, that would have been pretty significant in your view, isn't that right?

A. I guess so.

Q. And you would remember such a statement, isn't that right?

A. I suppose so.

Contrast, from the plaintiff's perspective, how to avoid getting trapped by such questioning:

Q. Are you aware of any other facts that lead you to believe that you were terminated because you were pregnant?

A. That's a difficult question to answer. Obviously I was not present when the reasons for my termination were discussed by management, nor have I seen the documents that we requested from the company. I expect that when the depositions of my managers and fellow employees occur, their testimony will show that I was an employee who was well regarded, worked hard, and performed at a satisfactory level. The only thing that separated me from the others in the department was that I got pregnant.

3. Reliability and Admissibility of Discovery

When exploring the evidence that is relied upon by an opposing party, it is insufficient simply to elicit a list of facts. After the opposing party lists his or her evidence, the reliability and admissibility of that evidence must then be tested. Typically, because this process requires a certain level of fluidity and spontaneity, the deposition once again is the favored discovery device for these purposes. Where circumstances preclude a deposition, however, interrogatories or, to a much lesser degree, requests for admissions, may also be helpful.

The "reliability" of evidence, as measured by all of the circumstances surrounding the particular alleged fact or occurrence, is another way of describing its persuasiveness. Frequently lawyers believe that, because courts are reluctant to make credibility determinations at the summary judgment stage, the reliability of evidence cannot have any impact on a motion for summary judgment. This is not entirely accurate. First, because human nature cannot be removed entirely from the summary judgment process, to the extent that certain evidence can be shown to be "incredible," a judge is more likely to analyze a summary judgment motion so as to achieve the "fair" or "correct" result. Second, according to the Supreme Court's decision in *Anderson v. Liberty Lobby, Inc.*, 77 U.S. 242 (1986), and the lower court decisions that followed,[11] the proper summary judgment standard is whether "a reasonable jury could return a verdict for the nonmoving party."[12] The Court in *Anderson* went on to hold that "[i]f the evidence is merely colorable, or is not significantly probative, summary judgment may be granted."[13] Implicit in this standard is the fact that courts must evaluate at some level the reliability of evidence in order to determine how it might be viewed by a reasonable jury.[14] As such, where the moving party has identified facts during discovery that severely undermine the reliability of certain evidence, summary judgment becomes a more distinct possibility.

The various methods of testing the reliability of evidence are restricted only by the lawyer's creativity. There are, however, a few time-honored methods that should normally be considered. These include (1) identifying the source of the information upon which the nonmoving party relies (that is, was he or she an eyewitness, or did he or she hear about it from someone else); (2) determining the degree to which an allegation rests on the nonmoving party's belief, rather than objective facts (at summary judgment, a plaintiff's "belief" unsubstantiated by fact will be insufficient to defeat summary judgment);[15] (3) determining the extent to which other witnesses may have interpreted the circumstances or events in question in the same manner as the nonmoving party; (4) evaluating the amount of corroborating evidence that the nonmoving party has, whether in the form of contemporaneous notes or other witnesses; and (5) determining whether the nonmoving party's recollection is consistent with relevant documents. Other effective means of discrediting evidence are dictated by the facts of the particular case.

Closely related to the concept of reliability is the law of evidence. In light of the language of Fed. R. Civ. P. 56(e), all lawyers should be mindful of the evidentiary rules as they proceed through the discovery process. Fed. R. Civ. P. 56(e) expressly requires that

> [s]upporting and opposing affidavits shall set forth such facts as would be admissible in evidence, and shall show affirmatively that the affiant is competent to testify to the matters stated therein.[16]

The law of many states closely mirrors this same standard.[17]

The courts have expanded this principle beyond affidavits so that all evidence that is proffered in connection with a motion for summary judgment must be admissible.[18] Any evidence that is inadmissible, for whatever reason, should be stricken.[19] Thus, evidence will not be considered in connection with a summary judgment motion if it is, for example, speculative or hearsay.[20]

In view of this principle, both parties must be certain during discovery to establish the admissibility of evidence that may be useful at the summary judgment stage of litigation. To this end, lawyers should be certain that depositions and other discovery tools are properly utilized to overcome evidentiary hurdles. Normally, for example, one might wait for trial to elicit testimony that will establish the admissibility of a document. Yet, if the document is to be used on summary judgment, and there is no friendly witness who can provide the necessary information by means of an affidavit, the discovery process may be the only means of gaining the document's admission and ensuring that it is considered in connection with the motion.

Accordingly, a lawyer who hopes to introduce a business record on summary judgment motion should either seek a stipulation or obtain admissions during discovery that will establish all of the elements of the business records exception under Fed. R. Evid. 803(6). Similarly, where a party wishes to use certain statements of a corporate party's employee as admissions under Fed. R. Evid. 801(d)(2), his or her lawyer should be certain that the individual who made the statement is identified specifically (See *Jefferson Construction Co. v. United States*, 283 F.2d 265, 267 (1st Cir. 1960)), and that there is sworn testimony confirming that the statements were made within the scope of the individual's employment.[21]

A similar requirement is set out in Fed. R. Civ. P. 56(e), which provides that "[s]worn or certified copies of all papers or parts thereof referred to in an affidavit shall be attached thereto or served therewith." In order to satisfy this requirement, deponents with knowledge of documents should be asked routinely to authenticate documents. In this way, one can be assured that all documents that might be used at summary judgment can be certified simply by reference to deposition testimony.

IV. Other Discovery Issues

A. Privacy Concerns regarding Discovery of Records from Plaintiff

It becomes quite clear very quickly in employment litigation that the discovery process can be grueling. Defendant employers, in attempting to confirm or explore various damage allegations that the plaintiff has asserted, seek to compel the plaintiff to produce documents that may shed light upon any changes in the plaintiff's living habits or actual damages. For example, it is common for employers to request copies of the plaintiff's checkbook registers, bank statements, credit card bills, receipts, and various financial statements. Plaintiff's lawyers have begun to attempt to limit what information a defendant may obtain in litigation; they argue that privacy concerns and interests should prevail over certain discovery practices.

Regarding plaintiff's records and privacy concerns, some courts will consider plaintiff's privacy interests, the specificity of the defendant's request in light of the plaintiff's allegations, the defendant's alternative methods of obtaining the information, and the effect of discovery on future plaintiffs. The circumstances of the case may not warrant the discovery of plaintiff's specific financial information or documents such as checking and banking accounts or credit card records.[22] Privacy interests may be sufficient to bar or limit unlimited intrusion. An additional concern is that such unlimited discovery of personal records might have a chilling effect on other employees' filing meritorious discrimination suits.

Defendant employers should first focus on less invasive means of obtaining personal and private information. The mere convenience and expediency to the employer does not establish a sufficient need to overcome the plaintiff's privacy interest. Nonetheless, employers should continue to pursue such discovery and be prepared to address these issues on a case-by-case basis.

B. Discovery of Unemployment Records, Tax Returns, and Other Financial Records

1. Unemployment Records

An employer may want the unemployment records of a former employee who has sued because of a termination, because in some state jurisdictions unemployment compensation reduces a back pay award.[23] Unemployment records are not protected under any federal discovery privilege.[24] Even if state statutes make unemployment compensation records confidential, such laws do not control their use in federal court, especially when federal rights are at issue.[25] Additionally, a claimant can usually request a copy of his own unemployment file in order to facilitate discovery.[26]

In some jurisdictions, under Title VII or the Age Discrimination in Employment Act, an employer cannot reduce a back pay award with unemployment benefits.[27] Individual state statutes, however, may provide relief to employers seeking to mitigate these benefits. In New Jersey, for example, an employer may argue that the Law against Discrimination permits such mitigation. In *Sporn v. Celebrity, Inc.*, 324 A.2d 71 (N.J. Law Div. 1974), the trial court refused to deduct unemployment benefits from a wrongful discharge back pay award (noting that "[r]educing recovery by the amount of the benefits received by plaintiff would be granting a windfall to defendant by allowing him an undeserved credit on his own wrongdoing from a source never so intended"); later, however, in *Willis v. Dyer*,[28] the New Jersey appellate Division awarded plaintiff back pay reduced by any amounts he received as unemployment compensation during that period.[29]

2. Tax Returns, Financial Records, and Other Information

a. From Plaintiffs With increased damages to terminated employees, a growing issue is proving (or disproving) an employee's emotional distress. One increasingly popular and effective method to reduce or eliminate plaintiff's emotional distress claims is to rebut plaintiff's emotional distress with records of plaintiff's finances. For example, if an employee contends that his recreational or social life has suffered dramatically since termination, the employer may refute with the plaintiff's checkbook registers, bank statements, credit card bills, receipts, or financial statements.

The conflict between an employer's desire for this financial information and an employee's wish to maintain his or her privacy interests may evolve through discovery motions. Where such records are relevant, courts will order their production.[30] In *Harmon v. Great Atlantic & Pacific Tea Co., Inc.*, 642 A.2d 1042 (N.J. App. Div. 1994), an employer's request for extensive financial records of the plaintiff for a five-year period was overbroad. The court rejected the employer's access based upon deposition testimony regarding dramatic changes in the plaintiff's lifestyle and difficulty in sleeping and eating. The court identified and relied on "[l]ess invasive means of obtaining facts to test objectively plaintiff's allegations."[31] As an alternative, the *Harmon* court suggested exploring plaintiff's specific activities during deposition. The employer could independently investigate these activities. Afterwards, where appropriate, the employer could seek authorizations for the release of specific information. The *Harmon* court thus struck a balance: While an employee's privacy interests can overcome an employer's "[m]ere convenience or expediency" in making broad discovery requests, an employee's privacy interests may not protect financial records that relate to particular issues in the litigation.

A plaintiff frequently puts his or her income at issue when seeking back pay. Tax returns can show interim earnings and mitigation of damages. Public policy may weigh against disclosure of a person's tax records. A court may deny such disclosure if the sought-after information is available through any other financial records.[32] Alternatively, a court may order such records remain under seal.[33]

> **b. From Defendants** Plaintiffs also often seek financial information relating to the defendant for use at trial. This information allows the plaintiff to show the wealth of the defendant employer, in connection with punitive damages. Before access, the plaintiff usually must establish entitlement to punitive damages and a prima facie showing of malice. Lacking this proof, the defendant may withhold financial information.[34] So, although an employee may prove a right to financial disclosure, he is not automatically entitled to any financial record.

The New Jersey Supreme Court in *Herman v. Sunshine Chemical Specialties, Inc.*, 627 A.2d 1081 (N.J. 1993) addressed the conflicting rights of the plaintiff to seek broad financial discovery and the privacy of corporate records. Publicly held corporate defendants must disclose annual shareholder reports or file reports with regulatory bodies. Privately held corporations may be required to disclose certified financial statements. The court also suggested that disclosure of corporate income tax returns may be resisted.[35]

Courts may differ as to whether plaintiff is required to make any showing in order to be entitled to such financial discovery. Although some courts will permit the financial discovery based simply on plaintiff's pleadings, other courts may require the plaintiff to make a prima facie showing of the defendant's liability. Some courts even bifurcate trial and disclose such financial records only after a jury has actually determined the defendant's liability.[36] (See chapter 6, "Pretrial Motions," regarding bifurcation.) Accordingly, if the confidentiality of certain documents is important to a corporate defendant, it may resist disclosure, especially if the employee's case is weak.

C. Psychological Evaluation of the Plaintiff*

A defendant may request a psychological examination of the plaintiff, pursuant to Rule 35(a) of the Federal Rules of Civil Procedure. Rule 35(a) permits such an evaluation if the plaintiff's mental condition is in controversy and good cause is shown.[37]

Most cases ordering mental examinations have involved either a separate tort claim for emotional distress or an allegation of ongoing

---

* See also Emotional Distress Issues, chapter 4, "Experts," and Protective Orders, Especially from Mental Examinations, later in this chapter.

severe mental injury.[38] The courts have generally ordered that the plaintiff undergo a psychological evaluation where the plaintiff alleges that the employer's discrimination caused emotional distress damages.[39] Courts have also ordered the plaintiff to undergo psychological evaluation by the defendant's expert when the plaintiff has alleged ongoing severe mental injury.[40]

Other courts have denied requests for psychological evaluations when the plaintiff has not alleged current emotional damage from alleged discrimination.[41] In some instances where courts have permitted psychological evaluations, they have placed conditions on the examination either by permitting a third party to be present in the evaluation[42] or by precluding the defendant from choosing the mental examiner.[43] (See chapter 4, "Experts," regarding examinations of plaintiffs, and Protective Orders, Especially from Pretrial Examinations, later in this chapter.)

D. Discovery of Personnel Records of the Plaintiff and Other Employees

In order to evaluate a cause of action or identify potential defenses, plaintiffs seek their personnel records from their employers. Such records would be discoverable during litigation, but an interesting issue arises for a request prior to any litigation. Several state statutes provide employees with the right of access to their personnel files.[44] So review state statutes (or case law, in the absence of a statute) to determine authority for an employee (or former employee) to have access to these files.

Plaintiffs may seek personnel files of other employees to establish a pattern or practice, motive, or other evidence in a discrimination case. Employers should be extremely cautious in permitting the discovery of such files and information. Discovery of the personnel files of other employees may lead to claims for invasion of privacy, defamation, or interference with economic advantage. In the absence of consent by these other employees, employers usually refuse to produce such co-workers' files without a court order.[45]

E. Protective Orders, Especially from Mental Examinations

Plaintiffs and defendants in employment actions must be prepared to fight for protective orders or orders compelling discovery. To protect legitimate privacy rights and to prevent harassment, counsel should object. If necessary, counsel should move for protective orders limiting or forbidding discovery into nonrelevant and intrusive areas.

Because many federal and state discrimination statutes allow damages for emotional distress, it is routine for plaintiff to seek emotional distress damages. In response to claims for damages for emotional distress, defendants may seek to have plaintiffs submit to mental examinations. The trend appears to be away from the automatic allowance of such examinations, unless the plaintiff seeks to present psychological testimony or makes specific claims for psychological disability.

Illustrative of this point is *Turner v. Imperial Stores*, 161 F.R.D. 89 (S.D. Cal. 1995), a Title VII action claim based on gender and race discrimination. After the plaintiff sought to recover damages for lost earnings, other employment benefits, and damages for "humiliation, mental anguish and emotional distress," the defendants sought to compel the mental examination of the plaintiff. The plaintiff objected on the ground that she had not received professional psychological care, that the examination would violate her right to privacy and that expert testimony regarding her emotional distress claim "would invade the province of the jury."[46] The court agreed and denied the defendant's motion. The court noted that even in those cases where mental examinations were ordered, it was because there were special circumstances, such as

> 1) a cause of action for intentional or negligent infliction of emotional distress; 2) an allegation of a specific mental or psychiatric injury or disorder; 3) a claim of unusually severe emotional distress; 4) plaintiff's offer of expert testimony to support a claim of emotional distress; or 5) plaintiff's concession that his or her mental condition is "in controversy" within the meaning of [Federal Rule of Civil Procedure] Rule 35(a).

The court concluded that "emotional distress" is not synonymous with the term "mental injury" as used by the Supreme Court in *Schlagenhauf v. Holder*, 379 U.S. 104 (1964) for purposes of ordering a mental examination of a party under Rule 35(a).[47] (See the discussion earlier in this chapter regarding psychological evaluation of the plaintiff and emotional injury and chapter 4, "Experts," on the issue of the use of expert medical examinations in employment cases.)

F. Discovery of Similar Discrimination Charges

Plaintiff's counsel may attempt to introduce evidence of discrimination charges brought by other people against the same employer as a method of proving defendant's discriminatory conduct against plaintiff. This evidence may usually be discovered.[48]

V. Conclusion

In many employment cases, discovery is the most important aspect of the entire litigation. The reason discovery is so vital is that in addition to discussing the other party's case, it is in the discovery phase that the case is shaped for resolution either by settlement or by trial. Planning and follow-through are essential to effective discovery. More often than not the case is resolved favorably either through settlement or trial because of the effective planning and implementation of focused efforts throughout discovery.

VI. Appendixes

A. Sample Interrogatories to Be Served on the Employer

- **Plaintiff's Employment History**
1. State for the named plaintiff the following information:
   a. Date of hiring
   b. Job title, grade or salary level, and rate of pay at date of hire
   c. All salary increases given since date of hire and the dates of each increase
2. Please state the name and job title of any and all employees of defendant who evaluated plaintiff and/or made job decisions concerning plaintiff. Please state whether or not there exist any written or recorded memoranda or documents of any sort with reference to such evaluations and job decisions. If so, provide copies of any and all such documents.
3. Until the date plaintiff stopped working for you, was there ever any complaint relative to his ability to do his work? If so, please detail and provide copies of documents reflecting or referring to such complaints.
4. Please describe each and every written reprimand issued by defendant to plaintiff regarding his performance.
5. State and describe in detail the operation of any seniority system in use, including salary by labor grade, specifically stating:
   a. its effect on merit earned salary increases;
   b. its effect on promotional opportunities;
   c. its effect on discharge, termination, or layoff.
- **Defendant's Reduction in Force or Reorganization**
6. Please state the number of department employees that defendant had for each of fiscal years _____, both for the company in its entirety and by division within the company. Explain the methods that defendant utilized to compare the performance of department employees, and with regard to each such method, how plaintiff was evaluated relative to other department employees, that is, how his performance compared with that of other members of his department.

   In answering, indicate and describe the correlation between performance evaluation of plaintiff relative to any documentation or other basis used in selecting plaintiff for discharge and that of the other employees retained by the defendant.
7. Please state if you have compiled any documents that contain statistics, charts, or reports relative to the ages of department employees for the years _____. If so, please provide any and all such documents.
8. Identify all individuals and their job titles who participated in or attended any meetings or discussions regarding termination of plaintiff's employment.
   a. State the date of each such recommendation, whether written or oral.
   b. If oral, state the substance of each such recommendation.
   c. If written, attach a copy of each such recommendation.

- **Performance Evaluations**
9. Does defendant maintain a system or procedure for employee performance evaluation? If so, provide separately for the defendant the following:
    a. A description of the system or procedure.
    b. The name, office address, and title of the custodian of the files or documents set forth in your answer to subparagraph (a) of this interrogatory.
       (1) Provide copies of any and all evaluations of the plaintiff during the term of his employment.
       (2) Provide copies of any and all evaluations of those employees who were terminated in the reduction in force for the last three years of their employment. (For example, the timing of a bad performance review may be a pretext for age discrimination if the employees selected for terminated were ostensibly chosen because of their poor performance. See e.g. *White v. Westinghouse Electric*, 862 F.2d 56 (3d Cir. 1988).)
- **Plaintiff's Damages**
10. Please state the value of all fringe benefits that the plaintiff was receiving at the time of his termination, based on a monthly or yearly calculation.
- **Other Evidence of Bias**
11. State whether any civil action or administrative charge has been filed charging the defendant with [age discrimination.] If so, for each such action state:
    a. The name of the court or administrative agency in which the action was instituted or is pending and the action number
    b. The names of all parties and decision makers to the action
    c. The disposition of the action or its current status
12. State separately for each year, the number of department employees and their ages, who were discharged, terminated, or laid off, including temporary layoffs, commencing with _____ and for each year thereafter through the present.

B. Plaintiff's Requests for Documents

The following are excerpts from a request for document production that was served with the above-excerpted interrogatories in a reduction-in-force case.

1. Provide copies of any and all evaluations of the plaintiff prior to his termination.
2. Provide a copy of any and all recommendations that plaintiff's employment should be terminated.
3. Provide copies of any and all documents reflecting or referring to complaints relative to plaintiff's ability to do his work.
4. Provide copies of any and all reprimands issued to the plaintiff regarding his performance.
5. Provide copies of any and all documents on which you base your denial that plaintiff's termination was not based on age.

6. Provide any and all documents relative to your contention that plaintiff's claims are time barred.

7. Provide copies of any and all documents you have compiled that contain statistics, charts, or reports relative to the ages of your department employees for the years ————————.

C. Sample Cover Letter and Client Intake Questionnaire*

The Plaintiff Employee Perspective

ATTORNEY-CLIENT PRIVILEGE

Re: Possible Case Against Former Employer

Dear ————————:

At your request, we are sending you the enclosed questionnaire and several other forms. Before you begin to work on these forms, there are several things that you should know.

We emphasize that *we have made no decision* on whether we think you have a case and/or whether we will represent you, as yet. We cannot make any such decision until after we have had a chance to evaluate the information that you will supply. Your cooperation with the above instructions therefore is essential, and we appreciate it.

Thank you for your patience, understanding, and cooperation.

Very truly yours,

[FIRM]

By: ————————————————

D. Possible Case Intake Questionnaire†

ATTORNEY-CLIENT PRIVILEGE

1. *Directions for Completing Questionnaire*:

Please answer *every* question in the questionnaire. If you need more space, add additional pages. Write on only one side of each additional page. Do *not* write on the back of the questionnaire or any additional page.

---

*See also Initial Consultation Confirmation Letter and Consultation Follow-up Letter, chapter 13, "Professionalism and Ethics."

†See also Employment Discrimination Questionnaire, chapter 1, "Commencing the Lawsuit," and Telephone Inquiry Form, chapter 13, "Professionalism and Ethics."

2. *History*:

Next, do a chronological memo of what your complaint is about. This memo is absolutely *essential* to our evaluation of your situation. We need to see *everything* that happened to you, in order, and what facts there are to back this up.

It is best *not* to do the memo in a single sitting. A good technique is to make an outline of the major events. Start with the first event and continue to the last, in order. Then put the outline aside for a day or two. Then go back to it, at which time you will begin to fill in the details. After doing a first draft, put the chronology aside again for another day or so. Then go back to it a third time, and add and revise as necessary. This is an excellent technique for making sure that you give us the most information possible in the best organized fashion.

Each time you describe something that happened, think of how you would *prove it* if asked; include the names of anyone present (who could be a potential witness) and anything else along this line. Be as direct as possible; for example, do not say "My supervisor ordered me to fix the machine" if you could say "My supervisor gave me a *written order* to fix the machine." This shows that there was a piece of paper concerning the order and that paper could back up the fact that the order was given. In addition, show us what *specific facts* there are to back up what you think was the *real* reason for your termination. For example, if a supervisor had it in for you, tell us *why* this came about, *when* it happened, *how* any dispute arose, over what incident, and so forth.

If you feel that you were talked into leaving another job and/or place of residence to take the job in question, it is essential that you tell us in detail about each and every conversation—who was there, when, who said what, and so on—that led you to make the job change.

Include in the chronology your thoughts, feelings, and emotions. It is important for us to know how you felt when the events occurred, as well as to know what the events were.

These directions have been given to you to help you complete the materials. Remember that you should be as complete and as *candid* as possible. We emphasize that we *must* have all the above materials, including a complete memo, before we can evaluate your situation. Thank you for your cooperation.

3. *Directions for Gathering and Submitting Documents.*

Gather documents or any written or printed materials that will back up or verify what happened to you.

We need to see the following:

    a. Any employee handbooks, personnel regulations, or memoranda concerning termination, discipline, or grievance procedures

    b. Any and all written evaluations of your performance that you have received from the company

    c. Your resume—an old version, a current version, or preferably both

    d. Any and all memoranda, letters, and so on concerning the events leading up to your termination

    e. If applicable, any decision of an unemployment insurance hearing officer or other unemployment papers

f. If applicable, copies of your complaint to, or any document from, the Human Rights Commission and/or Equal Employment Opportunity Commission, Department of Labor, or any other governmental agency

This list is not exclusive; send in *any and all* other documents that pertain to this matter.

Do *not*, however, contact the company to obtain additional documents. If you know that a certain document exists but the company has it, tell us what the document is and who has it.

DO NOT MAKE ANY MARKS OR WRITING ON A DOCUMENT ITSELF. If you need to tell us something about the document, attach a separate piece of paper to it by a staple or self-stick removable note and write your comments on that piece of paper or note.

Remember, make a set of copies for you, and give the *original* documents to us. Should we decide to take your case, these records will become a part of your file. Should we decide we are unable to help you with your claim, all original materials submitted will be returned to you.

Notes

1. *See, e.g.,* Maresco v. Evans Chemetics, Div. of W.R. Grace & Co., Inc., 964 F.2d 106, 110–11 (2d Cir. 1992).
2. United Steel Workers of Am. v. N.J. Zinec, 828 F.2d 1001, 1007–08 (3rd Cir. 1987).
3. Bridges, 64 Fair Empl. Prac. Cas. (BNA) at 1100.
4. *See* Chambers v. Capital Cities/ABC, 64 Fair Empl. Prac. Cas. (BNA) 581 (S.D. N.Y. 1994); Finch v. Hercules, Inc., 62 Fair Empl. Prac. Cas. (BNA) 295 (D. Del. 1993).
5. State *ex rel.* Swyers v. Romines, 65 Fair Empl. Prac. Cas. (BNA) 1663 (Mo. Ct. App. 1993).
6. Collins v. J.C. Nichols Co., 56 Fair Empl. Prac. Cas. (BNA) 1713 (W.D. Mo. 1991).
7. *See* Siguel v. Tufts College, 52 Fair Empl. Prac. Cas. 697 (D. Mass. 1990).
8. *See, e.g., In re* Opinion 668, 633 A.2d 959 (N.J. 1993); N.J.R.P.C. 4.2 and 4.3 effective September 1, 1996.
9. Normand v. Research Inst. of Am., 927 F.2d 857 (5th Cir. 1991) (noting that seven circuits had ignored discriminatory statements attributed to non–decision makers); Carter v. City of Miami, 870 F.2d 578 (11th Cir. 1989) (holding that "only the most blatant remarks, whose intent could be nothing other than to discriminate on the basis of age, . . . constitute direct evidence of discrimination"; E.E.O.C. v. Clay Printing Co., 955 F.2d 936 (4th Cir. 1992) (ignoring the decision-maker's comments concerning the need for "young blood" and the need to attract younger employees).
10. *See, e.g.,* Darnell v. Target Stores, 16 F.3d 174 (7th Cir. 1994); Sinskey v. Pharmacies Ophthalmics, Inc., 982 F.2d 494 (Fed. Cir. 1992); Davidson & Jones Dev. Co. v. Elmore Dev. Co., 921 F.2d 1343 (6th Cir. 1991); *but see* Ramos v. Geddes, 137 F.R.D. 11 (S.D. Tex. 1991) (where possible contradiction between deposition testimony and affidavit presented credibility issue, entry of summary judgment was precluded).
11. *See, e.g.,* NASCO, Inc. v. Public Storage, Inc., 29 F.3d 28, 32 (1st Cir. 1994) (court holds that factual disputes are "genuine," as that term is used in Fed. R. Civ. P. 56(c), only if they would allow a reasonable jury to resolve the issues in the nonmoving party's favor).
12. Anderson, 477 U.S. at 248.
13. *Id.* at 249–50.
14. *See* Losch, 736 F.2d at 903 (court will evaluate the evidence to determine if reasonable minds could draw only one conclusion).

15. *See* Herbert v. Mohawk Rubber Co., 872 F.2d 1104, 1106 (1st Cir. 1989).

16. Fed. R. Civ. P. 56(e).

17. *See, e.g.*, D.C. R. Civ. P. 56(e); Mass. R. Civ. P. 56(e).

18. Horta v. Sullivan, 4 F.3d 2, 8 (1st Cir. 1993); Aguilera v. Cook County Police and Corrections Merit B., 760 F.2d 844, 849 (7th Cir. 1985); Brown v. Trans World Airlines, Inc., 746 F.2d 1354, 1358 (8th Cir. 1984).

19. *See* Over the Road Drivers, Inc. v. Transport Ins. Co., 637 F.2d 816, 819 (1st Cir. 1980); 6 MOORE'S FEDERAL PRACTICE § 56.22[1] at 56–737 to 755 (2d ed. 1995).

20. Automatic Radio Mfg. Co. v. Hazeltine Research, Inc., 339 U.S. 827, 831 (1950); Sellers v. M.C. Floor Crafters, Inc., 842 F.2d 639 (2d Cir. 1988); Roslindale Coop. Bank v. Greenwald, 638 F.2d 258, 261 (1st Cir. 1981); MasMarques v. Digital Equip. Corp., 637 F.2d 24, 29 (1st Cir. 1980).

21. *See* Oreck Corp. v. Whirlpool Corp., 639 F.2d 75 (2d Cir. 1980); United States v. Bensinger Co., 430 F.2d 584 (8th Cir. 1970); Sec. & Exch. Comm'n v. Glass Marine Indus., Inc., 194 F. Supp. 879 (D. Del. 1961).

22. *See, e.g.*, Harmon v. Great Atl. & Pac. Tea Co., 642 A.2d 1042 (N.J. App. Div. 1994).

23. *See generally* Goodman v. London Metals Exch., Inc., 429 A.2d 341 (N.J. 1981) (discussing mitigation principles).

24. EEOC v. Illinois Dept. of Employment Sec., 995 F.2d 106, 107–08 (7th Cir. 1993).

25. EEOC v. Illinois Dept. of Employment Sec., 995 F.2d 106 (7th Cir. 1993) (allowing discovery of unemployment claims documents despite state law declaring documents confidential); Gallavdo v. Bd. of County Comm'rs, 881 F. Supp. 525 (D. Kan. 1995) (same); Thorne v. Big D Discount Auto Parts of Daleville, Inc., 92 F.R.D. 55 (M.D. Ala. 1981) (same); Mardis v. Robbins Tire & Rubber Co., 628 So. 2d 605 (Ala. 1993).

26. Rojas v. Ryder Truck Rental, Inc., 641 So. 2d 855 (Fla. 1994).

27. Craig v. Y & Y Snacks, Inc., 721 F.2d 77 (3d Cir. 1983); Taylor v. Central Pa. Drug and Alcohol Servs. Corp., 890 F. Supp. 360, 370 (M.D. Pa. 1995).

28. 394 A.2d 383 (N.J. App. Div. 1978).

29. *Id.*

30. Dunlap v. Midcoast-Little Rock, Inc., 166 F.R.D. 29 (E.D. Ark. 1995); Scott v. Alex, Inc., 124 F.R.D. 29 (D. Comm. 1989); Morton v. Harris, 86 F.R.D. 437 (N.D. Ga. 1986).

31. Harmon v. Great Atl. & Pac. Tea Co., Inc., 642 A.2d 1042, 1045 (N.J. Super Ct. App. Div. 1994).

32. *See* DiMasi v. Weiss, 669 F.2d 114, 119–20 (3d Cir. 1982).

33. Werner v. Bache Halsey Stuart, Inc., 76 F.R.D. 624 (S.D. Fla. 1977); Payne v. Security Savings & Loan, 924 F.2d 109 (7th Cir. 1991).

34. *See* Newport v. Facts Concerts, Inc., 453 U.S. 247 (1981); Herman v. Hess Oil Virgin Islands Corp., 524 F.2d 767 (3d Cir. 1975).

35. Herman v. Sunshine Chemical Specialties, Inc., 627 A.2d 1081, 1089 (N.J. 1993); Gumowitz v. First Fed. Savings & Loan Ass'n, 160 F.R.D. 462 (S.D.N.Y. 1995); Tele-Radio Sys. Ltd. v. DeForest Elec., Inc., 92 F.R.D. 371, 375 (D.N.J. 1981).

36. *See* Wilson v. Gillis Adver. Co., 60 Fair Empl. Prac. Cas. (BNA) 1078, 1079–80 (N.D. Ala. 1993).

37. *See* Schlangenhauf v. Holder, 379 U.S. 104 (1964).

38. *See* Bridges v. Eastman Kodak, 850 F. Supp. 216 (S.D.N.Y. 1974).

39. *See* Zabkowicz v. West Bend Co., 585 F. Supp. 635 (E.D. Wis. 1984); Lowe v. Philadelphia Newspapers, Inc., 101 F.R.D. 296 (E.D. Pa. 1983).

40. *See* Jansen v. Packaging Corp., 158 F.R.D. 409 (N.D. Ill. 1994).

41. *See, e.g.*, Curtis v. Express Inc., 868 F. Supp. 467 (N.D.N.Y. 1994); Robinson v. Jacksonville Shipyards, 118 F.R.D. 525 (N.D. Fla. 1988); and Cody v. Marriott Corp., 103 F.R.D. 421 (D. Mass. 1984).

42. *See* Zabkowicz v. West Bend Co., 585 F. Supp. 635 (E.O. Wis. 1984).

43. Jansen v. Packaging Corp. of Am., 158 F.R.D. 409 (N.D. Ill. 1994).

44. *See, e.g.*, ARK. CODE ANN. §§ 25-19-104, 105 (1987); CONN. GEN. STAT. §§ 31-128(a), 231–128(h) (1987); DEL. CODE ANN. tit. 19, §§ 730–35 (1988); MICH. COMP. LAWS ANN. §§ 423.501–512 (West 1988).

45. *See* Lee v. Hutson, 600 F. Supp. 957 (N.D.Ga. 1984); Tavoulareas v. Piro, 93 F.R.D. 35 (D.D.C. 1981).

46. *Id.* at 91.

47. *Id.* at 95.

48. Mister v. Illinois Central Gulf R.R., 639 F. Supp. 1560, 42 Fair Empl. Prac. Cas. (BNA) 1716 (S.D. Ill. 1985), *rev'd in part on other grounds*, 832 F.2d 1427, 45 Fair Empl. Prac. Cas. (BNA) 178 (7th Cir. 1987), *cert. denied*, 485 U.S. 1035 (1988); Jackson v. Alterman Foods, 37 Fair Empl. Prac. Cas. (BNA) 837 (N.D. Ga. 1984); Whalen v. McLean Trucking Co., 37 Fair Empl. Prac. Cas. (BNA) 835 (N.D. Ga. 1983).

CHAPTER 4

Experts

HERBERT E. GERSON[*]
CHRISTOPHER P. LENZO[†]
MAUREEN M. RAYBORN[‡]
NANCY ERIKA SMITH[§]

[*] *McKnight Hudson Ford & Harrison; Memphis, Tennessee.*

[†] *Francis, Lenzo & Manshel; Millburn, New Jersey.*

[‡] *Ballard Spahr Andrews & Ingersoll; Philadelphia, Pennsylvania.*

[§] *Smith Mullin; Montclair, New Jersey.*

I. Introduction

It is well known that the expert witness occupies an unusual position that in numerous ways is of a judicial character. In his testimony in many cases he is in fact deciding the case and should be as carefully selected as the judge, not only as to technical qualifications, but as to character and reliability.[1]

As a general rule, expert testimony should play only a limited role in the trial of any case because its sole function is to assist judges and juries in determining what they generally cannot determine on their own ability.[2] Admissibility of expert testimony is predicated upon whether the experts have peculiar knowledge or experience not common to the world that renders their opinions (based on such knowledge or experience) aids to the court or jury in determining the questions at issue.[3] It is within the discretion of the trial court to determine the necessity and propriety of the admission of expert testimony and whether such testimony will competently fulfill its function in aiding the jury.[4] In federal court, Rule 702 of the Federal Rules of Evidence governs this issue. *See infra* section V, for discussion of Rule 702 and *Daubert v. Merrell Dow Pharm., Inc.*, 509 U.S. 579 (1993).

In deciding whether to admit an expert witness at trial, the court must determine whether the expert will actually assist the jury or simply impinge upon the jury's role altogether. The ultimate determination of whether the defendant employer has breached a duty owed to the plaintiff must be made by the fact finder in the context of the circumstances of each case, and not by the expert witness.[5] Nevertheless, despite the trial judge's admonition that a jury is to determine the weight to be given to an expert's testimony, the combination of the expert testimony along with the court's instruction clearly has the potential to influence the jury's determination unduly. Expert witnesses are often key witnesses in employment law cases.[6] Litigators on both sides of an employment dispute must therefore select and prepare their experts with extreme care regarding both their body of knowledge and their jury appeal. Counsel must also identify all methods for minimizing the impact of the experts of their opponents. This chapter addresses strategies of plaintiffs' and defendants' counsel for the use of experts in employment litigation.

II. Do You Need Experts for Your Case?

A. In General

In employment law cases, experts generally fall into one of six classifications: statistical experts, labor economists, psychological experts, sociological experts, medical experts, and human resources professionals. The use of any expert requires a clear understanding of the claims and defenses raised, the admissibility of the testimony, and its impact on the jury.

The most common use of experts is in employment discrimination cases, where parties often will rely on psychiatrists, psychologists, and physicians to support or discredit claims of emotional distress. Economists and accountants can be used to establish or to challenge prospective lost earnings and benefits. Career counselors and job search experts can be used to assess the plaintiff's employability and the job market.

Both plaintiffs and defendants should also consider retaining other types of experts who will not actually testify but will assist in preparing the case for trial. These individuals include jury consultants and graphic arts specialists.

For both parties, potential experts should be identified early in the litigation. Consideration should also be given to engaging the expert for the purpose of drafting appropriate discovery and preparing questions to be used in deposing the opponent's expert. At this stage, the experts may also be valuable as a part of the litigation strategy team. Experts no doubt will be used aggressively in disability cases by both plaintiffs and defendants to address a variety of issues, ranging from whether a person is disabled to what a reasonable accommodation is. Increasingly experts are being used in nondiscrimination employment cases, such as in whistle-blower cases, and trade secret and noncompetition litigation to present particular substantive testimony.

The extent to which the defendant may wish to use an expert at trial will depend heavily on whether the plaintiff engages an expert for the purpose of testifying and what is learned from the plaintiff's expert report. The use of an expert may also depend upon the extent and timing of disclosures and discovery required under the applicable version of Rule 26 of the Federal Rules of Civil Procedure or the applicable state rules of discovery.

Experts should be identified and retained early in the litigation. From the defendant's perspective, the decision regarding experts is often determined by whether the plaintiff uses an expert at all. In large cases, counsel should consider using one set of experts to assist in discovery and preparation for trial and another set to testify as trial witnesses. The reason is that opinion of a "consulting" expert is usually nondiscoverable. In contrast, opposing counsel can routinely depose a "testifying" expert. (See Section IV in this chapter for discussion of expert discovery.)

B. Checklist for Retention of Experts

Counsel should be fully aware of a potential expert's qualifications, credentials, and potential weaknesses. To that end, counsel should interview potential experts and consider the following factors:

1. the expert's history of trial and/or deposition testimony;
2. all promotional and marketing materials, articles, written opinions, and books prepared by the expert (or his or her firm) within the last ten years;
3. whether the witness's opinions or testimony might be beneficial to the opposing party;
4. whether, and the extent to which, the expert has previously testified for the opposing position and if so, whether there is a conflict;
5. all deposition and trial transcripts of the expert's testimony within the last four years;
6. how much of the expert's vocation is being a litigation "expert";
7. the expert's billing, support staff, and present and anticipated case load;
8. whether the expert continues to practice in the field;
9. any awards/accomplishments and/or sanctions issued to the expert;
10. whether the expert has been the subject of litigation regarding his or her practice;
11. whether the expert considers the industry standard in formulating his or her opinion and/or conclusions;
12. the expert's communication skills;
13. the expert's cooperation with counsel, including a willingness to listen to counsel and the theory of the case;
14. the expert's availability and willingness to spend the time to be an effective witness and withstand cross-examination; and
15. the expert's ability to relate to jurors.

Counsel should also check with other members of their firms and other lawyers in the community to obtain "intelligence" on the potential expert.

III. Traditional Uses for Expert Testimony in Employment Cases

A. The Occurrence of Discrimination

Because matters of discrimination are considered to be within the understanding of the average juror, courts will generally not permit either employees or employers to have experts testify as to whether discrimination occurred in a particular instance.[7] Nevertheless, experts can be successfully employed to testify on several different types of critical issues in discrimination cases.

At least one decision permits a plaintiff to utilize expert testimony to establish his or her prima facie case. In *Robinson v. Jacksonville Shipyards, Inc.,* 760 F. Supp. 1486, 1505 (M.D. Fla. 1991), the court, in a Title VII bench trial, permitted plaintiff's expert to testify about "common practices and responses to sexual harassment and remedial steps." Having reviewed the discovery in that case, plaintiff's expert testified that a hostile work environment existed; she based her conclusion

> on the presence of indicators of sexually harassing behaviors and of a sexually hostile work environment, including evidence of a range of behaviors and conditions that are considered sexually harassing, evidence of common coping patterns by individual victims of sexual harassment, evidence of stress effects suffered by those women, evidence of male worker behavior and attitudes, and evidence of confused management response to complaints of sexual harassment.[8]

Relying upon this testimony, the court concluded that "the cumulative, corrosive effect of this work environment over time affects the psychological well-being of a reasonable woman placed in these conditions."[9]

B. Disparate Impact Issues

Experts have also been used in disparate impact discrimination cases to testify as to the meaning of statistics regarding the composition of a workforce or to assess the validity of tests used by employers to determine hiring or promotions.[10]

C. Bona Fide Occupational Qualification Issues

In an age or gender discrimination case, an expert can be used to testify as to whether an employer's prohibition against the hiring or promoting of covered individuals can be considered a bona fide occupational qualification.[11]

D. Disability Issues

An expert can testify as to whether an employer made a reasonable accommodation of an employee's disability[12] or as to the effect of a person's disability on his ability to perform his job.[13]

E. Emotional Distress Issues

Expert testimony is almost indispensable to establishing a plaintiff's claim for emotional damages. If a plaintiff seeks an award of damages for emotional distress, expert testimony may be critical. To recover for emotional harm the plaintiff must generally prove actual injury.[14] Still, the U.S. Supreme Court has unanimously held that a plaintiff need not assert a "psychological injury" as part of a Title VII hostile environment action.[15] Some state courts have reached the same conclusion regarding state law hostile environment claims.[16]

Even if expert testimony is not necessary to prove emotional distress, employment discrimination plaintiffs often have used an expert to establish emotional distress and a chain of causation between the discrimination, the emotional injuries, and all damages (including lost earnings) to try to avoid tax liability for the damages award. It should be noted that a recent amendment to the federal tax code provides that, in the absence of physical injury, all compensatory damages, including emotional distress damages, and punitive damages are taxable.[17]

To the extent that plaintiffs have suffered physical injury as a result of an employer's actions, plaintiffs should utilize psychiatrists, psychologists (or other therapists), and physicians who can testify as to the specific physical injury. The expert preferably should be one with whom the plaintiff has consulted or treated over an extended period of time (ideally before the onset of litigation)—rather than a "hired gun" who has examined the plaintiff only on a few occasions. In addition, the testimony of an independent forensic expert can buttress the testimony of the plaintiff's treating professional.

Plaintiffs' lawyers should be aware of a practical drawback in attempting to assert emotional distress as a means of establishing a "personal injury" for taxation purposes. Once the plaintiff puts his or her emotional or mental state in issue, the court will order a mental examination of the plaintiff upon the request of the defendant. To prevent such an examination is very difficult; plaintiffs' counsel have succeeded in doing so only on rare occasions.[18]

If the court does not bar the mental examination of the plaintiff, he or she has three options: (1) withdraw the claim for emotional distress damages; (2) seek mental examinations of any individual defendants to determine their biases regarding the protected group to which the plaintiff belongs; or (3) attempt to minimize the invasion of the plaintiff's privacy by seeking court-ordered controls on the examination. The first option is extremely unattractive because it will likely reduce potential damages dramatically. The second option is very difficult to attain. The third option is the most realistic response.

To control the mental examination of the plaintiff, counsel should try one or more of the following approaches: (1) attend the examination; (2) have a forensic expert or the plaintiff's treating professional attend the examination; (3) record the examination via stenography, videotaping, or audiotaping. All of these mechanisms operate as a form of "expert repellent" by discouraging experts from manipulating the plaintiff.[19]

The best preventive measure is the presence of plaintiff's counsel at the examination. One court has recognized that

> [Because a] physician selected by defendant to examine plaintiff is not necessarily a disinterested, impartial medical expert, indifferent to the conflicting interests of the parties[,] [t]he possible adversary status of the examining doctor for the defense is, under ordinary circumstances, a compelling reason to permit plaintiff's counsel to be present. . . .[20]

Several courts have allowed attorneys to be present at the mental examinations of their clients.[21] Counsel's presence can be valuable to protect against the defendant's expert asking damaging hearsay questions that later may be admitted at trial as part of the basis for his or her opinion.[22]

Substantial case law has prevented counsel's or others' presence at the plaintiff's mental examination.[23]

From the defendant's perspective, consideration should be given to whether the examination is likely to confirm the plaintiff's position. Detailed analysis by defendant's medical expert of plaintiff's medical history and plaintiff's doctor's report should precede any effort to require plaintiff to submit to an examination by defendant's expert.

F. Economic Damages Issues

An employment discrimination plaintiff should always consider the use of the expert testimony of an economist or accountant to establish the extent of economic damages, particularly prospective lost earnings and benefits.

Most plaintiffs use economists to prove economic damages. Some plaintiff's lawyers favor the use of accountants as better suited to establishing an employment discrimination plaintiff's economic damages.[24]

The economic expert must create a model that projects future lost earnings and benefits for the plaintiff. The model should be based upon the plaintiff's historical earning pattern (salary increases, bonuses, commissions, and so on) and the earning patterns of persons in similar positions. The effect of inflation on future earnings must be calculated, and the final calculation must be discounted to establish the present value of the future earnings. The economic expert must also estimate the risk that the plaintiff's employment with the defendant would have been terminated at some point in the future for a reason other than discrimination. That risk factor should include the likelihood of layoffs, closings, and retirement due to disability, as well as the plaintiff's life expectancy.

The expert's manner and mode of presentation are critical. The methodology through which the expert arrived at his conclusion must be explained to the jury in clear and simple terms, through demonstrative evidence, if possible. It is imperative that the expert not bore the jury with long-winded, highly technical, overly detailed explanations communicated in professional jargon. In addition, although expert economic testimony is not indispensable to establish the appropriate amount of punitive damages, it can be helpful for that purpose as well.[25]

All of the above factors are equally important for the defense. Because of the significance of meaningful cross-examination of the plaintiff's economic, vocational, and medical experts, it is especially important for the defendant's lawyer to know how to get behind and get beyond the surface appeal of the plaintiff's expert reports. This area is more fertile for attack than many defense lawyers realize.

G. Issues regarding Plaintiff's Unemployability

If a plaintiff claims to be unemployable, an employability expert such as a career counselor or "headhunter" should be used to establish or challenge the extent of the plaintiff's obstacles to employment. Of course, when appropriate, expert psychiatric or psychological testimony can also establish a plaintiff's unemployability due to emotional problems resulting from the discrimination.

IV. Expert Discovery*

Under Rule 26(b)(4) of the Federal Rules of Civil Procedure, substantial amounts of information obtained by experts are discoverable. In 1993, amendments to Rule 26 established radical and sweeping changes regarding the treatment of expert testimony and the discoverability of their information. (While the 1993 amendments made broad changes to the discovery rules, they may not be as sweeping as they appear. The drafters of the new Rule provided that district courts may

---

* See also Discovery of Experts and Medical Condition, chapter 3, "Discovery."

opt out, in part or in whole, of the new requirements and maintain discovery as it had operated under the old Rule 26. Lawyers must check to determine which set of rules applies in any particular district.)

A. Initial Disclosures

Rule 26(a)(2)(A) requires disclosure of detailed information regarding the identity, opinions, and background of testifying experts. (See also Fed. R. Evid. 702, 703, and 705 for evidentiary rules relating to experts and their testimony.)

Rule 26(a)(2)(B) provides that if the witness is "retained or specially employed to provide expert testimony" or is an employee of the party "whose duties . . . regularly involve giving expert testimony," the required disclosure must be supplemented by a written report prepared and signed by the expert. This report must disclose

1. all opinions to be expressed and the bases and reasons therefor;
2. data or other information considered by the witness in forming the opinions;
3. any exhibits to be used as a summary of or support for the opinions;
4. the qualifications of the witness, including a list of all publications authored by the witness within the preceding ten years;
5. the compensation to be paid for the study and testimony; and
6. a listing of any other cases in which the witness has testified as an expert at trial or by deposition within the preceding four years.

No discovery, other than the expert's deposition, may be sought in connection with the expert.

Disclosure of this information may be directed by the court, or, in the absence of court direction, no later than ninety days before the date set for trial. If the expert testimony is to be used to contradict the testimony of an opposing party's expert, this disclosure must be made within thirty days of the disclosure made by the opponent. In addition, any party making such a disclosure is under a continuing obligation to supplement the disclosure with up-to-date information if and when needed.

B. Types of Experts

Rule 26(b)(4) divides experts into four classes and provides different standards of discovery for each class.

1. Experts Expected to Be Called at Trial

Under the 1993 amendments to Rule 26, testifying experts may be deposed as any other normal witness. Rule 26(b)(4)(A) provides that the expert's deposition may not be conducted until the voluntary report required by Rule 26(a)(2)(B) has been provided. The rationale for this provision is to maximize the effect of cross-examination and rebuttal at trial. Thus, an opposing party will be able to attack the testimony of a party's expert either through cross-examination or through the use of its own expert to rebut the opinion of the opposition's expert. Rule 26(b)(4)(C) requires the party seeking discovery to pay the expert a reasonable fee for the time spent in responding to discovery and pay the other party a fair portion of the fees and expenses reasonably incurred by the latter party in obtaining facts and opinions from the expert.

2. Experts Retained in Anticipation of Litigation or Preparation for Trial But Not to Be Called as a Witness

Under Rule 26(b)(4)(B), facts and opinions of experts who have been retained or specially employed to aid in preparing for the trial, but who will not actually testify, are protected and are not discoverable. Even though these experts are not to testify, they may still be privy to a party's information and strategy regarding the suit.

There are two exceptions to this rule. First, Rule 35(b) provides for interrogatories and depositions of examining physicians in the context of physical or mental examinations when the examination is requested by one of the parties. Second, if there is a showing of "exceptional circumstances under which it is impractical for the party seeking discovery to obtain facts and opinions of the same subject matter by other means," the information may be discoverable.

3. Experts Informally Consulted in Preparation of Trial But Not Retained

Rule 26 makes no provision for discovery of the identities or opinions of experts who have been informally consulted in preparation for trial but were not retained. The Advisory Committee Note to this rule precludes discovery about experts who were informally consulted in preparation for trial but were not retained or specially employed.

The logic of this rule is based on sound policy. If this information were discoverable, a party would be forced to retain these experts in order to protect any information that may have been disclosed between the party and the expert, especially when the expert has views that are contrary or detrimental to that party's case. Discovery of this type of expert would drastically increase the costs of litigation and reduce the number of witnesses available for consultation.

4. Experts Whose Information Was Not Acquired in Preparation for Trial

Rule 26 does not specifically address this type of expert. The rule indicates only that it was drafted to address discovery of information "acquired or developed in anticipation of litigation or for trial." There seems to be no restriction on the discovery of information that an expert may have had that was not acquired or developed in this manner. This type of expert includes regular employees of a party not specifically employed for the case, and experts who were actors in or witnesses to the events that led to the commencement of the suit. These individuals are not included within Rule 26(b)(4), and their identities and opinions may be freely discovered as ordinary witnesses.

Several courts have established some protection for "unaffiliated" experts. Parties often employ the use of a subpoena to discover information from disinterested experts who had done research in the area in question. As the use of experts has increased, the burden on researcher-experts has increased, disrupting the research process and hampering research development. Rule 45(c)(3)(B) provides that a subpoena for "an unretained expert's study not made at the request of any party" may be quashed or modified by the court unless the party seeking the information can show that substantial need for the information exists and guarantees the court that the expert providing the information will be reasonably compensated.

C. Penalties for Nondisclosure

Rule 37(c)(1) provides that a party who fails to make a required initial or supplemental disclosure under Rule 26 shall not be allowed to use such evidence at trial unless failure to disclose is found to be harmless. In addition, the court is free to impose other sanctions and even make the nondisclosure known to the jury.

D. Work Product and Attorney-Client Privilege*

Rule 26(b)(3) provides protection for the work product of both the attorney and the client, but the protection extends only to documents. In contrast, Rule 26(a)(2)(A) provides for mandatory disclosure of expert information, including "data or other information considered by the witness in forming [his] opinions." Thus, if a lawyer in preparing an expert for testimony discloses work product to the expert, the lawyer

---

* See also Work Product Doctrine and Attorney-Client Privilege, chapter 13, "Professionalism and Ethics," and Discovery of Experts and Medical Condition, chapter 3, "Discovery."

has an obligation under Rule 26(a)(2)(A) to disclose the information to the opposing party, but only if the expert actually considers the information in forming his opinions.

A question also arises as to the discoverability of oral communications. The attorney-client privilege protects communications between the lawyer and the client about the legal representation sought. The courts are split as to the treatment of oral communications once they have been disclosed to an expert witness. Following the provisions of Rule 26(a)(2)(A), some courts have ruled that any disclosure of attorney-client privileged information to an expert before the expert has formed his opinion waives the privilege and such information is freely discoverable. Other courts hold that the waiver doctrine does not apply because the privilege is extended to experts sought in the legal representation. The key issues are whether the expert used the information in forming his or her opinion and whether the court is willing to extend the attorney-client privilege to experts sought in the representation.

Rule 26 also protects "mental impressions, conclusions, opinions or legal theories of an attorney or a party" against discovery. Generally courts will not allow discovery of this type of information, even if it is relied upon by experts in the formation of their opinions.

Parties must proceed cautiously, carefully weighing the possibility of forced disclosure of confidential or privileged information. The only definite way to protect confidential or privileged work from disclosure is not to share it with experts, but this course of action may reduce the efficiency of the expert and reduce his or her impact on the suit.

E. Discovery Areas*

1. In General

Counsel for each party should, of course, depose the other party's experts. The areas and issues identified in the checklist for retention of experts presented earlier in this chapter should be explored in these depositions.

2. Discovery by Defendant

The deposition of the plaintiff's experts is especially important for the defendant's case. Initial investigation of the plaintiff's case should focus on identifying all experts who have any knowledge about the plaintiff's claims. To ensure that the plaintiff identifies all experts and not just those whom the plaintiff intends to call at trial, defense counsel

---

* See also Psychological Evaluation of the Plaintiff and Protective Orders, Especially from Mental Examinations, chapter 3, "Discovery."

should propound interrogatories to the plaintiff, requesting the identity of every expert who has knowledge of the plaintiff's claims and the nature of the knowledge that the expert possess.

a. Checklist for Documents Requests regarding Plaintiff's Experts Among the documents that the defendant's counsel should request are

1. statistical analyses;
2. damage calculations;
3. plaintiff's medical records;
4. all clinical notes of the treating and/or forensic expert;
5. plaintiff's health insurance claims and records of the plaintiff's health insurance carrier;
6. plaintiff's health insurance policies or benefits summaries;
7. expert opinion concerning the content and actual operation of the defendant's personnel policies and procedures;
8. plaintiff's psychological test records and results, including answer sheets;
9. workers' compensation records;
10. plaintiff's history of medication use;
11. plaintiff's prior employment records; and
12. Social Security disability records.

b. Checklist for Mental Health Practitioner Documents If the expert retained or seen by the plaintiff is a mental health practitioner, the defense should also request documentation regarding

1. the expert's recorded evaluations of the plaintiff or of the plaintiff's case,
2. identification of all sources of information and/or data relied upon by the expert in forming opinions or conclusions, and
3. identification of the expert's history of trial and/or deposition testimony.

V. New Trends in the Use of Expert Testimony*

Rule 702 of the Federal Rules of Evidence has superseded the traditional *Frye* rule of evidence under which expert evidence was not admissible if it was not generally accepted in its field.[26] Rule 702 provides:

---

* See also Opinion Testimony of Experts and Nonexperts (Coworkers), chapter 6, "Pretrial Motions."

If scientific, technical or other specialized knowledge will assist the trier of fact to understand the evidence or to determine a fact in issue, a witness qualified as an expert by *knowledge, skill, experience, training, or education*, may testify thereto in the form of opinion or otherwise. (emphasis added).

The liberalization of the standard for admission of expert testimony has significantly affected employment litigation. Because federal courts, under *Daubert*, and several state supreme courts (see for example, *Rubanick v. Witco Chemical Corp.*, 593 A.2d 733 (N.J. 1991)) have eliminated the "general acceptance" requirement for the admission of expert testimony, either party has an improved likelihood of admission into evidence of expert testimony for novel purposes in employment cases.

These new uses include (1) proof that the defendant's conduct would have offended (or would not have offended) a reasonable person of the same gender as the plaintiff in sexual harassment cases, (2) proof of the presence (or absence) of stereotyping, (3) assessment of a discrimination plaintiff's failure to complain, (4) proof of the adequacy (or inadequacy) of an employer's antidiscrimination policies and procedures, and (5) explanation of what constitutes retaliation.

Daubert puts a special obligation on the trial judge to act as a "gatekeeper" in determining whether expert testimony is admissible. Therefore, even under *Daubert*, counsel for defendants can still attempt to exclude, or limit the scope of, plaintiffs' experts through motions in limine and/or motions for summary judgment directed at the reliability of the expert report.

Other modes of attack can include:

1. bias;
2. reliance on accuracy of or acceptance of history given by plaintiff;
3. credentials;
4. previous experience as an expert;
5. fees;
6. failure to obtain adequate history of plaintiff, including failure to obtain past medical records;
7. testimony that invades the province of the jury;
8. prior inconsistent testimony in similar cases;
9. violation of professional standards of analysis used as a basis for the expert's opinion or testimony;
10. use of theory rejected by the courts; and
11. the subjectivity of expert's opinion and lack of credible supporting evidence.

The following identify some of the potentially more creative use of experts, particularly by plaintiffs.

A. Hostile Environment in Sexual Harassment Litigation

In its second sexual harassment decision, *Harris v. Forklift Systems, Inc.*, 510 U.S. 17 (1993), the United States Supreme Court established a two-prong test for proving a hostile or abusive work environment:

> Conduct that is not severe or pervasive enough to create an *objectively* hostile or abusive work environment—an environment that a reasonable person would find hostile or abusive—is beyond Title VII's purview. Likewise, if the victim does not *subjectively* perceive the environment to be abusive, the conduct has not actually altered the conditions of the victim's employment, and there is no Title VII violation.[27]

Neither prong of the *Harris* hostile environment test requires the plaintiff to proffer expert testimony; however, expert testimony can aid in establishing the presence (or absence) of either prong of the test.

With regard to the objective prong, the plaintiff can use a social psychologist or sociologist to prove that a "reasonable person" would find the work environment hostile or abusive.[28]

At this time, the question of whether the gender of the "reasonable person" is that of the victim depends upon where the case is filed. The Supreme Court did not explicitly rule on that issue in *Harris*. The Equal Employment Opportunity Commission has issued an enforcement guideline, finding the *Harris* decision to be consistent with the agency's position that the "reasonable person" at issue is a person of the same gender as the plaintiff.[29] Consequently, some jurisdictions use a gender-specific standard.[30] Regardless of whether the "reasonable person" standard is gender-specific or not, however, the use of experts on the issue of hostile environment may become more common because of the trend toward more lenient standards for the admission of expert testimony. Defense counsel will be required to shift their efforts toward preparing effective cross-examination rather than attempting to bar the expert's testimony altogether.

With regard to the subjective prong of the *Harris* hostile environment standard, expert psychiatric, psychological, or medical testimony may be central to harassment plaintiffs in establishing emotional distress as evidence of their subjective perception that the environment was abusive.

Consulting physicians or mental health professionals may be particularly effective in this respect because they can chart the development of symptoms based on their knowledge of the plaintiff's condition before the harassing conduct purportedly began.

B. Stereotyping

In gender discrimination cases generally, including sexual harassment cases, expert testimony regarding the pervasive nature of sexual stereotyping can be invaluable to the plaintiff's case. (This statement would seem to be true with respect to other types of discrimination cases as well, although a review of the relevant reported decisions does not reveal any cases in which expert testimony has been admitted to establish stereotyping on the basis of a criterion other than gender.) In four federal decisions, expert testimony was admitted to establish sexual stereotyping: *Jenson v. Eveleth Taconite Co.*, 824 F. Supp. 847 (D. Minn. 1993); *Stender v. Lucky Stores, Inc.*, 803 F. Supp. 259 (N.D. Cal. 1992); *Robinson v. Jacksonville Shipyards, Inc.*, 760 F. Supp. 1486 (M.D. Fla. 1991); and *Hopkins v. Price Waterhouse*, 618 F. Supp. 1109 (D.D.C. 1985), *aff'd in relevant part*, 825 F.2d 458 (D.C. Cir. 1987), *rev'd on other grounds*, 490 U.S. 228 (1989).

In *Hopkins*, the plaintiff sued her former employer, an accounting firm, for gender discrimination. She sought to establish that illicit sexual stereotypes had played a role in the defendant's partnership decisions. For that purpose, the plaintiff proffered the expert testimony of a social psychologist who had interviewed the partners at the firm. The expert testified that "situations, like that at Price Waterhouse, in which men evaluate women based on limited contact with the individual in a traditionally male profession and a male working environment foster stereotyping" and that "[o]ne common form of stereotyping is that women engaged in assertive behavior are judged more critically because aggressive conduct is viewed as a masculine characteristic."[31]

In *Jenson*, a social psychologist testified that the major effect of sex stereotyping is "sexual spillover," that is, "the sexual dimension that characterizes male-female relationships outside of a work environment spills over . . . into the work environment, and . . . becomes part of the working environment."[32] In *Stender*, a sociologist, testifying on "the organization of work and its relationship to gender" on behalf of plaintiffs, concluded that initial job assignments and subsequent promotions at certain supermarkets run by defendant Lucky Stores, Inc. were motivated by sexual (and racial) stereotypes. He testified that "some jobs . . . have come to be perceived as 'men's work'; while other jobs . . . come to be perceived as 'women's work.' "[33] In addition, he stated:

> Stereotypes are most consequential in situations where evaluative criteria are ambiguous. . . . [W]hen the required qualifications for a job are ambiguous and information on the decision making process is unavailable to candidates, subjects were likely to recommend candidates of their own race and sex. In contrast, when evaluative criteria are clear and the decision making process is public, race and sex were less likely to factor into choices.[34]

Defense counsel should argue against any expert testimony regarding sexual stereotyping, especially in jury cases.[35]

The verdicts and decisions based on this type of evidence demonstrate the high impact that expert testimony on stereotyping may have on the finder of fact, whether judge or jury.

C. The Issue of Plaintiff's Failure to Complain

In at least two reported sexual harassment decisions, *Snider v. Consolidation Coal Co.*, 973 F.2d 555 (7th Cir. 1992), *cert. denied*, 506 U.S. 1054 (1993), and *Stockett v. Tolin*, 791 F. Supp. 1536 (S.D. Fla. 1992), the courts (in nonjury trials) have relied upon expert testimony explaining the plaintiffs' failure to complain about the harassment during their employment. This type of expert testimony would seem to be helpful in all types of discrimination cases; a review of the relevant decisions, however, discloses only sex discrimination cases in which such testimony has been admitted.

The plaintiff in *Snider* alleged a quid pro quo, nonconsensual sexual relationship with her former supervisor. Her expert testified that "over 95 percent of the victims of nonconsensual relationships—whether sexual or merely social—did not complain or report the problem due to a fear of reprisal or loss of privacy."[36]

In *Stockett*, a clinical psychologist, whose expert testimony on behalf of the plaintiff was allowed, testified:

[S]exual harassment is an example of a process known as victimization that ranges from the consequences of rape to family violence to spouse abuse to sexist slurs and low grade mistreatment of others. In less violent, more chronic situations, . . . a person slowly evolves a sense of helplessness in coping with the situation. This results in anxiety, depression, feelings of personal incompetence, loss of a sense of self confidence and worth, and the inability to develop strategies for handling the treatment.[37]

A plaintiff's explanation of her failure to complain may be indispensable in convincing a finder of fact that her allegations are credible, especially where the allegations involve physical assaults or other severe harassment.[38]

D. The Employer's Antidiscrimination Policies and Procedures

In at least one reported case, an employment discrimination plaintiff has successfully proffered expert testimony regarding the inadequacy of the employer's antidiscrimination policies and procedures. In *Shrout v. Black Clawson Co.*, 689 F. Supp. 774 (S.D. Ohio 1988), a human resources consultant, qualified as an expert on corporate policy and procedure, testified regarding the employer's "open door" policy as a sexual harassment policy. On the basis of her testimony, the court, noting that the policy was inadequate in virtually every respect, found that a harassed woman could reasonably fail to complain under such circumstances.[39]

E. Retaliation

In a retaliation decision not involving discrimination, the Texas Court of Appeals has held that a plaintiff could proffer the expert testimony of two professors to establish that the defendant's acts against the plaintiff constituted retaliation and to demonstrate the importance of deterring retaliation against whistle-blowers.[40] In reaching its decision, the appellate court held that the trial court did not err in admitting the testimony, even though the testimony concerned the ultimate issue before the jury, because "[i]t is not error for an expert witness to testify on a mixed question of law and fact."[41] The appellate court also recognized that the issue of the deterrence of egregious conduct is tied to the issue of the adequacy of exemplary damages.[42]

VI. Expert Trial Preparation Assistance

A. Jury Consultants*

In a case to be tried to a jury, a professional trial consultant can be very useful for two purposes: (1) to conduct trial simulations and (2) to assist in actually picking the jury. Counsel should be aware, however, that jury consultants can be very expensive. Counsel should examine this issue as part of the overall cost/benefit analysis for the case.

Jury consultants become much more important in jurisdictions where voir dire is severely limited and/or conducted by the judge. When an important case will be tried in such a jurisdiction, the input from a trial simulation conducted by a professional jury consultant can be invaluable; however, the costs associated with such services can be prohibitive.

Trial simulations serve several practical purposes:

1. identify the issues that jurors will consider most important,
2. determine the profiles of the most desirable and least desirable jurors,
3. determine the most effective theme and trial strategy,
4. gauge the effectiveness of opening and closing statements,
5. measure the effectiveness of various witnesses,

---

* See also chapter 9, "Juries," on jury consultants.

6. determine the value of demonstrative evidence,
7. assess the effectiveness of the lawyer's presentation, and
8. evaluate and negotiate settlement realistically.[43]

According to Paul D. Tieger, personality typing is a much more accurate predictor of juror behavior than demographic stereotypes based on variables such as gender, race, and even occupation.[44] On the other hand, however, "demographic stereotypes" may be more accurate predictors in employment discrimination cases. For example, would plaintiff's counsel in a race discrimination case brought by an African-American female secretary want a white male executive on the jury? (See chapter 9, "Juries," regarding discriminatory peremptory juror strikes.)

In a trial simulation, the consultant screens potential volunteer jurors and chooses a jury reflective of the actual jury pool and unfamiliar with the parties or their counsel. Usually, to limit cost, the mock jurors are shown videotaped summaries of the testimony of only the most important witnesses. (These summaries can be videotaped deposition testimony or simulated trial examination.) The jurors' responses are measured through written questionnaires before and after each significant trial event to determine at what points the lawyer succeeded or failed. At the conclusion of the presentation, the consultant instructs the jurors regarding the law before deliberations begin. During the deliberation (which is videotaped), the lawyer observes through a one-way mirror or on closed-circuit television. After the verdict, the consultant debriefs the jurors by asking a series of questions about their impressions of the case and how and why they reached their decision. Finally, the consultant issues a written report to the lawyer.[45]

Although such jury simulations generally cost several thousand dollars, their value often outweighs their cost in a significant case because the lawyer may learn that his or her expectations as to what is persuasive are incorrect.

B. Graphic Arts Specialists

Plaintiffs should use demonstrative evidence to the greatest extent possible because juries normally take such evidence into their deliberations with them. Demonstrative evidence is particularly significant in presenting expert economic testimony and statistical evidence regarding the composition of the workforce.

VII. Conclusion

Despite the temptation to think of the expert as a panacea in litigation, it is important to keep in mind that in its involvement in a case with opposing experts, the jury may very well believe both or believe neither, thus canceling out the testimony of both. As Justice Jayne stated in *International Pulverizing Corp. v. Kidwell*, 71 A.2d 151 (N.J. Ch. Div. 1950):

> This testimony . . . has been profuse and illuminating. The experts, as too often happens, disagree, leaving the problem, as Tennyson might say, dark with excessive brightness.

Notes

1. ALBERT OSBORN, THE MIND OF THE JUROR AS JUDGE OF THE FACTS 49 (1937).
2. State v. Zola, 548 A.2d 1022 (N.J. 1988), *cert. denied*, 489 U.S. 1022 (1989).
3. *Id.* (*citing* Butler v. Acme Mkts, Inc., 445 A.2d 1141 (N.J. 1982)).
4. *Id.*
5. *See, e.g.*, Burroughs v. Atlantic City, 560 A.2d 725 (N.J. App. Div. 1989).
6. *See e.g.*, Nesmith v. Walsh Trucking Co., 589 A.2d 596 (N.J. 1991).
7. *See, e.g.*, Smith v. Color. Interstate Gas Co., 794 F. Supp. 1035, 1044 (D. Colo. 1992).
8. *Id.* at 1506.
9. *Id.* at 1524–25.
10. *See, e.g.*, Daniels v. Pipefitters' Ass'n Local Union No. 597, 945 F.2d 906 (7th Cir. 1991); McAlester v. United Air Lines, Inc., 851 F.2d 1249 (10th Cir. 1988); Vulcan Pioneers, Inc. v. N.J. Dept. of Civil Serv., 625 F. Supp. 527 (D.N.J. 1985).
11. *See* Western Air Lines, Inc. v. Criswell, 472 U.S. 400 (1985).
12. Carrozza v. Howard County, 847 F. Supp. 365 (D. Md. 1994), *aff'd*, 45 F.3d 425 (4th Cir. 1995).
13. Burris v. City of Phoenix, 875 P.2d 832 (Ariz. Ct. App. 1993).
14. Cary v. Piphus, 435 U.S. 247, 255, 98 S.Ct. 1042, 1048 (1978); Patterson v. P.H.P. Healthcare Corp., 90 F.3d 927, 937–41 (5th Cir. 1996) ("hurt feelings, anger and frustration are part of life"); EEOC Policy Guidance No. 915.002 § II(A)(2) at 10 (July 14, 1992) ("existence, nature, and severity of emotional harm must be proved"); Tobey v. Excel/ JWP, Inc., 985 F.2d 330, 333 (7th Cir. 1993) ("the expert evidence of a psychologist might have established a plausible linkage between sexual harassment that ended in August 1988 and a seemingly voluntary resignation in April 1990"); Harrison v. Edison Bros. Apparel Stores, Inc., 146 F.R.D. 142 (M.D.N.C. 1993) (requiring expert testimony to establish causation of emotional distress by sexual harassment).
15. Harris v. Forklift Sys., Inc., 510 U.S. 127 (1993).
16. *See, e.g.*, Lehmann v. Toys 'R' Us, Inc., 626 A.2d 445 (N.J. 1993).
17. *See* Internal Revenue Code § 104(a)(2) (1998). *See also* Commissioner v. Schleier, 115 S.Ct. 2159 (1995) (holding that back pay damages under ADEA are not excludable from gross income because they constitute "damages received . . . on account of personal injuries or sickness").
18. *See, e.g.*, Curtis v. Express, Inc., 868 F. Supp. 467 (N.D.N.Y. 1994) (holding that even if good cause for mental examination of plaintiff, examination can be precluded if plaintiff merely asserted "garden variety" emotional distress claim rather than claim of continuing severe mental injury).
19. Wayne N. Outten & Jack A. Raisner, *The Role of Experts in Sexual Harassment Litigation: Plaintiff's Perspective*, 505 Practicing Law Institute/Litigation 107 (1994).
20. Jakubowski v. Lengen, 450 N.Y.S. 2d 612, 614 (App. Div. 1982).
21. *See, e.g.*, Jansen v. Packaging Corp., 158 F.R.D. 409 (N.D. Ill. 1994); Vreeland v. Ethan Allen, Inc., 151 F.R.D. 551 (S.D.N.Y. 1993); Zabkowicz v. West Bend Co., 585 F. Supp. 635 (E.D. Wis. 1984).
22. Outten and Raisner, *supra*.
23. Duncan v. Upjohn Co., 155 F.R.D. 23 (D. Conn. 1994); Tomlin v. Holecek, 150 F.R.D. 628 (D. Minn. 1993) (counsel's presence would impede the dynamics of the examination); Ali v. Wang Lab., Inc., 162 F.R.D 165, 168 (M.D. Fla. 1995) (no special need

for third-party presence); Shirsat v. Mutual Pharm. Co., 169 F.R.D. 68, 70 (E.D. Pa. 1996) ("distraction during the examination works to diminish the accuracy of the process"); Bradenberg v. El Al Israel Airlines, 79 F.R.D. 543, 546 (S.D.N.Y. 1978) (examination relies on unimpeded communications); Baba-Ali v. City of New York, No. 92 Civ. 7957, 1995 WL 752904, at *3 (S.D.N.Y. 1995) (plaintiff's experts conducted examinations without defense experts or defense counsel present).

24. *See, e.g.*, Edward N. Tucker & Steven R. Freemen, *Economic Damages under the 1991 Civil Rights Act: The CPA as Expert Witness*, 24 Fall Brief 59 (1994) (CPA work involves real-world, specific analyses of individuals' and businesses' tax returns and financial records; economists are usually from academic world and rely on more theoretical approaches, and regional, national, and global trends).

25. *See* Tucker & Freemen, *supra*, at 62–64.

26. *See* Daubert v. Merrell Dow Pharm., Inc., 509 U.S. 579 (1993).

27. *Id.* at 21.

28. *See, e.g.*, Eide v. Kelsey-Hayes Co., 397 N.W. 2d 532 (Mich. Ct. App. 1986), *modified on other grounds*, 427 N.W. 2d 488 (Mich. 1988) (holding expert testimony of sociologist admissible in sexual harassment case to assist trier of fact).

29. *See* Mark S. Dichter et al., *Use of Experts in Sexual Harassment Litigation*, 505 Practicing Law Institute/Litigation 27 (1994).

30. *See, e.g.*, Ellison v. Brady, 924 F.2d 872 (9th Cir. 1991); Lehmann v. Toys 'R' Us, Inc., 626 A.2d 445 (N.J. 1993); others do not, *see, e.g.*, Lipsett v. University of Puerto Rico, 740 F. Supp. 921 (D.P.R. 1990).

31. *Hopkins*, 618 F. Supp. at 1118.

32. 824 F. Supp. at 881.

33. 803 F. Supp. at 302.

34. *Id. See also* Robinson, 760 F. Supp. at 1503–05 (citing expert testimony that evaluation of women employees by coworkers and supervisors improperly takes place in terms of sexuality of women and their worth as sex objects rather than their merit as craft workers).

35. *See e.g.*, Lipsett v. University of Puerto Rico, 730 F. Supp. 921 (D.P.R. 1990).

36. 973 F.2d at 558.

37. 791 F. Supp. at 1549.

38. *See generally*, Sarah E. Burns, *Is The Law Male?: The Role of Experts*, 69 CHI.-KENT L. REV. 389, 394 (1993).

39. *Id.* at 777.

40. Texas Dept. of Human Serv. v. Green, 855 S.W. 2d 136 (Tex. Ct. App. 1993).

41. *Id.* at 149.

42. *Id.*

43. Paul D. Tieger, *Trial Simulations: The Next Best Thing to a Crystal Ball*, TRIAL DIPLOMACY JOURNAL, Spring 1991, at 119, 120–22.

44. *Id.* at 120.

45. *Id.* at 122–24.

CHAPTER 5

Summary Judgment

KENNETH BELLO*
JON W. GREEN†
BRUCE S. HARRISON‡

* Mintz, Levin, Cohn, Ferris, Glovsky & Popeo; Boston, Massachusetts.

† Deutsch, Resnick, Green & Kiernan; Springfield, New Jersey.

‡ Shawe & Rosenthal; Baltimore, Maryland.

I. Introduction

The increase in jury trials as a result of the passage of the Civil Rights Act of 1991 has placed additional emphasis upon the importance of summary judgment motions in such cases. Furthermore, recent decisions of the Supreme Court suggest that the federal courts are more receptive toward consideration of motions for summary judgment as a legitimate vehicle for dispensing with nonmeritorious lawsuits thereby sparing the parties unwarranted cost and effecting judicial economies.

II. Summary Judgment and the Discovery Process*

From the employer's perspective, summary judgment may provide an early and best opportunity for prevailing. Because this procedure also allows the defendant's case to be evaluated in a more dispassionate legal context, the danger of sympathy for the little guy and a host of other emotional reactions becomes minimized.

Conversely, surviving summary judgment is clearly one of the critical moments for the plaintiff/employee in that the opportunity for settlement is enhanced, and the opportunity to seek victory from a jury is now guaranteed. In some cases, however, a plaintiff may actually seek summary (or partial summary) judgment on certain claims in the case. Because the material factual allegations are almost always disputed by the employer, it is rare in employment cases for a plaintiff to file a motion for summary judgment. Yet, there will be situations where a cross-motion for summary judgment is viable and tactically desirable.

Given the critical nature of summary judgment to each of the parties, it is plain that each should address the summary judgment process long before the actual motion is filed. From a defendant's perspective, a preliminary determination as to whether the case is susceptible to dismissal on summary judgment should be made shortly after the lawsuit has been served. Once that decision is made, all elements of the litigation, and especially discovery, must be geared towards maximizing the likelihood of achieving summary judgment. Plaintiff's counsel, by contrast, must assume that the goal of the employer is to file a motion for summary judgment. Counsel, therefore, must craft discovery requests and responses with defendant's goal in mind.

---

* See also Discovery regarding Summary Judgment, chapter 3, "Discovery."

III. Legal Principles

A. The Respective Burdens of Proof Imposed by Rule 56

In federal court, the procedural requirements for summary judgment are set forth in the Federal Rules of Civil Procedure at Rule 56. Fed. R. Civ. P. 56(c) provides that summary judgment "shall be rendered forthwith if the pleadings, depositions, answers to interrogatories, and admissions on file, together with the affidavits, if any, show that there is no genuine issue as to any material fact and that the moving party is entitled to judgment as a matter of law." Rule 56 requires that judgment be granted when there is no genuine dispute with respect to a material fact and that based upon such facts, no trier of fact could reasonably find for the other party. In the application of that standard, the court is to consider all of the evidence in the light most favorable to the party opposed to the motion, drawing all inferences in that party's favor.

When the moving party has carried its burden of demonstrating the absence of a genuine issue of material fact, the opposing party must go beyond the pleadings and designate specific facts supported by discovery or affidavit showing that there is a genuine issue for trial. Indeed, Rule 56(e) expressly requires the opposing nonmovant to submit affidavits or other admissible evidence. Rule 56(f) protects the nonmoving party against premature summary judgment by giving the trial court discretion to deny summary judgment if adequate discovery has not been conducted.

B. The Supreme Court's Guidance

In 1986 the Supreme Court handed down three cases, commonly referred to as the "summary judgment trilogy," that clarified the legal standards by which motions for summary judgment must be evaluated. *Matsushita Electric Industrial Co. v. Zenith Radio Corp.*, 475 U.S. 574 (1986) addressed the quantum of evidence necessary to withstand summary judgment. The Court held that when a moving party has carried its burden under Rule 56(c) of showing that no disputed material facts exist, the nonmovant must do more than simply show that there is some "metaphysical doubt as to the material facts" because "[w]here the record taken as a whole could not lead a rational trier of fact to find for the non-moving party," there is no "genuine issue for trial." The Court added that if the factual context renders the plaintiff's claim implausible, the plaintiff must come forward with more persuasive evidence to support a claim than would otherwise be necessary.[1]

Next, in *Celotex Corp. v. Catrett*, 477 U.S. 317 (1986), the Supreme Court held that the moving party is not required to support its motion with affidavits or other like materials negating the nonmovant's claim. Instead, Rule 56 requires the non-moving party to (1) identify the essential elements of its case for which it bears the burden of proof at trial,[2] and (2) produce admissible evidence "sufficient to establish the existence of an element essential to that party's case, and on which that party will bear the burden of proof at trial."[3] The Court emphasized that Rule 56 is not limited to isolated and extraordinary circumstances, and that it is properly regarded not as a disfavored procedural shortcut, but rather as an integral part of the federal rules as a whole, which are designed "to secure the just, speedy, and inexpensive determination of every action."[4]

Finally, *Anderson v. Liberty Lobby, Inc.*, 477 U.S. 242 (1986) held that the standard in reviewing a summary judgment motion is analogous to that applied in reviewing a request for a directed verdict under Fed. R. Civ. P. 50(a). The Court stated: "there is no issue for trial unless there is sufficient evidence favoring the nonmoving party for a jury to return a verdict for that party."[5] Summary judgment would be proper, the Court said, if the evidence were merely colorable or was not significantly probative.[6]

Anderson also addressed an argument that is particularly important in employment cases: whether summary judgment should be granted where the defendant's state of mind is at issue and the jury might disbelieve a witness as to this issue. The Court held that a party may not defeat a motion for summary judgment by merely asserting that the jury might disbelieve the defendant's denial of the state of mind attributed to him by the nonmovant. The Court stressed that while the movant has the burden of showing that there is no genuine issue of fact, the nonmovant is not thereby relieved of his own burden of producing evidence that would support a jury verdict.[7]

C. What Constitutes a "Genuine" Issue of "Material Fact"?

A material fact is a fact that a party who bears the burden of proof must prove in order to establish a legal element of a civil cause of action.

A genuine issue of material fact is created when the nonmoving party produces sufficient evidence for a reasonable jury to return a verdict for the nonmoving party. In other words, a genuine issue of material fact is a dispute that legally affects the legal elements of the lawsuit. If resolution of the facts at issue will not materially affect the outcome of the challenged claim or defense, summary judgment should not be denied.[8] As noted previously, the quantum of evidence necessary has been equated to the standard that applies to a motion for directed verdict at trial. Thus, "the inquiry involved in a ruling on a motion for summary judgment . . . necessarily implicates the substantive evidentiary standard of proof that would apply at the trial on the merits."[9]

Where intent is an element of the cause of action, as in disparate treatment employment discrimination cases, the nonmoving party cannot avoid summary judgment by asserting that the jury might disbelieve defendant's denial of discriminatory intent.[10] Rather, the nonmoving party must adduce "concrete evidence from which a reasonable juror could return a verdict in his favor." This burden is not satisfied by arguing without supporting evidence that the movant's evidence is not worthy of belief.[11]

D. Different Federal Courts of Appeal and States Apply Summary Judgment Differently

This chapter cannot exhaustively discuss all employment summary judgment cases. A guiding principle is to check summary judgment precedents from your trial court and appellate court. A general theme in this chapter is that different courts reach opposite summary judgment results in factually similar decisions.

IV. Integrating the Summary Judgment Standard with the Burden of Proof in Discrimination Cases

In drafting a summary judgment motion, the legal standards set out in both Rule 56 and the summary judgment trilogy must be integrated with the burden of proof scheme established by the U.S. Supreme Court in the Civil Rights Act of 1964.[12] One or all of the summary judgment trilogy are often cited when a court grants or affirms the grant of summary judgment in an employment discrimination case.[13] Similarly, the trilogy has been applied in denying summary judgment in employment discrimination cases.[14] The merger of the two strands of legal doctrine produces some recurring or standard fact situations, legal issues, and arguments.

A. Issues Related to Intent and Motive

Historically, various federal courts have tended to view summary judgment as especially questionable in discrimination cases, since they usually necessarily involve examining motive and intent.[15] The rationale for that reluctance has been articulated as follows:

> [I]t is inappropriate to resolve issues of credibility, motive, and intent on motions for summary judgment. It is equally clear that where such issues

are presented, the submission of affidavits or depositions is insufficient to support a motion for summary judgment. . . . Summary judgment simply may not be granted when such matters as the defendant's motive and intent are questioned. . . . Just as summary judgment is inappropriate in qualified-immunity cases and in defamation cases, it is inappropriate here. Because petitioner raised issues going to respondent's motive and intent, it was error to grant a motion for summary judgment.[16]

Notwithstanding those concerns, a growing number of courts have declined to proscribe the reach of summary judgment solely on the basis that the ultimate issue involves a question of intent.[17] The non-movant will be required to show specific and provable facts to support a claim and may not rest on pleadings even if issues of motive or intent are involved.[18]

The rationale for summary judgment in disparate treatment cases (that is, discrimination claims affecting a particular employee) does not apply to disparate impact (that is, companywide) discrimination claims, since intent is not an element of proof in disparate impact cases. Furthermore, to establish a prima facie case of disparate impact, the plaintiff must actually prove that the challenged policy or practice discriminates against his or her statutory protected group.[19] By contrast, disparate treatment plaintiffs need only produce sufficient evidence to support an inference of discrimination against that plaintiff personally because of his or her protected status.[20]

B. Creating a Genuine Issue of Material Fact

The typical case of alleged intentional employment discrimination involves a plaintiff who either has been discharged during a reduction in force or for some more personalized reason. A plaintiff may prove his or her case either through direct, or "smoking gun," evidence or through circumstantial evidence. Generally the plaintiff will be able to establish the requisite prima facie showing under *McDonnell Douglas*; that is, the employee had a statutory protected status, there was an adverse employment action, and facts suggest discriminatory motivation. In turn, the employer will normally be able to express a legitimate, nondiscriminatory reason for the discharge, for example, an economically motivated reduction in force or some other legitimate reason for the adverse action against the employee. At that point, the case is at the "pretext" stage, and the plaintiff must create a genuine dispute of material fact with respect to the proffered legitimate reason. It is at this stage that the quality, quantity, and caliber of the employer's and employee's evidence is most often in dispute.

The Supreme Court's 1993 decision in *St. Mary's Honor Center v. Hicks*, 509 U.S. 502 (1993) is a case of particular import with respect to the application of the summary judgment standards in employment discrimination cases where the claims turn on the issue of pretext. Prior to the decision in *Hicks*, some courts required employees to produce at the pretext stage additional evidence of discriminatory "animus," that is, "pretext-plus."[21]

In *Hicks*, the Court addressed the consequences of the nonmoving party's production of evidence of pretext, holding judgment for plaintiff did not automatically result from proof of pretext. When the plaintiff proves through admissible evidence, even if only "vaguely suggested" in such evidence, that the defendant's articulated reasons are not the true reasons, the finder of fact must then determine whether the challenged action was more likely the result of intentional discrimination than not. The Court added, however, that the fact-finder's disbelief of the reasons put forward by the defendant may, together with the elements of the prima facie case, suffice to show intentional discrimination. The plaintiff is not legally required to put on any more evidence to avoid summary judgment, and the fact-finder is allowed but not required to draw the inference of discrimination without any direct evidence, and without any circumstantial evidence other than the evidence used to prove the prima facie case and the proof of pretext.[22]

A number of federal courts of appeals have construed *Hicks* as supporting the proposition that a plaintiff may now avoid summary judgment by casting doubt upon or refuting the articulated reasons of the defendant (provided that the employee has also submitted sufficient evidence to satisfy the prima facie elements under *McDonnell Douglas*).[23] In short, the issue of pretext becomes a question for the trier of fact where there is sufficient evidence to support a reasonable belief that the employer's proffered reason is false or not the true reason for the personnel decision. In the absence of smoking-gun evidence on the issue of pretext, a plaintiff may meet the burden of demonstrating pretext by indirect means, including showing (1) that the alleged legitimate reasons had no basis in fact; (2) if the alleged legitimate business reasons had a basis in fact, they were not really factors motivating the discharge; or (3) if the alleged legitimate reasons were truthful, nevertheless they were jointly insufficient to motivate the discharge. For example, in *Aungst v. Westinghouse Elec. Corp.*, 937 F.2d 1216 (7th Cir. 1991), the court held that the plaintiff needed to attack the company's claim of plaintiff's "lack of versatility" by showing (1) that the company was not really concerned with versatility; (2) and if it was, plaintiff was fired for reasons other than lack of versatility; or (3) if lack of versatility was the actual reason, then plaintiff must show that lack of versatility should not have caused him to be chosen for the reduction in force. The plaintiff's evidence of pretext, however, "must extend beyond casting doubt on the reasonableness of the employer's action; otherwise the law would be converted to a 'just cause' provision for the protected class of employees, an effect that Congress clearly did not intend." Moreover, in attempting to cast significant doubt upon the significance of an employer's proffered reasons, an employee's view of his own performance is immaterial.[24]

Where the employer is able to offer detailed historical records supporting its proffered reason, such objective evidence may render a claim of pretext implausible and hence a viable candidate for summary judgment.[25] Correspondingly, lack of records or ambiguous records may preclude summary judgment.[26] The fact that an employer's proffered reason is based upon subjective considerations by itself may not significantly advance the plaintiff's required showing.[27] However, an employer's subjective criticism such as the employee is not a "team player" or is "not cooperative" may under the right circumstances constitute evidence of pretext.[28]

Similarly, the fact that a plaintiff's past evaluations were good may not suffice to establish that the current bad evaluations are suspicious, because "[t]o hold otherwise would be to hold that things never change."[29] But a sudden and drastic decrease in an employee's performance evaluation may, under certain circumstances, be a significant factor with respect to pretext.[30]

A plaintiff cannot avoid summary judgment, however, by merely showing that the employer was mistaken as to the factual predicate for its decision or made a decision that was later shown to have been bad business judgment. An employer is entitled to make bad business decisions so long as they are not tainted by discriminatory motives. This is true even with respect to subjective business decisions.[31]

Finally, it is extremely important that counsel be aware that after *Hicks* the circuit courts of appeal have split as to the evidence that a plaintiff is required to submit during the pretext stage. Compare *Sheridan v. E.I. DuPont de Nemours and Co.*, 100 F.3d 1061 (3d Cir. 1996) (en banc) with *Fisher v. Vassar College*, 114 F.3d 1332 (2d Cir. 1997) (en banc), cert. denied, 1998 U.S. LEXIS 477 (1998) and *Rhodes v. Guiberson Oil Tools*, 71 F.3d 989 (5th Cir. 1996) (en banc).[32] The Third Circuit in *Sheridan*, held that all *Hicks* requires to defeat summary judgment is proof of the prima facie case together with evidence of pretext.[33] The Second and Fifth Circuits in *Fisher* and *Rhodes*, respectively, held that in certain cases evidence of a prima facie case and pretext may not be enough for a plaintiff to defeat summary judgment and that the employee may be required to produce additional evidence of discrimination during the pretext stage.[34] Since the Supreme Court has not resolved this apparent conflict between the circuits as of the date when this chapter and book went to press, it is important for counsel to meticulously research the pertinent jurisdictions for the required evidence necessary to defeat summary judgment.

C. Issues Related to Direct Evidence of Discrimination

Intentional discrimination claims may be established by either direct or circumstantial evidence of discriminatory animus.[35] Where the plaintiff can present direct evidence of discrimination, it is not necessary to establish a prima facie case according to the proof scheme outlined in *McDonnell Douglas*.[36] Biased statements by employers or their agents is the sort of direct evidence of discrimination makes the *McDonnell Douglas/Burdine* framework unnecessary.[37]

Where a plaintiff is able to adduce discriminatory statements made by the decision makers close to the time of the adverse decision concerning the employee, then such evidence is normally held under *Price Waterhouse* to create a "dual motive" case where the burden of proof shifts to the employer that it would have taken the same action absent the impermissible motive.[38]

The direct evidence must, however, be distinguished from comments or statements that are regarded as "stray remarks" under *Price Waterhouse*, or remarks made in jest, in the distant past, or by non–decision makers. Evidence of such remarks is often viewed as too weak to raise a genuine issue of material fact.[39] However, the 1991 Civil Rights Act has overruled *Price Waterhouse* to the extent that once a jury finds that the direct evidence was credible and that a discriminatory motive was "a motivating" factor, then judgment on liability must be entered in favor of the employee.[40] At that point, the employer then has the burden of proof to establish a nondiscriminatory motive that may reduce plaintiff's legal damages.[41]

V. Drafting a Motion for Summary Judgment

To draft a motion for summary judgment, counsel must have accurately identified the type of discrimination claim at issue and ascertained and reviewed the most definitive authority within the circuit where the case is pending, that describes the elements of a prima facie case in the type of claim asserted by the plaintiff.

A. The First Step—Prima Facie Case

A defendant generally will be unable to prevail on summary judgment by arguing that the plaintiff cannot establish a prima facie case. This is because in the majority of discrimination cases the plaintiff is able to produce evidence of membership in a protected group and evidence that he or she was the victim of an adverse employment decision. Plaintiffs also are usually able to produce evidence that they satisfy objective and job-related qualifications for the position applied for or that they were discharged from, although this element of the prima facie case is sometimes fertile ground for a defendant's motion. For the most part, the crucial element of the prima facie case of employment discrimination will be whether facts exist that are sufficient to raise an inference of discrimination. Generally it is evidence that suggests an inconsistency between the employer's actions and its representations.

In a case involving an allegedly discriminatory discharge, for example, if the plaintiff was not replaced by a person outside his or her protected class, a motion for summary judgment for failure to establish a prima facie case may be appropriate. (Note that a plaintiff proves a prima facie claim of age discrimination even if her replacement is within the protected class—over age 40.)[42] Keeping in mind that the elements of a prima facie case are flexible, however, the evidence revealed in discovery should be scrutinized to determine if there is an alternative basis for raising an inference of discriminatory intent. If not, a motion for summary judgment for failure to establish a prima facie case should be strongly considered.

B. The Second Step—The Employer's Legitimate Reason for the Personnel Decision

A plaintiff's proof of a prima facie case is not enough, however, to defeat a motion for summary judgment if the employer expresses through admissible evidence a nondiscriminatory reason for the challenged action.[43] Correspondingly, where an employer cannot state any legitimate reason for its treatment of the plaintiff, the plaintiff's establishment of an unrebutted prima facie case warrants summary judgment for the plaintiff. Since the plaintiff has the burden of proof at trial, however, it is incumbent upon a plaintiff to present affidavits, deposition testimony, interrogatory answers, or admissions from the employer confirming the absence of a legitimate explanation for its treatment of the plaintiff.

When the employer is moving for summary judgment, evidence of a legitimate reason for the employment decision at issue serves two purposes. First, it removes the inference created by the plaintiff's prima facie case and shifts to the plaintiff the burden of proving that the articulated reason is false or did not really motivate the employer and that the true reason is discriminatory. If no evidence of discriminatory intent exists beyond that necessary to establish a prima facie case, the employer will be justified in asserting that there is no genuine issue of fact for trial and summary judgment should be granted.

In addition to rebutting the plaintiff's prima facie case, evidence sustaining the employer's intermediate burden is pertinent to existence of a genuine issue of fact on the ultimate issue of discriminatory intent. Under *Matsushita*, a nonmovant with the burden of proof must produce "more persuasive evidence" to support a claim that seems implausible. Thus, to the degree that an employer moving for summary judgment produces evidence of legitimate reasons for the employment practice at issue, the burden on the plaintiff to raise a genuine issue of intent to discriminate is increased.[44]

C. The Third Step—Pretext

As discussed in IV.B. ("Creating a Genuine Issue of Material Fact") above, counsel must carefully consider whether there are sufficient facts to show that the employer's articulated reason for the challenged employment practice cannot be accepted at face value and to create a genuine issue of fact over pretext. Pretext is typically established by (1) conflicting explanations by the employer for its treatment of the plaintiff; (2) evidence that the facts identified by the employer in support of its articulated reason are false; (3) evidence that the employer knew that the employee was not responsible for deficiencies or problems identified for disciplining or discharging the employee; and (4) evidence that the employer did not have knowledge of the facts that allegedly formed the basis of its articulated reason when its decision was made; or (5) the employer's articulated reason was not the actual reason for the employer's decision. Additionally, and perhaps most commonly, an employment discrimination plaintiff may show pretext that he or she was treated more harshly than similarly situated employees.

Where an employer has proffered multiple reasons on the theory that "more is better," the employer often increases the potential for the plaintiff to create an issue for trial. Invariably some of the proffered reasons are weaker than others, and plaintiff must identify, and then focus on, the weakest links in the chain. If the plaintiff is able to prove pretext as to at least some of the reasons, an inference is raised as to the bona fides of the remaining reasons.

D. The Ultimate Question—Intent

Summary judgment analysis in a discrimination case should not end with focus on proof and rebuttal of a prima facie case. Counsel must thoroughly consider whether or not there is any basis for raising a genuine issue of intent to discriminate before filing a motion for summary judgment.[45] If the plaintiff can turn the issue of pretext into a credibility issue, summary judgment may not be available.[46]

In evaluating whether a case is a viable candidate for summary judgment, particular attention must be focused on determining whether there is any evidence of (1) comments by management decision makers indicative of animus toward members of the plaintiff's protected group; (2) evidence that the plaintiff was treated more harshly, subjected to more demanding work requirements, or was denied privileges and opportunities extended to nonprotected employees; and (3) statistical evidence indicating that employees in the plaintiff's protected group have been adversely affected by the employment practice at issue with disproportionately greater frequency than nonprotected employees.

In many disparate treatment cases, evidence that similarly situated nonminorities were treated more favorably than the plaintiff will be the only or principal evidence for claiming that the employer acted unlawfully. When the plaintiff has identified employees outside the protected group who were treated more favorably, the availability of summary judgment will turn on the existence of a genuine fact issue as to two facts: (1) whether the comparison employees are similarly situated to the plaintiff; and, if so, (2) whether there is a nondiscriminatory explanation for the differing treatment.

Direct evidence is proof that does not require the drawing of any inferences in order for it to support the proposition for which it is offered. For example, a statement by the manager or supervisor responsible that the challenged action was made alone for a discriminatory reason is direct evidence of discrimination. Absent a viable bona fide occupational qualification defense, liability will turn solely on credibility and, consequently, summary judgment will not be available. If the same statement is offered but is attributed to someone other than the decision maker or is offered to support an allegation that a subsequent employment action was unlawful, the evidence is no longer accurately characterized as "direct" evidence. In those circumstances, the evidence is circumstantial, as an inference must be drawn in order for the evidence to advance the proposition for which it has been offered.

E. The Mixed Motive Case

Where a plaintiff has adduced direct evidence that is sufficiently probative to permit the trier of fact to find that the employer's actions were tainted by an unlawful motivation, the *McDonnell Douglas/Burdine* framework gives way to what has been referred to as the "mixed motive test." Under this test, the most an employer can do is to limit its liability; it cannot escape it altogether. In order to limit its liability, the employer has the burden of proving by a preponderance of the evidence that it would have made the same decision even if it had not taken the impermissible factor into account.[47] Under the Civil Rights Act of 1991, the plaintiff prevails on the issue of liability if he or she shows that discrimination was a "motivating," as opposed to a "determining," factor in the challenged employment decision.[48] Summary judgment is less likely in a mixed motive case, as plaintiff's showing that the employer was at least partially motivated by discriminatory animus supports an inference that the legitimate reason proffered by the employer is pretextual.

In situations where an employee has alleged the existence of sufficient evidence of a discriminatory motivation, an employer-movant's best opportunity for summary judgment is to attempt to establish that even if each of the events alleged by the plaintiff did occur, they do not establish that impermissible factors impacted on the employment decision. This can be accomplished, for example, by allowing that while a manager may have said that plaintiff had "been around too long," this was not equivalent to stating that age motivated plaintiff's termination. Another frequently used method is to establish that the individual who made the remark played no role in the decision to take the job action.

F. Secondary Considerations

In moving for summary judgment, an employer should always argue that under *Celotex*, the plaintiff bears the burden of coming forward with evidence on all issues for which the plaintiff would bear the burden of proof at trial. The plaintiff is forced to come forward with evidence of a prima facie case and pretext or risk not surviving summary judgment.

In opposing summary judgment, plaintiffs often rely upon affidavits from cooperative individuals. Such affidavits are an inexpensive way of satisfying the plaintiff's burden. In addition, if submitted after discovery has closed, the affidavits will educate the defendant to the least possible extent. To be effective for purposes of establishing a dispute of material fact, however, an affidavit must be based on personal knowledge and the facts set forth in the affidavit must be admissible evidence.

Where the facts do not favor a motion for summary judgment of the entire case, a movant may wish to consider moving for partial summary judgment. Such a motion could have the effect of paring the case down to its essential core for trial and may also resolve certain issues that are impeding settlement. On the other hand, unsupported motions for summary judgment often result in a loss of the movant's credibility with the trial judge, which may extend beyond resolution of the motion.

G. The Drafter's Art

The best summary judgment motions are "good reads," telling a story that will catch and retain the reader's interest. The motion should begin with a crisp, interesting preliminary statement or introduction

123

that sets the theme, introduces the parties and claims, and describes clearly why the motion should be granted.

In painting the picture of the case, the drafter should take into consideration the intended audience. Judges are only human, and the drafter's theme and recitation of the facts should be tailored to the known proclivities and predisposition of the judge who will decide the motion, where possible. To that end, review the judge's prior summary judgment decisions, as well as any bench decisions, new trial orders, or judgments as a matter of law involving similar claims and factual scenarios.

1. Just the Facts

A moving party need not negate unsupported claims by plaintiff; the moving party's burden is met by showing to the court that there is an absence of evidence of some element on which the opposing party bears the burden of proof.[49] It is good practice, however, for the moving party to affirmatively prove every fact necessary to establish summary judgment.

In setting forth the statement of material facts, the operative word is that the facts be material to the disposition of the motion. Hence, many facts that would be presented at trial will be omitted. That consideration notwithstanding, a balance must be struck with regard to including facts that have limited materiality in a summary judgment context, but would help to give the court the flavor of the case. Facts that cast the opposing party in an unfavorable light with respect to the equities of the case may be included.

A movant does not want to have to argue in the reply brief, however, that a fact it set forth is not really material after all, in the event it proves to be subject to dispute. To avoid that possibility, the facts can be referenced outside the statement of undisputed material fact, that is, in the supporting memorandum of points and authorities. Or the facts can be expressly acknowledged as being in dispute, but immaterial, and included only for narrative purposes.

2. Identifying and Applying Persuasive Authority

In order for the motion to be persuasive, the advocate must apply the law to the facts and demonstrate the result that must follow. In setting forth the legal precedent in support of summary judgment, the movant should identify the best case for each of the specific grounds upon which the motion is based, and that case should be displayed prominently. Of course, persuasive authority within the jurisdiction and prior decisions of the same judge that are on point are the first preference. In citing to any authority, emphasis should be placed on the factual similarity to the present case and on a decision's dispositive language.

VI. Opposing the Motion

Plaintiff's counsel should take defendants' motions for summary judgment very seriously since they are often granted.

A plaintiff must emphasize the legal standard for summary judgment, that is, that all inferences are to be drawn against the moving party and in favor of the party opposing the motion for summary judgment.[50] Plaintiffs should assert that the movant's position should be more closely scrutinized than the opposing papers, which are to be "indulgently treated," to determine whether the moving party has satisfied its burden.[51] Furthermore, it should be stressed that the burden is on the moving party at all times despite the fact that plaintiff ultimately has the burden of proof in establishing his or her claim.[52]

When opposing summary judgment, considerable attention should be directed to the existence of disputes as to material facts. Consideration should be given to whether the opposing party's factual representations are based upon admissible evidence and, if not, whether a motion to strike should be filed, as opposed to simply drawing the court's attention to the matter. It is also important to separate the wheat from the chaff and properly identify for the court any disputed facts that are not material and, hence, the dispute irrelevant.

Where critical facts are disclosed to a party for the first time in the summary judgment context, it is appropriate to request that the court provide additional opportunity for discovery. The rules specifically provide for that alternative.[53] Further discovery would be futile, however, to the extent the motion is based on plaintiff's own admissions.[54]

Where the case involved is to be proved through circumstantial evidence, it is critical for plaintiff's counsel to submit all admissible evidence of both plaintiff's prima facie case as defined under the *McDonnell Douglas/Burdine/Hicks* framework and evidence of pretext. As discussed above, if the plaintiff does not submit evidence that the employer-expressed nondiscriminatory reason is a pretext for discrimination, then summary judgment will be granted to the employer.

Additionally, every plaintiff's counsel should be well versed in the Third Circuit decision of *Marzano v. Computer Science Corp., Inc.*, 91 F.3d 497 (3rd Cir. 1996). In that case, the Third Circuit held that summary judgment should not be granted to the employer where the employee "can then produce enough evidence to cast doubt on the employer's stated reason, [then] the case should go to trial."[55]

Employment discrimination cases center around a single question: why did the employer take an adverse employment action against plaintiff?

125

Because this "is clearly a factual question," *Chipollini*, 814 F.2d at 899, summary judgment is in fact rarely appropriate in this type of case. Simply "by pointing to evidence which calls into question the defendant's intent, the plaintiff raises an issue of material fact which, if genuine, is sufficient to preclude summary judgment." Id. See *Sempier*, 45 F.3d at 732–33 (cases in which plaintiff attacks employer's stated reasons for adverse employment action "must be resolved by a jury and cannot be resolved on summary judgment").[56]

VII. When Should a Plaintiff Cross-Move for Summary Judgment?

It is not uncommon that certain cases develop facts that help establish plaintiff's claims. In fact, sometimes discovery will reveal that a certain employer's practice may have disproportionately affected the plaintiff-employee, which would be impermissible under federal and state law and sometimes these unintended revelations of such facts may warrant a plaintiff to cross-move for summary judgment. Many times such a motion, while not often granted, will force the employer to reveal interesting evidence that was not produced during the discovery process. That is usually the biggest reward when plaintiff cross-moves for summary judgment on some material element of the legal claim.

The other beneficial effect from a plaintiff cross-moving for summary judgment is that it puts the employer on the defensive before the summary judgment judge. Once the employer is on the defensive, it changes the whole tenor of the motion and makes it much less likely that the motion judge will grant summary judgment. Thus, a properly made cross-motion for summary judgment could (1) pry loose discovery from the employer that may prove helpful in your case at trial and (2) change the tenor of the summary judgment process and ultimately lead to a denial of the employer's motion for summary judgment.

VIII. Conclusion

Both the employee and employer must recognize that the summary judgment motions to be made are absolutely critical in employment litigation. Usually, when an employer loses a summary judgment motion, it is more likely to settle since it faces exposure of a jury verdict and lawyer's fees under the appropriate statutes. Conversely, the plaintiff will lose the benefit of a jury trial if summary judgment is granted, and federal and state judges are increasingly more inclined to grant summary judgment as employment claims have proliferated. Thus, it is extremely important for both plaintiff's and defendant's counsel to prepare from the outset of the litigation to come to legal blows in summary judgment motions after discovery has been completed. Those counsel who are most prepared to meet this test will most likely obtain a more successful outcome for their client.

Notes

1. *Id.*
2. *Id.* at 322.
3. *Id.*
4. *Id.* at 324.
5. *Id.* at 248.
6. *Id.* at 249–50.
7. *Id.* at 255.
8. *Anderson v. Liberty Lobby* at 247.
9. *Id.* at 248–49.
10. *Id.* at 251.
11. *Id.*
12. McDonnell Douglas Corp. v. Green, 411 U.S. 792 (1973); Texas Dept. of Community Affairs v. Burdine, 450 U.S. 248 (1981).
13. *See e.g.,* Beard v. Whitley County REMC, 840 F.2d 405 (7th Cir. 1988) (involving claims of sex discrimination in wages); Dea v. Look, 810 F.2d 12 (1st Cir. 1987) (involving claim of age discrimination arising from his termination of employment); Williams v. Williams Elecs., Inc., 856 F.2d 920 (7th Cir. 1988) (involving claim of race-based termination); Menard v. First Security Servs. Corp., 848 F.2d 281 (1st Cir. 1988) (claim of age-based termination); Goldberg v. B. Green & Co., 836 F.2d 845 (4th Cir. 1988) (involving claim of age); Pierce v. Marsh, 859 F.2d 601 (8th Cir. 1988) (involving failure to promote based upon race and sex).
14. *See, e.g.,* Chipollini v. Spencer Gifts, Inc., 814 F.2d 893 (3d Cir. 1987), *cert. denied,* 483 U.S. 1052 (1987) (involving claim of age-based termination); Jackson v. University of Pittsburgh, 826 F.2d 230 (3d Cir. 1987), *cert. denied,* 108 S. Ct. 732 (1988) (involving claim of race-based termination); Reynolds v. Brock, 815 F.2d 571 (9th Cir. 1987) (involving claim of disability-based termination).
15. *See, e.g.,* Gallo v. Prudential Residential Serv., 22 F.3d 1219, 1224 (2nd Cir. 1994), Hayden v. First National Bank of Mount Pleasant, 595 F.2d 994 (5th Cir. 1979).
16. *See* Hardin v. Pitney-Bowes, Inc., 636 F.2d 1217 (6th Cir. 1980), *cert. denied,* 451 U.S. 1008 (1981) (Justice Rehnquist dissenting from the denial of certiorari).
17. *See, e.g.,* MacDonald v. Eastern Wyo. Mental Health Ctr., 941 F.2d 1115 (10th Cir. 1991) (commenting that after the "trilogy," summary judgment was no longer in disfavor in discrimination cases). *See also* Steckl v. Motorola, Inc., 703 F.2d 392 (9th Cir. 1983) (finding that allegations of wrongful motive, "without substantial factual evidence," are insufficient and that summary judgment is proper even when the plaintiff has established a prima facie case); Kohler v. Ericsson, Inc., 847 F.2d 499 (9th Cir. 1988) (holding that while the plaintiff did not need to directly prove the existence of a hidden motive, he must bring forth facts sufficient to raise a genuine issue of the existence of bad faith); Meiri v. Dacon, 759 F.2d 989, *cert. denied,* 474 U.S. 829 (2d Cir. 1985) (finding that conclusory allegations of discriminatory intent or state of mind are insufficient to satisfy the requirements of Rule 56(e)); Munson v. Friske, 754 F.2d 683 (7th Cir. 1985) (finding summary judgment is proper in cases involving conflicting questions of motive and intent where the plaintiff presents no evidence of motive and intent supportive of his position).
18. *See* Friedel v. City of Madison, 832 F.2d 965 (7th Cir. 1987).
19. *See* Thomas v. MetroFlight, Inc., 814 F.2d 1506 (10th Cir. 1987).
20. *See* Johnson v. Uncle Ben's, Inc., 657 F.2d 750 (5th Cir. 1981), *cert. denied,* 459 U.S. 967 (1982).
21. *See, e.g.,* Connell v. Bank of Boston, 924 F.2d 1169 (1st Cir. 1991), *cert. denied,* 501 U.S. 1218, (1991) (criticizing the adoption of a three-prong approach for avoiding summary judgment: the prima facie case, proving the proffered reasons are pretextual, and adducing additional evidence of age animus and surveying cases from the other circuits with respect to requiring "additional" evidence of animus); Villanueva v. Wellesley College, 930 F.2d 124 (1st Cir. 1991), *cert. denied,* 502 U.S. 861 (1991) (holding that when the

employer has articulated a presumptively legitimate reason for discharging an employee, the latter must elucidate specific facts that would enable a jury to find that the reason given was not only a sham, but a sham intended to cover up the employer's real motive: . . . discrimination").

22. *Hicks*, 509 U.S. at 511.

23. *See also*, Goetz v. Farm Credit Servs., 927 F.2d 398 (8th Cir. 1991) in which the Eighth Circuit stated that "as a matter of both common sense and federal law, an employer's submission of a discredited explanation for firing a member of a protected class is itself evidence that may persuade the finder of fact that such unlawful discrimination actually occurred." *Compare* Visser v. Packer Eng'g Assocs., Inc., 924 F.2d 655 (7th Cir. 1991) (en banc); Shager v. Upjohn Co., 913 F.2d 398 (7th Cir. 1990).

24. *See, e.g.*, Billet v. Cigna Corp., 940 F.2d 812 (3d Cir. 1991) (holding that "what matters is the perception of the decision maker").

25. *See* Danielson v. City of Lorain, 938 F.2d 681 (6th Cir. 1991); Wheeler v. McKinley Enters., 937 F.2d 1156 (6th Cir. 1991); Medina-Munoz v. R.J. Reynolds Tobacco Co., 896 F.2d 5 (1st Cir. 1990); Billet. *But see* Sischo-Nownejad v. Merced Community College Dist., 934 F.2d 1104 (9th Cir. 1991).

26. *See, e.g.*, Kraus v. Sobel Corrugated Containers, Inc., 915 F.2d 227 (6th Cir. 1990) (criticizing the employer for failing to produce contemporaneous records of the plaintiff's unsatisfactory work or that she was even put on notice of the fact). *See also* Moody v. Pepsi-Cola Metro. Bottling Co., Inc., 915 F.2d 201 (6th Cir. 1990) (finding that notations of "age" and "minority" made in personnel files could be viewed by a jury as evidence of discriminatory motive).

27. *See, e.g.*, Conkwright v. Westinghouse Elec. Corp., 933 F.2d 231 (4th Cir. 1991) (holding that subjective poor evaluations could possibly tend to show that an employer's proffered reasons were actually pretexts, but that such proof is "close to irrelevant" absent evidence showing that the ratings were otherwise out of line).

28. Weldon v. Kraft, 896 F.2d 793, 799 (3rd Cir. 1990).

29. Billet v. Cigna Corp., 930 F.2d 812 (3d Cir. 1991).

30. *See e.g.*, White v. Westinghouse Elec. Co., 862 F.2d 56 (3rd Cir. 1988); Colgan v. Fisher Scientific Co., 935 F.2d 1407 (3rd Cir. 1991), *cert. denied*, 502 U.S. 941 (1991); Shager v. Upjohn Co., 913 F.2d 398 (7th Cir. 1990) (trial court ignored plaintiff's outstanding record).

31. Hankins v. Temple Univ., 829 F.2d 437 (3d Cir. 1987) (finding that evidence that an employer's decision is erroneous is insufficient to create an inference of discriminatory intent).

32. *See also* Combs v. Plantation Patterns, 106 F.3d 1519, 1529–36 (11th Cir. 1997) (discussing split among panels within Eleventh Circuit on interpretation of *Hicks*).

33. *See also* Kolstad v. American Dental Ass'n, 108 F.3d 1431 (D.C. Cir. 1997) (evidence of pretext sufficient to create a jury issue); Anderson v. Baxter Healthcare Corp., 13 F.3d 1120 (7th Cir. 1994) (same); Washington v. Garrett, 10 F.3d 1421, 1433 (9th Cir. 1993) (same).

34. *See also* Woods v. Friction Materials, Inc., 30 F.3d 255, 260–61 n.3 (1st Cir. 1994) (more than mere pretext required); LeBlanc v. Great American Ins. Co., 6 F.3d 836, 842–43 (1st Cir. 1993), *cert. denied*, 114 S. Ct. 1398 (1994) ("In this circuit we have always required not only 'minimally sufficient evidence of pretext' but evidence that overall reasonably supports a finding of discriminatory animus.").

35. Haskins v. Temple Univ., 829 F.2d 437 (3rd Cir. 1987); Billet v. Cigna Corp., 930 F.2d 812 (3rd Cir. 1991).

36. Price Waterhouse v. Hopkins, 490 U.S. 228, 109 S. Ct. 1775 (1989) ("[T]he entire purpose of the *McDonnell Douglas* prima facie case is to compensate for the fact that direct evidence of intentional discrimination is hard to come by."). *See also* Ang v. Proctor & Gamble Co., 932 F.2d 540 (6th Cir. 1991).

37. *See* Sennello v. Reserve Life Ins. Co., 872 F.2d 393 (11th Cir. 1989) (manager's statement that "we can't have women in management because women are like Jews and [pejorative term] they hire like themselves, and the trouble with that is that when they leave they take them with them" is direct evidence of discriminatory motivation).

38. *See* Sischo-Nownejad v. Analysis & Tech., Inc., 934 F.2d 1104 (9th Cir.); Starceski v. Westinghouse Elec. Corp., 54 F.3d 1089 (3rd Cir. 1995).

39. *See, e.g.*, Levin v. Analysis & Tech., Inc., 960 F.2d 314 (2nd Cir. 1992).

40. See 42 U.S.C. § 2000e-2(m).

41. *See e.g.* 42 U.S.C. § 2000e-5(g)(2)(B).

42. O'Connor v. Consol. Coin Caterers, 116 S. Ct. 1307 (1996).

43. *See, e.g.,* Smith v. American Express Co., 853 F.2d 151 (2d Cir. 1988) (granting summary judgment where employer articulated legitimate nondiscriminatory reason for discharge and plaintiff failed to offer admissible evidence of pretext); Dea v. Look, 810 F.2d 12 (1st Cir. 1987) (holding that plaintiff cannot prove pretext "simply by refuting or questioning the defendants' articulated reason"); Grisby v. Reynolds Metals Co., 821 F.2d 590 (11th Cir. 1987) (granting summary judgment in sex discrimination claim based upon evidence that more males were laid off than females and that the male who was promoted was better qualified); Carey v. U.S. Postal Service, 812 F.2d 621 (10th Cir. 1987).

44. *See, e.g.,* Mechnig v. Sears Roebuck & Co., 1988 U.S. App. LEXIS 18024; 48 Fair Empl. Prac. Cas. (BNA) 1218 (7th Cir. 1988) (granting summary judgment despite evidence of inconsistent past practice because evidence not sufficient to prove that those who made termination decision relied on anything other than company policy.); Fowle v. C&C Cola, 868 F.2d 59 (3rd Cir. 1989) (granting summary judgment and finding that plaintiff's certification that defendant's officers used improper standard to evaluate his performance did not raise a genuine issue of material fact as to whether the articulated reason was pretext). *But see* Ramseur v. Chase Manhattan Bank, 865 F.2d 650 (2d Cir. 1989) (grant of summary judgment reversed because the trial court failed to draw all factual inferences in favor of nonmovant, which would have raised genuine issues of material fact as to plaintiff's performance and as to disparate treatment).

45. *See also* Paolillo v. Dresser Indus., Inc., 821 F.2d 81 (2d Cir. 1987); DeCintio v. Westchester County Medical Ctr., 821 F.2d 111 (2d Cir. 1987), *cert. denied,* 108 S. Ct. 455; Hillebrand v. M-Tron Indus., Inc., 827 F.2d 363 (8th Cir. 1987) (summary judgment should be used only sparingly and where there can be only one conclusion from the evidence).

46. *See* Section IV.B. above, discussing the split in the circuits on the effect of pretext. *See also, e.g.,* Chipollini v. Spencer Gifts, 814 F.2d 893 (3rd Cir. 1987), *cert. denied,* 483 U.S. 1052, 108 S. Ct. 26 (plaintiff challenged employer's conclusion as to poor performance and bad attitude; because pretext issue turned on credibility, court reversed summary judgment).

47. Price Waterhouse v. Hopkins, 109 S. Ct. 1775, 1795 (1989).

48. *See* 1991 Civil Rights Act § 107, 42 U.S.C. § 2000e-2-(m).

49. Celotex Corp. v. Catrett, 477 U.S. 317, 322–23 (1986).

50. U.S. v. Diebold, Inc., 369 U.S. 654, 655 (1962).

51. 6 JAMES WM. MOORE ET AL., MOORE'S FEDERAL PRACTICE, § 56.15[3], at 469–72.

52. *Id.* § 56.15, at 405.

53. Fed. R. Civ. P. 56(f).

54. 6 MOORE'S FEDERAL PRACTICE § 56.15[4], at 286 & n.7 (1988) (there is no need for cross-examination of defendant's witnesses when the motion is based on plaintiff's admissions).

55. 91 F.3d at 509.

56. 91 F.3d at 509–10.

CHAPTER 6

Pretrial Motions

BURTON KAINEN*
ANNE K. MILLHAM†

* Kainen, Starr, Garfield, Wright & Escalera, P.C.; Hartford, Connecticut.

† Law Office of Judith A. Ravel; Branford, Connecticut.

I. Introduction

Pretrial motions, such as motions in limine, motions to bifurcate, and motions to sever, are critical instruments in shaping how a jury will hear a case. A litigator has only so much control over when, how, and what evidence is presented to the jury once a case is at trial. Therefore, it is useful to try to gain as much control as possible over the most important evidence before the trial begins. In virtually any case there will be evidence that will be damaging if admitted, or in the alternative, evidence that must be ruled admissible because it is essential to the case. When there is powerful yet questionably relevant evidence that can be very harmful or helpful to the case, or when it is important that the jury hear evidence in a particular context, these devices can become powerful and critical tools in shaping the outcome of the case before the trial even begins. Equally important, motions in limine streamline and shorten the trial by simplifying the issues presented and reducing the possibility of mistrial.

II. Motions in Limine

A motion "in limine" is a motion "on the threshold" of trial to obtain a ruling before trial. Usually these motions rely on evidentiary principles. They seek to exclude or admit evidence; however, the possibilities for use are as varied as the evidence in the case and the ingenuity of counsel. Motions in limine are extremely effective pretrial devices. They can accomplish multiple objectives that can determine the outcome. Most frequently, a motion in limine seeks to exclude harmful evidence. Such motions can be equally effective to admit evidence, however, thus permitting reference to the evidence in the opening statement. Further, a motion in limine may produce a legal ruling from the court that may not have been raised or addressed at the summary judgment stage. In limine motions alert the court to important legal standards that ultimately affect admissibility of particular evidence.

There are many advantages to motions in limine. First and most importantly, a successful motion in limine avoids the irreversible prejudice that occurs when excludable evidence is presented to a jury. Any corrective or limiting instruction may not be sufficient. Indeed, objections often are too little, too late. They frequently serve only to highlight the dangerous evidence. Picture, for example, the following scenario: Your opponent produces evidence that is devastating for your case; you object; juror number four, who has been busy counting ceiling tiles for the last twenty minutes suddenly wakes up and starts paying attention; if your objection is successful, the judge then makes a curative instruction. That instruction tells juror number four exactly what important information he just missed. The instruction highlights the objectionable material for all of the other members of the jury. Once Pandora's box has been opened, there is no way to remove the evidence's impact on the minds of the jurors. Frequently, however, a motion in limine may exclude the damaging evidence.

Second, a written motion can educate the judge and focus on critical issues of proof necessary at trial. In addition, it is a useful tool for planning any necessary rebuttal testimony with more certainty.[1]

Third, a motion may prevent the unnecessary expense of preparing special exhibits. Or it may avoid the need to produce distant witnesses for rebuttal or the case in chief.

Fourth, a motion in limine avoids repeated objections at trial. Objections tend to reduce counsel's credibility with the jury. Jurors may doubt counsel who are interfering with hearing all the evidence.[2] A successful motion avoids the prejudicial effect of both prejudicial questions and answers. Further, during trial a successful motion requires an opponent to constantly avoid violating the order. The successful motion forces counsel to instruct witnesses not to discuss the excluded evidence.

Fifth, a motion assists counsel in evaluating settlement. Knowing how a court will rule on a significant evidentiary or legal issue can provide important information on the likelihood of success or of potential damages.

There are, of course, some disadvantages. A motion in limine may strengthen an opponent's case. The motion may highlight overlooked evidence.[3] Thus it is always important to consider how strong the evidence really is. Weigh the potential hazards before filing a motion in limine.

A. Motions in Limine in Employment Litigation

Motions in limine can be particularly advantageous in employment litigation. Employment evidence often proves emotional and inflammatory. Even if a motion in limine fails to definitely admit or exclude evidence, the motion may expand or limit the scope of the opening statements. For example, in a sexual harassment case, similar complaints of coworkers are likely to have a significant impact on a jury. From an employer's perspective, there is an advantage to excluding this highly prejudicial (although arguably probative) evidence. At a minimum the employer wants to prevent the plaintiff's counsel from mentioning similar harassment in the opening statement. In the motion in limine, an employer can argue that "bad acts" are irrelevant, prejudicial, remote, cumulative, and excludable character evidence under Fed. R. Evid. 403 and 404(b).

Conversely, plaintiff's counsel may want to exclude the plaintiff's sexual history, provocative dress or behavior, and prior discrimination complaints or other lawsuits. Even an indecisive motion may limit the opening statement.

The scope of motions in limine does not follow any specific rule of evidence. Indeed, these motions can be as broad as warranted by the case and the creativity of counsel. The following illustrative examples identify some of the more frequent types of motions in limine.

1. Time-Barred Events

Motions in limine may exclude evidence that is too remote in time to be relevant, or a statute of limitation may bar the evidence.[4]

2. Excluding Evidence Relating to Employees Other Than the Plaintiff*

Motions in limine may exclude testimony from other employees claiming similar wrongful conduct. In discrimination cases, plaintiffs seek to present evidence of alleged discriminatory conduct directed towards other employees. Courts have broad discretion to admit or exclude such evidence as the facts warrant. A motion in limine will encourage the court to resolve the issue up front rather than during the middle of the trial.

Defense motions to exclude such evidence often rely on irrelevance under Fed. R. Evid. 401 and 402. The statements of the other employees may not relate to the decision to terminate the plaintiff. Or the evidence may not establish a policy or pattern of discrimination.[5] Under Rule 403 the evidence also may be unfairly prejudicial, or confusing.[6] Also, the employer would want to present rebuttal evidence. Such a minitrial would waste time and cause confusion and prejudice.[7] An employer may move to exclude comparative evidence relating to claimed disparate treatment. If the employee in the other case was not similarly situated in all respects to the plaintiff, the evidence may be irrelevant and confusing.[8] An employer also may seek to exclude such evidence as cumulative, particularly with marginal relevance.

3. Unduly Prejudicial Statements

Employment cases often turn on the alleged statements from a supervisor, manager, or even the plaintiff. For example, a plaintiff may offer generalized statements reflecting a discriminatory animus (for ex-

---

* See also Evidence of Discrimination against Other Employees, chapter 7, "Special Evidentiary Concerns," and chapter 8, "Trial Preparation," regarding evidence of similar discrimination.

ample, "this company has too many employees that are out of date"). The speaker may have played no role in the disputed employment decision. The impact of such a statement can be enormous for both parties. There are numerous arguments for excluding this type of evidence. An employer might argue that the speaker was not acting as an agent of the employer or within the scope of his employment. Therefore the statement was not an admission by the employer. A statement from a non–decision maker may be irrelevant. Such a statement was not tied to the challenged employment decision; likewise, the statement relates to events that are not in issue. Hearsay may bar other statements.[9]

4. After-Acquired Evidence

Either party may use a motion in limine to admit or contest the after-acquired evidence of wrongdoing by the employee in an attempt to justify the termination or reduce damages. From the plaintiff's perspective, the after-acquired evidence is relevant only to back pay. Such evidence would be irrelevant in determining liability. On the other hand, the employer may rely on wrongdoing to attack the plaintiff's credibility.[10] For example, *Vichare v. AMBAC Inc.*, 106 F.3d 457 (2nd Cir. 1996) allowed evidence of kickbacks to the plaintiff to impeach the plaintiff's creditability in a Title VII suit. The plaintiff was a crucial witness. (See After-Acquired Evidence, chapter 7, "Special Evidentiary Concerns.")

5. Damages

Motions in limine can be a very effective tool to define the scope of damages in an employment case. For example, a plaintiff has a duty to mitigate damages, such as lost pay.[11] So mitigating back pay may be critical to the ultimate value of the case, regardless of liability. Often the facts (but not the legal conclusions) of mitigation are substantially undisputed. Mitigation may be ripe for ruling from the court. Framed as a motion in limine, counsel can clarify if a plaintiff is or is not entitled to back pay or front pay.

Emotional distress damages often are a significant element of a plaintiff's damages. A motion in limine can address critical evidentiary and legal damages issues. Counsel can resolve whether expert testimony is necessary (or barred), whether friends and relatives can testify about the plaintiff's emotional distress and the impact of non-employment-related stress on any emotional distress. In Age Discrimination in Employment Act cases, a motion in limine should exclude evidence of emotional distress since the statute does not authorize compensatory or punitive damages.

If punitive damages are not available (for example, in a typical breach of contract case), a motion in limine may exclude evidence of the worth of a company, its individual officers, and senior employees and other evidence suggestive of a "deep pocket." Another way to handle this type of issue is bifurcation, which is discussed below.

6. Opinion Testimony of Experts and Non-experts (Coworkers)

A motion in limine may limit opinion testimony of coworkers. The jury may be just as competent as the witnesses to form an opinion based on the evidence. Certain subjects are not technical enough to require expert testimony. Or an expert's opinions may not be generally accepted in the field of expertise.[12]

7. Other Matters

There are few legal boundaries for motions in limine. Motions in limine may help a defendant to exclude the following: affirmative action goals, settlement offers, prior consistent statements from the plaintiff in journals or logs, flawed statistical evidence, flawed tape or video recordings, and so forth. Similarly, a plaintiff may seek to exclude evidence relating to prior or subsequent work history, nonemployment bad acts such as prior arrests and convictions (see Fed. R. Evid. 401(b)), and a plaintiff's personal wealth, including other sources of income.

B. How to Bring a Motion in Limine

No specific rule expressly authorizes a motion in limine. A court has general authority to manage the pretrial process. A court can make preliminary evidentiary rulings under Rule 16 of the Federal Rules of Civil Procedure (as well as the rules of most state courts).[13] Motions in limine also are a proper extension of the trial judge's authority to administer and conduct the trial.

Depending on the purpose of the motion, timing may be important. In most cases, motions in limine are right before trial or the beginning of trial, often along with a pretrial memorandum. Motions come almost always before jury selection. Bringing a motion before the trial judge shortly before the trial highlights the issues.[14] One reason not to move too early is to avoid premature disclosure of trial strategy to an opponent. Yet, because a critical goal of the motion is to limit opening statements (or framing questions in the voir dire that might suggest the evidence), it is important to give the court sufficient time to consider the motion. Early motions minimize the time a jury waits while the court resolves these issues. It is preferable to bring the motion before the judge who will hear the case. Judges do not like to make evidentiary rulings that another judge can better resolve during trial.

There may, however, be reasons for bringing the motion well in advance of trial. Where settlement is a serious objective, resolving critical evidentiary issues can help settlement.

Although there is no requirement in many federal courts (or in many state jurisdictions) for a written motion, the preferred practice is a written motion. By preparing a written motion, you can clearly outline the disputed evidence. In addition, the judge is more likely to adopt the reasoning of a memorandum. Even if the motion fails at trial, a written motion may change the judge's initial rulings as trial progresses.

The motion should broadly describe the challenged evidence. Opposing counsel may try to introduce the same information or prejudice in another way. Yet the motion must be specific enough so that the court has a clear presentation of what should be excluded and why. Provide a clear path for the court to follow during the trial. To illustrate the importance of scope, consider the following. Plaintiff's motion in limine excludes evidence about the plaintiff's termination from another employer. At trial the defendant calls a former employer to testify about the character of the plaintiff. This evidence is arguably outside the scope of the court's earlier ruling. Plaintiff's counsel will object to the character evidence. But a broader motion in limine could have addressed the issue up front. At the same time, counsel must be careful not to frame a motion too broadly or to make it too complicated. Broad orders in limine may be more difficult for both counsel and the trial judge to follow during the course of the trial. Remember, an order in limine is not a device to preclude an entire claim or defense.

A motion in limine should include materials substantiating any facts necessary for the motion. Such evidence may include deposition testimony, interrogatory answers, admissions, and/or an affidavit. Draft a proposed order clearly outlining the challenged evidence to be excluded or admitted. Your draft order should ideally clarify that all direct and indirect forms of communication such as pleadings, questions, testimony, remarks, and arguments are within the scope of the court's order. Plus all parties, all witnesses, and all lawyers must follow the order.

C. How to Handle a Motion in Limine at Trial

Orders on motions in limine are interlocutory orders. These orders are subject to revision or even reversal at trial. Therefore, be prepared to deal with the evidence admitted. There are various ways to handle a motion in limine at the trial stage. When a motion in limine has failed and the evidence is damaging, object, object, object when an opponent offers the evidence. Courts are split on whether an objection at trial is necessary to preserve appeal. So, play it safe and object on the record.[15] Beyond the issue of record preservation, events during the trial can cause the court to reconsider. A reason for exclusion or admission becomes more clear during trial. Remember also that often trial judges will reserve ultimate ruling on the motion in limine until the evidence has developed at trial. Renew the motion before the challenged evidence has been offered, even by way of a suggestive question.

If an opponent's motion in limine excludes important evidence, make an offer of proof outside the presence of the jury. It is always possible that the judge may then see the relevance of the evidence and admit it. Even if the judge holds firm, the offer of proof gives the reviewing court a clear view of the evidentiary issue. When an opponent violates an in limine order, object. Ask for a curative instruction or even a mistrial if the evidence is of that level of significance.

D. Available Sanctions for Violation of a Motion in Limine

The court has discretion in ruling on violations of the order in limine. Therefore, many sanctions are available. The court may find the violator in civil contempt or may grant a request for mistrial during or at the conclusion of trial. The court may allow the case to go to the jury and then reverse if the verdict is in the favor of the offending party. Or the court may simply direct a finding against the party willfully violating the order on the issue of liability. A violation may also be a basis for reversal on appeal.[16]

Whether to grant a motion in limine and whether to punish a violation of an order in limine are both discretionary issues. Accordingly, the trial court will not be reversed unless the decision was patently erroneous. The trial court is therefore reviewed on the abuse of discretion standard.[17]

III. Motions to Sever and Motions to Bifurcate

When the court admits problematic evidence on a motion in limine, consider severance or bifurcation. Both severance and bifurcation will allow litigators, and especially defendants, increased control of the trial. Some use the terms bifurcation and severance interchangeably. They are different concepts. A severance divides a lawsuit into two or more independent causes, each of which results in a separate judgment. A bifurcation separates the issues of a case, trying some first, and leaving the rest for further proceedings. Generally, a bifurcated case will try the issue of liability separately from, and before, the issue of damages.[18]

A. Deciding Whether to Sever the Trial

Usually, severance in employment litigation is more to the benefit of the defendant than the plaintiff. For instance, when many plaintiffs are suing the defendant, it is to the defendant's advantage to try to sever each action. Severance will prevent the plaintiffs from marching to the stand one after another recounting employer mistreatment. Severance will prevent the jury from concluding that the employer must have done something wrong to have so many people sue the employer. In addition, severance can avoid confusion of the facts, issues, and defenses of each plaintiff's or each defendant's case in multiparty actions.

Plaintiffs may find severance helpful too. Examples include when a plaintiff wants to disassociate from a class action to receive a faster trial. Or a plaintiff may want to distance himself from a coplaintiff because of the coplaintiff's character or bad acts. Severance may also separate individual issues for trial that are factually unrelated to each other.

The problem with severance is that it takes more time to try each case separately. Therefore, it is more expensive and more inconvenient for most parties concerned.

Finally, in considering severance, both plaintiffs and defendants must carefully analyze whether the damages will be more convincing all together or separately. If all the plaintiffs have strong cases on liability, the total of each individual damage award may exceed what a jury deciding the cases together would be willing to allow.

B. Deciding Whether to Bifurcate the Trial

One difference between bifurcation and severance is that bifurcation has the potential to shorten the trial. Assuming the usual scenario of bifurcation of liability from damages, when the defendant prevails on liability, no evidence of damages is needed.

Bifurcation can also clarify and simplify the trial when complex damages issues might confuse the jury on the liability issues. Damage issues may involve expensive but unnecessary expert witnesses if the defendant wins the liability issues. In addition, claims for punitive damages often involve the plaintiff's use of financial information about the defendant's net worth or profits. Bifurcation avoids this financial evidence until after proving liability.

Plaintiffs may find bifurcation useful when the defendant will invoke after-acquired evidence of wrongdoing by the plaintiff. The plaintiff may limit the wrongdoing evidence to the second stage of damages, excluding the wrongdoing from the liability stage.

Like severance, however, bifurcation tends to be more favorable for the defendant because it usually reduces the impact of the plaintiff's case. Defendants should pursue bifurcation where there is concern that the jury might find for the plaintiff due to sympathy, for example, when liability may be doubtful but the plaintiff's damages are devastating.

If, however, the damage claims are exaggerated or there is after-acquired evidence of employee wrongdoing, the defendant may oppose bifurcation. In that situation, the defendant may want to demonstrate to the jury that the plaintiff suffered little injury or the plaintiff deserved the actions of the defendant.

Bifurcation avoids the compromise verdict outcome in which pro-plaintiff and prodefendant jurors trade off liability for low or minimal damages.

C. How to Sever or to Bifurcate Trials

Under Rules 21 and 42(b) of the Federal Rules of Civil Procedure, and many state court rules, the judge can bifurcate or sever trials for convenience, expedience, economy, or to avoid prejudice. Severance may avoid prejudice because the various claims do not arise from the same transaction or occurrence. A bifurcation also may avoid prejudice, promote expedience and economy, and avoid confusion. The court can order separate trials for any claim or issues, so long as the court preserves the right to a jury trial.

Motions to bifurcate or to sever are more likely to succeed when filed early. The closer to trial, the more prejudicial such motions are to the other side in preparing for trial, and the less likely the motions will win.

D. Opposing Motions to Sever or to Bifurcate

In deciding motions to sever or to bifurcate, the court has wide discretion. A court may deny a motion to sever because evidence would have to be duplicated or because severance is unnecessary to avoid prejudice. A motion to sever may also fail because it will prejudice a party if it is brought too close to trial. Severance may take more time or money and may be more inconvenient for all parties involved.

Motions to bifurcate may fail due to the nature of injuries. Certain injuries have an important bearing on the issue of liability. Courts may also deny motions to bifurcate if evidence will have to be duplicated or if bifurcation is unnecessary to avoid prejudice.

Like motions in limine, a decision to bifurcate or to sever will not be reversed unless prejudice is shown. The decision is within the discretion of the trial judge.

IV. Conclusion

Motions in limine, motions to sever, and motions to bifurcate can be extraordinarily useful in controlling the shape of the trial. Consider such motions as part of your strategic analysis of every case.

V. Appendixes

A. Pretrial Motions Checklist

1. Motions in Limine

- Put the motion in writing with supporting materials (for example, deposition testimony, interrogatory answers, admissions, supporting affidavits) verifying the facts and a written proposed order.
- Bring the motion before the judge who will hear the trial.
- File the motion early enough to be heard before trial begins.
- As a minimum file the motion before jury selection.
- Make sure the motion is clearly drafted to cover only the evidence you want allowed or excluded.
- Make sure a favorable order clearly states that all direct and indirect forms of communication are within the order and that all parties, witnesses, and attorneys are bound by the order.
- At trial, after your motion is denied, renew your motion; and object to preserve appeal.
- At trial, when you want to get in evidence covered by an order, make an offer of proof outside the presence of the jury. If your opponent brings up the evidence, you must follow up.
- At trial, when an order has been violated, object and request a curative instruction or a mistrial.
- Do not rely on an order in limine even if granted. It may be reversed at trial, so be prepared to defend the motion at trial and be prepared to have the evidence come in.

2. Motions to Sever

- Consider a motion to sever if there are several plaintiffs, several defendants, or unrelated issues being tried together.
- Make your motion in writing.
- Make your motion as early as possible to avoid an argument of prejudice.

3. Motions to Bifurcate

- If defending, consider this motion if the evidence concerning damages is strong, but the claim for liability is weak.
- Make your motion in writing.
- Make your motion as early as possible to avoid an argument of prejudice.

B. Motion to Bifurcate Trial

[Note: Follow your local pleading rules and practices.]

UNITED STATES DISTRICT COURT
DISTRICT OF _____

[PLAINTIFF],	:
Plaintiff, :	Civil Action No.
v. :	
[DEFENDANT], :	Date
Defendant. :	

[DEFENDANT'S] MOTION TO BIFURCATE TRIAL

Defendant hereby requests that the trial in the above-captioned matter be bifurcated into a liability proceeding followed, if necessary, by a damages proceeding, for the following reasons:

1. Bifurcation of liability and damages will expedite the hearing of this case, lead to judicial economy, and avoid prejudice;

2. Bifurcation of liability and damages phases of a trial is appropriate in an action for [age discrimination];

3. Bifurcation is necessary since only the court is empowered to grant relief in the instant action;

4. Bifurcation is necessary because [the issue of what types of damages available in the instant action has not yet been resolved]; and

5. Bifurcation is necessary due to the possibility of [medical testimony at trial].

A memorandum of law in support of this motion is attached.

Respectfully Submitted,

[DEFENDANT],
By: [Counsel]

C. Motion in Limine

[Note: Follow your local pleading rules and practices.]

UNITED STATES DISTRICT COURT
DISTRICT OF _____

[PLAINTIFF],	:	
Plaintiff,	:	Civil Action No.
	:	
v.	:	
[DEFENDANT],	:	
Defendant.	:	

[DEFENDANT/PLAINTIFF'S] MOTION IN LIMINE

[Defendant/Plaintiff] moves this court in limine to determine the evidentiary issue, set forth below, in advance of trial in order to prevent the presentation of inadmissible and prejudicial testimony or materials to the jury that will jeopardize [defendant's/plaintiff's] opportunity for a fair hearing.

[Defendant/plaintiff] requests an order precluding any evidence, testimony, mention or reference of [employment decisions affecting individual employees of defendant other than plaintiff.]

As a basis for such a motion [Defendant/Plantiff] cites: _____.

Respectfully Submitted,

[DEFENDANT/PLAINTIFF],

By: [Counsel]

143

D. Motion to Sever

[Note: Follow your local pleading rules and practices.]

UNITED STATES DISTRICT COURT
DISTRICT OF _____

[PLAINTIFF],	:	
	:	
Plaintiff,	:	Civil Action No.
	:	
v.	:	
	:	
[DEFENDANT #1]	:	
[DEFENDANT #2]	:	
	:	
Defendants	:	

<u>MOTION TO SEVER</u>

    Pursuant to Rule 21 of the Federal Rules of Civil Procedure, Defendant [#1] moves to sever the defendants in the above-entitled action. For the reasons set forth in Defendant [#1's] accompanying memorandum of law, Plaintiff's claims against Defendant [#2] are misjoined with those against Defendant [#1] and should be severed. Such a Motion is without intended prejudice to the right of Defendant [#1] to alternatively seek relief pursuant to Rules 20(b) and 42(b) of the Federal Rules of Civil Procedure, or Rule _____ of this Court's Local Rules of Civil Procedure at some later juncture.

    As a basis for severance Defendant cites: _____.

[DEFENDANT #1]

By: [Counsel]

Notes

1. Edna Selan Epstein, *Motions in Limine—A Primer*, LITIGATION, Spring 1982, at 34.

2. James W. McElhaney, *Creative Objecting, What Evidence Gets in Can Determine How the Case Will Turn Out*, A.B.A. Aug. 1994, at 81.

3. Epstein, *supra* note 1, at 35.

4. Malarkey v. Texaco, Inc., 983 F.2d 1204, 1211 (2d Cir. 1993).

5. Haskell v. Kaman Corp., 743 F.2d 113 (2d Cir. 1984).

6. Schrand v. Fed. Pac. Electric Co., 851 F.2d 152 (6th Cir. 1988).

7. Moorhouse v. Boeing Co., 501 F. Supp. 390 (E.D. Pa. 1980), *aff'd*, 639 F.2d 774 (3d Cir. 1980).

8. Darvin v. Delta Air Lines, 678 F.2d 567 (5th Cir. 1982). *See* William F. Gardner, *Narrowing the Trial: Motions in Limine and Other Options*, AMERICAN EMPLOYMENT LAW COUNCIL SECOND ANNUAL MEETING, Oct. 26–29, 1994, at 3–5.

9. Arbruster v. Unisys Corp., 1994 U.S. App. LEXIS 1983, 65 Fair Empl. Prac. Cas. (BNA) 828 (3d Cir. 1994); Boyle v. Mannesmann, 1993 U.S. App. LEXIS 8682 (6th Cir. 1993); Carden v. Westinghouse Elec. Corp., 850 F.2d 996, 47 Fair Empl. Prac. Cas. (BNA) 446 (3d Cir. 1988); Gardner, *supra* note 8, at 6–10.

10. McKennon v. Nashville Banner Publ'g Co., 513 U.S. 352, 115 S. Ct. 879, 130 L. Ed. 2d 852 (1995).

11. *See* Ford Motor Co. v. EEOC, 458 U.S. 218 (1982).

12. *See* Daubert v. Merrell Dow Pharm., Inc., 509 U.S. 579 (1993) and New Trends in the Use of Expert Testimony, chapter 4, "Experts," and Beware Lay Opinion Testimony, chapter 8, "Trial Preparation."

13. Epstein, *supra* note 1, at 35.

14. Epstein, *supra* note 1, at 35.

15. *See* Colleen R. Courtade, Annotation, *Sufficiency in Federal Court of Motion in Limine to Preserve for Appeal Objection to Evidence Absent Contemporary Objection at Trial*, 76 A.L.R. FED. §§ 1–5 (1986).

16. Epstein, *supra* note 1, at 63.

17. 75 AM. JUR. 2D *Trial* § 97 (1991).

18. 75 AM. JUR. 2D *Trial* § 115 (1991).

CHAPTER 7

Special Evidentiary Concerns

Domenick Carmagnola[*]
Wayne J. Positan[*]
Kyle Francis[†]
Nancy Erika Smith[‡]

I. Introduction

This chapter will discuss and outline various issues, strategies, problems, and developments that may arise regarding special evidence concerns. Counsel may address these issues during the discovery phase

---

[*] *Lum, Danzis, Drasco, Positan and Kleinberg; Roseland, New Jersey.*

[†] *Francis, Lenzo and Manshel; Millburn, New Jersey.*

[‡] *Smith Mullin; Montclair, New Jersey.*

See also chapter 3, "Discovery," regarding related discovery and evidentiary issues.

of the litigation or as part of in limine applications. (See chapter 3, "Discovery," and chapter 6, "Pretrial Motions.") Counsel should also consider how these evidence issues may arise during trial.

II. Evidence of Discrimination against Other Employees*

Evidence of discrimination against employees other than the plaintiff may be admissible for the purpose of proving plaintiff's case. Although defendants often seek to exclude such evidence (usually through motions in limine, as discussed in chapter 6, "Pretrial Motions"), such motions frequently fail.[1]

The reasoning behind the admission of such evidence has been succinctly articulated by the *Stair* court:

> To prove that discrimination was intentional, the plaintiff must show the defendant's state of mind. *Texas Department of Community Affairs v. Burdine*, 450 U.S. 248, 255 (1981). A plaintiff can prove the defendant's state of mind through circumstantial evidence such as evidence of past conduct or prior incidents. *United States Postal Service Board of Governors v. Aikens*, 460 U.S. 711, 714 n.3, 715 (1983). Thus, evidence of past conduct or prior incidents of alleged discrimination has a tendency to make the existence of a fact that is of consequence—the defendant's discriminatory motive or intent— more probable than it would be without the evidence, and therefore such evidence is, as a general rule, relevant.[2]

Thus, courts from various jurisdictions have allowed the use of such evidence on behalf of the plaintiff.[3]

Employer's evidence of the fair treatment of similarly situated employees often allows the plaintiff to offer rebuttal of the employer's evidence. For example, in *Rendine v. Pantzer Realty*, 661 A.2d 1202 (N.J. 1995), the New Jersey Supreme Court held that the plaintiff's evidence that other pregnant employees suffered discriminatory treatment was admissible when the defendant produced eight employees who returned to work after short maternity leaves. If, however, the coworker evidence is not probative because the coworker's circumstances vary greatly from those of the plaintiff, the plaintiff may not admit evidence concerning other employees.[4]

In reviewing whether the testimony of other victims of discrimination by the same employer is admissible, courts generally look to Rule 403 of the Federal Rules of Evidence.[5] Courts have interpreted Rule 403 to provide broad discretion to the trial judge in determining

---

* See also chapter 6, "Pretrial Motions," regarding motions in limine excluding evidence relating to employees other than the plaintiff, and chapter 8, "Trial Preparation," evidence of similar discrimination.

the admissibility of testimony by other employees. In reviewing the probative value of other discriminatory acts, the court must analyze the relevance of those acts to the acts of which plaintiff complains, as well as the nature of the discrimination charged.[6]

Although plaintiffs in employment discrimination cases will consistently argue that evidence of discriminatory actions against employees other than the plaintiff is admissible for the purpose of proving the plaintiff's case, such evidence is not always admissible.[7] Defendants may seek to exclude this evidence by way of motions in limine. (See chapter 6, "Pretrial Motions," regarding motions in limine, and chapter 8, "Trial Preparation," regarding evidence of similar discrimination.) To the extent that such applications fail, the court's ruling may create an issue for appeal and will certainly alert defense counsel to the scope of evidence facing rebuttal.

III. Evidence of Other Lawsuits and Settlements against the Employer

Many times plaintiffs attempt to introduce evidence of prior litigation or claims against the employer. Plaintiffs seek to establish a pattern, practice, or motive with such evidence. Courts must balance the tension between past discriminatory behavior and undue prejudice when evaluating admissability of such evidence.[8]

It is widely accepted that settlement negotiations have no legal relevance to liability, regardless of whether the offer was made in the same case or in a related case.[9] The parties, however, should always be cautious in relating or discussing evidence during settlement negotiations. Such evidence may be admissible, notwithstanding the fact that it was presented and exchanged during the course of such negotiations.[10]

Some courts have excluded potentially prejudicial evidence regarding the filing of a lawsuit against the employer. Other courts have restricted such evidence to include only alleged prior acts of discrimination by the employer. In theory, these limits permit the plaintiff to show a pattern of discrimination without creating undue prejudice against the defending employer.

IV. Admissibility of Administrative Agency Findings*

A. In General

Many times, litigants find themselves in court after the underlying claim has gone through an administrative agency process. For example, most employment discrimination suits start with charges with the Equal Employment Opportunity Commission (EEOC) or with a state civil rights agency.

If the administrative agency has made a finding or determination of any kind, counsel should review whether the finding prohibits re-litigating the dispute in court.[11] Jurisdictions vary on this issue. Counsel must review the applicable statute. The preclusion issue is complex. Discrimination litigants must examine this threshold question whenever there has been an administrative ruling or finding (whether made by a civil rights enforcement agency or not) and any judicial review of such a ruling or finding to determine whether either res judicata or collateral estoppel precludes the civil action.

The party who won during the administrative process usually wants to admit the findings of the agency in support of its case. Several factors determine whether findings of an administrative agency are admissible. A long line of cases address the admissibility of EEOC determinations or findings in Title VII or Section 1981 actions, under Rules 8034(b) and 403 of the Federal Rules of Evidence. First, the report or findings must fall under one of the exceptions to the hearsay rule, such as public records and reports under Rule 803(8)(C).[12] Second, the trial judge must evaluate the trustworthiness of the administrative finding.[13] Third, some courts balance the probative value of the report against the danger of prejudice, as required under Rule 403.[14]

B. Federal Rule of Evidence 803(8), Public Records and Reports

Rule 803(8)(c) of the Federal Rules of Evidence admits hearsay of factual findings contained in public records and reports unless the sources of information or circumstances lack trustworthiness.[15]

C. Federal Rule of Evidence 403, Probative Value versus Prejudice

Courts often weigh the probative value versus the prejudice, confusion, or delay under Rule 403 in admitting or excluding findings of administrative agencies.[16]

---

* See also chapter 8, "Trial Preparation," regarding other administrative agency determinations of violations.

D. Admissibility of Equal Employment Opportunity Commission Findings

In *Chandler v. Roudebush*, 425 U.S. 840 (1976), the Supreme Court noted that prior administrative findings regarding an employment discrimination claim may be admissible as evidence at a subsequent federal trial under Title VII. Subsequent appellate decisions have split over whether administrative findings, particularly EEOC findings, are admissible per se or in the court's discretion.

Some courts have held that such findings are admissible per se in light of the fact that such findings would be highly probative of the ultimate issue in a discrimination case since a trained and experienced investigator found an unlawful practice had likely occurred.[17] Other courts have held that the admissibility of such findings is left to the sound discretion of the trial court.[18] Once the EEOC findings are admitted into evidence, the amount of weight to be given to them is also left to the discretion of the fact finder.[19]

In addition, litigants should review their specific state law to determine whether such administrative findings are admissible. Although federal courts generally admit EEOC findings in employment litigation—either per se or at the discretion of the trial court—some states have ruled that findings of administrative agencies are inadmissible hearsay.[20]

V. Emotional Injury*

In many instances, a key element to plaintiff's case is the recovery of emotional damages. In federal courts, plaintiffs may prove emotional damages through their own testimony without corroboration from expert witnesses.[21] Plaintiffs should be wary, however, as some courts continue to require expert testimony in proving emotional damages.[22] Moreover, where a plaintiff alleges state court claims, such as intentional infliction of emotional distress, counsel must determine whether applicable state law requires medical evidence of emotional injury.

Harris v. Forklift Systems, Inc., 510 U.S. 17 (1993), held that a discrimination plaintiff need not establish a psychological injury in order to recover emotional distress damages. The Court stated that "[a] discriminatorily abusive work environment, even one that does not seriously affect employees' psychological well-being, can and often will detract from employees' job performance, discourage employees from remaining on the job, or keep them from advancing in their careers."[23]

---

* See also chapter 3, "Discovery," regarding psychological evaluation of plaintiff, and chapter 4, "Experts," regarding emotional distress issues.

While an expert may not be necessary to a recovery for emotional distress, a plaintiff would be well advised to employ one. As one court has noted, a number of different types of injuries can result from sexual harassment, such as work performance stress, emotional stress, and physical stress.[24] Similarly, a defendant should consider hiring an expert witness to rebut the existence or extent of emotional damage.

VI. Termination of Back Pay and Front Pay

In a discrimination case, the plaintiff has a duty to mitigate damages by taking reasonable steps to find comparable employment.[25] The defendant, however, has the burden of establishing that the plaintiff failed to mitigate his damages.[26]

Termination or reduction of the back-pay period may occur

1. as of the time that the plaintiff begins comparable employment;[27]
2. for any period in which the plaintiff did not reasonably mitigate his damages;[28]
3. when after-acquired evidence of prior employee misconduct is discovered.[29] (see also section VIII, After-Acquired Evidence, in this chapter and chapter 6, "Pretrial Motions" regarding the same topic);
4. as of the time that the plaintiff would have been laid off or discharged for some nondiscriminatory reason, such as the close or sale of the employer's business;[30] and
5. rejection of an unconditional offer of reinstatement.[31] (See chapter 2, "Responding to the Lawsuit," regarding corrective actions such as unconditional reinstatement offers.)

Termination of the front-pay period is appropriate under the same circumstances as for back pay. In addition, front pay cannot be unduly speculative. It must reflect a realistic period of time for the plaintiff to obtain comparable employment, in light of his or her skills, age, the job market, and the nature of the position at issue.[32]

VII. Admissibility of Plaintiff's Prior Conduct and Lawsuits, Including Sexual Behavior

Defendants may want to admit evidence of the plaintiff's prior conduct and any prior litigation. The courts generally apply Rule 404 of the Federal Rules of Evidence, regarding character evidence and wrongs, in determining whether to admit evidence regarding the plaintiff's prior conduct.[33] An individual's prior acts are often not admissible to prove that he or she engaged in similar conduct on a particular occasion. Some courts have admitted such evidence when the plaintiff has "opened the door" by addressing the subject in his or her own testimony or evidence.[34] A sexual harassment plaintiff's sexually provocative speech, dress, or personal fantasies are "obviously relevant" on the issue of whether plaintiff welcomed advances.[35]

Rule 412 limits evidence of a victim's past behavior in civil cases alleging "sexual misconduct." The rule provides that evidence "proving the sexual behavior or sexual predisposition of an alleged victim is admissible if it is otherwise admissible . . . and its probative value substantially outweighs the danger of harm to any victim and of unfair prejudice to any party. Evidence of an alleged victim's reputation is admissible only if it has been placed in controversy by the alleged victim." The rule requires a written motion fourteen days before trial specifying the evidence and its purpose. The trial court must conduct an in camera hearing and allow the victim and parties to attend. The court must generally seal the motion and related papers and record. The Notes of the Advisory Committee on the December 1, 1994 Amendments clarified: "Rule 412 will . . . apply in a Title VII action in which the plaintiff has alleged sexual harassment."

A plaintiff's sexual history is often not admissible in sexual harassment suits, absent extraordinary circumstances. Such information has been barred as inadmissible to prove any propensity to act in conformity with such prior acts.[36]

VIII. After-Acquired Evidence

McKennon v. Nashville Banner Publishing Company, 513 U.S. 352 (1995) ended the conflict among the federal circuit courts about the admissibility and effect of after-acquired evidence of a plaintiff's misconduct. Under *McKennon*, if a former employee's misdeeds are discovered after termination, such misdeeds may be admissible. But "the factual permutations and the equitable considerations they raise will vary from case to case." As a general rule, where the plaintiff proves a termination claim, after-acquired evidence of misdeeds can bar reinstatement and front or back pay.[37]

The burden is on the employer to prove that the after-acquired evidence was severe enough for termination if the employer had known of it. If the employer cannot meet this burden, after-acquired evidence does not affect the plaintiff's entitlement to full damages.[38] (See chapter 6, "Pretrial Motions," regarding after-acquired evidence.)

IX. Conclusion

As these materials demonstrate, discrimination, harassment, and wrongful discharge cases depend on indirect or circumstantial evidence (or the lack thereof). It is incumbent on both plaintiff's counsel and defendant's counsel, first, to undertake thorough investigations to ascertain whether there are any evidentiary "skeletons" in their own client's closets or those of their adversary; second, to identify, early on, the legal and tactical issues raised by those skeletons; and finally, to decide what strategy to follow in dealing with them.

Notes

1. *See, e.g.,* Stair v. Lehigh Valley Carpenters, 813 F. Supp. 1116 (E.D. Pa. 1993) (evidence of discrimination against other employees admissible unless too remote in time or too dissimilar from plaintiff's situation).

2. 813 F. Supp. at 1118–19.

3. *See, e.g.,* Heyne v. Caruso, 69 F.3d 1475 (9th Cir. 1995) (sexual harassment of others may prove manager's motive); Ryther v. Karell, 864 F. Supp. 1510 (D. Minn. 1994) (evidence concerning discrimination against other employees admitted); Taylor v. Cummins Atl., Inc., 852 F. Supp. 1279 (D.S.C. 1994), *aff'd,* 48 F.3d 1217 (4th Cir. 1995) (evidence admissible generally but not probative in this instance); Herber v. Boatmen's Bank of Tenn., 781 F. Supp. 1255 (W.D. Tenn. 1991) (evidence admitted on motion for summary judgment); Buscemi v. Pepsico, Inc., 736 F. Supp. 1267 (S.D.N.Y. 1990) (evidence of other discriminatory acts admitted on motion in limine).

4. *See* Jardien v. Winston Network, 888 F.2d 1151 (7th Cir. 1989) (trial court properly excluded testimony offered by defendant in age discrimination action where older employees did not work in same division or perform jobs comparable to plaintiff's).

5. *See* Spulak v. K-Mart Corp., 894 F.2d 1150 (10th Cir. 1990); Schrand v. Fed. Pac. Elec. Co., 851 F.2d 152 (6th Cir. 1988); and Hunter v. Allis-Chalmers Corp. Engin. Div., 797 F.2d 1417, 1423 (7th Cir. 1986).

6. *See* Spulak v. K-Mart Corp. 894 F.2d at 1156 (circumstances under which other individuals were terminated were so similar to plaintiff's as to be probative of defendant's discriminatory intent toward its older employees).

7. *See, e.g.,* Moorhouse v. Boeing Co., 501 F. Supp. 390 (E.D. Pa.), *aff'd,* 639 F.2d 774 (3d Cir. 1980).

8. *See* Philip v. ANR Freight Sys., Inc., 945 F.2d 1054 (8th Cir. 1991); Massie v. Ind. Gas Co., 752 F. Supp. 261 (S.D. Ind. 1990); and Scaramuzzo v. Glenmore Distillers Co., 501 F. Supp. 727 (N.D. Ill. 1980).

9. *See* Fed. R. Evid. 408.

10. *See* Scaramuzzo v. Glenmore Distillers Co., 502 F. Supp. 727 at 733 (N.D. Ill. 1980).

11. *See, e.g.,* Hermann v. Fairleigh Dickinson Univ., 444 A.2d 614 (N.J. App. Div.), *cert. denied,* 453 A.2d 884 (N.J. 1982) (finding of no probable cause by the New Jersey Division on Civil Rights precludes filing of claim in state court; complainant limited to review by the Superior Court of New Jersey Appellate Division).

12. *See* Local Union No. 59 v. Namco Elecs., 653 F.2d 143 (5th Cir. 1981); Cohen v. Illinois Inst. of Tech., 524 F.2d 818 (7th Cir. 1975).

13. *See* Chandler v. Roudebush, 425 U.S. 840 (1976).

14. *See* Barfield v. Orange County, 911 F.2d 644 (11th Cir. 1990).

15. *See* Local Union No. 59 v. Namco Elecs., 653 F.2d 143 at 145 (5th Cir. 1981) (National Labor Relations Board findings admissible; nothing in record indicated board's findings lacked trustworthiness); Pugh v. State of Wis. Dept. of Natural Resources, 749 F. Supp. 205 (E.D. Wis. 1990) (district court in Title VII race discrimination case adopted as its own Wisconsin Personnel Commission findings of fact).

16. *See* Barfield v. Orange County, 911 F.2d 644, at 649–51 (11th Cir. 1990); Johnson v. Yellow Freight Sys., Inc., 734 F.2d 1304 (8th Cir. 1984).

17. *See* Smith v. Universal Servs., Inc., 454 F.2d 154 (5th Cir. 1972). *See also* Plummer v. Western Int'l Hotels Co., Inc., 656 F.2d 502 (9th Cir. 1981).

18. *See* Barfield v. Orange County, 911 F.2d 644, at 650 (11th Cir. 1990); Johnson v. Yellow Freight Sys. Inc., 734 F.2d 1304, at 1308–10 (8th Cir. 1984); Cox v. Babcock & Wilcox Co., 471 F.2d 13 (4th Cir. 1972).

19. *See, e.g.,* Abrams v. Lightolier Inc. 50 F.3d 1204 (3d Cir. 1995); Hilton v. Wyman-Gordon, 624 F.2d 379 (1st Cir. 1980).

20. *See, e.g.,* Muench v. Haddon, 605 A.2d 242 (N.J. App. Div. 1992).

21. *See* Wiscatoni v. Mich. Nat'l Bank, 716 F.2d 378 (6th Cir. 1988); Brockelhurst v. PPG Indus., Inc., 865 F. Supp. 1253 (E.D. Mich. 1994); Rendine v. Pantzer, 661 A.2d 1202 (N.J. 1995).

22. *See* Glover v. McDonell Douglas Corp., 981 F.2d 388 (8th Cir. 1992).

23. *Id.* at 22.

24. Robinson v. Jacksonville Shipyards, Inc., 760 F. Supp. 1486, 1506–07 (M.D. Fla. 1991).

25. *See, e.g.,* Payne v. Sec. Savings & Loan, 924 F.2d 109 (7th Cir. 1991).

26. *See, e.g.,* Normand v. Research Inst., 927 F.2d 857 (5th Cir. 1991).

27. *See, e.g.,* Griffin v. Buck Consulting Actuaries, Inc., 566 F. Supp. 881 (S.D.N.Y. 1983).

28. 42 U.S.C. § 2000e-5(g)(1); *see, e.g.,* EEOC v. Delight Wholesale Co., 765 F. Supp. 583 (W.D. Mo. 1991).

29. *See, e.g.,* McKennon v. Nashville Banner Publ'g Co., 513 U.S. 352 (1995).

30. *See, e.g.,* Bartek v. Urban Redevelopment Auth., 882 F.2d 739 (3d Cir. 1989).

31. *See, e.g.,* Ford Motor Co. v. EEOC, 458 U.S. 218 (1982).

32. *See e.g.,* Hybert v. Hearst Corp., 900 F.2d 1050 (7th Cir 1990).

33. *See* Neuren v. Adduci, Mastriani, Meeks & Schill, 43 F.3d 1507 (D.C. Cir. 1995); EEOC v. Bermuda Star Line Inc., 744 F. Supp. 1109 (N.D. Fla. 1990).

34. *See* EEOC v. General Dynamics Corp., Inc., 999 F.2d 113 (5th Cir. 1993).

35. Meritor Savings Bank FSB v. Vinson, 477 U.S. 57, 68–69, 106 S. Ct. 2399, 2406–07 (1986).

36. *See, e.g.,* Priest v. Rotary, 98 F.R.D. 755 (N.D. Cal. 1983).

37. *See, e.g.,* Wehr v. Ryan's Family Steak Houses, Inc., 49 F.3d 1150 (6th Cir. 1995) (after-acquired evidence rule did not preclude back pay in Title VII action, but remand was necessary for further factual determination and balancing of equities to determine whether plaintiff was entitled to reinstatement, in light of employer's allegation that plaintiff had lied on application resume).

38. Shattuck v. Kinetic Concepts, Inc., 49 F.3d 1106 (5th Cir. 1995) (in age discrimination action, former employer not entitled to judgment based on after-acquired evidence that former employee had falsely represented himself as a college graduate, where employer presented no evidence that it would have terminated employee for misrepresentation).

CHAPTER 8

Trial Preparation

JON W. GREEN*

BARBARA RYNIKER EVANS†

* *Deutsch Resnick Green & Kiernan; Springfield, New Jersey.*

† *Barbara Ryniker Evans & Associates; New Orleans, Louisiana.*

I. Introduction

Trial preparation of an employment case begins when you first receive it. Both plaintiff and defense counsel should assess each step of the litigation with the trial in mind. From the initial evaluation of an employment claim, through the pleadings, discovery, and motion phases of the case, trial preparation should be the focus. Witnesses not timely subpoenaed and documents not properly exchanged in employment cases will be excluded from trial in most jurisdictions. The extensive testamentary, documentary, statistical, and other evidence, which make modern employment litigation far more complex than the traditional unfair labor practice hearings of yesteryear, also make early trial preparation essential.

This chapter explores trial preparation from the perspective of both the plaintiff and defendant. The first time to think about trial strategy is not when the judge asks how many trial days are needed at the first status conference in the case. Trial planning starts from the initial meeting with your client. Even after all of the pretrial preparation is completed, however, employment counsel should be aware that last-minute motion practice may change the case. Thus the watchword in pretrial preparation of an employment case is to expect the unexpected!

A number of related issues that must be considered in the pretrial phase are covered in much greater detail in other chapters of this book. Selection and use of experts is covered in chapter 4. Voir dire, jury selection, and instruction and verdict forms, which must be considered in the pretrial phase, are covered in chapter 9. Opening statements, which should be prepared in the pretrial phase, are discussed more fully in chapter 10.

II. Explaining Your Case

A. Plaintiff's Perspective

1. *A Simple, Hard-Hitting Case Will Be That Much More Persuasive*

Although the typical employment case usually involves complicated fact patterns, scores of documents, and intricate legal and evidentiary issues, the successful plaintiff's trial counsel will have molded the case into one that any six-year-old can understand. Thus your trial preparation should be guided by three words: simplify, simplify, simplify.

The overriding theme that makes your case "sing" is the injustice that the employer has visited upon your client. To show this you must ensure that the following three events occur: (1) the jury likes and believes your client, (2) the jury believes your client was a good employee, and (3) the jury believes the employer's supposed business reason is a pretext for wrongful conduct. If you succeed in accomplishing these three objectives, your client will prevail. If you lose on any of these, then you are headed for defeat.

Once your discovery is completed, there should be no doubt whether you have a direct or a circumstantial evidence case. If you have a direct evidence case, that is, "you're fired because you are too old" or "you're fired because you are a trouble-making whistle-blower," your case is very straightforward. This is especially true if you have a "smoking gun," such as a company document or a tape recording proving the direct evidence. If the direct evidence involves conflicting verbal testimony, then your goal is to present credible witnesses whose testimony is consistent with all the documentary evidence produced and with their deposition testimony. As for the employer's witnesses who dispute the direct evidence, you should be prepared to undermine their credibility during cross-examination with contrary memos, documents, or prior deposition testimony.

As a practical matter, the vast majority of employment cases are circumstantial evidence cases that entail satisfying the evidentiary requirements developed by the U.S. Supreme Court in employment discrimination cases such as *McDonnell Douglas Corp. v. Green*, 411 U.S. 792 (1973), *Texas Department of Community Affairs v. Burdine*, 450 U.S. 248 (1981), and *St. Mary's Honor Center v. Hicks*, 509 U.S. 502, 113 S. Ct. 2742 (1993).

While proving the necessary legal elements of your case, you must humanize your client. Although your case may leap off the page in your opposition brief to the employer's summary judgment motion or in your trial brief, if the jury comes to dislike your client or concludes that your client was not performing up to the employer's reasonable expectations, you are sunk. One of the most reliable ways to test your client's likability is to ask those in your firm who have frequently interacted with your client how they feel about her or him; if they do not like your client, then it is very likely that the jury will not either. Also, if you, as trial counsel, do not like your client, you will give that message to the jury subconsciously no matter how hard you try to hide your feelings.

Another way to test your client's likability is to conduct a mini–mock trial using a jury focus group where your client testifies for about ten to fifteen minutes. You then observe the jury focus group deliberating behind a two-way mirror, paying special attention to juror reactions and perceptions. Although an expensive exercise that can cost upwards of $10,000–$15,000, a jury focus group will prove invaluable in preparing your client's direct testimony, in determining at what point in your witness order you want your client to testify, and in measuring the emphasis to place on certain liability and damage issues.

Second, you must convince the jury that your client was or is a competent employee, or the jury will have no reason to believe that your client was treated wrongfully. This can be done in a number of ways. First, if your client is articulate and creates the impression that he or she knows his or her job inside and out and is adaptable to new situations, you are almost home. Second, your client's performance reviews, especially if they are excellent, may prove invaluable. Third, former bosses, coworkers, colleagues, customers, or other third-party witnesses may help to dispel false employer criticisms; however, be careful that these witnesses don't have their own agendas and that there are no skeletons in their closets.

Next, you must be prepared to discredit the business reason that the employer is using to justify the adverse action against your client. If your discovery has been conducted properly, the depositions of the decision makers have locked in their supposed business reason for taking the adverse action against your client. If the decision makers are lying, then company documents will usually contradict the decision makers' deposition testimony at trial. Thus you must come to know intimately every word in every company document along with every word in every deposition. Remember, you need not necessarily prove the employer's alleged business reason is false as long as it is not the true reason for the adverse personnel action against your client.[1]

To recapitulate, you must convince the jury of three themes: (1) your client is likeable and believable, (2) your client was or is a good employee, and (3) the employer's supposed business reason is a sham or pretext for the illegal personnel action taken against your client. In all likelihood, if you persuade the jury of the first two themes, then they will be open to persuasion on the third theme.

The shorter and more tightly organized you make your case in chief, the more persuasive it will be. A trap that ensnares many plaintiff's counsel is putting on a long and tiresome case in chief, especially when there are numerous documents in the case. Keep in mind that the typical juror has probably watched many television courtroom drama shows where testimony and opening and closing arguments are presented in 60-second sound bites. Consequently, juror attention spans are usually short, requiring you to make your presentation short and to the point.

2. Using a Trial Outline

It is absolutely critical that you have a thorough mastery of the relevant statutes and interpretive case law that pertain to your case. Employment law cases typically involve different and shifting burdens of proof that govern what evidence is relevant. This makes developing and using a trial outline essential because it helps keep you focused on what you have to prove. Once you know what you have to prove, the evidence you need to prove your case becomes clear and you will be able to identify, in advance of trial, what evidentiary problems you may face.

Put another way, your trial outline should serve as a road map to proving your case and to helping identify potential evidentiary problems that may arise. The outline will also help you devise alternative ways to prove each element of your case. You should organize your trial outline so that it enables you to identify the elements of the cause of action to be proved, the necessary evidence to prove each element, and the different ways to introduce the supporting proofs into evidence. Doing so will keep you focused on your themes and at the same time able to meet cogently the inevitable motion to dismiss your case.

A good example illustrating the need for a trial outline are the proofs needed to establish an age discrimination case in a reduction-in-force setting. Reduction-in-force cases usually involve proof through circumstantial evidence, thus utilizing the *McDonnell Douglas/Burdine/ Hicks* approach. Typically a plaintiff must make out a prima facie case by showing that he or she was (1) in the protected class or over forty years of age; (2) that the plaintiff was qualified for the job for which he or she was employed and was performing competently; (3) that the plaintiff was removed from the job either through demotion or termination; and (4) either that the plaintiff was replaced by someone significantly younger or that the discharge occurred under circumstances suggesting age discrimination.[2] If the employer counters by alleging (remember that the employer need not prove but only articulate its legitimate business reason once the plaintiff establishes a prima facie case) that plaintiff's job was eliminated, the plaintiff then must prove either that the job duties actually remained and that the employer is mounting a musical chairs or "three-card monte" defense with plaintiff's job duties or that other, younger employees' jobs were also eliminated but that other jobs were found for them while older employees were terminated.[3]

Your trial outline should set forth each element of proof and the evidence necessary to establish that element. In the example above, you may use the employer's organizational chart to prove that your client's job survived intact. Or the younger person replacing your client may be subpoenaed to testify that he or she indeed performs your client's job duties. An evidentiary problem may arise in authenticating the employer's organizational chart; this may be solved a number of ways. You can either serve a request to admit the authenticity of the chart (Rule 36 of the Federal Rules of Civil Procedure) or subpoena persons with knowledge about the chart. If you decide on the latter course, you should make sure the testimony of the witnesses you are subpoenaing is locked in through depositions or documents that back up what you are trying to prove.

B. Defendant's Perspective

1. Develop a Theme

The most substantial challenge of an employment lawyer is explaining the employment case to the jury. Every juror has either experience in the working world or some preconceived notions about "the job" based upon reports from parents, siblings, or offspring. Thus establishing a theme early in the employment litigation and understanding how it will be presented to the jury later at trial is absolutely critical. And making last-minute pretrial revisions to the theme is one of the keys to a successful defense.

Defense counsel must proffer a logical explanation for their client's actions toward plaintiff that is consistent with the jurors' own views of employment relationships. And unlike other types of litigation, the race, sex, and level of education of jurors may not accurately predict their views. Defense counsel generally believe that a conservative, sophisticated juror with management experience is the best prospective juror. Plaintiff's counsel frequently seek a liberal juror similar in race, sex, and socioeconomic level to the plaintiff. Yet the nature of the facts in a particular employment case may challenge counsel's preconceived notions on jury selection.

Sexual harassment, mental anguish, psychological well-being, and similar issues involve the jurors' own views of normal, appropriate behavior and responses. Any theme developed by either party in employment litigation that contradicts such juror views will have perilous sledding. Thus, defense counsel should emphasize aspects of the case that conform with these juror preconceptions. Neither party can prevail unless the jury believes that real people, like themselves, acted logically. And no defense counsel will prevail unless the jury believes that the plaintiff was treated fairly.

2. Develop a Cohesive Master Plan

The trial outline, or other master plan directing trial preparation in an employment case, must comply with the pretrial requirements of the jurisdiction. But it also must be a flexible document. Pretrial preparation and examination of witnesses and exhibits may require quickly revising the trial outline.

Once the trial outline has been developed, employment counsel should decide how they want to organize their trial materials. The key materials targeted in the trial outline can be divided into trial files that are labeled and include the documents pertinent to that phase of the case. This method is particularly suited to complex employment trials where the documents are too voluminous to be kept in a trial notebook. Another method of organizing the trial outline materials is through a trial notebook. Many employment lawyers use this three-ring-binder method for smaller trials where all of the materials can be organized and easily retrieved.

3. Use the Opening Statement Wisely

The opening is defense counsel's first chance to explain an employment case to the jury. The theme will be introduced to the jury, and the jury will get its first impression of the case. A forceful opening can be the best way to explain an employment case to the jury and present the defense's uncontroverted facts.

This is not the time for the defendant in an employment case to argue or raise defenses that may elicit plaintiff's objections. The opening statement should be a clear, forceful statement of the facts, presented in a logical manner that personalizes the defendant. Any exhibits that the defense will be using in the employment case can be effectively introduced to enforce the theme in the jurors' minds.

4. Know Your Jurors

Venue is a critical issue in considering the juror biases and the juror profile needed in the effective defense of an employment case. A white-collar conservative in an urban jurisdiction may possess an entirely different view of the case than a similarly credentialed white-collar conservative in a rural jurisdiction.

The local employers, commuting patterns, demographics, and related information are important in jury selection in an employment case. None of these factors, however, can be viewed in isolation. A university community will not produce the same type of juror as a heavy industry community, although both jurisdictions may have the same demographic composition.

Your client's other litigation in the venue is also relevant. If your client just lost a high-profile toxic tort case, its image in the community may be tarnished and your jury selection may be affected. Similarly, if Greenpeace barricaded the entrance to your client's facility recently, alleging environmental violations, your "good guy" defense may be in jeopardy.

III. Selection and Preparation of Witnesses

A. Plaintiff's Perspective

Direct testimony during the plaintiff's case in chief is probably the most difficult part of the trial to control. Unlike opening and closing statements, where you have control over what you are going to say, or cross-examination, where you can ask leading questions to control the witness, direct examination involves asking open-ended questions with open-ended answers. In other words, direct examination can be a potential minefield into which your witness may wander—potentially destroying your case in the process.

1. The Plaintiff

The most important witness in your case is the plaintiff, and you must take time and care to prepare him or her for both direct examination and cross-examination. First, it is vital that both you and your client know your client's entire deposition. Second, it is essential that your client's testimony be consistent with the information he or she has produced during discovery.

But most importantly, your client's testimony should tell a compelling story of injustice. This may be done by developing your client's background to create a positive impression with the jury. Despite our society's prevailing cynicism, people still are impressed with those who lifted themselves up by their own bootstraps to become successful. This Horatio Algier theme highlights the employer's illegal adverse action because the jury becomes convinced that the very competent employee's demise was not of his or her own doing, but rather the employer's evil act.

2. Nonparty Fact Witnesses

Nonparty fact witnesses are even harder to control because they do not necessarily agree with your client's version of the facts. When this occurs, you have to weigh the positive aspects of the fact witnesses' testimony against the negative aspects and decide whether to use them. It is absolutely critical that your nonparty fact witnesses are locked into their testimony through memos created on the job, written statements, or deposition testimony. Of course, written statements are the most desirable way to lock in testimony. However, if the witnesses are either hostile or current employees who may also be decision makers concerning your client's employment status, you may have no alternative but to take their deposition. Also, the ethical canons may prohibit counsel from having ex parte conversations with those witnesses. (See Witness Interviews/Ex Parte Contacts, chapter 13, "Professionalism and Ethics.")

You are playing with fire if you put a nonparty witness on the stand without having a written statement, a memo, or deposition testimony to keep the witness in line. If your nonparty fact witness starts to deviate from the desired testimony on the stand, you can use the documents or testimony to gently remind the witness what his testimony should be. If the witness appears to be turning on you, you may have no choice but to impeach that witness and may, with the prior inconsistent statement, ask the judge for permission to treat the witness as hostile and to ask leading questions.[4] Again, it is extremely important that you have confidence in what your witnesses will testify to and that you ensure that testimony with prior memos, written statements, or deposition testimony that lock them into the testimony you want.

3. Adverse Witnesses

If, after preparing your trial outline, you decide that you must establish pretext for the employer's illegal action, you may want to consider calling the employer's decision makers during your case in chief, provided the trial judge allows you the latitude of asking leading questions (Fed. R. Evid. 611(c)). However, if you make this decision, it is extremely important that these witnesses be locked into that testimony which proves your case in chief. You must make sure that you are prepared to exercise total control over the witness during the course of the direct examination. It is also highly recommended that you utilize live testimony because a live witness helps make the case more interesting and more lively for the jury. However, if you think that the adverse witnesses you wish to call would prove difficult to control, you should resort to using their deposition testimony as permitted by the rules of your jurisdiction.[5]

4. Expert Witnesses

Because chapter 4 deals extensively with expert witnesses, this section will be brief. The important point is to make sure that expert witnesses' reports and curricula vitae have been timely served on defense counsel and that their opinions are based on the facts in this case, or your expert testimony could be barred.[6]

B. Defendant's Perspective

1. Humanize, Organize, and Dramatize the Defense

The challenge to defense counsel explaining an employment case to the jury is to humanize, organize, and dramatize the workplace and the personnel actions in the case. A large part of the defense of an employment case will be presented through the corporate representatives involved in the disputed employment action. The defense must **humanize** management, **organize** carefully the case they are presenting, and **dramatize** the case to credibly support the defendant's theme.

This presents a considerable challenge since many management representatives earn more than triple the average juror and come from a different ethnic background than some jurors. In addition, management representatives usually have a different work history and level of education than the typical juror. Even where they are contemporaries in age of the typical juror, the very assurance, determination, and achievements propelling the manager's rise in corporate America may alienate him or her from the jury.

Compounding the problem are juror biases about the employment arena that exist in most jurisdictions. Many jurors may have experienced an employment-related problem similar to the plaintiff's or have a close friend or family member who has. Such problems are exacerbated in defending layoff decisions in communities that have experienced substantial downsizing.

Many jurors believe that the employer and its representatives spend most of their time either trying to figure out ways to hurt the "little guy" or acting in reckless disregard of their interests. The defense must **humanize** management making the disputed decisions, **organize** their decision making as it relates to the plaintiff, and **dramatize** that process into a believable presentation of the theme.

2. Choose Witnesses Carefully

Overcoming juror bias against management may be a formidable task in some cases. That bias will be lessened by selecting witnesses with the best juror appeal. The defense has no choice as to critical witnesses who were pivotal to the disputed incidents in the employment litigation. But witnesses who explain personnel practices, processes, and procedures may be numerous, so select the strongest witness.

Defendants have considerable leeway in employment litigation to select witnesses who have had favorable experiences at the employer. These witnesses, although unacquainted with the plaintiff, may effectively **humanize, organize,** and **dramatize** the company as a good place to work.

3. Prepare the Witness Thoroughly

An imperative in helping defense witnesses overcome some of the innate prejudice against them in employment litigation is relentless and thorough witness preparation. Include in the preparation all elements of the trial outline the witness is expected to cover.

Witnesses should be prepared individually with the lawyer who will be presenting their testimony. Witnesses should review the relevant testimony rendered in depositions and parallel proceedings, as well as in answers to interrogatories, requests for admission, and written or oral statements and affidavits. Any inconsistencies with other witnesses' testimony, conflicting documents, and impeachment data must be explained.

Witnesses should know beforehand the exhibits they will identify or authenticate. The fundamentals of laying a foundation should be explored on each exhibit. Witnesses also must understand the importance of thinking before speaking. They must thoroughly understand why employer's counsel cannot ask them leading questions. Witnesses also need to become familiar with all of the rules about listening to questions, asking for repetition of questions where appropriate, being serious and dignified, waiting until objections are resolved to resume testifying, answering questions on personal observations, and not volunteering.

Witnesses should also be counselled against being argumentative. This is a particular problem in employment cases, where those who have been used to making decisions and see themselves as impartial may be angered by plaintiff's questioning of their authority and accusations of discrimination.

165

Witnesses should be made aware of the importance of jury eye contact, attire suitable in that venue, appropriate language, and related comportment issues. This is particularly important in employment cases where management faces considerable prejudice.

Mock examinations after all of the review has occurred will reinforce these principles with the defense witness in employment litigation. At a minimum, you or a colleague should cross-examine as plaintiff's counsel can be expected to proceed to permit the witness to understand the trial process. Videotaping the direct and cross-examination of critical witnesses is advisable. This permits the witness to view his or her testimony and correct whatever problems appear. A full-blown mock trial, while far more costly, lets the witness see how the process works and allows defense counsel to evaluate how the witness is perceived by the mock jurors.

Defense witnesses should be given specifics including date, time, location of, and directions to the courthouse, as well as layout, personnel, and functions of the courtroom. Flustered witnesses who have been lost for thirty minutes will not be effective regardless of the preparation time spent with them.

4. Prepare Simple, Clear Testimony

All employment litigation involves myriad facts, many of which are only tangentially relevant. Once the most effective defense witnesses are chosen, they should be prepared to carry the defense theme to the jury in simple, effective language. Witnesses should know those critical elements of the case about which they are to persuade the jury. Excessive time should not be spent in preparation on extraneous facts. Logical, paced testimony can be riveting to the jury, where the meandering witness can lose the jury.

It is important in the employment case that defense counsel anticipate cultural and/or language problems and potential disability problems. This is especially true where discrimination cases are being tried to urban, minority juries who may be particularly sensitized to such slights.

Narrative testimony that clearly describes the critical facts makes the best direct testimony. Getting the general description of the scene, followed by the action is usually a good approach. Short, open-ended questions can elicit adequate facts and start the pace of the narrative. Defense counsel must listen carefully to the answers, setting the example for the jury.

5. Avoid Cumulative Testimony

Proving the necessary facts without overkill is essential to a successful defense. Cumulative testimony is a particular problem in employment litigation, where there are many other employees who could testify to the same facts. Both plaintiff and defense counsel may be harmed by reliance upon cumulative testimony of lay witnesses in employment cases that adds nothing new to the record[7] or that repeat the testimony of multiple witnesses.[8]

6. Alternate Lay and Expert Witnesses

The use of expert witnesses is discussed in chapter 4. Also key to expert testimony in employment cases is the order in which you present expert testimony. Medical, statistical, economic, vocational rehabilitation, and other experts can present critical testimony that will be difficult for the jury to absorb if not presented in the proper context. Thus, it is wise to alternate the order of fact and expert witnesses to ensure that the jury can place the expert's testimony in the proper context. The order of witnesses also is important in avoiding juror tedium and lack of interest in the defense.

7. Beware Lay Opinion Testimony*

A particular difficulty defense counsel may encounter in defending an employment case is lay opinion evidence. Explaining the case and effectively presenting the theme may be hampered by the court allowing innumerable lay witnesses to testify as to their opinion of how bad the employer is.

Lay opinion testimony is limited under Fed. R. Evid. 701 to opinions or inferences rationally based on the perception of the witness and helpful to a clear understanding of his testimony or a fact in issue. Lay opinions on whether discrimination existed, for example, can be stricken if the witness "is not someone with expertise in evaluating age discrimination claims of salaried employees."[9] Such errors are so prejudicial as to warrant reversal of the trial court's order denying a new trial, as where the failure to exclude the testimony of two former employees who were told they were discharged because they were too old was grounds for granting a new trial.[10] Lay witnesses are plainly not qualified under Rule 701 of the Federal Rules of Evidence to render an opinion on the employer's discriminatory practices, and defense counsel should ensure that they do not. They are not experts on discrimination, and their testimony to a legal conclusion would invade the province of the court and the jury. In *Torres v. Oakland*, 758 F.2d 147, 37 Fair Empl. Prac. Cas. (BNA) 535 (6th Cir. 1985), the court held that it

---

* See chapter 4, "Experts," and chapter 6, "Pretrial Motions," regarding motions in limine for opinion testimony of experts and non-experts (coworkers).

was reversible error to allow testimony of employees who believed plaintiff experienced discrimination.

Such testimony may also be excluded under Rule 403 of the Federal Rules of Evidence because its probative value is substantially outweighed by the danger of prejudice, confusion, and undue delay. For example, opinions of employees that the employer was sexist were excluded as prejudicial to the employer in a sex discrimination case.[11]

Defense counsel should not ignore this important area when preparing for trial, and care should be taken to ensure that defense witnesses are not being relied upon to render opinion testimony that will be ruled inadmissible.

8. Consider Other Administrative Agency Determinations of Violations*

Findings by state agencies, state courts, or the Equal Employment Opportunity Commission (EEOC) on the same and other matters should be evaluated for collateral estoppel purposes or as evidence.

a. Preclusive Effect of Findings on the Same Matter

A state court judgment of no discrimination (including a state court refusal to reverse a state agency finding of no discrimination) may bar a federal lawsuit based on the same facts. Defense counsel must ensure, however, that all Fourteenth Amendment procedural due process rights were satisfied, the state law is at least as broad as the applicable federal law, and the judgment would have preclusive effect in that state's own courts.[12]

But whether defense counsel can argue that a federal suit is estopped by the findings of a state or local agency depends on the nature of the federal suit. In *University of Tennessee v. Elliott*, 478 U.S. 788, 106 S. Ct. 3220, 92 L. Ed. 2d 635, 41 Fair Empl. Prac. Cas. (BNA) 177, 180 (1986), the Supreme Court held that "unreviewed state administrative proceedings [do not] have preclusive effect on Title VII claims" (footnote omitted). On the other hand, a state or local agency's determination will preclude a section 1983 claim in federal court if the determination would have preclusive effect in that state.[13]

EEOC findings are never given preclusive effect. As explained in *Gilchrist v. Jim Slemons Imports, Inc.*, 803 F.2d 1488, 42 Fair Empl. Prac. Cas. (BNA) 314, 322 (9th Cir. 1986), the EEOC generally determines only whether there is "probable cause" to conclude that a violation

---

* See Admissibility of Administrative Agency Findings, chapter 7, "Special Evidentiary Concerns."

occurred. The Ninth Circuit there concluded that an EEOC "letter of violation" in an Age Discrimination in Employment Act case is more probative than a "probable cause" finding but, for that reason, may be excluded as evidence. Nor would the court give it preclusive effect. (See chapter 7, "Special Evidentiary Concerns," regarding these topics.)

b. Evidentiary Use of Findings on the Same Matter
Although a prior finding may not have preclusive effect, it may have evidentiary value. EEOC findings in Title VII cases on the presence or absence of "probable cause" are automatically admissible in some appellate circuits,[14] while in others their admissibility is subject to trial court discretion.[15]

In a jurisdiction where admission is discretionary, defense counsel should argue for exclusion of an adverse finding on grounds that its prejudicial effect would outweigh its probative value, as in *Smith v. MIT*, 877 F.2d 1106, 50 Fair Empl. Prac. Cas. 169, 174–75 (1st Cir. 1989), *cert. denied*, 493 U.S. 965 (1989). Defense counsel should also be cautious when seeking admission of a favorable finding of "no probable cause." Prevailing on this point at trial could create a basis for reversal on appeal. In *Estes v. Dick Smith Ford*, 856 F.2d 1097, 47 Fair Empl. Prac. Cas. 1472, 1479 (8th Cir. 1988), admission of the EEOC's letter finding no probable cause was an abuse of discretion because the letter was conclusory rather than analytical, and the conclusion was based on a different defense than was raised at trial.

State agency findings may also be subject to exclusion, as in *Hall v. W. Prod. Co.*, 988 F.2d 1050, 61 Fair Empl. Prac. Cas. (BNA) 554 (10th Cir. 1993), where the court affirmed the trial court's refusal to admit the finding of the Wyoming Fair Employment Commission (WFEC) that no age discrimination occurred. Because the defendant could offer the jury the same evidence that the WFEC examined in reaching its conclusion, "the only purpose to be served by admitting into evidence the WFEC report 'would be to suggest to the jury that it should reach the same conclusion' as the WFEC."[16] (See chapter 7, "Special Evidentiary Concerns," regarding this topic.)

c. Preclusive Effect of Findings on Related Matters
Preclusive effects need not arise from findings in the same lawsuit between the same parties. In particular, collateral estoppel should be evaluated where the litigation involves an employment policy or practice encompassed by an already litigated policy or practice. In *EEOC v. American Airlines*, 67 Fair Empl. Prac. Cas. (BNA) 754 (5th Cir. 1995), the court affirmed dismissal, on collateral estoppel grounds, of a challenge to defendant's age-related policy of hiring as cockpit personnel

only pilots with potential to become captains by age 55. Since the prior judgment was rendered in a federal Age Discrimination in Employment Act case, the court applied federal collateral estoppel principles.

The court found that litigation in the early 1980s of defendant's former age-based policy (American generally would not hire anyone over 30) in *Murnane v. American Airlines, Inc.*, 667 F.2d 98, 26 Fair Empl. Prac. Cas. (BNA) 1537 (D.C. Cir. 1981), *cert. denied*, 456 U.S. 915, 102 S. Ct. 1770, 72 L. Ed. 2d 174 (1982), presented an essentially identical issue that was crucial to the outcome of *Murnane*. The *Murnane* court held that American's age-30 policy was a bona fide occupational qualification and reasonably necessary to its goal of developing a highly experienced captains corps. The Fifth Circuit in 1995 found the new policy less age-restrictive than the age-30 policy (and thus encompassed within it). Since the court also found no circumstances rendering collateral estoppel inappropriate or unfair, it affirmed dismissal. (See chapter 7, "Special Evidentiary Concerns," regarding this topic.)

d. Evidence of the Discrimination Charges by Coworkers This type of evidence may also be introduced at trial.[17] Defense counsel should argue for exclusion under Fed. R. Evid. 403 because of prejudice or delay. Such evidence can confuse the jury and, on that basis, was excluded in *Czajka v. Hickman*, 703 F.2d 317, 320 (8th Cir. 1983). It might also be excluded as prejudicial to the employer.[18]

If it is not possible to exclude such evidence, defense counsel must craft its explanation of the case around this serious impediment, and the appropriate witnesses need to be prepared on the critical issues to prevent these determinations from tainting the current case. (See Evidence of Discrimination against Other Employees, chapter 7, "Special Evidentiary Concerns.")

IV. Selection and Preparation of Exhibits

A. Plaintiff's Perspective

1. Keep the Documents to a Minimum

Plaintiff's counsel should avoid the seductive trap of putting in a large number of documents to prove plaintiff's case in chief. The jury will probably hear the entire case in a period that stretches from a few days to three or four weeks and will have tremendous difficulty absorbing all of the information introduced. If there is document overload, plaintiff's counsel will obscure the themes that he is trying to put forward to the jury: the client suffered an injustice because of illegal treatment by the employer. It is extremely important not to lose sight of "the forest for the trees" when selecting documents.

2. Essential Documents

Essential documents include performance reviews of your client showing good job performance and key documents authorized by the decision makers that affected your client's personnel status. Many times a decision-maker's memos concerning material facts in your case will prove to be the decisive factor in persuading the jury that the employer acted illegally. Moreover, such documents will box in the employer when it comes to the employer's own case in chief. Once the employer tries to explain away or run away from its own documents you know you are on the way to a verdict for the plaintiff.

Additionally, plaintiff's counsel may want to consider either creating document books for each juror so they have access to the documents or, if the trial judge would not permit that, enlarging key documents or using overhead projectors so that the jurors will be able to read and absorb their contents while they are displayed during the course of the testimony of the various witnesses.

3. Time Lines, Chronologies, and Organizational Charts

Plaintiff's counsel should utilize a time line and/or chronology concerning the facts in the lawsuit. More likely than not the timing of an employer's personnel decision will be probative of the employer's illegal motive, as in a retaliation case or the sudden lowering of a performance appraisal right before a reduction in force. Plaintiff's counsel can prepare enlarged documents that indicate the chronology and the time line. Jury consultants advise using both tools since not all jurors absorb information the same way. Plaintiff's counsel should also request that these documents be used during the opening statement. Additionally, organizational charts, as long as they are clear and easy to understand, help the jury visualize what is going on in the reporting structure of an employer. Again, these documents should be enlarged for easy viewing.

B. Defendant's Perspective

1. Avoid Overproving the Case

A frequent problem in defending employment cases is overproving the case. Overproving a case can bore the jury, create conflicts, and lose the effect of key defense documents. Give the jury the key exhibits early in the defense of an employment case. Presenting the most pertinent documents early in the case can help the defense focus upon the best evidence available. These critical documents can be emphasized repeatedly to the jury as the defense progresses and can be woven into the theme in an effective closing argument.

2. Solve Evidentiary Problems Early

Defense counsel should review the appropriate rules of evidence, rules of procedure, and local rules again before trial to ensure that all evidentiary problems with critical exhibits have been anticipated. Foundation and relevancy should be considered in developing the order of proof. Unless the exhibit has the proper foundation, proof problems will arise.

3. Use Show-and-Tell Techniques

Most jurors remember much more of what they see than of what they hear. A significant problem exists for the defense, however, in that most employment cases are defended with evidence that includes corporate policies, handbooks, personnel evaluations, warnings, suspensions, work rules, statistics, and the like—not the stuff of which dreams are made! The combined effect of management arrogance and dry corporate documents can be deadly.

One way to overcome the dry aspects of corporate decision making is with the use of photographs, charts, graphs, videotapes, diagrams, and other demonstrative evidence. The jury may sleep through a defense litany of declining profit figures, but a multicolor graphic or videotape capturing the same data may be riveting. Enlarged exhibits, properly highlighted for emphasis, can also be very effective. Where the witness explaining the exhibit is necessary but obtuse, a well-done graphic can pick up the slack. Defense testimony that the discriminatory comments could not have been heard by the plaintiff is predictable. But a photograph of the facility indicating the distance between the work station of the alleged perpetrator and the plaintiff may make the point stick.

4. Intersperse the Depositions with Other Testimony

Depositions, stipulations, and other ponderous exhibits should be interspersed with the more lively parts of the case. This evidence may be critical to the defense and should not be lost because of juror inattention.

Depositions should be excerpted to get the key testimony without the irrelevant testimony. Clearing the testimony in advance with opposing counsel can also speed the defense.

5. Beware Exhibit Traps

Exhibits should be examined to be sure that they actually help the defense. Many employment records contain conflicting, impeaching, and inconsistent information. Such records can often be used effectively by plaintiff's counsel to attack the defense.

Choosing the right witness to introduce the exhibit can be the difference between scoring an effective point in the defense theme and losing the point totally. Jurors should not be distracted from the most effective witnesses by exhibits. Conversely, jurors should be distracted from the weaker witnesses by strong exhibits.

Jurors should be given time to examine all of the most effective exhibits. Defense counsel should be sure that all of the sterling exhibits are referred to repeatedly throughout the trial and woven into the opening and closing statements.

V. Preparing for Cross-Examination

A. Plaintiff's Perspective

Preparing your witnesses for cross-examination is extremely important. It is advisable to put your client and your nonparty fact witnesses through a mock cross-examination that is as uncomfortable and as unpleasant as possible. You will want to tell your witnesses to concede what they have to concede and not to fight with the cross-examiner but at the same time not to concede what they should not concede during the course of their cross-examination. You should go over the most salient points and make sure their testimony is consistent with their prior statements, whether they be memos, written statements, or deposition testimony.

Because most employment cases require proof through circumstantial evidence and thus evidence of pretext, cross-examination of the employer's witnesses will be absolutely critical to winning your case. Consequently, you should prepare meticulously for cross-examination of these witnesses, keeping in mind the theme of your case. Cross-examination should be short, to the point, and easy to understand, and it should promote the theme of your case: namely, that your client was a victim of a discriminatory attitude by the company.

In fact, serious thought should be given to calling the employer's decision makers as adverse witnesses under Rule 611(c). After establishing with the trial judge that the witness is adverse to your client's interests, all preparation should be made to control that witness by knowing that witness's deposition backwards and forwards and all

173

documents offered by that witness. Again, themes should be developed in your cross-examination preparation, and cross-examination should be no longer than 20 to 30 minutes. Because of the short attention span of today's jurors—remember that 30-second devastating cross-examination that took place on *L.A. Law* every Thursday night—cross-examination should be kept short and sweet.

B. Defendant's Perspective

A defendant in an employment case can effectively use cross-examination with the realization that it is useful only if it advances the theme of the case. Totally passing on cross-examination may be in order when there is nothing to gain in the process. This may be particularly effective in those cases where plaintiff has presented cumulative testimony that adds little to their case.

1. Index Prior Proceedings

There are always surprises in employment litigation. And the well-written, thoughtfully prepared cross-examination will have to be seriously modified where there was surprise testimony on direct or where there have been last-minute modifications of the theme.

Defense counsel should have all of the prior proceedings clearly indexed by topic, witness, and document name for easy reference. All prior testimony at deposition or in a parallel proceeding, and all statements, affidavits, or other evidence on the same topic should be readily accessible. Unemployment, discrimination agency, workers' compensation, and other proceedings in which the witness may have testified should also be indexed. All discovery, pleadings, and other documents listed in the pretrial order should also be indexed and readily accessible. Without the ability to quickly target these items when impeachment is needed, a vital opportunity for effective cross-examination can be lost.

2. Structure the Order of Cross-Examination

The order of cross-examination should be easy for the jury to follow. The cross-examination should bolster the defendant's theme or in the very least create some chinks in the armor of plaintiff's case.

The order need not be chronological or follow the order of direct examination. But the fact that jurors usually remember the first and last things that they have heard should not be overlooked. All recent studies suggest that the beginning and the end of the testimony will have the most impact upon the jury.

A hard-hitting opening line of questions on a topic highly favorable to the defense may be all that the jury remembers. Any areas of questionable inquiry can either be buried in the middle or abandoned totally if the key points have already been scored.

3. Prepare Simple, Leading Questions

Defense counsel approach preparation for cross-examination differently. Some counsel prefer the question-and-answer method of preparation. This requires the preparation of all written questions and their proposed answers. An alternative method involves the broader outline approach. Outline the witnesses' anticipated testimony, then develop direct questions based on the outline of expected testimony. A combination of the two approaches works in cases where the witnesses vary in the complexity of their testimony.

Regardless of which preparation means is employed, a defendant in an employment case should lead each of plaintiff's witnesses into helpful testimony without permitting repetition, embellishment, or explanation of direct testimony. Brief, leading questions in plain language should highlight a few key points to which the response is already known.

The basic cross-examination questions should be prepared in advance. If there is some question about which version of the facts the witness may render on direct, the questions should be drafted in the alternative and grouped around the issue that will be covered.

The cross-examination questions should **show** the jury what their conclusion should be without **telling** them the conclusion. An effective series of well-prepared cross-examination questions should light up the defense theme without insulting the common sense of the juror. The defense may be subjected to more rigid scrutiny for demeaning the intelligence of the jury if the cross-examination is too inane or belittling.

Defense counsel should be sure to obey the cardinal rule and avoid asking "one question too many" on cross-examination. If there is any question at all as to what the response will be, avoid that area. Contingency plans should be developed for the talkative or evasive witness, and surprises should be covered where possible.

4. Control, Control, Control

It can be a very costly mistake for defendants in employment litigation to lose control of a witness during cross-examination. Asking nonleading questions, becoming quarrelsome, or permitting the witness to recite direct examination again are common means of losing control. Trying to get too much from the reluctant witness on cross-examination can also lead to a loss of control. The defense must control all aspects of the cross-examination in a thorough and thoughtful manner whenever cross-examination is undertaken.

Employers are especially vulnerable to juror criticism when they are argumentative, do not allow witnesses to finish their answers, and do not listen to the witness's answers. As most employment litigation involves some aspect of inequitable treatment, any apparent inequities in witness treatment by the defense is often magnified in the jurors' eyes.

But these pitfalls should not cause the defense to shrink from the opportunity to weaken plaintiff's case. Many of plaintiff's witnesses in employment litigation will be coworkers who have their own personal "axe to grind." The opportunity to inform the jury through cross-examination of the coworker witness's personal agenda should not be missed. Usually the coworker's personnel file is a source of irrefutable evidence for effective cross-examination.

5. Attacking the Plaintiff

Seldom would a defendant forego the opportunity to cross-examine the plaintiff in an employment case. The discovery process inevitably leads to areas where the plaintiff is vulnerable, either as to past or current employment, credentials, or on some aspect of the plaintiff's credibility on critical facts. Those vulnerabilities should be developed in the case theme and brought home through the plaintiff's cross-examination.

Limiting plaintiff's cross-examination to those issues where the plaintiff is most vulnerable is usually the most effective approach. Topics covered should closely relate to those areas of the trial outline where the plaintiff's case must be assailed.

The plaintiff's cross-examination should be tightly controlled and, in most cases, brief. The best means of controlling the testimony is using plaintiff's testimony in a deposition, parallel proceeding, statement, or affidavit. Unemployment, EEOC, workers' compensation, and other proceedings in which the plaintiff may have testified are excellent sources for preparing impeachment data for cross-examination of the plaintiff in an employment case.

Helpful data for cross-examination of the plaintiff is usually found in his or her employment records. This is especially true where the plaintiff claims a pattern and practice of improper treatment over the course of employment. Employment records can seriously undermine the plaintiff's credibility in such circumstances.

Plaintiff's cross-examination may also be a good time to impress upon the jury the inconsistencies between plaintiff's version of some critical facts and the version rendered by the remainder of plaintiff's witnesses. Plaintiff may be at a loss to explain inconsistencies in the testimony of the coworkers who render damaging testimony on critical issues in the case as to which they were ill prepared.

6. Preparing Witnesses for Cross-Examination

The index to prior proceedings in your trial outline should be an effective first step in determining the expected direction of the cross-examination. The witness should be familiar with all of his prior testimony at depositions or in a parallel proceeding. Statements, affidavits, or other evidence on the same topic should be readily accessible. All discovery, pleadings, or other documents referring to the witness, written by the witness or germane to the witness's testimony, should also be thoroughly reviewed.

VI. Appendixes:
Checklists and Samples for the Practitioner

A. Plaintiff's Checklist

1. Witnesses—subpoenas, phone numbers

NOTE: You should have a witness list with telephone numbers handy. This way, you can contact witnesses on a moment's notice should the need arise. You should have all your subpoenas with you in the courtroom so that if a subpoenaed witness does not show or refuses to show, you can immediately request the judge to enforce the subpoena.

2. Trial brief
   a. Liability
   b. Damages
   c. Anticipated evidentiary issues

NOTE: This chapter has not mentioned the importance of preparing the trial brief, proposed jury instructions, proposed jury voir dire for selection of the jury, proposed jury verdict forms, or memos of law regarding potential evidentiary issues because they are covered in depth in chapters 9 and 10. However, it is extremely important that you have all of these ready for trial. Doing so tells the trial judge that you are well prepared and have a command of the law. Also, it usually results in the trial judge treating you with more respect, which may prove critical in certain evidentiary rulings and during the jury charge conference. Therefore, you should create a checklist of everything you need to give to the trial judge before you even start the case. Of course, federal rules and many federal district courts require you to provide many of these items anyway. Moreover, even though state courts often do not impose these requirements formally, you should be prepared to provide these materials to a state court judge upon his or her request.

3. Jury instructions
4. Judge's opening statements to jury before voir dire
5. Proposed voir dire
6. Jury consultant for jury
7. Documentary evidence
   a. Blowups
   b. Time lines and chronologies
   c. Exhibit books for witness box, adversary, yourself, judge, jury members
8. Verdict forms

B. Defendant's Checklist*

1. Notice last-minute motions.
2. Organize all court papers in order filed or entered.
3. Ensure all exhibits are prepared, marked, and labeled.
4. Index all prior proceedings by topic, witness, and document name for easy reference, including
   a. prior testimony at deposition or in a parallel proceeding
   b. witness statements
   c. affidavits
   d. unemployment files
   e. Equal Employment Opportunity Commission files
   f. workers' compensation files
5. Index all discovery, pleadings, and other documents listed in the pretrial order.
6. Consult indexed trial folders or trial notebooks for completeness, accuracy, and last-minute changes, including
   a. your trial outline
   b. order of proof
   c. pleadings
   d. motions
   e. discovery
   f. jury selection
   g. witness examination files
   h. opening and closing arguments
   i. jury instructions
   j. evidence
   k. objections
   l. depositions
   m. transcripts
   n. legal research, including photocopies of critical cases
7. Confirm that all exhibits are authenticated as required by applicable rules of evidence.
8. Audit trial outline and all pretrial preparation to ensure they conform with rulings on motions for summary judgment, motions in limine, and other pretrial motions.
9. Subpoena all witnesses in advance.
10. Prepare cross-examination of plaintiff's witnesses, organizing critical documents, points for fruitful cross-examination and impeachment, and potential evidence favorable to your position.
11. Consider rebuttal evidence.
12. Check all rules for admission of expert reports, testimony, and related issues in your jurisdiction.
13. Review rules of civil procedure, rules of evidence, and local rules and have them available for use in pretrial preparation

---

*See, Defense Litigation Checklist and Timetable, chapter 2, "Responding to the Lawsuit."

and trial.
14. Examine all exhibits, charts, and physical evidence personally where possible.
15. Revisit significant locations before the trial if necessary to re-fresh witness.
16. Excerpt appropriate deposition testimony.
17. Expect the unexpected and be ready for it.

C. Witness Preparation Checklist

1. Review with the witness prior depositions, answers to interrogatories, written or oral statements, affidavits, testimony in parallel proceedings, and anything usable for impeachment.
2. Explain the trial process to the witness, including impeachment and entering exhibits in court. Anticipate cultural and/or language problems and potential disability problems.
3. Review any inconsistencies with other witnesses' testimony.
4. Thoroughly prepare direct examination on all elements of the trial outline the witness is expected to cover, then have a colleague cross-examine as opposing counsel can be expected to proceed, and videotape the cross-examination for witness review if necessary.
5. Outline eye contact, attire, demeanor, dignity, temper control, courtesy, language, and related comportment issues.
6. Give witness courthouse specifics, including location and directions, as well as information on the layout, personnel, and functions of the courtroom.
7. Reiterate testimony rules from deposition preparation, including no volunteering, asking for explanations of vague questions, handling objections, and answering questions on personal observations.

D. Sample Trial Outline

Legal Elements of Proof Required	Evidence Needed to Prove Element	Evidence Rule Justifying Admission

Notes

1. *See, e.g., Burdine*, 450 U.S. at 256; Hagelthorn v. Kennecott Corp., 710 F.2d 76, 82 (2d Cir. 1983).

2. *See, e.g.*, Woroski v. Nashua Corp., 31 F.3d 105, 108 (2d Cir. 1994); Mansfield v. Sinclair Int'l, 766 F.2d 788 (3d Cir. 1985).

3. *See, e.g.*, Cronin v. Aetna Life Ins. Co., 46 F.3d 196 (2d Cir. 1995).

4. *See, e.g.*, Fed. R. Evid. 611(c).

5. *See, e.g.*, Fed. R. Civ. P. 32(a)(2).

6. Daubert v. Merrell Dow Pharm., Inc., 113 S. Ct. 2786 (1993).

7. Mercado v. Austin Police Dept., 754 F.2d 1266, 1268, 37 Fair Empl. Prac. Cas. (BNA) 532 (5th Cir. 1985).

8. McLaurin v. Fischer, 768 F.2d 98, 104, 41 Fair Empl. Prac. Cas. (BNA) 1012 (6th Cir. 1985); Donovan v. Burger King Corp., 672 F.2d 221, 225, 25 Wage & Hour Cas. (BNA) 428 (1st Cir. 1982).

9. Mitroff v. Xomox Corp., 797 F.2d 271, 275–76, 41 Fair Empl. Prac. Cas. (BNA) 290 (6th Cir. 1986).

10. Schrand v. Fed. Pac. Elec. Co., 851 F.2d 152, 47 Fair Empl. Prac. Cas. (BNA) 273 (6th Cir. 1988).

11. Feazell v. Tropicana Prod., Inc., 819 F.2d 1036, 1041, 44 Fair Empl. Prac. Cas. (BNA) 101 (11th Cir. 1987).

12. Kremer v. Chem. Constr. Corp., 456 U.S. 461, 102 S. Ct. 1883, 72 L. Ed. 2d 262, 28 Fair Empl. Prac. Cas. (BNA) 1412 (1982) (relying on 28 U.S.C. § 1738).

13. *Id.*

14. Gilchrist v. Jim Slemons Imports, Inc., 803 F.2d 1488, 42 Fair Empl. Prac. Cas. (BNA) 314, 322 (9th Cir. 1986).

15. Georater Corp. v. EEOC, 592 F.2d 765, 19 Fair Empl. Prac. Cas. (BNA) 70 (4th Cir. 1979).

16. *Id.* at 560.

17. LaDolce v. Bank Admin. Inst., 585 F. Supp. 975, 36 Fair Empl. Prac. Cas. (BNA) 1820 (N.D. Ill. 1984).

18. Haskell v. Kaman Corp., 743 F.2d 113, 35 Fair Empl. Prac. Cas. (BNA) 941 (2d Cir. 1984); Moorhouse v. Boeing, 501 F. Supp. 390, 24 Fair Empl. Prac. Cas. (BNA) 589 (E.D. Pa. 1980), *aff'd*, 639 F.2d 774, 25 Fair Empl. Prac. Cas. (BNA) 714 (3d Cir. 1980).

CHAPTER 9

Juries

DANIEL C. EMERSON*
SAMUEL M. MATCHETT†

* *Bose McKinney & Evans; Indianapolis, Indiana.*

† *Powell, Goldstein, Frazer & Murphy; Atlanta, Georgia.*

I. Introduction

Since the enactment of the Civil Rights Act of 1991, trial by jury has become a fact of life for employment lawyers. The management bar has uneasily regarded plaintiffs' expanded right to jury trials with trepidation about runaway jury verdicts swayed by sympathy for the downtrodden employee mistreated by the heartless corporation. Conversely, the plaintiffs' bar has viewed juries as an opportunity to access justice by "peers" who are more likely than a judge to empathize with their client and to punish wayward employers through substantial compensatory and punitive damage awards.

The truth of the matter probably lies somewhere short of the advocates' expectations. Although juries are certainly not infallible and are more susceptible to emotional entreaty than the average federal district judge, they do not check their brains at the courthouse door and are not necessarily inclined to disregard cogent presentations of legitimate, nondiscriminatory reasons for adverse job actions.

As such, a jury trial in an employment case is not merely a perfunctory exercise preceding the inevitable enormous award to the plaintiff. If the outcome were foregone, there would be no need for either party to undertake the effort and expense of trial—the case would have been settled or concluded by dispositive motion. Facts, inferences, and applications of law are at issue and it is the lawyer's job to persuade the jury that it should resolve those issues in favor of his or her client.

Success at trial, however, is rarely the result of the pure trial skills of counsel. Much more often it is the product of exhaustive preparation and the intelligent use of tools and techniques designed to persuade a receptive jury that one interpretation of a particular set of facts is more plausible than another. It is therefore incumbent upon the lawyer facing a jury trial to at least consider the use of consultants, methods, and procedures designed to improve the likelihood of impaneling a receptive jury and to minimize the adverse effect of jurors' extraneous prejudices and preconceptions.

II. Jury Consultants*

The use of consultants and mock or simulated trials to assist lawyers in the selection of jurors and to help lawyers communicate more effectively to a jury is an interesting phenomenon. Just when, how, and whether to use trial consultants or some other method of assessing the strengths and weaknesses of one's case is the aim of this section.

Jury consulting dates back to the late 1960s when a group of social scientists formed the National Jury Project.[1] Amidst the widely publicized criminal cases involving Vietnam War protestors, the National Jury Project's aim was to find whether the defendants could receive a fair trial given the extensive media coverage. The National Jury Project used sociological and psychological research, dwelling on jurors' attitudes to find impartial jurors. With the National Jury Project's effectiveness in those early trials, it continued to grow and is now a full-service trial consulting firm. The growth of the National Jury Project fueled growth in the consulting industry. In 1982 the American Society of Trial Consultants was formed with 15 members; it now has over 350.

A. What Is Jury Consulting?

Jury consulting is not an intuitive hunch or speculation based on stereotypes. It involves scientific and analytical research into the attitudes of potential or impaneled jurors. Jury consultants use statistical analysis to develop a model of desirable and undesirable jurors.

Although the Sixth Amendment mandates an impartial jury, jurors are everyday people who bring to the courtroom their preconceptions, prejudices, and life experiences. All of these elements affect how jurors will view a case. Jury consultants believe that understanding these factors will help a lawyer develop effective case strategies.

Jury consulting began in the basic realm of social science research—sociology and psychology—but now involves people from a variety of disciplines, including communications specialists, linguists, handwriting experts, and even lawyers. While jury consulting has its origins in criminal trials, it is now used primarily in complex civil litigation. Consultants offer their service not only in the selection of jurors, but in evaluating venue, lawyers, witnesses, case themes, trial strategies, and exhibits.

---

* See Expert Trial Preparation Assistance, chapter 4, "Experts."

While a lawyer is well versed in the law and is trained to analyze the facts and apply legal principles, jury consultants may offer a different perspective. Consultants test the facts and theories of a case before it ever reaches a jury. Although they cannot read a juror's mind, consultants attempt to piece together how a person is likely to react based on his or her background, answers to certain questions, and overall community attitudes. Anticipating jurors' reactions is a primary focus of jury consulting.

B. What Do Jury Consultants Do?

There are a variety of techniques used and services offered by jury consultants. The consultant may use one, all, or a combination of techniques or services for a particular case. Some of the major techniques include (1) community attitude surveys, (2) focus groups, (3) demographic surveys, (4) juror investigations, (5) deliberation groups, (6) mock trials, (7) shadow juries, and (8) postverdict surveys. Services offered by consultants typically include (1) strategy development, (2) witness preparation, (3) jury selection, (4) persuasion techniques, (5) preparation of demonstrative exhibits, and (6) evaluation of counsel.

1. Techniques Employed by Jury Consultants

a. Community Attitude Surveys Community attitude surveys are used to get a feel for community biases and to address the problem that potential jurors are prone to be less than candid about their own biases during voir dire. The survey is usually conducted over the telephone and seeks information on the community members' reaction to certain trial issues and their awareness of the case, parties, and issues.

Results may be used to support a change of venue if large numbers indicate bias in the community. If the case is highly emotional or well publicized, the consultant may conduct an individual study tailored to address venue concerns. The results may also be used in determining which jurors to strike. During voir dire, if a potential juror gives an answer to a question that is inconsistent with his or her socioeconomic profile, the lawyer may question the juror more closely or choose to strike. A drawback to using a community attitude survey is that it tends to group people together without taking into account individual personalities.

b. Focus Groups Focus groups are traditionally used by social scientists and are the beginning process for many research projects. The groups consist of people from the same area where the case is being tried. The consultant/lawyer presents one or two issues to the group, then the group is divided into smaller groups for a response. Lastly, participants are interviewed on what factors affected their decisions, what they liked and disliked about the presentation, and what they understood and did not understand.

The information is compiled and compared with corresponding personalities and demographic types. The focus group involves ongoing discussion among the participants. Often the focus group is moderated by a consultant but viewed on monitors by lawyers. Two or three groups are used to assure that the opinions and reactions offered by the groups reflect the general population.

c. Demographic Surveys Like focus groups, demographic surveys are also a staple of jury research. Most of the information is gathered by phone and can help pinpoint local biases, psychological profiles, and demographic characteristics. This kind of survey is particularly useful when counsel believes a certain attitude exists within the community already.

Demographic surveys are not helpful when the case involves a limited number of people, intercompany relationships, or relationships not of a community interest. Demographic surveys are broad and should not be used if the lawyer or client wants to minimize exposure in the community, because there is little control over who is contacted.

d. Juror Investigations Juror investigation is a somewhat controversial technique used to find out information about potential jurors. Two types of investigations used are community network models and home surveillance. The community network model combines general neighborhood demographic information and interview responses to provide a network profile.

The controversy involving juror investigations is in the use of home surveillance techniques. This practice is simply observing a potential juror's home and monitoring his or her activities. Critics argue that this invades the privacy of the jurors. However, some lawyers have long used this practice.

e. Deliberation Groups Deliberation groups are mini-mock trials. As with the focus group, a presentation is made by the lawyer either personally or on videotape. The presentation includes each side of the case. At the end of the presentation, the group is left unattended to reach a decision. Although the participants deliberate without contact with the consultant or lawyer, they are usually videotaped or observed through a monitor mirror.

Deliberation groups provide a view similar to that of the actual trial. However, deliberation groups require a lot of time and effort from the trial team. A lawyer is well advised to exercise caution when using deliberation groups early in the trial process to avoid jumping to conclusions about important issues, thus misjudging the direction in which the trial should move.

f. Mock Trials The mock trial, or trial simulation, is considered the most comprehensive technique used in jury research. It is a dress rehearsal of the actual trial. It encompasses lawyers' opening and closing arguments, witness testimony, and verdict results. It is the best opportunity for a litigator to assess and restructure the presentation before trial. Often a large group is used to hear the case, then broken into smaller groups for deliberations. Mock trials can be extremely expensive and, as with deliberation groups, lawyers are warned to avoid making assumptions about presentation and strategy. If the cost can be justified, mock trials are a certain method of assessing the strengths and weaknesses of one's case, as well as the strengths and weaknesses of counsel's overall verbal and physical presentation.

g. Shadow Juries Shadow juries, or feedback juries, are likely to be the final step in the process (some consultants offer followup surveys with jurors after a case is tried if there is the potential for similar litigation). Participants of the same gender, age, ethnicity, and socioeconomic background as the actual jurors sit in the courtroom and hear the testimony. The shadow jury hears only what the actual jury hears.

A major concern with using shadow juries is the distraction of third-party information going to the lawyer while he or she is concentrating on the events of the trial. Another drawback is the attention that shadow juries draw inside the courtroom. Opposing counsel may try to point out use of the shadow jury to actual jurors, which could create a negative impact on an actual juror's decision-making process.

h. Postverdict Surveys Postverdict surveys are interviews conducted with the actual jurors after the verdict has been decided. The jurors are questioned about the verdict and why they decided the way they did. Postverdict surveys are useful if there is a potential for similar litigation.

2. Services Offered by Consultants

a. Strategy Development Several techniques may be analyzed together to develop a strategy plan. Research data will help point out themes, arguments, and counterattacks that are helpful to the client's case. Techniques can be helpful to test strategies before and during the trial.

b. Witness Preparation Most jury consultants offer witness preparation services, and a few even specialize in this area. Witness preparation is important in familiarizing the witness with the trial team, making the witness comfortable under courtroom examination, and simply providing an opportunity for practice and feedback.

Body language, eye contact, verbal pacing, and vocabulary are all characteristics as to which a consultant or lawyer can coach a witness. Because it is important that jurors understand the witness, witness preparation can be vital to a case. The downside is that the witness may appear stiff and rehearsed.

c. Jury Questionnaires and Selection Through focus groups and other techniques, the jury consultant will have compiled the best- and worst-case profiles of jurors. Consultants may draft helpful questionnaires for prospective jurors. The lawyer and consultant will set objectives for voir dire to obtain sufficient information from the jurors. The consultant may even observe voir dire and give feedback or make suggestion as to additional questions. After the entire jury is impaneled, the consultant may evaluate its overall composition and compare it to already established profiles.

d. Persuasion Techniques and Evaluation of Counsel Lawyers are well trained in the law and how to apply it to the facts of a case. This is usually the primary focus of the lawyer. The focus of the jury consultant is the jury. Some consulting firms hire linguistics and communications specialists to assist counsel in developing effective communication skills and techniques. Even the best and most well reasoned argument can be lost if the person on the receiving end is distracted by the lawyer's mannerisms, dress, or vocal delivery.

Consultants also evaluate lawyers' written and oral arguments to translate legal jargon into terms that nonlawyers will understand. The consultant may also observe the lawyer during trial and give feedback on jurors' responsiveness to arguments. Witness and voir dire questions may be carefully drafted to evoke a certain physical response that exposes a juror's true feelings. The consultant may serve as a second set of eyes in the courtroom.

C. Advantages and Disadvantages of Using Jury Consultants

Jury consulting is comparable to the test marketing that a manufacturer does when introducing a new or revised product. Most manufacturers choose to conduct some type of survey to find out whether the product will be acceptable to the general public. Similarly, jury consultants are testing the "market" with trial themes and arguments. As with the market testing of products, there are advantages and disadvantages.

1. Arguments for Using Consultants

Consultants can give objective views of arguments, presentation skills, and persuasion techniques. Research shows that no one is more than 50 percent accurate in knowing how others perceive him or her.[2] Communicating to jurors is an important skill that consultants can help lawyers improve.

The use of a consultant can be cost-effective. Lawyers who have used consultants with positive results maintain that although some services are expensive, in the long run they can result in tremendous savings for a client. A consultant's research may help determine whether a case should be tried or settled. Likewise, time and money can be saved by avoiding certain themes and arguments that jury research indicates the community does not favor.

A basic advantage of consulting is assistance with jury selection. The most experienced trial lawyers are able to pick out jurors who will be unfavorable to their clients' positions. It is more difficult, however, to identify those "fringe" jurors who could go either way. A jury consultant's in-depth analysis may help counsel recognize these jurors and develop strategies to persuade them to favor his or her client's position. This of course must be balanced against the actual opportunity to influence jury selection, depending on the availability and scope of voir dire in any particular jurisdiction.

Jury research may help uncover bias. Most potential jurors will not admit to bias during voir dire. Studies show that people tend to give socially acceptable answers when questioned by an authority figure.[3] Jury research techniques help ensure impartial juries by identifying jurors who fall into certain profiles.

A consultant's research may lessen the effect of stereotyping. Stereotypes based on race and class have long been used by lawyers in determining favorable and unfavorable jurors. Jury research shows, however, that education and the type of books one reads are far more indicative of a person's feelings than race or class.[4]

2. Arguments against Using Jury Consultants

Critics argue that jury consulting and research are nothing more than high-tech methods of jury tampering because the consultant's efforts are focused on weeding out unfavorable jurors and selecting jurors favorable to the client's case. Hence, the argument goes, the Sixth

Amendment's "impartial jury" mandate is frustrated when a lawyer stacks the jury with people favorable to his case, rather than with jurors who are simply impartial. Although this characterization is not favorable from any perspective, it must be balanced against the risk of an adverse jury verdict and the attendant negative impact of such a result.

Critics also argue that the cost of consulting separates the rich from the poor. Consulting is very expensive. The bare minimum for employing a consultant is somewhere between $10,000 and $50,000.[5] Many lawyers are not persuaded that jury consultants are cost-effective, particularly when there is pressure to reduce legal costs associated with litigation.

The reliability of a jury consultant's research is questionable. Many feel that the extensive analysis and statistical information provided by consultants is still merely guesswork. Social science, by nature, is imprecise, yet it is the basis of jury research and consulting. The system may be based on a faulty assumption that a correlation exists between juror characteristics and the favoring of one party and that a particular juror will behave according to that relationship. Some experts have shown that the relationship between verdict and background characteristics is too weak to be of significance.[6]

There is no regulation of jury consultants. Although the American Society of Trial Consultants has hundreds of members, no credential, certification, or special training is required. Also, there is no governing body that monitors the performance or professional ethics of jury consultants. Because most consultants are not lawyers, they are also not aware of the ethical standards of the American Bar Association or local bar associations.

When using a consultant, there is the potential of exposing information that a trial team or client may not want exposed. The use of some techniques may lead to disclosure of information to a variety of people over whom the consultant has no control. Some themes or arguments could be inadvertently revealed to opposing counsel. Also, exposure could possibly lead to discovery problems, although most experts say the risk is minimal.[7]

Use of a consultant may have an adverse impact on witnesses, lawyers, and jurors. Witnesses may come off as rehearsed and overprepared. Actual jurors may feel manipulated by research results or shadow juries and react negatively. Lawyers may also respond negatively when they are told to change trial strategy at the last minute based on a consultant's research.

D. What to Look for in Choosing a Consultant

When looking for a jury consultant, the key factor should be the consultant's experience in the industry. Some consultants boast about high success or accuracy rates, although the Code of Professional Standards of the American Society of Trial Consultants states that no member shall claim a win-loss record as a way of advertising. However, the society has no credentials or rules, thus a member who does boast about a win-loss record is not barred or reprimanded. Most professionals agree that because of the type of research conducted, outcome is not a good measure of success.[8] Also, a lawyer should seek out a jury consultant who is recommended by another lawyer who has used that consulting firm previously. A positive referral from a colleague whose opinion is valued is the most natural and reliable method of choosing a consultant to work with. Additionally, it is important to consider what types of services the consultant offers. If the lawyer is going to utilize the consultant only for witness preparation or jury selection, a consultant who specializes in those areas should be considered. Finally, cost is an important consideration. The cost and use of a consultant should always be the decision of the client.

E. The Bottom Line—When to Use Jury Consultants

Jury consulting and mock trials are not new, but excessive verdicts appear to have increased their popularity in recent years. There is an observable increase in the number of consultants and in the number of services they offer. Lawyers, however, give the use of jury consultants mixed reviews. Some lawyers believe consultants can make or break a big case, while others believe that the cost of utilizing a consultant is not justifiable. Many lawyers, in fact, find it more reasonable to become their own consultants and stage their own simulated trials. Not surprisingly, consultants warn that while lawyers may be able to conduct some of their own studies, lawyers are ill-suited to be as objective as a third person.

The use of jury consultants can be very broad or narrow. It is critical to determine up front exactly what the engagement can achieve and to use the jury consultant in a manner consistent with that goal. For example, the lawyer must decide if the jury consultant is being used to support a change in venue because of community bias, to determine whether the case should be settled at an early stage, to evaluate witness and presentation styles, to assist in the selection of a particular type of jury, to assist in posttrial analysis where other similar cases may be pending, and so forth. Focused use of jury consultants based on the particular case presented will be more economical and is more likely to achieve the desired goal. The jury selection rules in the particular state or federal jurisdiction must be considered carefully. Voir dire analysis and assistance is not particularly helpful where a court permits only limited or no questions to potential jurors by counsel.

III. Jury Selection—Pointers

It is no secret that winning or losing a case at trial may depend almost entirely on the jurors hearing the case. When assessing juror qualifications, the court looks for the ability to be impartial; lawyers look for "ringers" who will win or lose the case for them during deliberation.

The ability to influence jury selection is quite limited in many jurisdictions. In many federal courts, the presiding judge will typically pose all or substantially all of the voir dire examination, and counsel has only a very limited number of peremptory strikes from the panel. In some state courts, lawyers are given more information and latitude in the juror selection process than in federal court. Whatever the court, a lawyer is well advised to familiarize himself or herself with the court's rules and practices regarding jury selection and meticulously prepare for this critical process.

How does one marshal the complexities of the process? The following tips should be helpful.

A. Be the Master of the Jury Pool

To the extent possible, the lawyer should attempt to influence the jury pool selection. For plaintiff's counsel, it may be possible to file a lawsuit in multiple districts within a state, each of which may draw a substantially different jury pool. For employer's counsel, there often is the opportunity to remove state court actions to federal court based on federal question or diversity jurisdiction. Federal district courts generally draw jurors from a much different pool than do state courts. The former is generally viewed as more favorable for the defense because the jury pool in federal court is culled from numerous counties in the district. State court is frequently perceived to be more advantageous for plaintiffs, probably because the jury pool is more localized and because urban jurors are regarded as more likely to be generous with a company's money than are rural jurors. Additionally, state court juries are frequently comprised of twelve people instead of the usual six in federal court. With more jurors on the panel, there seems to be a greater tendency to compromise on a verdict, which usually does not inure to the benefit of a company. It is important for the lawyer to consider this "forum" issue at the outset of the litigation.

B. Consider Use of a Jury Consultant

Evaluate whether a jury consultant can assist in identifying favorable jurors or disqualifying potentially harmful jurors based on factors such as education and economics. The expense associated with jury consultants may not be practical in garden variety cases but may make sense in very large cases. An alternative to professional jury consultants is to enlist the help of an experienced local trial lawyer who has tried cases in the locality of the trial.

C. Know Your Jury Pool

It is critical to determine as much as possible about the particular court and judge's jury selection process. Find out from the judge's law clerk whether or not a jury questionnaire can or will be used and, if so, whether you will be allowed to provide questions, and exactly how to proceed. Prepare specific questions for the questionnaire that elicit the information needed to identify the "ideal" juror for your type of case. Verify with the court's clerk the exact number of jurors in civil cases in that court, as well as the permitted number of peremptory strikes. Surprises in this area must be avoided. As early as possible, obtain a copy of the venire from which the jury will be chosen. This list typically contains very helpful identification and demographic information on each juror: name, address, marital status, educational background, occupation, residency, and so on. With this information, together with that gleaned from the juror questionnaires, you should prepare a juror profile sheet that ranks jurors in order of raw demographic desirability. Having immediate access to this information, including through use of a laptop computer in court, can prove invaluable. Once in court, the time between voir dire and jury selection is very short. Thus, whatever you can prepare in advance will be very helpful.

In districts that provide only the limited information of juror names in advance of trial, it is important to devise a system in advance to help capture critical information while the jurors are responding to voir dire. It is important to have co-counsel or a skilled paralegal at the table to assist while lead counsel actively conducts the voir dire.

D. Managing Information during Voir Dire

It is critical to know exactly how a particular judge will proceed to select jurors, including the number of peremptory strikes and the specific method the judge will employ. Remember also that some jurors can be struck for cause. Therefore, if a juror appears to be improperly predisposed one way or the other, that witness is subject to be stricken for cause. Any discussion regarding the striking of a juror should be conducted outside the presence and hearing of the jury panel to avoid antagonizing the subject juror or other potential jurors.

Prepare in advance a voir dire witness seating chart that can be quickly completed at counsel's table. Handwritten charts also may be helpful, but may waste valuable time.

E. Introduce Yourself to the Jury

Whether or not a court allows lawyer-directed voir dire, at some point the judge is likely to request counsel to address the pool. Use this as an opportunity to present and ingratiate yourself to the jury. Speak to the jury as though you are addressing a respected, nonlawyer family member. Never talk down to the jurors or patronize them. If the court permits counsel to conduct voir dire, be ready to proceed. Ask open-ended questions ("Please tell me about. . . .") that prompt jurors to tell you who they really are, what they feel, and what their experiences have been. Make it your aim to establish a trusting relationship with the jury. One lawyer suggests that the following three questions be asked in every employment discrimination case:

- Tell me about any employee/management dispute concerning age, sex, or racial discrimination that has occurred in your workplace.
- We have all heard horror stories about people not getting promoted or even fired because of their age, sex, or race. Tell me about the worst instance that you have personal knowledge of. (How did that make you feel? In what way did you change your behavior because of that instance?)
- Tell me about an instance where you think an employee made an unfounded claim that he or she was discriminated against in the workplace.

Most important, though, is the admonition for you to *watch* and *listen*. Listen to what the prospective jurors say and how they say it. Listen to what they *do not* say. Pick up on any visual or aural cues you can about their predispositions and get a gut feel for them.

F. Think before You Choose

Make sure that you have the opportunity to absorb all of the information that you have gathered before making your ultimate selections. If necessary, ask the judge for a few moments to review your notes on the jurors before the actual selection process begins. Any amount of time the court permits can be put to effective use, particularly if your notes are organized.

Remember that your primary goal in jury selection is to *deselect*, through the use of peremptory strikes (or for-cause dismissal), those jurors who you believe will be most likely to hurt your case. Jurors are human beings who bring to court all of their predispositions based on their experiences, their exposures, and their religious, political, economic, and philosophical beliefs. Specifically, the types of jobs jurors hold, their educational backgrounds, and their similarities or empathy with a party in the case or a party's counsel are powerful factors that may result in partiality. These are all important in deciding who to strike. The lawyer should visualize prior to trial what the characteristics are of the jurors he or she does not want and utilize peremptory strikes accordingly.

IV. Challenges

In employment cases, where the plaintiff's race or gender is often central to the controversy, the composition of the jury may have a substantial effect on the trial's outcome. Many lawyers have traditionally preferred to try these cases to a jury composed of people of a race or gender that they believe to be sympathetic (or at least not antagonistic) to their position by way of their peremptory challenges. However, a series of Supreme Court decisions over the last decade have substantially eroded the use of preemptory challenges in cases where the racial or gender composition of a jury is a source of contention.

At one time lawyers were free to use peremptory challenges to strike potential jurors because of the person's race or gender.[9] The courts rejected attacks on the use of peremptory challenges for this reason because it was believed that peremptory challenges should be "exercised without a reason stated, without inquiry, and without being subject to the court's control."[10]

The beginning of the end of the unfettered use of peremptory challenges came in 1986 with the Supreme Court's decision in *Batson v. Kentucky*, 476 U.S. 79, 106 S. Ct. 1712, 90 L. Ed. 2d 69 (1986). In *Batson*, the Supreme Court held that jury selection based upon an individual's race violates a defendant's fundamental right to equal protection.[11] The Supreme Court has followed *Batson* in several other decisions that have further restricted the use of discriminatory peremptory challenges.[12]

To successfully oppose a peremptory challenge, a party must satisfy a three-part test.[13] First, the party opposing the peremptory challenge must establish a prima facie showing that the challenge because the juror's race or gender.[14] Once that party makes a prima facie showing, the burden shifts to the party who asserted the peremptory challenge to offer either a race- or gender- neutral reason for challenging the juror that is clear, reasonably specific, and related to the case.[15] The court must then determine whether the objecting party has proved the existence of intentional discrimination.[16]

In *Batson*, the Court stated that a prima facie case of racial discrimination is established when the defendant is a member of a cognizable racial group and that the prosecutor has exercised peremptory challenges to remove from the venire members of the defendant's race.[17] While the defendant may rely on the fact that peremptory challenges are a vehicle that allows those who would discriminate to discriminate, it also must be shown that the relevant circumstances raise an inference that the prosecutor used the practice to exclude people from the panel because of their race.[18] The Supreme Court in *Edmonson* further held that the same approach applies in a civil context, and "we leave it to the trial court in the first instance to develop evidentiary rules for implementing our decision."[19] Nevertheless, despite the requirement that a party present a prima facie case to initiate a *Batson* challenge, some courts seemingly have eliminated this requirement.[20]

The Supreme Court decision in *Purkett v. Elem*, 514 U.S. 765, 115 S. Ct. 1769, 131 L. Ed. 2d 834 (1995), provides insight into how the second and third steps in the *Batson* test will be implemented. In *Purkett*, the Supreme Court explained that the burden of coming forward with a race-neutral explanation does not demand an explanation that is persuasive, or even plausible. At this point in the inquiry the issue is nothing more than the facial validity of the explanation. Unless a discriminatory intent is inherent in the explanation, the reason offered is to be deemed race-neutral and the court is to proceed to the third step, in which it evaluates the persuasiveness of the justification. At that stage, "implausible or fantastic justifications may (and probably will) be found to be pretexts for purposeful discrimination." Through the entire process the burden of persuasion regarding racial motivation rests with, and never shifts from, the opponent of the peremptory challenge.

Although there is not a large body of case law, the tests enunciated in these decisions have been utilized by lower courts in civil litigation involving employment discrimination claims.[21] While the dearth of authority addressing *Batson* challenges in the employment discrimination context makes it unclear whether courts will strictly adhere to *Batson* when race or gender is such a fundamental element of the case, courts have not yet evidenced any propensity to shift away from a traditional *Batson* analysis in civil cases.

Recent cases also reflect the importance of other elements of preemptory challenges, including making timely objections, being prepared to articulate the reasons for an objection, and knowing how to defend against an objection.[22]

Finally, if a litigant exercises a peremptory challenge against a minority or female prospective juror, the litigant must provide a reason that is not shared by prospective jurors who are not challenged. It is well established that peremptory challenges cannot be lawfully exercised against potential jurors of one race unless potential jurors of another race with comparable characteristics are also challenged.[23]

As the cases discussed above demonstrate, there is no bright-line test for determining when a peremptory challenge will be held to be discriminatory under *Batson* in any case, much less in employment discrimination litigation. The determination must be made by the trial judge and be based on the facts and circumstances of the controversy at issue. It is clear, however, that lawyers selecting juries in employment cases must be fully prepared to deal with the issues raised by *Batson*.

V. Jury Instructions

Many instructors of trial advocacy rate the drafting of concise, impartial, and understandable jury instructions as one of the most critical, if not *the* most critical, aspects of trial preparation. The task of drafting instructions has been made somewhat easier by the general availability of books of pattern jury instructions. Most states have compilations of jury instructions that are generally accepted, officially or unofficially, by the state courts. In the federal system, the three-volume *Federal Jury Practice and Instructions* is accepted as authoritative by virtually every district court, and the Fifth, Sixth, Eighth, Ninth, and Eleventh circuits have each adopted manuals of pattern jury instructions. Another excellent source is the American Bar Association's *Model Jury Instructions: Employment Litigation* (1994). (All the federal district courts throughout the country have copies.)

No compilation of sample jury instructions, however, should be swallowed whole. All are aids to and road maps for the preparation of appropriate instructions. Each case has its own peculiar facts and twists to which instructions must be tailored, and no compilation should be regarded as a substitute for ingenuity and thorough research.

VI. Special Verdicts and Interrogatories

Employment litigators should give careful consideration to taking advantage of the very effective alternative methods for submitting fact issues to juries provided by Rule 49 of the Federal Rules of Civil Procedure. The rule provides:

(a) **Special Verdicts**. The court may require a jury to return only a special verdict in the form of a special written finding upon each issue of fact. In that event the court may submit to the jury written questions susceptible of categorical or other brief answer or may submit written forms of the several special findings which might properly be made under the pleadings and evidence; or it may use such other method of submitting the issues and requiring the written findings thereon as it deems most appropriate. The court shall give to the jury such explanation and instruction concerning the matter thus submitted as may be necessary to enable the jury to make its findings upon each issue. If in so doing the court omits any issue of fact raised by the pleadings or by the evidence, each party waives the right to a trial by jury of the issue so omitted unless before the jury retires the party demands its submission to the jury. As to an issue omitted without such demand the court may make a finding; or, if it fails to do so, it shall be deemed to have made a finding in accord with the judgment on the special verdict.

(b) General Verdict Accompanied by Answer to Interrogatories. The court may submit to the jury, together with appropriate forms for a general verdict, written interrogatories upon one or more issues of fact the decision of which is necessary to a verdict. The court shall give such explanation or instruction as may be necessary to enable the jury both to make answers to the interrogatories and to render a general verdict, and the court shall direct the jury both to make written answers and to render a general verdict. When the general verdict and the answers are harmonious, the appropriate judgment upon the verdict and answers shall be entered pursuant to Rule 58. When the answers are consistent with each other but one or more is inconsistent with the general verdict, judgment may be entered pursuant to Rule 58 in accordance with the answers, notwithstanding the general verdict, or the court may return the jury for further consideration of its answers and verdict or may order a new trial. When the answers are inconsistent with each other and one or more is likewise inconsistent with the general verdict, judgment shall not be entered, but the court shall return the jury for further consideration of its answers and verdict or shall order a new trial.

Rule 49 is a variation on the old common law special verdict procedure still in use in many states, and it allows two different alternatives to the general verdict by which the jury may express its findings. Under subdivision (a), the court dispenses with the general verdict altogether and instead submits the various fact issues in the case to the jury. Under subdivision (b), the court requests the jury to return a general verdict, accompanied by answers to interrogatories relating to particular issues in the case.

Both forms of the special verdict procedure are designed to permit the jury to make decisions on each of the dispositive issues of the controversy while avoiding personalities, prejudice, and bias.[24] The special verdict form is generally drafted as a series of questions addressing ultimate facts in the case. For example, was the plaintiff qualified for the job for which she applied? Would a reasonable person in the position of the plaintiff find her workplace to be hostile and offensive? With these findings, the court applies the law and directs the entry of judgment. Thus, the jury is expected to answer each question regardless of the effect or supposed effect of the answer on the ultimate result of the case.

A. Discretion of the Court

A party is not entitled to a special verdict or the submission of interrogatories with a general verdict as a matter of right. The rule is permissive and whether Rule 49 procedures are used rests in the complete discretion of the trial court.[25] Likewise, the court is vested with considerable discretion as to the nature, scope, and form of special verdicts or interrogatories.[26] The arguments for and against the use of Rule 49 procedure go to the fundamental notions of the appropriate role of the jury. Proponents of special verdict practice urge that its use avoids possible errors by the jury in considering questions of law, provides for a more efficient presentation to the jury of both sides of the controversy, and furnishes a practical, concrete basis for the appellate court's evaluation of the case on review. On the other hand, those litigators who view the jury's role as something nearly metaphysical, bought and paid for at Runnymede, argue that special verdict and interrogatory practice tend to make the law cold and mechanistic, without the flexibility and susceptibility to human foibles permitted by the general verdict form. Moreover, on a more practical level, opponents of special verdicts and interrogatories point out that special verdicts and interrogatories almost inevitably lead to more lengthy jury deliberations because it is inherently more difficult for the jury to reach separate compromise agreements on several fact findings of a special verdict than it is to agree on one all-inclusive general verdict.

Notwithstanding the debate, special verdicts should be particularly appropriate for employment litigation because of the numerous and often sequential issues of proof attendant to most claims. The complementary advantages of the special verdict to both sides of an employment controversy arise from compelling the jury to articulate its reasoning in a logical and systematic manner. The methodology makes it tougher for a jury, motivated by racial prejudice or employer animus, to hide behind a general verdict.

B. Form and Sufficiency of the Special Verdict

Under Rule 49(a), the special verdict may consist of (1) "yes" or "no" or other brief answer to the question or issue submitted, (2) findings on written forms submitted by the court, or (3) findings in such other form as the court deems appropriate. A special verdict is sufficient if it clearly and unambiguously determines the relevant issues of the case. The parties should, however, exercise care in assuring that questions or interrogatories covering all the issues raised by the pleadings or the evidence are submitted because Rule 49(a) specifically provides that if the court in submitting the issues to the jury "omits any issue of fact raised by the pleadings or by the evidence, each party waives the right to a trial by jury of the issue so omitted unless before the jury retires the party demands its submission to the jury."[27]

C. General Verdict with Written Interrogatories

Rule 49(b) authorizes the court, where general verdicts are used, to submit written interrogatories to the jury on one or more of the fact issues essential to the verdict. The rule thus contemplates requiring the jury essentially to double-check its work by comparing its ultimate conclusion expressed in the general verdict with the reasoning process necessary to reach that conclusion.

The rule goes on to provide specifically the procedure to be followed to resolve inconsistencies between answers to interrogatories and the general verdict. If the general verdict and the answers to the written interrogatories are harmonious, judgment should ordinarily be entered on the verdict pursuant to Rule 58. If the answers are internally consistent but one or more of them are irreconcilably inconsistent with the general verdict, the answers trump the general verdict and the court may either enter judgment pursuant to Rule 58 in accordance with the answers, return the jury for further consideration of its answers and verdict, or order a new trial.[28] If the answers are internally inconsistent and one or more are inconsistent with the general verdict, the court cannot enter judgment and must either return the jury for further consideration or order a new trial.[29]

VII. Appendixes: Sample Forms

A. Jury Questionnaire/Voir Dire—*Weeks v. Baker & McKenzie, et al.* [As modified]

SUPERIOR COURT OF THE STATE OF CALIFORNIA
IN AND FOR THE COUNTY OF SAN FRANCISCO

RENA WEEKS,	)	Case No. 943 043
	)	
Plaintiff,	)	
	)	
v.	)	JURY QUESTIONNAIRE/
	)	VOIR DIRE
	)	OF ALL PARTIES
BAKER & MCKENZIE,	)	
MARTIN R. GREENSTEIN	)	[California Code of Civil
AND DOES 1–10,	)	Procedure § 222.5]
Defendants.	)	
	)	
	)	
_____	)	

JUROR NUMBER   PRINT NAME

DIRECTIONS

The integrity of our legal system depends upon the fairness and impartiality of jurors. This questionnaire has been prepared to assist the Court and the parties in determining whether or not you may have had personal experiences or knowledge about the issues to be decided by the jury. Acquaintance with any of the parties, the lawyers or potential witnesses should also be disclosed.

This questionnaire is part of the public record of a public trial. Please answer the questions honestly and with great care. Your full and complete answers are desired. Please note that there are no right or wrong answers to any question. In the event that the questions call for sensitive personal information that you do not wish to disclose, please indicate that in your response. You will be provided an opportunity to speak with the judge and the attorneys outside the presence of other jurors.

Please fill out this questionnaire completely in pen or ink. Since we need to make copies, *do not* write on the back of any page. If you need more room to answer any question, continue on the bottom or side of the page or on the last page (noting the question number). Please complete this questionnaire by yourself and do not consult with anyone else.

_____

JUDGE OF THE SUPERIOR COURT

PART I: BACKGROUND INFORMATION

PLEASE ANSWER THE FOLLOWING QUESTIONS ABOUT YOURSELF

1. Name

_____

2. Age

_____

3. Marital Status

PLEASE CHECK ALL THAT APPLY

(   ) Single
(   ) Married
(   ) Living with partner
(   ) Separated
(   ) Divorced
(   ) Widowed

4. Please check one   Male _____   Female _____

5. Place of residence

PLEASE LIST THE LOCATION OF YOUR CURRENT ADDRESS AND THE PART OF TOWN OF YOUR RESIDENCE AND HOW LONG YOU HAVE LIVED THERE.

CITY	PART OF TOWN	FROM	TO

6. Current employment status

(   ) Employed full-time
(   ) Employed part-time
(   ) Homemaker
(   ) Student
(   ) Unemployed—looking for work
(   ) Unemployed—not looking for work
(   ) Retired

7. If you are employed:

(a) Where do you work?

_____

(b) What is your occupation?

_____

(c) What is your job title?

_____

(d) How long have you had this job?

_____

(e) Do you supervise other employees?

( ) Yes   ( ) No

(f) If yes, how many employees do you supervise directly (_____)
and indirectly (_____)?

(g) Do you have the authority to hire or fire other employees?

( ) Yes   ( ) No

(h) Briefly describe your responsibilities at work.

_____

_____

_____

(i) Has anybody ever made a complaint about you as a supervisor?

( ) Yes   ( ) No

If yes, please describe.

_____

_____

_____

(j) Have you ever made a complaint to a supervisor?

( ) Yes   ( ) No

If yes, please describe.

_____

_____

_____

(k) Has anybody ever made a complaint within a company that you discriminated against a person on the job?

( ) Yes   ( ) No

If yes, please describe.

_____

_____

_____

(l) Have you ever made a complaint within a company that you or someone else had been discriminated against on the job?

( ) Yes   ( ) No
If yes, please describe.

_____

_____

_____

(m) Has anybody filed a lawsuit or a complaint with a government agency that you discriminated against a person on the job?

( ) Yes ( ) No

If yes, please describe.

_____

_____

_____

(n) Have you filed a lawsuit or a complaint with a government agency that you had been discriminated against on the job?

( ) Yes ( ) No

If yes, please describe.

_____

_____

_____

8. (a) Have you ever owned your own business?

( ) Yes ( ) No

If yes, how many employees did you have?

_____ 0 employees _____ 4–9 employees
_____ 1–3 employees _____ 10 or more employees

(b) Have you ever worked for someone else as an independent contractor?

( ) Yes ( ) No

If yes, please describe.

_____

_____

_____

(c) Have you ever been an officer or member of the Board of Directors of a corporation?

( ) Yes ( ) No

If yes, please describe.

_____

_____

_____

9. Have you ever been employed in any of the following occupations or has your work ever included any of the following responsibilities or have you ever received any training in any of these areas?

Human Resources/Personnel _____ Yes _____ No
Labor Relations _____ Yes _____ No

10. Please list any other jobs you have held during the past ten years that you can recall.

EMPLOYER	JOB TITLE	FROM	TO
_____	_____	_____	_____
_____	_____	_____	_____
_____	_____	_____	_____
_____	_____	_____	_____
_____	_____	_____	_____

11. Education
PLEASE CHECK THE HIGHEST GRADE YOU COMPLETED
  ( ) Grade school
  ( ) High school
  ( ) Vocational or technical school
  ( ) Junior college (two year)
  ( ) College (four year)
  ( ) Post-graduate or professional school

12. If you attended college, vocational or technical school, what was your:

(a) Major subject(s)?

_____

_____

(b) Name and location of school(s)?

_____

_____

13. (a) Please list and briefly describe any classes, correspondence courses, seminars or workshops you have taken since you left school.

_____

_____

(b) Have you ever had any training, advanced education, or employment in any aspect of finance, economics, accounting, or business administration?

( ) Yes   ( ) No

If yes, please describe.

_____

_____

_____

14. (a) Have you ever served in any branch of the U.S. military?

( ) Yes   ( ) No

(b) If yes, please list the branch of service and your highest rank.

_____

15. Are you a member of any trade or professional association, union, civic club, religious, or other organization?

( ) Yes   ( ) No

(a) If yes, please list all of the organizations to which you belong.

_____

_____

_____

(b) Please list any office you currently hold or have held in the past in these or other organizations.

ORGANIZATION	OFFICE HELD	FROM	TO
_____	_____	_____	____
_____	_____	_____	____
_____	_____	_____	____

16. (a) Do you belong to any private club, civic, professional, or fraternal organization that limits its membership on the basis of race, ethnic origin, sex, sexual orientation, national origin, or religion?

( ) Yes   ( ) No

(b) If yes, please list the organization(s).

_____

_____

17. Do you have children?

( ) Yes   ( ) No

18. If you have adult children, please list their names, ages, and occupation, if any:

NAME	AGE	OCCUPATION
_____	_____	_____
_____	_____	_____
_____	_____	_____
_____	_____	_____

19. If there are other adults living in your home other than your spouse, partner, or children, please list their occupations and employers.

OCCUPATION	EMPLOYER
_____	_____
_____	_____

20. If you have children living at home, will caring for them interfere with your ability to serve on this jury?

( ) Yes   ( ) No

21. (a) Do you have any health problems which could affect your ability to serve on this jury?

( ) Yes   ( ) No

(b) If yes, please explain.

_____

_____

22. (a) Have you or any members of your household ever had any health problems that were caused by stress?

    ( ) Yes   ( ) No

    (b) If yes, please explain.

    _____

    _____

23. (a) Have you ever filed a workers' compensation claim?

    ( ) Yes   ( ) No

    (b) If yes, please briefly describe the complaint.

    _____

    _____

    _____

24. (a) Have you or your spouse/partner ever been under stress because of problems at work?

    ( ) Yes   ( ) No

    (b) If yes, when did this problem(s) take place?

    _____

    _____

    _____

25. (a) Do you take any prescription medication of any kind?

    ( ) Yes   ( ) No

    (b) If yes, does the medication affect your mental alertness or cause any physical discomfort?

    ( ) Yes   ( ) No

26. (a) Do you have any religious or other beliefs that would make it difficult for you to sit in judgment on another person?

    ( ) Yes   ( ) No

    (b) If yes, please explain.

    _____

    _____

27. Please list your hobbies.

    _____

    _____

    _____

    _____

28. (a) Which television programs do you watch most often?

    _____

    (b) Which television talk shows, if any, do you watch?

    _____

    (c) Which magazines do you read?

    _____

(d) Do you read business news or business periodicals three or more times a week?

( ) Yes   ( ) No

PART II: YOUR SPOUSE OR PARTNER'S BACKGROUND

PLEASE ANSWER THE FOLLOWING QUESTIONS ABOUT YOUR SPOUSE OR PARTNER.

29. Name

_____

30. Current employment status

( ) Employed full-time
( ) Employed part-time
( ) Homemaker
( ) Student
( ) Unemployed—looking for work
( ) Unemployed—not looking for work
( ) Retired

31. If he or she is employed:

(a) Where does he or she work?

_____

(b) What is his or her occupation?

(c) What is his or her job title?

(d) How long has he or she had this job?

_____

(e) Does he or she supervise other employees?

( ) Yes   ( ) No

(f) Does he or she have the authority to hire or fire other employees?
( ) Yes   ( ) No

(g) Has anyone ever made a complaint about him or her as a supervisor?

( ) Yes   ( ) No

If yes, please describe.

_____
_____
_____

(h) Has your spouse or partner complained within the company that he or she has been discriminated against on the job?

( ) Yes   ( ) No

If yes, please describe.

_____
_____
_____

(i) Has your spouse or partner filed a lawsuit or a complaint with a government agency that he or she has been discriminated against that person on the job?

( ) Yes ( ) No

If yes, please describe.

_____
_____
_____

(j) Briefly describe his or her responsibilities at work.

_____
_____
_____

(k) Has anybody complained within the company that your spouse or partner discriminated against that person on the job?

( ) Yes ( ) No

If yes, please describe.

_____
_____
_____

(l) Has anybody filed a lawsuit or a complaint with a government agency that your spouse or partner discriminated against that person on the job?

( ) Yes ( ) No

If yes, please describe.

_____
_____
_____

32. Please list any other jobs he or she has held during the past ten years.

EMPLOYER	JOB TITLE	FROM	TO

33. Has your spouse or partner owned his or her own business?

( ) Yes ( ) No

If yes, how many employees did the business have?

_____

34. Has your spouse or partner been an officer or director of a corporation?

( ) Yes   ( ) No

If yes, please describe.

_____

_____

_____

35. Has your spouse or partner ever been self-employed or worked for some-one else as an independent contractor?

( ) Yes   ( ) No

(a) If yes, please briefly describe the nature of his or her work.

_____

_____

_____

36. Education

PLEASE CHECK THE HIGHEST GRADE YOUR SPOUSE OR PARTNER COMPLETED.

( ) Grade school
( ) High school
( ) Vocational or technical school
( ) Junior college (two year)
( ) College (four year)
( ) Post-graduate or professional school

37. If your spouse or partner attended college, vocational or technical school, what was his or her:

(a) Major subject(s)?

_____

(b) Name and location of school(s)?

_____

38. Please list and briefly describe any classes, correspondence courses, seminars or workshops your spouse or partner has taken relating to sexual harassment, employment law, or psychology.

_____

_____

_____

_____

39. (a) Has your spouse or partner ever served in any branch of the U.S. military?

( ) Yes   ( ) No

(b) If yes, please list the branch of service and his or her highest rank.

_____

40. (a) Is your spouse or partner a member of any trade or professional association, union, civic club, religious, or other organization?

( ) Yes   ( ) No

(b) If yes, please list all of the organizations to which he or she belongs.

_____

_____

_____

41. Does your spouse or partner belong to any private club, civic, professional, or fraternal organization that limits its membership on the basis of race, ethnic origin, sex, sexual orientation, national origin, or religion?

( ) Yes ( ) No

(a) If yes, please list the organization(s).

_____

_____

42. (a) Which magazines does your spouse or partner read?

_____

(b) Does your spouse or partner read business news or business periodicals three or more times a week?

( ) Yes ( ) No

43. (a) Has your spouse or partner ever been under stress because of problems at work?

( ) Yes ( ) No

(b) If yes, when did your spouse or partner experience problems like this?

_____

_____

_____

PART III: FAMILIARITY WITH JUDICIAL SYSTEM

44. (a) Have you ever served as a juror before?

( ) Yes ( ) No

(b) If yes, please list the court(s), the type of case(s), and the approximate date(s).

COURT (state/federal)	Criminal or Civil	Type of Case	Date
_____	_____	_____	____
_____	_____	_____	____

(c) Were you ever the foreperson?

( ) Yes ( ) No

(d) Have any of the juries on which you have served been "hung" (unable to reach a verdict)?

( ) Yes ( ) No

(e) Did you enjoy your previous experience(s) as a juror?

( ) Yes ( ) No

213

45. (a) Have you ever been to court before, other than for jury service?

     ( ) Yes   ( ) No

    (b) If yes, please describe the circumstances.

    _____

    _____

46. Have you ever testified in a trial or court proceeding?

     ( ) Yes   ( ) No

47. Have you ever had your deposition taken?

     ( ) Yes   ( ) No

48. (a) Have you or any member of your household or family, or any close friends, ever sued or been sued?

     ( ) Yes   ( ) No

    (b) If yes, how was the case resolved?

    _____

    _____

49. (a) Have you ever thought you might have a reason to file a lawsuit but decided not to?

     ( ) Yes   ( ) No

    (b) If yes, please describe the circumstances.

    _____

    _____

50. During trial, it may become necessary for the attorneys to approach the bench or discuss a point of law outside the hearing of the jury. Will it bother you that the law sometimes does not allow jurors to hear discussion of legal points?

     ( ) Yes   ( ) No

PART IV: MISCELLANEOUS

51. Which of the following is your main source of news?

    ( ) Television
    ( ) Radio
    ( ) Newspaper(s)
    ( ) Magazine(s)

52. Please rate how much you agree or disagree with each of the following statements.

    (a) Sexual harassment in the workplace is being blown way out of proportion.

        ( ) Strongly Agree
        ( ) Somewhat Agree
        ( ) Somewhat Disagree
        ( ) Strongly Disagree

(b) There are too many lawsuits today.

( ) Strongly Agree
( ) Somewhat Agree
( ) Somewhat Disagree
( ) Strongly Disagree

(c) Sexual harassment in the workplace is one of the most serious problems facing female employees today.

( ) Strongly Agree
( ) Somewhat Agree
( ) Somewhat Disagree
( ) Strongly Disagree

(d) Most women are sexually harassed in the workplace.

( ) Strongly Agree
( ) Somewhat Agree
( ) Somewhat Disagree
( ) Strongly Disagree

(e) Not enough is being done to eliminate sexual harassment in the workplace.

( ) Strongly Agree
( ) Somewhat Agree
( ) Somewhat Disagree
( ) Strongly Disagree

(f) Most individuals accused of sexual harassment at work probably did it.

( ) Strongly Agree
( ) Somewhat Agree
( ) Somewhat Disagree
( ) Strongly Disagree

(g) To what extent do you think attorneys are trustworthy or untrustworthy?

( ) Very Trustworthy
( ) Somewhat Trustworthy
( ) Somewhat Untrustworthy
( ) Very Untrustworthy

Why is that?

_____

_____

53. (a) Have you ever had any dealings with an attorney?

( ) Yes   ( ) No

(b) If yes, please explain.

_____

_____

54. Do you think lawyers feel that the rules others have to live by do not apply to them?

( ) Yes　　( ) No

55. What is your main complaint or annoyance about lawyers?

_____

_____

56. (a) How do you feel about the size of money awards given in trial today?

( ) Too large
( ) OK
( ) Too small

(b) Please explain.

_____

_____

57. Have you or anyone close to you ever worked for:

	YES	NO	Who was the worker?
(a) A lawyer or law firm?	____	____	_____
(b) A counselor, psychotherapist, psychologist or psychiatrist?	____	____	_____
(c) The court system?	____	____	_____

58. (a) Have you, or has anyone close to you, ever been falsely accused or written up by a supervisor at a place of employment?

( ) Yes　　( ) No

(b) If yes, what happened and how did you feel?

_____

_____

_____

59. Do you feel that lawyers are more likely than other employers to sexually harass their employees?

( ) Yes　　( ) No

60. Do you think there is more, less, or about the same amount of sexual harassment today as there was 10 years ago?

( ) More
( ) Less
( ) Same amount

61. (a) Have you ever read any books or magazine articles about sexual harassment?

( ) Yes　　( ) No

(b) If yes, please explain.

_____

_____

_____

62. Do you feel that employers nowadays have gotten the message about the seriousness of sexual harassment in the workplace?

( ) Yes   ( ) No

PART V: ABOUT THIS CASE

63. (a) In this case, the plaintiff (the person who filed the lawsuit) claims that she has been harassed on the basis of her sex while she worked for defendant. Do you have any preconceptions or feelings one way or the other about how this kind of situation should be decided?

( ) Yes   ( ) No

(b) If yes, please explain.

_____

_____

_____

64. (a) Have you heard, seen, or read anything about this case?

( ) Yes   ( ) No

(b) If yes, please explain.

_____

_____

_____

65. (a) Do you know anyone who may be involved in a situation like what you have heard so far about this case?

( ) Yes   ( ) No

(b) If yes, please explain.

_____

_____

_____

66. (a) Do you have a supervisor of the opposite sex?

( ) Yes   ( ) No

(b) If yes, how do you feel about that supervisor?

_____

_____

_____

(c) If yes, do you think that supervisor treats men and women equally?

_____

_____

67. (a) Are you familiar with the Anita Hill–Clarence Thomas hearing?

    ( ) Yes   ( ) No

   (b) If yes, have the Anita Hill–Clarence Thomas hearings changed your opinions or perceptions regarding allegations of sexual harassment in the workplace?

    ( ) Yes   ( ) No

68. (a) Are you familiar with Paula Jones's allegations against President Clinton?

    ( ) Yes   ( ) No

   (b) If yes, has Paula Jones's claim against President Clinton changed your opinions or perceptions regarding allegations of sexual harassment in the workplace?

    ( ) Yes   ( ) No

69. (a) Have you ever been involved in a situation at work involving sexual harassment?

    ( ) Yes   ( ) No

   (b) If yes, please explain in general terms.

   _____

   _____

   _____

70. (a) Have you ever felt that you or someone you worked with had been sexually harassed at work?

    ( ) Yes   ( ) No

   (b) If yes, please explain in general terms.

   _____

   _____

   _____

71. (a) Have you ever had to quit a job because you felt you were being treated unfairly?

    ( ) Yes   ( ) No

   (b) If yes, please describe generally.

   _____

   _____

72. Have you, your spouse/partner, close friend and/or member of your family/household ever been employed as a legal secretary or paralegal?

    ( ) Yes   ( ) No

73. (a) Have you, your spouse/partner, close friend and/or member of your family/household ever had any training on the handling of sexual harassment in the workplace?

    ( ) Yes   ( ) No

(b) If yes, please describe what training you received.

_____

_____

74. (a) Do you feel that most large businesses discriminate against women?

( ) Yes   ( ) No

(b) If yes, please explain.

_____

_____

_____

_____

75. If you work for a business, has your employer implemented a policy against sexual harassment?

( ) Yes   ( ) No

76. Has your employer implemented an internal complaint procedure to investigate and respond to sexual harassment complaints?

( ) Yes   ( ) No   ( ) Does not apply

77. Have you ever been accused of sexual harassment?

( ) Yes   ( ) No

78. Have you, your spouse, partner, close friend, or any member of your family/household ever made a complaint of sexual harassment at work?

( ) Yes   ( ) No

79. Have you or has any one close to you, i.e., spouse, partner, significant other, sibling, parent, child, ever been sexually harassed, discriminated against, sexually assaulted, or victim of a sex crime by a man?

( ) Yes   ( ) No

80. (a) Given the nature of this case, is there anything in your background and experience that would make it difficult for you to be fair and impartial?

( ) Yes   ( ) No

(b) If yes, please explain.

_____

81. Do you feel people should be awarded money for psychological pain?

( ) Yes   ( ) No

82. Do you feel that too much money is awarded for claims of emotional distress?

( ) Yes   ( ) No

83. (a) Do you believe there is any limit of money that should be awarded for emotional distress?

( ) Yes   ( ) No

(b) If yes, please explain.

_____

_____

84. Do you know what punitive damages are?

( ) Yes   ( ) No

85. (a) Is there any reason why you could not award punitive damages, that is, damages to punish the defendant or deter the defendant from engaging in this behavior again?

( ) Yes   ( ) No

(b) If yes, please explain.

_____

_____

_____

86. When you read about large punitive damages, do you feel that the juries awarded too much in punitive damages?

( ) Yes   ( ) No

87. (a) Are there any matters that you would like to bring to the attention of the judge and lawyers that you do not want to discuss in the presence of other potential jurors?

( ) Yes   ( ) No

(b) If yes, please describe.

_____

_____

_____

88. (a) Will you agree to obey the judge if you are ordered not to read, view, or discuss any news media coverage of this case?

( ) Yes   ( ) No

(b) If no, please explain.

_____

_____

_____

_____

_____

I declare under penalty of perjury that all of my answers to the questions in this questionnaire and the attached explanation sheets are true to the best of my knowledge.

Executed at _____ (city), _____ (state), this _____ day of _____, 199___.

_____

(SIGN YOUR FULL NAME)

_____

(PRINT YOUR FULL NAME)

EXPLANATION SHEET

Please use this space to complete your answers to any of the questions or to provide any additional information that you think may be important to the judge or the attorneys in this selection process. Please feel free to add additional sheets if necessary.

Thank you very much for your cooperation.

_____

_____

_____

_____

_____

_____

_____

_____

_____

_____

_____

_____

_____

_____

_____

_____

B. Jury Instructions [Partial]—
Weeks v. Baker & McKenzie, et al.

SUPERIOR COURT OF THE STATE OF CALIFORNIA
IN AND FOR THE COUNTY OF SAN FRANCISCO

RENA WEEKS,	)	Case No. 943 043
	)	
Plaintiff,	)	
	)	
v.	)	JURY INSTRUCTIONS
	)	
BAKER & MCKENZIE, MARTIN R.	)	
GREENSTEIN AND DOES 1–10,	)	[PARTIAL]
	)	
Defendants.	)	
	)	
	)	
	)	

The plaintiff in this case is Rena Weeks. The defendants are Martin R. Greenstein and Baker and McKenzie. Plaintiff makes two claims in this case. The first claim is that defendants harassed her at work. I will now instruct you as to this first claim.

It is an unlawful employment practice for an employer or any person, because of sex, to harass an employee.

To establish a claim of environmental sexual harassment against defendants, plaintiff must prove, by a preponderance of the evidence, each of the following elements:

1. That plaintiff was subject to unwelcome sexual harassment;
2. That the harassment complained of was based upon sex;
3. That the harassment complained of was sufficiently severe or pervasive so as to alter the conditions of employment and create a hostile or abusive working environment; and
4. That plaintiff suffered injury, damage, or harm which was caused by the sexual harassment.

"Preponderance of the evidence" means evidence that has more convincing force than that opposed to it. If the evidence is so evenly balanced that you are unable to say that the evidence on either side of an issue preponderates, your finding on that issue must be against the party who had the burden of proving it.

You should consider all of the evidence bearing upon every issue regardless of who produced it.

Sexual harassment is either unwelcome sexual advances or other unwelcome verbal or physical conduct of a sexual nature. In order to constitute harassment, the conduct must be unwelcome in the sense that the employee did not solicit or invite it and the employee regarded the conduct as undesirable

223

or offensive. In this connection, you may consider, among other factors, plaintiff's speech and conduct and Mr. Greenstein's speech and conduct.

Plaintiff must prove by a preponderance of the evidence that gender was a substantial factor in the claimed harassment and that if the plaintiff had been a man, she would not have been treated in the same manner.

To recover for sexual harassment, plaintiff must prove by a preponderance of the evidence that the unwelcome sexual advances or other unwelcome sexual conduct was either sufficiently severe or sufficiently pervasive to alter the conditions of her employment and to create an objectively hostile or abusive work environment. In other words, plaintiff must prove by a preponderance of the evidence that the environment in issue was such that a reasonable person would find it to be hostile or abusive and further that plaintiff herself subjectively perceived it to be hostile or abusive.

As respects the issue whether unwelcome sexual advances or conduct were "sufficiently severe," you are to consider the seriousness and intensity of the advances or conduct. As respects the issue whether unwelcome sexual advances or conduct were "sufficiently pervasive," plaintiff must show a concerted pattern of harassment of a repeated, routine, or generalized nature. In other words, on the issue of pervasiveness, it is not enough for plaintiff to prove merely the existence of acts of harassment which were occasional, isolated, sporadic, or trivial.

In making the determination as to whether the environment was hostile or abusive, you should look to the totality of the circumstances. Factors to consider include:

1. The nature of the sexual advances or conduct; that is, whether they were verbal or physical;
2. The frequency and severity of the sexual advances or conduct;
3. The context in which the sexual advances or conduct occurred;
4. Whether the sexual advances or conduct unreasonably interfered with an employee's work performance.

On the subject of damages, I have told you that plaintiff must prove by a preponderance of the evidence that she suffered injury, damage, or harm which was caused by sexual harassment. The law defines "cause" in its own particular way. A cause of injury, damage or harm is something that is a substantial factor in bringing about an injury, damage, or harm.

All parties agree that plaintiff chose to leave Baker and McKenzie, and there is no claim that she was terminated or constructively terminated from her employment at that firm. The term "constructive termination" means actions and conditions so intolerable or aggravated at the time of the employee's resignation that a reasonable person in the employee's position would have resigned. In short, no damages may be awarded due to the fact that plaintiff terminated her employment with Baker and McKenzie.

Plaintiff claims to have suffered injury, damage, or harm in one respect. Her claim is that she suffered that kind and degree of emotional distress which is usually associated with sexual harassment, and she seeks damages for that claimed emotional distress.

Plaintiff does not make any of the following claims in this lawsuit:

1. That she suffered any emotional distress beyond that usually associated with sexual harassment;
2. That she suffered any emotional distress after October of 1993; or
3. That she has suffered or will suffer any loss of wages or earnings or other economic injury.

You may not award damages for any of the matters not claimed by plaintiff in this lawsuit.

I have instructed you that there is no claim in this case that plaintiff lost any wages or earnings at any time. In this regard, you are further instructed that a plaintiff who makes a claim of sexual harassment need not prove loss of tangible job benefits. That is not a necessary element of such a claim.

The law provides that an employer is liable for the actual injury, damage, or harm which is caused by an employee who also is a supervisor. Martin R. Greenstein was an employee of Baker and McKenzie, and also was a supervisor. Therefore, if you should find that plaintiff suffered actual injury, damage, or harm caused by unlawful sexual harassment on the part of Mr. Greenstein, then your verdict must be against both Mr. Greenstein and Baker and McKenzie for the amount of the damages caused thereby.

If you find that plaintiff is entitled to a verdict in her favor, then you must award plaintiff damages in an amount that will reasonably compensate plaintiff for any emotional distress of the degree and kind claimed by her, provided that you find that such emotional distress was suffered by her and caused by the act or omission upon which you base your findings of liability. The amount of such award shall include reasonable compensation for such pain, discomfort, fear, anxiety, and other mental and emotional distress. No definite standard is prescribed by law by which to fix reasonable compensation for pain and suffering. Nor is the opinion of any witness required as to the amount of such reasonable compensation. In making an award for pain and suffering, you shall exercise your authority with calm and reasonable judgment and the damages you fix shall be just and reasonable in the light of the evidence.

A person who has a condition or disability at the time of an injury is not entitled to recover damages therefor. However, a plaintiff is entitled to recover damages for any aggravation of such preexisting condition or disability caused by the injury.

This is true even if a condition or disability made plaintiff more susceptible to the possibility of ill effects than a normally healthy person would have been, and even if a normally healthy person probably would not have suffered any substantial injury.

Where a preexisting condition or disability is so aggravated, the damages as to such condition or disability are limited to the additional injury caused by the aggravation.

It is the duty of a person who has been injured to use reasonable diligence in caring for her injuries and reasonable means to prevent their aggravation and to accomplish healing.

When one does not use reasonable diligence to care for her injuries, and they are aggravated as a result of such failure, the liability, if any, of another whose act or omission was a cause of the original injury, must be limited to the amount of damage that would have been suffered if the injured person herself had exercised the diligence required of her.

No matter whether you decide in favor of the plaintiff or the defendants, you may not make an award of attorney's fees for any party.

I previously told you that plaintiff makes two claims in this case. Now I turn to the second claim. It is a claim against defendant Baker and McKenzie alone, and the claim is that Baker and McKenzie failed to take all reasonable steps to prevent the alleged harassment of plaintiff by Mr. Greenstein from occurring. In order to recover on this claim, plaintiff must prove by a preponderance of the evidence each of the following elements:

1. That plaintiff was subject to sexual harassment as defined by the instructions which I previously gave you with respect to plaintiff's first claim in this case;
2. That Baker and McKenzie failed to take all reasonable steps to prevent the harassment of plaintiff by Martin R. Greenstein; and
3. That plaintiff suffered injury, damage or harm which was caused by Baker and McKenzie's failure to take all reasonable steps to prevent the harassment.

It is an unlawful employment practice for an employer to fail to take all reasonable steps necessary to prevent harassment from occurring. When an employer has received any complaint, notice, or knowledge of facts such as to place the employer on notice of any sexual harassment by any employee, the employer has a duty to take all reasonable steps necessary to end such sexual harassment and to prevent any further occurrence.

If you find that Mr. Greenstein sexually harassed women before plaintiff became employed at Baker and McKenzie and that Baker and McKenzie had knowledge of such acts, you may consider whether the conduct was sufficiently severe or pervasive so as to warrant his termination or other action by Baker and McKenzie to put a stop to such conduct. If you find that the conduct was sufficiently severe or pervasive to warrant such action by Baker and McKenzie, you may consider the evidence in question in connection with plaintiff's second claim in the case, that is, the claim against Baker and McKenzie alone. However, if you find that the conduct was not sufficiently severe or pervasive to warrant such action by Baker and McKenzie, then you may not consider the evidence of prior acts directed against other women in connection with plaintiff's second claim.

If you find that plaintiff is entitled to damages, you must also consider the following: Even though plaintiff is claiming damages from two defendants, she may only have one recovery, that is, she may not recover duplicate damages. Therefore, if you find that she is entitled to damages, you may not double the amount because there are two defendants.

The amount of damages claimed, either by the written pleadings or in the argument of counsel, must not be considered by you as evidence of reasonable compensation.

With respect to plaintiff's claims against defendant Baker and McKenzie, if you find that plaintiff suffered actual injury, harm, or damage caused by sexual harassment, you must decide whether by clear and convincing evidence you find that there was oppression or malice by Baker and McKenzie in the conduct on which you base your finding of liability on the part of the law firm. You may find Baker and McKenzie guilty of such oppression or malice if, but only if, you find by clear and convincing evidence that:

Baker and McKenzie had advance knowledge of the unfitness of Mr. Greenstein and with a conscious disregard of the rights or safety of others continued to employ him, or

Baker and McKenzie authorized or ratified the conduct of Mr. Greenstein which is found to be oppression or malice.

The advance knowledge and conscious disregard, authorization, ratification, or act of oppression or malice must be on the part of a managing agent of Baker and McKenzie. A "managing agent" is a person who has sufficient discretion in the firm to make decisions that will ultimately determine policy.

C. Special Verdict—*Weeks v. Baker & McKenzie, et al.*

SUPERIOR COURT OF THE STATE OF CALIFORNIA
IN AND FOR THE COUNTY OF SAN FRANCISCO
DEPARTMENT NO. 3

RENA WEEKS,	)	Case No. 943 043
	)	
Plaintiff,	)	
	)	
v.	)	SPECIAL VERDICT
	)	
BAKER & MCKENZIE, MARTIN R.	)	
GREENSTEIN AND DOES 1–10,	)	
	)	
Defendants.	)	
	)	
	)	
	)	

We, the jury, in the above-entitled action find the following Special Verdict on the following questions submitted to us:

QUESTION NO. 1:

Did plaintiff Rena Weeks prove by a preponderance of the evidence that she was sexually harassed by defendant Martin R. Greenstein?

ANSWER: Yes _____   No _____

If you answered Question No. 1 "No," skip the remaining questions, and date, sign, and return this Verdict. If you answered Question No. 1 "Yes," then answer Question No. 2.

QUESTION NO. 2:

Did the sexual harassment cause injury, damage or harm to plaintiff Rena Weeks?

ANSWER: Yes _____   No _____

If you answered Question No. 2 "No," skip the remaining questions, and date, sign, and return this Verdict. If you answered Question No. 2 "Yes," then answer Question No. 3.

QUESTION NO. 3:

Did defendant Baker & McKenzie fail to take all reasonable steps to prevent the sexual harassment of plaintiff from occurring?

ANSWER: Yes _____   No _____

If you answered Question No. 3 either "Yes" or "No," please answer Question No. 4.

QUESTION NO. 4:

What amount do you award to plaintiff Rena Weeks for emotional distress caused by the sexual harassment?

ANSWER: $_____

After you have answered Question No. 4, please answer Question No. 5.

QUESTION NO. 5:

Has plaintiff Rena Weeks proved by clear and convincing evidence that defendant Martin R. Greenstein was guilty of oppression or malice in his conduct upon which you base your finding of sexual harassment?

ANSWER: Yes _____   No _____

If you answered Question No. 5 either "Yes" or "No," please answer Question No. 6.

QUESTION NO. 6:

Has plaintiff Rena Weeks proved by clear and convincing evidence that defendant Baker & McKenzie either (a) had advance knowledge of the unfitness of defendant Martin R. Greenstein and with a conscious disregard of the rights or safety of others continued to employ him, or (b) ratified the conduct of Mr. Greenstein which is found to be oppression or malice?

ANSWER: Yes _____   No _____

If you answered Question No. 6 either "Yes" or "No," please date, sign and return this Verdict.

Dated: _____

_____
FOREPERSON

SUPERIOR COURT OF THE STATE OF CALIFORNIA
IN AND FOR THE COUNTY OF SAN FRANCISCO
DEPARTMENT NO. 3

RENA WEEKS,	)	Case No. 943 043
	)	
Plaintiff,	)	
	)	
v.	)	SPECIAL VERDICT PHASE II
	)	
BAKER & MCKENZIE, MARTIN R.	)	
GREENSTEIN AND DOES 1–10,	)	
	)	
Defendants.	)	
	)	
	)	
	)	

WE, the jury in the above-entitled action, find the following special verdict on the questions submitted to us:

Write the answer "yes" or "no" after the name of each defendant.

Question No. 1: Shall punitive damages be assessed against

Answer: Yes or No

Defendant Martin R. Greenstein   _____
Defendant Baker & McKenzie   _____

If your answer is "no" for both defendants, have your foreperson sign and date this special verdict. If your answer is "yes" for either defendant or both defendants, answer the next question for that defendant or those defendants.

Question No. 2: We assess punitive damages against the following named defendant(s) as follows:

                                                      Amount

Defendant Martin R. Greenstein $_____
Defendant Baker & McKenzie $_____

Dated:_____

_____
                              FOREPERSON

D. Juror Profile Sheet

Juror # _____

Name _____
M F Race _____ Age _____
Married _____ Single _____
Occup. _____
Employer _____
Salaried _____ Hourly _____
Spouse Occup. _____
Education _____
Address _____
Prior Service _____
Verdict?   Yes   No
Filed a lawsuit? Yes   No
Acceptable   Yes   No

Juror # _____

Name _____
M F Race _____ Age _____
Married _____ Single _____
Occup. _____
Employer _____
Salaried _____ Hourly _____
Spouse Occup. _____
Education _____
Address _____
Prior Service _____
Verdict?   Yes   No
Filed a lawsuit? Yes   No
Acceptable   Yes   No

Juror # _____

Name _____
M F Race _____ Age _____
Married _____ Single _____
Occup. _____
Employer _____
Salaried _____ Hourly _____
Spouse Occup. _____
Education _____
Address _____
Prior Service _____
Verdict?   Yes   No
Filed a lawsuit? Yes   No
Acceptable   Yes   No

Juror # _____

Name _____
M F Race _____ Age _____
Married _____ Single _____
Occup. _____
Employer _____
Salaried _____ Hourly _____
Spouse Occup. _____
Education _____
Address _____
Prior Service _____
Verdict?   Yes   No
Filed a lawsuit? Yes   No
Acceptable   Yes   No

Juror # _____

Name _____
M F Race _____ Age _____
Married _____ Single _____
Occup. _____
Employer _____
Salaried _____ Hourly _____
Spouse Occup. _____
Education _____
Address _____
Prior Service _____
Verdict?   Yes   No
Filed a lawsuit? Yes   No
Acceptable   Yes   No

Juror # _____

Name _____
M F Race _____ Age _____
Married _____ Single _____
Occup. _____
Employer _____
Salaried _____ Hourly _____
Spouse Occup. _____
Education _____
Address _____
Prior Service _____
Verdict?   Yes   No
Filed a lawsuit? Yes   No
Acceptable   Yes   No

Notes

1. Jeremy W. Barber, *The Jury Is Still Out: The Role of Jury Science in the Modern Courtroom*, 31 AM. CRIM. L. REV. 1225 (1994).

2. David E. Beckwith & Theresa L. Zagnoll, *The Use of Trial Consultants*, 4 FED. LITIG. GUIDE 289, Oct. 1992.

3. Jeremy W. Barber, *The Jury Is Still Out: The Role of Jury Science in the Modern Courtroom*, 31 AM. CRIM. L. REV. 1225 (Summer 1994).

4. *Id.* at 1244.

5. *Id.* at 1241.

6. *Id.* at 1240.

7. Douglas A. Green & Robert W. Maxwell, *Jury Research: Reading the Road Map of Jury Thinking*, 16 AM. J. TRIAL ADVOC. 795 (1993); Gedes v. United States, 425 U.S. 80, 90 n.3 (1976) (use of witness consultant subject to cross-examination).

8. Green & Maxwell, *supra* note 7, at 815.

9. *See* Swain v. Alabama, 360 U.S. 202 (1965).

10. *Id.* at 219.

11. *Batson*, 90 L. Ed. 2d at 84.

12. *See* Powers v. Ohio, 499 U.S. 400 (1991) (holding that racially motivated use of peremptory challenges by a prosecutor was improper even if the defendant and the challenged juror did not share the same race); Edmonson v. Leesville Concrete Co., 500 U.S. 614, 111 S. Ct. 2077, 114 L. Ed. 2d 660 (1991) (*Batson* rationale extended to civil suits involving private parties by holding that a private litigant in a civil case who uses peremptory challenges to exclude prospective jurors because of race violates the prospective juror's rights to equal protection); Hernandez v. New York, 500 U.S. 352, 11 S. Ct. 1859, 114 L. Ed. 2d 395, 406, 409 (1991) (holding that a peremptory challenge is *not* discriminatory simply because it might have a disproportionate impact upon a racial group—intentional or purposeful discrimination, which will "largely turn on [an] evaluation of credibility" with respect to the explanation offered by counsel, is necessary for a successful *Batson* challenge); J.E.B. v. State *ex rel.* T.B., 511 U.S. 127, 114 S. Ct. 1419, 128 L. Ed. 2d 89 (1994) (upholding a father's challenge to the state's use of peremptory challenges to eliminate men from juries in paternity actions, thus prohibiting gender-based peremptory challenges).

13. *Batson*, 90 L. Ed. 2d at 87–88.

14. *Id.* at 87.

15. *Id.* at 88.

16. *Hernandez*, 114 L. Ed. 2d at 404.

17. *Id.*, 90 L. Ed. 2d at 87.

18. *Id.* at 87–88.

19. *Id.* at 680.

20. *See* Doe v. Village of Downers Grove, 834 F. Supp. 244 (N.D. Ill. 1992) (holding that in a civil rights action the failure to offer a race-neutral explanation in conjunction with a peremptory challenge of a black juror is grounds for denying the challenge).

21. Jackson v. City of Little Rock, 26 F.3d 88 (8th Cir. 1994); Dias v. Sky Chefs, Inc., 14 F.3d 1313, 1316 (8th Cir. 1994) (use of a peremptory challenge to exclude a juror on the basis of race violates the Equal Protection Clause); J.E.B. v. State *ex rel.* T.B., 114 S. Ct. 1419, at 1427 (suggesting that the same rule would appear to apply with respect to the exclusion of women from a jury in a sex harassment case).

22. *See* Dias v. Sky Chefs, Inc., 948 F.2d 534 (9th Cir. 1991) (challenge to preemptory exclusion of three males after adverse verdict in wrongful discharge and intentional infliction of emotional distress case in the context of alleged sexual harassment untimely and deemed waived; court notes that *Batson* objections must occur as soon as possible, preferably before the jury is sworn); Arch v. Schnur, 824 F. Supp. 1042, 1044 (S.D. Fla. 1993) (in nonemployment civil rights case, court denies preemptory challenge where defense counsel was provided with thirty minutes to supplement any voir dire questions posed by the court but failed to ask any questions of the black juror that the lawyer subsequently challenged, and further failed to provide a race-neutral reason for challenging her other than stating that he simply preferred other jurors who he felt would

be better equipped to understand the complexities of the case); Jackson v. City of Little Rock, 26 F.3d 88 (8th Cir. 1994) (upholding challenge to preemptory exclusion by defendants of prospective black juror in Title VII case where defendants provided satisfactory race-neutral explanation for exclusion); Doss v. Frontenac, 14 F.3d 1313 (8th Cir. 1994) (court of appeals sustains preemptory challenge even where prior challenge that resulted in mistrial had been rejected by court under *Batson*, rejecting argument that because the employer had improperly exercised one preemptory challenge the subsequent ones should have been viewed as part of a "pattern" of strikes that gave rise to an inference of purposeful discrimination).

23. *Doss*, 14 F.3d at 1316–17; *see also* Reynolds v. Benefield, 931 F.2d 506, 512 (8th Cir. 1989) (holding that a proffered race-neutral reason is pretextual if the challenger fails to strike potential jurors who have the same traits or qualities as the stricken jurors).

24. See 9A Charles A. Wright & Arthur R. Miller, FEDERAL PRACTICE AND PROCEDURE § 2505 (2nd ed. 1995).

25. *E.g.*, Edwards v. Sears Roebuck & Co., 512 F.2d 276 (5th Cir. 1975).

26. *E.g.*, Hibma v. Odegaard, 769 F.2d 1147 (7th Cir. 1985).

27. *See* Menue v. Celotex Corp., 861 F.2d 1453 (10th Cir. 1988); Stewart & Stevenson Servs. Inc. v. Pickard, 749 F.2d 635 (11th Cir. 1984).

28. *E.g.*, Wilks v. Reyes, 5 F.3d 412 (9th Cir. 1993).

29. *E.g.*, Waggoner v. Mosti, 792 F.2d 595 (6th Cir. 1986).

CHAPTER 10

The Trial

DOUGLAS DEXTER*
CHRISTINE MASTERS†
VICTORIA D. STRATMAN‡

* O'Melveny & Myers; San Francisco, California.

† Masters & Ribakoff; Santa Monica, California.

‡ California Institute of Technology; Pasadena, California.

I. Introduction

Trial should be the culmination of all the work and theorizing of counsel while the case developed through discovery. But too often trial counsel learns the case the week before opening argument or while calling the first witnesses. This wastes the time of the judge, jury, opposing counsel, and witnesses and stresses an already overburdened judicial system.

Trial is not the time to try theories. The lawyer must know his or her case and have supported theories of why the client should prevail. Success at trial cannot occur without early evaluation of the case and adequate discovery. Mere trial technique alone in never enough.

Try the entire case with the opening and closing statements in mind. Maintain a master outline incorporating factual and legal developments, which your opening statement will sketch. The master outline will assure themes consistent with the evidence you have developed and will present at trial.

The importance of the advocate's performance at trial, however, should not be underestimated. The lawyer's preparation and skill *can* be the difference between winning and losing. Jurors' perception of the case can be tainted by a lawyer who is unprepared or obnoxious. And critical evidence can be ignored or misunderstood unless the advocate presents it effectively.

This chapter highlights issues that every advocate should consider going into a trial. But since each case, each party, each judge and each lawyer is different, there are no hard and fast rules that apply in every case. For example, although it is against the rules to argue in opening statement, many trial lawyers frequently do so. Thorough and thoughtful preparation tailored to fit the facts and circumstances of each individual case is the key to winning at trial.

II. Preliminary Matters

Your client should be present throughout the trial. In the case of a plaintiff, the plaintiff must be there. In addition, trial counsel should consider if there are family members who should be present in the courtroom, keeping in mind that their presence could lead to a subpoena even if they were not previously identified as witnesses.

In the case of a corporate defendant, a representative should be present at counsel table throughout the trial. Selection of an appropriate client representative can be an important strategic decision. The client representative will be the first person the jury sees from the company, and he or she will hear all of the testimony and assist in the conduct of the trial. Thus, the defense may wish to avoid selecting an individual with no connection to the events simply because he is personable. Defense counsel may find it preferable to look for a representative connected to the case who will personify the corporation in a favorable way and be able to actively assist in the defense. Remember that the corporate representative's continuous presence and apparent relationship with trial counsel will disproportionately emphasize the representative's testimony.

Whether plaintiff or corporate representative, the client should dress plainly and remain impassive, but appear engaged in the trial effort. Notes and conferences with your client in moderation will tell the jury that you believe your client and that your presentation is based upon what your client believes really happened.

III. Opening Statements

Opening statement is the lawyer's opportunity to draw a road map to the desired verdict. If the road map is credible, memorable, and clear, the jury will understand the significance of each witness examination or exhibit. If not, the jury will lose the route on which you are attempting to lead them and follow your opponent's route.

In order to focus the jury on your road map, counsel must be conscious of the primary goals in an opening statement. First, you present yourself as sincere, forthright, and knowledgeable, while establishing your themes of the case. Second, you explain how each witness and exhibit fits into the overall trial structure to support your themes.

Going into trial, you should be able to describe your client's view of the case in one or two sentences—your primary themes. By the end of your opening statement, the jury should remember those sentences and be primed to appreciate how the evidence will support them.

The importance of the opening statement cannot be overemphasized. Although a spectacular opening may not guarantee victory, a poor opening may guarantee defeat because the jury will reject your argument and evidence. Studies suggest that jurors form their opinions about a case during or immediately after opening statement and that 80 percent do not sway from their initial opinion.[1] As a result, the plaintiff obtains a distinct advantage in setting the stage first. The defendant must have a strategy for recapturing juror open-mindedness despite the force of plaintiff's opening.

A. Presentation Style

Establishing credibility in an opening statement as a teacher, rather than a preacher, will encourage the jury to look to you throughout the trial as a reliable information source. Balancing the appearance of fairness toward both parties with your role as an advocate is a key to success in this area. Rather than referring to "plaintiff's case" or "defendant's case," create a perception that you are simply telling a credible story—thereby enhancing the jury's moral comfort in accepting your position.

Demonstrate your intimate familiarity with the facts (having "lived with the case"). Your familiarity confers confidence in your client's position. Reliance upon notes will create the opposite impression, as well as reduce critical eye contact with the jury. For defendants, notes also reduce the sense of spontaneity and flexibility in responding to plaintiff's opening. If the jury believes that you speak from the heart, they will care little whether you stumble over a few words or pause a few moments to find your place. Both jurors and lawyers should remember that trial is about these facts, not about lawyers' egos.

In fact, speaking deliberately and with pauses, even in midsentence, will allow jurors to absorb and understand. Rapidly reciting a prepared opening out of nervousness or concern for the jury boredom will undermine your credibility and impact. Jurors will lose the presentation thread if not allowed time to absorb the new information before counsel further builds on it.

Tone and volume variations, used in moderation, also create emphasis. Counsel should allow voice inflections to tell part of the story. Emotion creates great effect, if not overdone. On the other hand, jurors may stop listening to an advocate who expresses indignation or incredulousness without strong support.

Credibility and confidence will flow more naturally if your speaking style is consistent with your personality, rather than imitating opposing counsel or another great advocate. Content and sincerity should be emphasized over big words, flamboyance, or entertainment.

The court may place limitations on where lawyers may stand during opening and closing and require counsel both to use and remain at the lectern. If possible, the barrier of a lectern should be avoided. If not, you might center the lectern approximately six to eight feet from the jury box. While regular pacing is an undesirable distraction, break monotony with occasional movement for emphasis or reference to demonstrative evidence. In some cases, use the courtroom itself to demonstrate the location of various persons or objects.

B. Persuasive Content

Lawyers differ on the amount of detail they reveal in opening, and different cases call for different strategies. A detailed opening will better tune the jury into the purpose behind otherwise fragmented or weak testimony. Your opening may also distract your opponent into countering your themes rather than presenting his own themes. Yet, overstating the evidence during opening will severely damage your credibility. A favorable evidentiary surprise is better than an argued disappointment, which a diligent opponent will certainly highlight in closing. For this reason, take careful notes of all "promises" made by your opponent during opening. Better still, obtain a transcript of your opponent's opening, for possible use during closing.

Start your opening with a concise statement of your theme. Use what advertisers call a "hook." Catch the jury's attention and implant your theme. Base your hook upon your themes, rather than vice versa. Repeat the hook throughout your opening and once more at the end.

The prohibition against argument in opening statement clearly precludes pleas for sympathy or justice. Instead, organize and describe the facts without argument to lead the jury to a favorable conclusion. Moreover, jurors will have more conviction in conclusions they feel they have reached themselves. You probably have not yet earned sufficient credibility to effectively persuade and emotionally move the jury to the ultimate morality of your position.

Remember, however, that a bland and plodding recital of the facts will not capture your jurors' interest or memory. Be a storyteller; use graphic, descriptive, and favorable language rather than dry recitations of the facts. For example, plaintiff's counsel might refer to plaintiff's employment history as a "career of devotion to [defendant.]"

Another effective storytelling technique is to speak from a particular witness's perspective. For example, plaintiff might caricature the supervisor as arbitrary or vindictive. Defendant could portray plaintiff as forcing the supervisor to make tough decisions.

You may establish suspense early in the presentation through innuendo or rhetorical question. For example, suggest that you will later reveal an opponent's motive for otherwise inexplicable misconduct. If you do this, be sure that you follow up on your suggestion or promise.

Touch upon weak spots and awkward issues your opponent will raise. If you are at trial, some weaknesses probably exist. Acknowledge them and enhance your credibility as the "trustworthy teacher." Avoiding problems will undermine that credibility and leave a gaping hole in your theory by the end of the trial. Consider explaining problems in terms of benign human fallacies—such as failing to provide progressive discipline out of a natural reluctance to be critical or failing to report sexual harassment out of fear of being fired or of not being believed.

Preview critical cross-examination so that the jury understands its purpose and significance. Although counsel may refer to anticipated impeachment of opposing witnesses, disparaging witnesses or offering personal opinions on witness credibility is inappropriate argument in opening statement.[2]

Counsel should familiarize the jury with relevant employment law jargon such as "good cause," "notice," or "at-will" without explicitly discussing legal issues. For example, explain that the court will later instruct the jury with respect to certain critical issues, such as the significance of an "at-will" clause on a signed application.

Be sensitive to varying views on the controversial subjects that surround employment cases, such as sexual overtures, racial remarks, and what constitutes both workplace misconduct and appropriate progressive discipline. In defining these terms, many jurors will draw on their own experiences, including policies and practices of their own employers as well as those of the defendant. Remember what you learned about your jurors in voir dire.

You may wish to explain the significance of any anticipated expert testimony. Consider whether your detailed explanation might clarify an unavoidably technical recitation by your expert. You might also warn jurors about other anticipated special circumstances such as witnesses out of order, depositions to be read into the record, and interpreters.

Remember the individuals who constitute your jury. If you anticipate that a particular juror's special knowledge will be helpful, glance at that juror when referring to the subject issue. On the other hand, if a particular juror worries you, consider how to address that juror's concerns in opening or closing. But note that mentioning a juror's name after voir dire is misconduct.[3]

C. Visual Aids

Before appearing for opening statement, counsel should check local rules and the judge's preferences regarding the use of visual aids in opening statement. Courts may or may not require disclosure of such aids before opening. When in doubt, however, obtain court approval or your opponent's stipulation rather than risking interruption and admonishment, or possibly mistrial.

Where permitted, visual aids are invaluable during opening statements. Judicious use of enlarged offer letters, performance evaluations, or written warnings can publish and emphasize those critical documents early. Demonstrative exhibits such as time lines, maps, and calculations may also be helpful to the jury. Although some defense counsel worry that "high-tech" visual aids suggest superior financial resources, poster board enlargements or overhead projectors should suffice in most cases. On the other hand, prepared graphics and enlargements are a relatively inexpensive investment for plaintiff's counsel.

D. Timing

The party bearing the ultimate burden of proof normally opens first. Federal courts have discretion to establish the order of opening statements.[4] Thus, plaintiff usually speaks first, unless affirmative defenses are the only liability issues. While primacy has its advantages, defendant should appreciate the advantages of speaking second. Defendant can establish credibility by filling the gaps left by plaintiff's opening. More importantly, defendant presents its position and responds to plaintiff's opening without plaintiff directly addressing the jury again until closing arguments.

Although defendant may delay opening statement until after plaintiff's case in chief, this is rarely advisable. Delay allows plaintiff's opening to remain uncontested throughout plaintiff's evidentiary presentation. In delaying the opening, defendant loses the opportunity to temper the impact of plaintiff's evidence and present the employer's justification for its actions. The delayed opening statement by the defendant may be viewed as an afterthought concocted once defendant had heard plaintiff's evidence.

Delaying opening, however, may be tactically valid in limited circumstances. A defendant may use a delayed opening to present a blockbuster to surprise the plaintiff. Or where two defendants go to trial, one defendant might open before plaintiff's evidence and one might open before defendant's evidence to maximize the "bookend" approach to the trial.

E. Plaintiff's Opening

When communication experts speak of credibility, they emphasize the importance of the receiver's perception of the message. An effective communicator will be very aware of trying to present his message in the most favorable light. Three levels of communication work during the trial: verbal, vocal, and nonverbal. All can, and should, be used during opening statement.[5]

In addition to the verbal message, an effective opening relies on voice qualities, pitch and rhythm, pauses, and rate of speech, as well as eye contact and facial behavior (expression), movement, gestures, postural orientation, personal appearance, and environmental surroundings. Some studies show that as little as 7 percent of the actual impact of a message comes from verbal communication, while 38 percent relates to vocal qualities and 55 percent to nonverbal behavior.

Assuming you have been given an opportunity to conduct voir dire, the jury should already be aware that you are a sincere and honest lawyer who represents a person who has been seriously harmed by the actions of the defendant and that you are seeking just compensation for that harm. While each juror has formed certain initial impressions from things said during voir dire, the opening statement must get the jury "on board" with the plaintiff's primary issues: (1) the harm done to plaintiff by defendant, (2) the liability of defendant for that harm, and (3) damages to compensate plaintiff and punish defendant.

While effective voir dire may be the best opening statement in some cases, the opening statement itself is the most important part of the trial in most employment matters. By going first, plaintiff benefits from the fact that the first impressions have lasting effects on the outcome, and plaintiff can define the issues and occasionally get defense counsel off stride. Plaintiff also gets to begin the process of building up his or her credibility.

The opening can be used to introduce the plaintiff, his background, work experience, community involvement, and significant family members. Portray the plaintiff as sympathetic and honest and, if possible, highlight those aspects of plaintiff's experience that reflect the jurors' own experiences and background, as revealed during voir dire.

The first words of the opening statement must grab the jury's attention and interest, while informing them of the justness of the plaintiff's case. In describing the wrong done to plaintiff by defendant, keep the theme of your case in mind; for example, plaintiff was terminated by her boss because she refused his overt sexual advances and reported him to senior management. Describe the background of the plaintiff and the defendant, plaintiff's job duties, the harassment, and any policy or procedure on which plaintiff relied. Explain that sexual harassment is a form of sex discrimination, that discrimination and retaliation for protesting discrimination are against the law. Tell them of the witnesses and documents that will be presented to prove what happened. You must also alert them to the defenses that will be raised and explain how the evidence will show each defense to be pretextual.

Then focus on the harm suffered by plaintiff. Explain how plaintiff's normal activities were impaired, the effect the harassment had on her family life, and how she was made to feel inferior and powerless. Identify the treating doctors and describe medical terms and phrases that will be used during trial, including her diagnosis and prognosis.

You must generally address the issues of damages, identifying your expert economists. Explain that plaintiff is seeking back pay (past losses), front pay (predicted future losses), and postemployment benefits. Explain, too, that she is seeking compensation for emotional distress. Finally, explain plaintiff's motives in filing suit—that she does not want others (her daughter or sister or the jurors' daughters or sisters or spouses) to suffer what she did. Tell them that they have the power, based on the evidence, to stop the wrongdoing and punish the corporate wrongdoer, and individuals as well.

At the conclusion of the plaintiff's opening, all members of the jury should understand the overview of your position on the liability of defendant, the harm suffered by plaintiff, and your expectation of damages. In addition, they should know about any weaknesses in your case and how those weaknesses will be overcome.

F. Defendant's Opening

Defendant must counter the sympathy plaintiff has engendered by placing the jury in the employer's shoes and providing a moral justification for accepting the employer's decision through defendant's themes in the case. Defendant must also undermine plaintiff's themes, which will usually fall within the following categories: (1) insufficient cause, (2) insufficient notice, (3) ulterior motive, (4) disparate treatment, or, if all else fails, (5) sympathy. Counter these by proposing defendant's themes through rival facts and explanations, while dismissing plaintiff's theory as illogical, impractical, or dependant upon incorrect or unbelievable assumptions.

Defendant's initial "hook" should deflate plaintiff's theme. It may respond directly, such as:

> Plaintiff's counsel has told plaintiff's side well, but she has only told part of the story. If it were that simple, there would be no need for a trial. This is not only a case about plaintiff's termination. This case involves the difficult selection of 20 percent of Acme's workforce for layoff.

Defendant may wish to take an alternative route and avoid being too far distracted from defendant's own fairness themes. For example, to respond more indirectly to plaintiff's theme that he had been unfairly disciplined and terminated, defendant's opening statement might start:

> Plaintiff has suggested that this case is about harassment. But, actually, you will see that this is a case about plaintiff's indifference toward the responsibilities Acme entrusted to him. This indifference continued despite every effort by Acme management to assist him and encourage him to improve. Acme had run out of options.

Introduce the defendant employer and its representative, providing a brief background. Explain that the term "defendant" carries no stigma since anyone can file a lawsuit and complaints are merely allegations. After this, consider referring to the defendant as "we" rather than "defendant."

Describe defendant's business in a way that reminds jurors that it is composed of people who think, feel, and act just like them. In addition to establishing some bond with the jury, this will emphasize that the employer should not be held to any divine standard—that is, it need not be clairvoyant, impervious to economic realities, or infinitely patient. Indeed, later in your opening you may need to attribute undeniable management errors to normal human frailty rather than malice.

The heart of defendant's opening must provide a moral justification for defendant's position, countering the natural sympathy for an individual losing employment. This involves legitimizing management goals, while acknowledging that they may unavoidably lead to unpleasant choices. Allude to commonly accepted moral tenets, hopefully discussed in voir dire, such as personal responsibility, the employer's need to survive in a competitive business environment, an honest day's pay for an honest day's work, and fairness to other employees. You will argue these justifications more explicitly in closing argument.

Describe how plaintiff's job fit into defendant's business in a critical way. Where appropriate, explain how plaintiff's misconduct harmed defendant's business. Define the standards expected of persons in plaintiff's position and articulate the justification for those standards— such as high pay or prestige. Point to groups of employees who met those standards.

Identify the witnesses and documents supporting the termination. Recounting management's painstaking decision process to help jurors identify with the employer and to undermine plaintiff's efforts to portray the decision as having been imposed by a heartless, malicious, or arbitrary institution. If plaintiff's theme is directed at a specific supervisor, emphasize the participation of others in the decision—perhaps at the maligned supervisor's request.

Emphasize fairness provided to plaintiff, such as notification, similar treatment of other employees, and efforts to assist or accommodate plaintiff through training or job alteration. Note plaintiff's refusal to accept advice or unwillingness to improve. Suggest that plaintiff's lawsuit could be motivated by an inability to accept his or her own faults. Be wary, however, of unnecessarily maligning plaintiff, thereby alienating jurors and creating sympathy for plaintiff. Allow jurors to reach their own conclusions regarding plaintiff's character.

Toward the conclusion of your opening statement, remind the jurors of their obligations—(1) not to be swayed by passion or sympathy, (2) to apply common sense to the evidence and judge's instructions, and (3) to keep an open mind until hearing all evidence. But avoid preaching (for example, about the importance of jury service), which may sound insincere.

Instead, consider concluding your opening with a request that the jury keep your themes in mind during plaintiff's case. Explain that the employer has been waiting to vindicate itself in the face of plaintiff's accusations. Ask that the jury give the employer that chance by listening carefully when the employer's witnesses testify.

G. Objections

Objectionable behavior in opening statements includes argument and reference to facts that the party has no good faith expectation will be tendered and admitted into evidence,[6] as well as expression of personal opinions or suggestion that counsel has knowledge of the facts beyond the evidence.[7]

Objections are waived if not raised before or during the statement, unless an admonition would not have cured the prejudice created by the objectionable conduct. Courts rarely reverse jury decisions based upon opening statement misconduct, usually holding that it was insufficiently prejudicial or that a given admonition cured any prejudice.

Thus, other than interrupting the flow of your opponent's opening and hopefully obtaining an admonition (of questionable value) against opposing counsel, objections are of doubtful value. They may harm you in the jury's eyes by identifying you early as obstructionist, highlighting your objectionable behavior, creating jury sympathy for your opponent, and embarrassing you when you are overruled. Defendant's objections also invite the plaintiff to object during defendant's opening with little of the same risk since the defendant has legitimized the objection.

If you feel the need to object, you might ameliorate these problems by requesting a sidebar. The best course, however, is to anticipate issues and address them through motions in limine. On the other hand, if your opponent's behavior during opening statement is truly outrageous, you should consider moving for a mistrial or challenge your opponent to support arguments with evidence.

H. Nonsuit

Admissions in opening statement are binding on the presenting party.[8] If plaintiff makes a fatal admission or fails to discuss evidence supporting all necessary elements during opening, defendant may move for nonsuit. This oral motion should be made out of the jury's presence. Such motions are rarely granted because, similar to a demurrer, plaintiff is normally allowed to reopen and add missing elements. Defendant should weigh this edification of plaintiff against the value of undermining plaintiff's and the jury's confidence in plaintiff's counsel.

IV. Direct and Cross-Examination

A. Direct Examination

Direct examination of your own witnesses (along with the documents they present) provides the mechanism for making your case. Make sure the witnesses will do a good job for you. Credibility is the main issue. How the jurors perceive your witnesses will often determine the outcome of the trial. That perception often depends on the way counsel treats witnesses. One commentator likens direct examination to the movies—the lawyer must not only perform, but also direct. Hence, adequate time must be spent in preparation and rehearsal.

There are several ways to maximize credibility of your own witnesses. Ask open-ended questions that allow narrative answers. Allowing the witness to tell his or her own story will avoid having the jurors perceive that the lawyer is testifying or overcoaching the witness. An open question might be phrased, "Tell the jury exactly what your supervisor said to you," or "Can you explain to the jury how you came to conclude termination was necessary?" When the witness is allowed room to talk, he or she can begin to build rapport and credibility with the jury.[9]

Direct examination may bore the jury, particularly if redundant or repetitive. Keep the examination moving. Change the pattern of questions and the language you use to ask them. Intersperse a few yes/no questions with longer narrative questions. When an important series of questions is about to begin, change your position or tone of voice, engaging the jury's attention anew.

If your witness stumbles in answering a direct question, bring the focus back on you. "Let me rephrase that—I don't think my question was clear." If the witness becomes so confused or upset he or she cannot continue, ask for a short recess.

Learn to listen.

1. Direct Examination of the Plaintiff is Crucial

The plaintiff is undoubtedly the most important witness in any employment case. After all, it is the plaintiff who brought the case and is asking for money from the defendant. Everything that is done in the case should involve making sure the plaintiff is perceived in the best possible light.

2. Believe in Your Client

During direct examination, the jury must know that the lawyer believes wholeheartedly in the client. You should not try a case if you are not 100 percent committed to the client; your doubt will be conveyed to the jury. Most plaintiff's lawyers suggest referring to the plaintiff by first name during direct examination as a way to have the jury see the lawyer has accepted the client totally.

3. Soften the Impact of the High-Stress Courtroom

Most plaintiffs have never set foot inside a courtroom before and are understandably nervous and anxious about doing so. There is no way of knowing in advance how the client will react once the day of trial is upon him. The jury will be watching; the opposing counsel will be arguing; the judge will be listening; and in some cases, the cameras will be rolling.

To assuage the stress, you must prepare the plaintiff completely for the experience. Tell him exactly what will happen. If possible, the plaintiff should observe a trial, or at minimum, visit the courtroom where the case will be tried. Reassure the plaintiff that nervousness is natural; let him talk out his fears. Prepare, prepare, prepare—both the direct and the anticipated cross-examination—as aggressively as you can without risking the transference of hostility to the examiner that can result from aggressive simulated cross-examination. In this connection, counsel should be aware that the extent of witness preparation, including the use of witness consultants, may be a proper subject of cross-examination.[10]

Work with the plaintiff on voice control and body language. Many plaintiff attorneys videotape practice examination and review it with the plaintiff to smooth out any difficulties. Others say that seeing themselves on tape can cause witnesses to overreact and give a stilted, self-conscious performance. There is no right way to prepare your plaintiff; each individual will require individualized attention.

Work with the plaintiff on vocabulary and message content. Suggest that the use of qualifiers ("I'm pretty sure" or "I think") and adjective intensifiers ("it was very, very late" or "I was so extremely afraid") can cause the jurors to question the reliability of the plaintiff's testimony. To deal with this, instruct the plaintiff to pause before answering.

Also instruct the plaintiff to speak directly to the jury and make eye contact with them on occasion, especially for longer narratives. Addressing every answer to the jury may look silly and appear "coached." You can signal the plaintiff to focus on the jury by saying "Now, please tell the jury what happened next."

4. Direct Examination of the Decision Maker or Personnel Manager Presents the Defendant's Story

The testimony of the decision maker or personnel manager is the defendant's opportunity to educate the jury about the decisions affecting the plaintiff and about the defendant in general. This is also your opportunity to personalize a corporate defendant by reminding the jury that a corporation can act only through employees. The plaintiff is claiming that this person is the "bad" actor or wrongdoer, not the "corporation"; you must remind the jury that to find in favor of the plaintiff, they must decide that the decision maker is a bad actor. Defense counsel must be prepared, however, for a preemptive strike by the plaintiff's lawyer: some plaintiff's lawyers will call the decision maker in plaintiff's case in chief in order to take the witness by surprise and elicit testimony in a way that is most favorable to the plaintiff. Accordingly, when preparing your witness for direct examination, you must educate him or her on getting the defendant's story across, even if he or she is cross-examined by the plaintiff's lawyer first.

5. Assess Your Witnesses as Witnesses

Credibility of your witnesses turns on both the underlying attitudes of the jurors and the personal characteristics of your witnesses. Before preparing your witnesses for trial, think back to your first meetings and to the deposition and assess how your witnesses came across. As James W. McElhaney has noted, many of our clients find themselves in difficulty and in need of our help because they are disagreeable people who cannot solve their own problems. If you would characterize your witnesses as whiney, secretive, indifferent, selfish, boastful, or angry as opposed to brave, honest, pleasant, helpful, concerned, or modest, then you should plan on spending extra time with these witnesses and perhaps curtailing their testimony.[11]

6. Help Your Witnesses Convey Their Best Images

Your witnesses are not courtroom professionals and even if they have engaged in public speaking, sales, or other occupations that involve addressing audiences or convincing others, they will not be prepared for the tension that inevitably occurs when giving testimony in the courtroom. Help your witnesses anticipate the tension and deal with it effectively. Remind them that physical or verbal "squirming" conveys deceitfulness. Emphasize that straightforward answers using direct terms are more effective than answers couched with wiggle room. Avoid prefacing answers with phrases such as "I think" or "I believe" that suggest uncertainness, especially if it becomes a habit to preface every answer with these phrases. Remind your witnesses to talk loudly enough to be heard but not to express anger by a loud voice or uncertainty by talking too softly. Your witnesses should not avoid eye contact with the jury but also should not pretend that the questions are not coming from you. Finally, watch for personal habits and tendencies that are distracting, such as fiddling with hair or fingers, or using three syllable words when a one syllable word will do.

7. *Organize Your Witnesses*

Your prime witnesses must be prepared to tell the company's side of the story in an organized fashion. Usually, a chronological rendition of the facts makes the most sense and avoids the prospect of the jury missing a point because the significance was not yet readily apparent. You may want to have a partner or associate who is not familiar with the facts in your case listen to your direct examination to make sure your case comes across in the way you have planned. Because you are not to ask leading questions, you must make sure that your witnesses communicate clearly and effectively. In trying to achieve clarity, however, avoid endless repetitions of the same point—you will bore and antagonize the jury not to mention the judge.

Consider using graphics, visual aids, or diagrams to help your witnesses give testimony in a clear and organized manner and to keep the interest of the jury. Remember too that physical evidence such as documents, tape recordings, or pictures that show or support the veracity of your witnesses will enhance overall credibility. Make sure your witnesses are comfortable with aids and that you and your witnesses can present them in an assured way. Endless fumbling in front of the jury signals ineptness by you and your witnesses.

8. *Be Observant*

Listen to the testimony. Every lawyer has seen a fellow practitioner fall into the easily avoidable trap of not listening to the answer given by the witness. This is particularly easy when it is your own witnesses. You believe you know what the witnesses will say and you are thinking of the next question. Witnesses become confused and may not answer the question asked. Witnesses have been known to change their stories once they are in a courtroom. Your witnesses may simply have misunderstood the questions. If you are not listening, you have told the jury your witnesses are not that important to you, you have failed to get a point into evidence, and you have left either erroneous or misunderstood information in front of the jury.

Watch the jury. Testimony that seemed clear and concise to you that provokes puzzled frowns from several jurors should be revisited. Sleeping jurors are a good indicator that you are not being effective. In addition, by looking at the jury, you direct the attention of the witness to the jury in a natural way and encourage eye contact with the jurors.

Look at your witnesses. If your witnesses appear uncomfortable to you, the witnesses lose credibility with the jury. If the witnesses have been on the stand for a long time, perhaps breaks are in order. There are times when the phrasing of a question is confusing to the witnesses even if not confusing to you. It is far better to suggest that you have ineptly phrased a question than to leave your witnesses struggling on the witness stand.

9. Avoid Grandstanding

Although your thespian talents might be considerable, your witnesses should be the stars of the production. Your conduct should not detract attention from your witnesses or suggest that there might be a problem. Questioning conducted in a calm, moderate voice is far more effective than thundering oratory. At the conclusion of the testimony, you want the jury to know and like your witnesses. Do not be the impediment to that process.

B. Cross-Examination

The purpose of cross-examination is to elicit only that information that helps your case. This can be accomplished either by discrediting the witness, thereby limiting any harm caused by the witness's testimony, or by bringing out favorable information. Effective cross-examination requires a mind-set different from direct examination. For example, on direct examination the witness generally plays the starring role. Cross-examination provides a chance for the lawyer to star.

Trial is not the time to discover new information. The whole idea of cross-examination is to box the witness in, making him or her respond to short, yes/no questions where counsel already knows the answers. Avoid questions where the answer is not already known from previous depositions or other discovery devices. Also, avoid open-ended questions that allow the witness to be unresponsive or avoid revealing important facts.

Once you have scored a point on cross-examination, stop. If you are able to elicit an admission from a witness, allow the admission to linger. Do not rush into further questioning. Resist the temptation to ask just one more question.

1. Cross-Examination of the Plaintiff

The most important guideline in cross-examining the plaintiff is to remember that you should not be making your case with an adverse witness. Too often, lawyers rely on attempts to elicit damaging testimony rather than presenting their case through their own witnesses. Cross-examination should be focused, to the point, and limited.

The starting point for cross-examination is the deposition. Review the deposition and determine those material factual points to which the plaintiff has given unequivocal testimony. If the plaintiff was not locked down in the deposition, you will not lock the plaintiff down into a damaging admission at trial.

The points you cover should be material to the case and significant to the jury. Impeachment should be saved for those points on which any listener will conclude that the plaintiff is lying about a significant fact in the case. The fact that the plaintiff once called in sick when he or she was not in fact sick will not convince your jury in a layoff case that the plaintiff is a liar. Similarly, thundering impeachment on a point that is not important to the jury is usually a waste of time and often undermines your creditability. Repeated readings from deposition transcripts are boring and will soon become mundane and insignificant to the jury.

The points you intend to make in your cross examination should be obvious to the jury—if they are not significant enough to be obvious, you should not be wasting the time to ask about them. However, do not simply ask the ultimate question. If the plaintiff was discharged for falsifying expense reports, do not demand that the plaintiff admit that he attempted to steal from the company. Instead, confirm the underlying facts with the plaintiff, for example, plaintiff prepared the expense report, plaintiff submitted the receipt, the receipt was prepared by plaintiff's brother, plaintiff did not tell anyone that he had purportedly lost the original until confronted with the forgery. Do not ask the plaintiff to concede or admit the ultimate conclusion to be drawn from these facts. Your witnesses will testify to their conclusions; use the plaintiff to verify the facts or circumstances known to your decision makers when they drew their conclusions.

Once you have made your points with the plaintiff, sit down. Your client might well expect, and eagerly anticipate, an endless grilling of the plaintiff. If the grilling only permits the plaintiff to retell the plaintiff's story, however, you have done your client a disservice.

The attitude you adopt towards the plaintiff should depend on the type of case and the personality of the plaintiff. An elderly employee claiming age discrimination usually should be treated more gently than an employee claiming he was wrongfully discharged for sexual harassment. Make sure your style can change depending on the witness. Your inability to adapt could sway the sympathies of the jury against your client.

2. Cross-Examination of the Decision Maker or Personnel Manager

Employer witnesses, particularly senior management or human resources professionals, can be well-coached, articulate, and believable witnesses. The more attractive the decision maker or personnel manager is as a witness, the less time the plaintiff should keep him or her on the stand. Employer witnesses are also subject to juror skepticism as they remain in the company's employ and continue to be dependent upon the company for their livelihood.

Although your goal is to damage the testimony of any adverse witness, care should be taken to avoid making such a witness appear the underdog, thus invoking the sympathy of the jurors. Plaintiffs' cases are not typically won through impressive cross-examination. Rather, the strength of the plaintiff's own witnesses and their testimony is more often determinative.

What follows are suggested areas of inquiry. These areas are typically difficult for adverse employer witnesses to argue with or deny. The impression is thus generated that the witness is somehow aligned with the plaintiff and that there is really no dispute about the wrongness of the conduct alleged, and the company's obligations to the plaintiff.

Elicit admissions to the effect that treating similarly situated employees differently in the terms or conditions of their employment is illegal if a person's sex, race, age, and so on is the basis for the disparate treatment; that the employer has a duty to take an active role in eradicating harassment from the workplace, whether it exists from coworkers, clients with unlawful preferences, or management itself; that the company recognizes its duty and obligation to assure that the working environment is not tainted by sexually explicit or denigrating commentary; that a working environment free of discrimination is a right of every employee of the company.

Go through the offending conduct alleged by plaintiff, including comments reflecting negative stereotypes or other statements of bias, seeking an admission from the company witness that he would consider such treatment inappropriate and discriminatory. Elicit his belief that the perpetrator of such alleged treatment should be disciplined, specifically that discipline would be required under the practices of the employer. Emphasize that in this instance the company did not discipline the perpetrator.

Testimony should be sought that clarifies that the discriminatory actions of individuals in management legally bind the company: when a manager fails to take action to correct discrimination, the inaction could be perceived as condoning or approving of the unlawful conduct.

Begin to attempt to inoculate the jury from the frequent lack of corroborating witnesses to direct evidence of discrimination, particularly sexually harassing conduct.

- You know from workshops, your own work, and human experience that discrimination is a matter of attitude and therefore may not be expressed out loud; action/conduct can suggest prejudice or bias. "Actions speak louder than words" is true when investigating the validity of a complaint of discrimination.
- It is not unusual—and as a matter of fact, it is expected—that the alleged perpetrator of biased comments or harassing conduct would *deny* the conduct when confronted. Therefore, you cannot accept a denial at face value; but you need to conduct a thorough investigation.
- Since sexual harassment is so often secret, an employer has a duty to learn what is going on in its workplace.
- The employee-victim is not expected to tell you how to investigate. *You* must ask the questions.

Consider attacking the employer's "if we'd only known earlier" defense by getting the witness to admit that even if the plaintiff had complained prior to her termination, no meaningful action would have been taken. Set up your argument that the employer's action, or inaction, warrants the imposition of punitive damages by showing that the employer will do it again. For example, "I take it from your testimony that you are telling this jury, even in hindsight, that you would do it the same way today; that is, you wouldn't do anything differently, would you?" "Therefore, there will be no change in attitude at the company, because you have decided, and have come to this courtroom and testified, that your attitudes and handling of this situation were proper, haven't you?"

Start to corroborate plaintiff's damages for a lost or damaged career. Use the witness's loyalty to the company to obtain testimony that lauds the opportunity for advancement and other job benefits that are available from this employer, including job security and job satisfaction. Elicit testimony that establishes that this employer enjoys a particularly good reputation as the premier employer of its kind—a leader—in the industry.

V. Closing Argument

In closing argument, counsel explains why the evidence the jury has heard supports the themes introduced in opening statement and requires a favorable verdict under the court's instructions. Despite the conventional wisdom that most jurors have reached a decision before evidence concludes, the closing may solidify some jurors' resolve or convince the one or two remaining undecided jurors. At the very least, it arms jurors who are favorable to your position with arguments to convince undecided jurors.

A. Presentation Style

Your closing argument is your opportunity to capitalize on the credibility you have earning throughout the trial. It should be more animated and should more aggressively press the conclusions in your opening statement. But do not overstate the evidence, ignore difficult issues, or use blatant emotional pleas. Practice delivering your argument before audiences of nonlawyers. Consider using a focus group, if the value of the case merits the expense.

Your arguments should rely upon common sense, probability, and human nature. Counsel may assert any reasonable inferences from the evidence. Although you want to press your points, understatement is often effective. Respect juror intelligence by tactfully guiding them to reach the conclusions you desire.

Emphasize your strengths rather than your opponent's weaknesses. Jurors recognize that the latter approach suggests that you have little good to say about your own case. A positive approach will be better received.

The theme, and to the extent practical the factual sequence, of your closing should parallel your opening. Repeat words and phrases used in your opening and in your direct or cross-examinations. Remind the jury of what you assured them in opening you would prove and point out where you proved it.

But be certain that your closing addresses the actual events and tenor of trial. Acknowledge difficulties that arose during trial as well as highlighting pleasant surprises. Again, notes will undermine the impression of spontaneity and candor. Have "talking points" on a single sheet of paper. If the judge allows, be mobile, approach jurors.

Finally, keep your audience in mind. Call them ladies and gentlemen; do not refer to them as "the jury." Combine the information learned in voir dire with what you may have gleaned from observing each juror's reaction to evidence during trial. If you are able to determine who are the likely jury leaders or which jurors might have specific concerns, direct your pitch toward them.

B. Persuasive Content

After your prefatory remarks, restate the "hook" with which you began your opening. Thereafter, define the issues for the jury in a way most likely to secure a favorable answer. Next, discuss how applying the evidence to specific jury instructions text compels that answer, while more explicitly invoking the thematic moral tenets suggested in your opening.

Remind the jury of exhibit contents and which witnesses said what. Explain any evidence that might have been confusing, but do not be condescending to the jury. Selectively quote specific questions and answers directly from the trial transcript (you should have obtained a copy of choice testimony). To the extent that witnesses called by your opponent supported your theory, emphasize that testimony and use it to corroborate witnesses you called. You may even wish to display key transcript lines or transparencies or to blow up exhibits.

Many jurors do not like to think a witness is lying. Where possible, reconcile testimony and attribute discrepancies to faulty memory or witness misperception. This enhances your image as fair and reliable. If appropriate, explain how bias may subtly influence perception and memory. Avoid dwelling on minor or meaningless testimony discrepancies. Jurors will view this as petty lawyer tactics.

Personalities of the plaintiff and supervisors are usually critical to each party's theory in employment actions. Jurors will draw inferences about workplace relationships and environment from the demeanor of these witnesses. Your closing argument must be consistent with the displayed demeanor of the witnesses. Indeed, you should highlight displayed characteristics that corroborate your theories. You may need to explain unsupportive displays, characterizing your witnesses as understandably nervous or your opponent's as well prepared. Remember, however, that counsel may not suggest personal knowledge beyond the evidence.

Mention your opponent's failure to substantiate significant allegations raised in his or her opening, perhaps referring to them as "broken promises." Again, do not be petty. If your opponent uses this tactic against you, explain to the jury that your opening presented the evidence as you anticipated it and why the variation your opponent has raised was meaningless.

Weave specific jury instructions text into the corresponding portions of your factual arguments. This will demonstrate that, not only do commonly accepted moral tenets favor your client, the law does as well. You may also need to argue policy reasons behind instructions with which the jury might otherwise be uncomfortable. Remind jurors of voir dire promises to follow the law. Again, verbatim transparencies or blowups of critical instructions are often effective.

Consider diffusing unfavorable instructions by placing them in the context of other instructions or arguing their inapplicability to these facts. Yet, be wary of misstating the law and drawing an objection. In addition to substantive legal instructions, you may wish to emphasize instructions on witness credibility, reasonable inferences, and common sense. Discuss any special verdict form or interrogatories.

Visual aids will again be persuasive and provide a refreshing change of pace from straight oratory. The jury may be shown any admitted exhibits, but obtain the court's approval if using blowups of any exhibit. Additionally, summaries of the evidence may be used if not misleading or confusing.[12] Consider appropriating a visual aid that your opponent uses in closing. If that aid is not in evidence, you may even write on it.

Rhetorical questions may help set up your presentation or challenge your opponent. However, the latter tactic can be dangerous if you do not have a rebuttal opportunity. If your opponent challenges you with a rhetorical question, attempt to incorporate the answer within your prepared closing or challenge the materiality of the question by suggesting that your opponent has asked the wrong question.

Analogies can also be persuasive and engaging, but do not assert your personal beliefs. They should be based upon common experiences, reflect community values, and not be reversible against you by your opponent. Analogies suggested by witnesses during trial are best. If your opponent raises analogies, consider whether you can turn them against the opponent.

Finally, if your trial has been bifurcated on the issue of punitive damages, counsel should have prepared an argument on punitive damages in the event it becomes necessary. Counsel should spend the liability deliberation period adapting it to any changed circumstances.

C. Plaintiff's Closing*

The plaintiff's closing argument is the time to pull out the stops—it is the culmination of everything that has transpired since the day the plaintiff first contacted you. In fact, you should open a file at the start of the case called "Closing." File your ideas/metaphors/homilies as they occur, and even prepare a working closing argument that you can tune as discovery proceeds.

Focus on the plaintiff as a real person, who made contributions and sacrifices for the defendant "corporation" or "company." Careful use of language can help reinforce your theme: Plaintiff was not "terminated," but "fired"; his or her job was not eliminated, plaintiff was eliminated. Often a chronological approach to the facts is best for the plaintiff as the jury can be induced to feel sympathy for an escalating

---

* The order of closing may vary. For example, in New York the defendant closes first. Check local rules and practices.

plight, which culminates in termination and/or unemployment. Anticipate defendant's closing and defuse its theme. Force defense counsel to respond to your theme, diverting from the defense script.

As with the opening statement, address the three primary issues: defendant's liability, the harm suffered by the plaintiff, and damages. In discussing damages, use the demonstrative evidence that was presented during the trial. For example, if your economist used a flip chart during trial to summarize damage calculations, use that chart. Also; give the jury a way to calculate emotional distress or punitive damages, for example, what is it worth to suffer an unwanted physical touching for a day, for a week, for a month? Ask for a percentage of the company's net worth or a percentage of its yearly profits.

Confront defendant's argument that damages are speculative. Reiterate that the jurors cannot and need not speculate. Explain in simple terms how you arrive at the dollars plaintiff is seeking. Plant numbers throughout the closing for the jurors to remember. This is the time to appeal to the jury's notions of industrial fairness. Highlight how in exercising its business judgment, defendant unfairly damaged the plaintiff. The larger the corporate defendant, the easier it is for defense counsel to personalize the individual decision makers. Therefore, it is crucial for plaintiff's counsel to explain why the actions of individuals are the actions of the corporate defendant.

Speak from your heart as well as your head. The jury should not walk away from your closing thinking, "What a great lawyer." Rather each juror should be thinking, "If that lawyer believes that his client was treated unfairly and truly damaged without justification, then maybe I should believe it too."

D. Defendant's Closing*

Defendant's closing argument must again defuse the mood of sympathy created by plaintiff's closing. Immediately restate your "hook" and refer to other facts favoring defendant. Reiterate the jury's duty to decide the case based upon the facts and law rather than sympathy. Point out that plaintiff's plea for sympathy changes neither the facts nor the law. If applicable, remind the jury that plaintiff's inflammatory language is designed solely to anger the jury. Consider a statement such as, "You've heard plaintiff's passionate presentation. But let's now look at the facts."

This is the time to more explicitly argue the moral justification for finding defendant's way; for example, personal responsibility, the com-

---

* The order of closing may vary. For example, in New York the defendant closes first. Check local rules and practices.

pany's need to flourish in a competitive business environment, a day's pay for an honest day's work, and fairness to other employees. If plaintiff has effectively emphasized defendant's contractual obligations, consider emphasizing plaintiff's reciprocal obligation to perform competently. Provide jurors a reason to overcome their natural tendency to assist an individual in apparent need.

Direct attacks on plaintiff may engender sympathy for plaintiff. Yet, you may want to suggest that plaintiff has an unrealistic perception of his or her own performance. You may argue that this lack of introspection in itself contributed to the performance problem—thereby reconciling your theme with plaintiff's courtroom demeanor.

Invoke sympathy for others whose interests diverge from plaintiff, such as alternative layoff candidates, the accused supervisor, or complaining customers or coworkers. Ask rhetorical questions such as, "If plaintiff were not laid off, then who instead?" or "How could our business survive with customers as unhappy as those for which plaintiff was responsible?"

Cite testimony of customers or nonmanagement employees to enhance your management witnesses. Plaintiff presumably will not have contended that all these people were biased against him or her. If he or she contends that they were, point to the most credible of these witnesses and suggest that plaintiff has lost perspective (again perhaps consistent with your theme).

If plaintiff has only attacked defendant's stated justifications but never postulated an ulterior motive, counsel may wish to point this out. Be wary, however, of pressing the point too hard. Plaintiff may be saving that revelation for rebuttal.

You want to reassure the jury of the moral justification for finding your way, then provide the legal justification. Defendant should stress instructions regarding plaintiff's burden of proving each element, employer discretion, and the jurors' obligation not to be influenced by passion, prejudice, or sympathy. Consider reminding the jury that the issue is not whether it might have treated plaintiff differently, but rather whether defendant violated the law.

If applicable, point out that plaintiff has failed to present significant evidence with respect to a specific element. For example, plaintiff's presentation may have addressed "good cause" without establishing a contractual requirement for good cause. Yet, recognize that many jurors will assume the duty to terminate only for cause, regardless of contrary jury instructions or contractual language.

Many defendants prefer to discuss damages early and move on. Note that, as with any other topic, plaintiff may not discuss damages in rebuttal if defendant does not discuss them in closing.[13] Thus, if plaintiff does not discuss damages in plaintiff's initial closing argument, defendant should avoid the topic, thereby precluding plaintiff from addressing it at all.

Defendants often conclude their arguments by noting that plaintiff has the last word and asking that the jury consider what defendant would say in response if given the opportunity. This can seem somewhat self-evident and condescending. It may be better to note simply that you will not speak again and thank the jurors for their careful attention.

E. Objections

As with opening statements, any misconduct that could have been cured with an admonition must be objected to immediately.[14] Exit polls indicate that jurors are annoyed by and suspicious of repeated objections. Thus, objections should be avoided if the jury's common sense or your subsequent argument would substantially ameliorate any prejudice. If objections are made to the use of certain visual aids, preserve any relevant visual aid that was not admitted into evidence.

Objectionable behavior on closing argument generally falls within three categories. The first is misstatement of the law. The second category is inadmissible or prejudicial matter. This includes counsel suggesting personal knowledge of facts beyond the evidence,[15] inviting the jury to speculate beyond reasonable inferences,[16] belaboring hypotheticals that are not based upon evidence,[17] references to insurance,[18] references to political influence of defense counsel,[19] disparaging opponent's objections,[20] encouraging prejudice against corporations,[21] stating counsel's personal belief in justice of client's position or vouching for witness,[22] emphasizing the absence of a witness equally available or unavailable to both sides,[23] effect on tax or insurance rates,[24] identifying a collateral source of recovery,[25] prejudicial references to party's race, religion, or national origin,[26] and referencing jurors by name.[27]

The third category of objections is improper form. This includes arguing that the jury should place itself in the parties' shoes (the "golden rule");[28] appeals to passion, prejudice, or sympathy or references to defendant's wealth or poverty absent punitive damages issue.[29] Also, many jurisdictions prohibit "per diem" damage calculation.[30]

VI. Closing Note

When the jurors retire to deliberate, they will frequently turn to the verdict form to see the questions they must answer. Those questions will provide the focal points and organization for the jurors' discussion.

Do not wait until the end of trial to draft what may be the most important document to the jury. Make sure the form submitted has received your attention not only in its drafting but also in your evidence and arguments: Your goal should be to educate the jury on each issue on the verdict form by the end of trial.

Develop your own style. You can learn from others, but unless you are relaxed and natural, you will be ineffective. It is not necessary to be a member of the Screen Actors Guild to be a good trial lawyer. You will find that being a skilled and effective teacher brings you more success before a jury than being a great orator.

VII. Appendix: Your Trial Checklist

1. See the forms and checklists at the end of chapter 8, "Trial Preparation," and chapter 9, "Juries."
2. Prepare proposed jury instructions early. See American Bar Association: *Model Jury Instructions: Employment Litigation* (1994). (Courts appreciate computer disks.) Weave key points from instructions into your opening and closing arguments. See the sample instructions at the end of chapter 9, "Juries."
3. Prepare verdict forms. (Courts appreciate computer disks.) See the sample special verdict at the end of chapter 9, "Juries."
4. Prepare suggested voir dire questions. Also a jury questionnaire may be appreciated. See the sample questionnaire at the end of chapter 9 "Juries."
5. Prepare trial brief, usually relying on motion for and opposition to summary judgment or dismissal motions.
6. Prepare exhibit list and exchange exhibits, perhaps initialing exhibits to confirm receipt and review. Mark exhibits and make copies for opposing counsel, judge, and witness.
7. Summarize and designate deposition excerpts.
8. Prepare motions in limine to admit or exclude evidence or witnesses. See chapter 7, "Special Evidentiary Matters."
9. Review and follow pretrial stipulation or pretrial order.
10. Consider and prepare bench briefs on potential or anticipated evidentiary or procedural matters.
11. Attempt to stipulate to joint admission of mutually acceptable exhibits. Consider juror exhibit books to expedite review of any exhibits.
12. Have originals of any disputed exhibits available for trial.
13. Prepare any demonstrative exhibits such as time lines, exhibit blowups, videos, or visual aids. Show opposing counsel and check with judge.
14. Select appropriate client representative for trial, or prepare your client to make his or her best presentation at counsel table.
15. Subpoena witnesses.
16. Reduce witnesses' trial stress by showing courtroom and witness box to clients or witnesses. Perhaps have witnesses observe earlier trial in the same courtroom.
17. Focus on telling an interesting story, not just a recital of facts or events. Organize the story chronologically. Use suspense and different points of view. Avoid legalese. Employ common-sense analogies.
18. Prepare a sample statement of claims or defenses for the judge's introduction to the jury.
19. Focus on themes for opening and closing statements. Identify and use in "hook" theme and repeat that theme.
20. Identify key issues and evidence for plaintiff and defendant.
21. Find out what the judge allows regarding speaking at a lectern or approaching the jury or witness. Check local rules and customs on trial.
22. Consider bifurcation of plaintiff's cases, liability and damages (especially punitive damages), or other aspects of the case.

23. Organize your presentation in order of witnesses and exhibits. Usually start strong and stop strong. Vary long witnesses with short witnesses. Make the presentation interesting and logical. What do jurors want to see and hear? Chronological order is often a good approach. See the sample trial outline at the end of chapter 8, "Trial Preparation."

24. State any objections and grounds for objections. Get a ruling. If a sustained objection, seek an admonition.

25. Listen to the testimony. Correct any testimony mistakes.

26. Be prepared as plaintiff's counsel to call employer's decision maker in plaintiff's case in chief. As defense counsel, anticipate and prepare witness for this strategy. Also, as defense counsel be prepared to go directly to your testimony from this decision maker right after plaintiff's counsel's questions.

27. Cross-examine with a purpose. You usually want to "box in" witnesses, obtain contradictory testimony, or obtain admissions or concessions. Lead witness. Do not ask "why" questions allowing witness to explain. Usually, ask only questions where you know and can prove desired answers. Stop while ahead on cross-examination. Do more than examine—crossly. Depositions are a great source for cross-examination.

28. Before resting, confirm that the court has admitted all your exhibits. Check that the court has legible and correct exhibits for jurors to review during deliberations.

29. In closing argument, walk jury through verdict form. Simplify jurors' job. Prepare blowup of jury form and show jury how to render your verdict.

30. If defending, make a motion for judgment as a matter of law or directed verdict at conclusion of case to preserve motions for new trial or judgment not withstanding the verdict.

31. Read along as judge charges jury. Correct any significant errors.

32. Consider posttrial motions and appeals. (See chapter 11, "Posttrial Motions," and chapter 12, "Appeals.")

Notes

1. Tom Riley, *The Opening Statement: Winning at the Outset*, 3 AM. J. TRIAL ADVOC. 225, 226 (1979).

2. Hallinan v. United States, 182 F.2d 880, 885–86 (9th Cir. 1950).

3. Neumann v. Bishop, 59 Cal. App. 3d 451, 473, 130 Cal. Rptr. 786, 801 (1976); People v. Davis, 46 Ill. 2d 554, 560, 264 N.E.2d 140, 143 (1970).

4. Commercial Iron & Metal Co. v. Bache Halsey Stuart, Inc., 581 F.2d 246, 250 (10th Cir. 1978).

5. LAWRENCE J. SMITH & LORETTA A. MALANDRO, COURTROOM COMMUNICATION STRATEGIES (1985).

6. Hawk v. Superior Court, 42 Cal. App. 3d 108, 121 (1974); Schwedler v. Galvan, 46 Ill. App. 3d 630, 640, 360 N.E.2d 1324, 1331 (1977); Timsah v. General Motors Corp., 225 Kan. 305, 315, 591 P.2d 154, 163 (1979); State v. Hill, 866 S.W.2d 160, 163 (Mo. 1993); Cincinnati Ins. Co. v. Maytag Co., 63 Ohio App. 3d 144, 147, 578 N.E.2d 478, 479–80 (1989).

7. Hossman v. State, 473 N.E.2d 1059, 1063 (Ind. Ct. App. 1985); State ex rel. Brown v. Howard, 3 Ohio App. 3d 189, 190, 444 N.E.2d 469, 471 (1981).

8. Standard Mgt. Realty Co. v. Johnson, 157 Ill. App. 3d 919, 924, 510 N.E.2d 986, 990 (1987). Contra Papke v. Tribbey, 68 Mich. App. 130, 137, 242 N.W.2d 38, 42 (1976).

9. See JAMES S. BELL, TOP COURTROOM PERFORMANCE (1994).

10. Geders v. United States, 425 U.S. 80, 90 n.3 (1976).

11. James W. McElhaney, *Witness Profiles*, 81-AprABA J-102 (1995).

12. Langlinais v. Figueroa, 636 So. 2d 983, 989 (La. App. 1994); State v. Doughty, 554 A.2d 1189, 1192 (Me. 1989); State v. Thompson, 73 Wash. App. 654, 663, 870 P.2d 1022, 1028.

13. Cortez v. Macias, 110 Cal. App. 3d 640, 658, 167 Cal. Rptr. 905, 915 (1980); Jenner v. Leapley, 521 N.W.2d 422, 429 (S.D. 1994); Hunter v. Kuether, 38 Wis. 2d 140, 156 N.W.2d 353, 357 (1968).

14. Horn v. Atcheson & S.F. Ry. Co., 61 Cal. 2d 602, 609–10, 394 P.2d 561, 565 (1964); Ellington v. Bilsel, 255 Ill. App. 3d 233, 238, 626 N.E.2d 386, 390 (1993); Baker v. Terex Div., 65 Ohio App. 3d 704, 708, 585 N.E.2d 441, 443 (1989); Moody v. Rasmussen, 274 Or. 605, 612, 547 P.2d 623, 627 (1976).

15. Garden Grove Sch. Dist. v. Hendler, 63 Cal. 2d 141, 143, 45 Cal. Rptr. 313, 314, (1965); Richardson v. State Hwy. & Transp. Comm'n, 863 S.W.2d 876, 881 (Mo. 1993); Commonwealth v. Villalobos, 7 Mass. App. Ct. 905, 906, 388 N.E.2d 701, 702 (1979).

16. Neumann v. Bishop, 59 Cal. App. 3d 451, 479, 130 Cal. Rptr. 786, 805 (1976).

17. Jensen v. Southern Pac. Co., 129 Cal. App. 2d 67, 79, 276 P.2d 703, 712 (1954); Smith v. JBJ Ltd., 694 P.2d 352, 353 (Colo. Ct. App. 1984); People v. Truss, 254, Ill. App. 3d 767, 778, 626 N.E.2d 1175, 1184, 1193 (1993).

18. Cook v. Anderson, 512 So. 2d 1310, 1311 (Ala. 1987); Price v. King, 255 Iowa 314, 322, 122 N.W.2d 318, 323 (1963).

19. Jonte v. Key System, 89 Cal. App. 2d 654, 658, 201 P.2d 562, 565 (1949).

20. Missouri K. & T. Ry. Co. v. Ridgway, 191 F.2d 363 (8th Cir. 1951); Love v. Wolf, 226 Cal. App. 2d 378, 391–92, 38 Cal. Rptr. 183, 190–91 (1964); Eisbrenner v. Stanley, 106 Mich. App. 356, 308 N.W.2d 209 (1981); Texas Employers' Ins. Ass'n v. Phillips, 255 S.W.2d 364, 366 (Tex. Civ. App. 1953).

21. Brokopp v. Ford Motor Co., 71 Cal. App. 3d 841, 860, 139 Cal. Rptr. 888, 899 (1977); Clark v. Yellow Cab Co., 195 So. 2d 39, 39–40 (Fla. Dist. Ct. App. 1967).

22. People v. Johnson, 121 Cal. App. 3d 94, 102, 175 Cal Rptr. 8, 12 (1981); Strout v. American Stores Co., 385 Pa. 230, 235, 122 A.2d 797, 799 (1956); Polk v. Kavelin, 332 Ill. App. 660, 76 N.E.2d 353 (1947).

23. Fleming v. Safeco Ins. Co., 160 Cal. App. 3d 31, 41–42, 206 Cal. Rptr. 313, 318 (1984); Heina v. Broadway Fruit Mkt., Inc., 304 Mass. 608, 611, 24 N.E.2d 510, 512 (1939); Gillespie v. Chrysler Motors Corp., 135 Ill. 2d 363, 373, 553 N.E.2d 291, 296 (1990).

24. Brokopp v. Ford Motor Co., 71 Cal. App. 3d 841, 861, 139 Cal. Rptr. 888, 899–900 (1977); Hall v. Chicago & N.W. Ry. Co., 5 Ill. 2d 135, 150, 125 N.E.2d 77, 88 (1955); Sanchez v. LeBlanc, 400 So. 2d 349, 352 (La. Ct. App. 1981).

25. Neumann v. Bishop, 59 Cal. App. 39 451, 476, 130 Cal. Rptr. 786, 803 (1976); Ferry v. Checker Taxi Co., 165 Ill. App. 3d 744, 751, 520 N.E.2d 733, 738 (1987).

26. McLemore v. International Union, 264 Ala. 538, 88 So. 2d 170 (1956); Kolaric v. Kaufman, 261 Cal. App. 2d 20, 27–28, 67 Cal. Rptr. 729, 733 (1968); Mindt v. Shavers, 214 Neb. 786, 795, 337 N.W.2d 97, 102 (1983).

27. Neumann v. Bishop, 59 Cal. App. 3d 451, 473, 130 Cal. Rptr. 786, 801 (1976); People v. Davis, 46 Ill. 2d 554, 560, 264 N.E.2d 140, 143 (1970).

28. Woods v. Burlington N. R.R. Co., 768 F.2d 1287, 1292 (11th Cir. 1985); Horn v. Atcheson & Santa Fe, 61 Cal. 2d 602, 609–10, 394 P.2d 561, 565 (1964); Dillon v. Bundy, 72 Ohio App. 3d 767, 775, 596 N.E.2d 500, 506 (1991).

29. Allison v. Actonia-Etheridge Coal Co., 289 Ala. 943, 447, 268 So. 2d 725, 729 (1972); Hoffman v. Brandt, 65 Cal. 2d 549, 553, 55 Cal. Rptr. 417, 428 (1966); Duke v. American Olean Tile Co., 155 Mich. App. 555, 562, 400 N.W.2d 677, 681 (1986).

30. Botta v. Brunner, 138 A.2d 713, 723 (N.J. 1958); Certified T.V. & Appliance Co. v. Harrington, 201 Va. 109, 115, 109 S.E.2d 126, 131 (1959). *Contra* Yates v. Wenk, 363 Mich. 311, 318–19, 109 N.W.2d 828, 831 (1961).

CHAPTER 11

Posttrial Motions

CAROL A. MAGER*

MAUREEN M. RAYBURN†

---

* *Mager Law Firm; Philadelphia, Pennsylvania.*

† *Ballard, Spahr, Andrews & Ingrsoll; Philadelphia, Pennsylvania.*

I. Introduction

Trial may be only the beginning. Significant posttrial motions may snatch defeat from the jaws of victory. Or vice versa.

II. Postverdict Motion for Judgment as a Matter of Law (Formerly JNOV)

After an employment case trial today, posttrial motion practice is almost inevitable. To ease the posttrial burden, trial counsel should prepare early for both filing and defending against such motions.

A. In General

Prior to 1991, under the Federal Rules of Civil Procedure, two different terms were used for motions seeking judgment as a matter of law: The preverdict motion, in which the mover asked the court to enter a judgment for the moving party as a matter of law, was called a motion for a directed verdict. The postverdict motion, in which the mover asked the court to replace what was considered to be an erroneous verdict with a decision as a matter of law, was known as a motion for judgment notwithstanding the verdict, or JNOV.

The 1991 amendments to the Federal Rules of Civil Procedure abolished this terminology distinction. The rules now refer to the motion formerly known as a directed verdict motion, as a motion for judgment as a matter of law. The former motion for a JNOV is now called a renewal of motion for judgment after trial.

Amended Rule 50 governs both preverdict and postverdict motions. Fed. R. Civ. P. Rule 50(a)(1) provides for preverdict judgment as a matter of law:

> If during a trial by jury a party has been fully heard on an issue and there is no legally sufficient evidentiary basis for a reasonable jury to find for that party on that issue, the court may determine the issue against that party and may grant a motion for judgment as a matter of law against that party with respect to a claim or defense that cannot under the controlling law be maintained or defeated without a favorable finding on that issue.

Such preverdict motions "for judgment as a matter of law" are allowed under Fed. R. Civ. P. 50(a)(2) at any time before submission of the case to the jury.

Rule 50(b) provides for postverdict renewal of motions for a judgment as a matter of law, previously known as a motion for JNOV. Movants must preserve the right to move for judgment as a matter of law *after* the jury has rendered a verdict by moving for judgment as a matter of law *before* the case is submitted to the jury.[1] The postverdict motion for judgment as a matter of law under Fed. R. Civ. P. 50(b) must be served and filed no more than ten days after entry of the judgment.

The grant of a postverdict motion for judgment as a matter of law does not necessarily result in a reversal of the jury's verdict. Renewal of a motion for judgment as a matter of law under Fed. R. Civ. P. 50(b) is often combined with a Fed. R. Civ. Rule 59 motion for a new trial. A renewed motion for judgment as a matter of law asks the court to reopen the verdict and either set aside the jury's verdict and enter judgment for the moving party or reopen the verdict for the purpose of vacating it and granting a new trial.

The court may conditionally grant a motion for judgment as a matter of law under Fed. R. Civ. P. 50(c)(1) that is joined with, or sought in the alternative to, a motion for a new trial:

> If the renewed motion for judgment as a matter of law is granted, the court shall also rule on the motion for a new trial, if any, by determining whether it should be granted if the judgment is thereafter vacated or reversed, and shall specify the grounds for granting or denying the motion for the new trial. In case the motion for a new trial has been conditionally granted and the judgment is reversed on appeal, the new trial shall proceed unless the appellate court has otherwise ordered.

B. The Standard

The standard of review to be applied by the court in reviewing a renewed motion for judgment as a matter of law is clear and has been often stated, as in *Brady v. Southern R.R.*, 320 U.S. 476, 479–80 (1943):

> When the evidence is such that without weighing the credibility of the witnesses there can be but one reasonable conclusion as to the verdict, the court should determine the proceeding by . . . judgment notwithstanding the verdict. By such direction . . . the result is saved from the mischance of speculation over legally unfounded claims.

This is a different, stricter standard of review than that which is applied on a motion for a new trial, which is generally committed to the sound discretion of the trial court.[2]

A postverdict motion for judgment as a matter of law is also distinguished from a motion for new trial as the court must consider "the evidence in the light and with all reasonable inferences most favorable to the party who secured the jury verdict."[3] This is generally not the standard applied on a motion for a new trial, discussed in more detail in Section III of this chapter. The grant of a postverdict motion for judgment as a matter of law is an extreme measure that displaces the jury's function and allows the court to substitute its judgment for that of the jury. Such motions are not often granted but may be granted in an employment discrimination case.

In *Gillespie v. First Interstate Bank*, 717 F. Supp. 649 (E.D. Wis. 1989), a male black employee sued the bank for race discrimination and retaliatory discharge under 42 U.S.C. §1981 and Title VII of the Civil Rights Act of 1964, as amended. He sued after he was denied a promotion in favor of a white female, filed a charge of discrimination with the Equal Employment Opportunity Commission, and was terminated three months later. The jury returned a verdict for plaintiff on the Section § 1981 claim, and defendant moved for JNOV, or in the alternative, for a new trial. The court granted the motion for JNOV on the issue of the promotion because no inference of pretext properly could have been drawn by the jury because plaintiff's circumstantial evidence had not adequately rebutted defendant's nondiscriminatory reason for denying plaintiff a promotion. Without an inference of pretext, and with no direct evidence of discrimination, the jury could not, as a matter of law, find that defendant had discriminated against plaintiff on the basis of race.

In contrast, the motion for JNOV was denied in *Valenti v. International Mill Serv., Inc.*, 634 F. Supp. 57 (E.D. Pa. 1985), where the jury found for three discharged employees who sued their former employer for age discrimination. Defendant argued that a JNOV was warranted because the jury's conclusions were based on speculation and emotion and consequently were contrary to the evidence; that no competent evidence was introduced to establish pretext, and that the finding of willfulness in the discharge decisions was "not supported by the evidence."[4]

The court denied the motion for JNOV stating:

> The purpose of a motion for JNOV is not to relitigate the case . . . it is not the court's function to review inconsistencies in the evidence and determine which testimony is credible; to do so would require de novo review of each credibility determination and would undermine the province of the jury. Accordingly, the defendant's motion for JNOV will be denied as the evidence was legally sufficient to warrant the verdicts reached.[5]

III. Motions for New Trial

A. In General

Fed. R. Civ. Pr. 59(a) provides the grounds upon which a new trial may be granted:

> A new trial may be granted to all or any of the parties on all or part of the issues (1) in an action in which there has been a trial by jury, for any of the reasons for which new trials have heretofore been granted in actions at law in the courts of the United States; and (2) in an action tried without a jury, for any of the reasons for which rehearings have heretofore been granted in suits in equity in the courts of the United States. On a motion

for a new trial in an action tried without a jury, the court may open the judgment if one has been entered, take additional testimony, amend findings of fact and conclusions of law or make new findings and conclusions, and direct the entry of a new judgment.

Rule 59(d) provides the circumstances under which a new trial may be granted by the court on its own initiative or upon motion by a party but for reasons not asserted by either party:

Not later than 10 days after entry of judgment the court of its own initiative may order a new trial for any reason for which it might have granted a new trial on motion for a party. After giving the parties notice and an opportunity to be heard on the matter, the court may grant a motion for a new trial, timely served, for a reason not stated in the motion. In either case, the court shall specify in the order the grounds therefor.

A motion for a new trial may be made in accordance with Rule 59 or it may, pursuant to Rule 50(b), be combined with a motion for judgment as a matter of law or sought in the alternative:

Whenever a motion for a judgment as a matter of law made at the close of all the evidence is denied or for any reason is not granted, the court is deemed to have submitted the action to the jury subject to a later determination of the legal questions raised by the motion. . . . A motion for a new trial under Rule 59 may be joined with a renewal of the motion for judgment as a matter of law, or a new trial may be requested in the alternative. If a verdict was returned, the court may, in disposing of the renewed motion, allow the judgment to stand or may reopen the judgment and either order a new trial or direct the entry of judgment as a matter of law. If no verdict was returned, the court may, in disposing of the renewed motion, direct the entry of judgment as a matter of law or may order a new trial.

The party making a motion for a new trial must be aware of certain time limits. Rule 59(b) provides that a "motion for a new trial shall be served not later than 10 days after the entry of the judgment."[6] A timely motion for a new trial stops the running of time within which an appeal may be taken. The time for appeal then begins to run from the date of entry of order denying the motion for new trial.[7] If the court grants a motion for a new trial, the order cannot be appealed until after the new trial is held and a final judgment has been entered.[8]

Note that a court may also consider motions for remittur or additur, to reduce or increase damages. A later portion of this chapter discusses these issues.

B. The Standard

It is not grounds for a new trial that the trial judge disagrees with the verdict reached by the jury, or that the judge would have decided differently had the trial been a nonjury trial. The standard of review for a motion for a new trial is one that has been referred to as the "manifest miscarriage of justice standard."[9] The district court may grant a motion for a new trial only if it is convinced that the jury's verdict is "against the clear weight of the evidence or is based upon evidence which is false or will result in clear miscarriage of justice."[10]

Courts apply the "manifest miscarriage of justice standard," holding that a new trial is justified where, for example, "the verdict is against the weight of the evidence, damages are excessive, or the trial was not fair to the moving party for some other reason."[11] New trials are granted in employment discrimination cases when substantial errors were made in admitting or excluding evidence,[12] or in giving jury instructions.[13]

However, "harmless errors" will not provide the basis for a new trial under Fed. R. Civ. P. 61:

> No error in either the admission or the exclusion of evidence and no error or defect in any ruling or order or in anything done or omitted by the court or by any of the parties is grounds for granting a new trial or for setting aside a verdict . . . unless refusal to take such action appears to the court inconsistent with substantial justice. The court at every stage of the proceeding must disregard any error or defect in the proceeding which does not affect the substantial rights of the parties.

In contrast with the postverdict motion for judgment as a matter of law, where the court must view the evidence in the light most favorable to the nonmoving party, the court considering a motion for a new trial need not view the evidence in the light most favorable to the party who prevailed at trial. On a motion for a new trial, the court is free to weigh the evidence and set aside the verdict where the evidence to support the verdict is insufficient, even if the level of insufficiency would not be enough to sustain a motion for judgment as a matter of law.[14]

While courts have generally applied a different, more lenient standard of review on a motion for a new trial, some courts deciding employment discrimination cases apply the same standard of review to both motions.[15]

IV. Petition for Lawyer's Fees and Other Costs

A. Lawyer's Fees

A prevailing party may recover lawyer's fees under Title VII, 42 U.S.C. § 2000e-5(k), and under the Age Discrimination in Employment Act (ADEA), 29 U.S.C. § 626. The plain language of § 2000e-5(k) allows the prevailing party—either plaintiff or defendant—to recover lawyer's fees. However, courts award prevailing defendant's lawyer's fees only in limited circumstances given the purpose behind the award of lawyer's fees. Lawyer's fees, costs, and expenses are available if counsel irrationally and unreasonably multiples litigation, 28 U.S.C. § 1927.

Local rules and practices usually control the practical aspects of seeking lawyer's fees. Fed R. Civ. Proc. 54(d)(2) generally requires a motion applying for fees within 14 days of entry of judgment.

1. Standard for an Award of Fees to Prevailing Plaintiff

A prevailing plaintiff is entitled to an award of lawyer's fees unless special circumstances would render the award unjust.[16]

There is no issue as to who is the "prevailing party" when a plaintiff is successful on all claims brought. But questions as to who is the "prevailing party" arise when plaintiff is successful on some, but not all, aspects of a claim, and did not get the relief requested. The Supreme Court in *Farrar v. Hobby*, 113 S. Ct. 566, 572–73 (1992), stated that to be considered a "prevailing party:"

> the plaintiff must be able to point to a resolution of the dispute which changes the legal relationship between itself and the defendant. . . . Therefore, to qualify as a prevailing party, a civil rights plaintiff must obtain at least some relief on the merits of his claim.

Normally, when the plaintiff is entitled to some form of injunctive relief or damages, the element is satisfied. The Court in *Farrar* further established that a plaintiff who recovers nominal damages qualifies as a prevailing party under the lawyer's fees provision of the Civil Rights Act.

Special circumstances may make an award of lawyer's fees unjust, but the Supreme Court has made clear that the special circumstances exception is extremely narrow.[17] For example, absence of bad faith or of specific intent on the part of the defendant does not constitute special circumstances.

Special circumstances may make the award of lawyer's fees unjust when the purpose of the statute—vigorous enforcement of antidiscrimination laws—would not be furthered by the plaintiff's suit. For instance, special circumstances might exist when a plaintiff brings an action for discrimination well after the employer has cured the discriminatory conduct for which the action was brought. In the vast majority of cases, however, a "prevailing party" qualifies for an award of lawyer's fees.

2. Standard for an Award of Lawyer's Fees to a Prevailing Defendant

Defendants are awarded lawyer's fees under Title VII and the Age Discrimination in Employment Act (ADEA) only when the claim brought by the plaintiff was frivolous, unreasonable, or without foundation.[18] The defendant is entitled to lawyer's fees when the plaintiff continued action despite knowledge of the statute of limitations bar.[19] The defendant may be awarded union lawyer's fees in an ADEA action.[20]

3. Calculating the Amount of the Lawyer's Fees— "The Lodestar"

Once a party qualifies for an award of fees, the court must calculate the amount. Courts have established a formula to arrive at the proper lawyer's fees awardable to a prevailing party, which can vary from zero to an amount greater than any damages recovered.

This formula, called "The Lodestar," is designed to further the statutory purpose of encouraging private enforcement of the civil rights statutes. To arrive at the fee award, the court multiplies a reasonable hourly rate by the number of hours reasonably expended on the litigation.

a. Reasonable Hourly Rate

The reasonable hourly rate is the market rate for a lawyer with similar skill, experience, and reputation in the relevant geographic area. Usually a court will use the lawyer's regular hourly billable rate.[21]

b. Amount of Time Reasonably Expended on Litigation

Accurate billing entries will be an exhibit to the fee petition and should contain detailed descriptions of the time billed by all lawyers and legal assistants. The court will begin by examining the record of the amount of time the attorney actually billed to the case in considering the "reasonableness" of the lawyer's fee application and may exclude any hours not supported by documentation.[22]

Three inquiries are conducted on the number of hours reported by a lawyer in a fee application. First, the court determines whether the hours should be reduced because they were not "reasonably expended." In this context, the test is basically whether the hours would be ethical if charged to a regular paying client: "Counsel for the prevailing party should make a good faith effort to exclude from a fee request hours that are excessive, redundant, or otherwise unnecessary, just as a lawyer in private practice ethically is obligated to exclude such hours from his fee submission."[23] The court will examine whether the litigation was overstaffed or whether the skill and experience of the lawyers on the case was in some way counterproductive.

Therefore, a lawyer should review the fee request with a specific eye toward "reasonableness." For example, the lawyer should be wary of billings that reflect long strategy conferences with multiple attorneys or bills that charge the time of a partner for work that is normally performed by a lower-billing associate, such as research. If the request appears unreasonable, there is a risk that the lawyer will provoke the judge to reduce the fees or possibly award no fee at all.

The second and third factors for adjustment turn on the results obtained. The court examines whether the plaintiff failed to succeed on any claims wholly unrelated to the claims on which he or she did succeed. A claim is wholly unrelated where there is no factual or legal similarity. Advancing different theories under Title VII normally does not implicate this factor because the claims are related both legally and factually.[24] If there were claims, however, for which the plaintiff was unsuccessful, but that were wholly unrelated, then the award should be reduced by the time expended on those claims.

Next the court examines whether there were any unsuccessful claims interrelated to the claims for which the plaintiff recovered. When such claims exist the court will determine whether the award should be reduced to compensate for such unsuccessful claims. The determination depends on plaintiff's overall level of success. If the plaintiff has obtained excellent results, then the court will not reduce the award based on unsuccessful interrelated claims. However, when the overall result was unimportant, and counter to the actual relief sought, the court may consider reduction. For example, when a plaintiff requests large compensatory and punitive damages, but the jury or the court awards only nominal damages, the court often will reduce the compensable hours to zero.[25]

c. Contingent Fee

The Supreme Court made clear in *City of Burlington v. Dague*, 112 S. Ct. 2638 (1992), that it will not enhance reasonable lawyer's fees that are recoverable under federal statutes because the lawyer represented the plaintiff on a contingent fees basis. The Court held that to do so would make the lawyer's fee determination more complex, arbitrary, and unpredictable, resulting in increased litigation. However, various states do allow contingency fee multipliers and counsel should check their local jurisdiction's statues and case law.

d. Multipliers (and Reducers)

Once a court has determined a lodestar, the court has discretion to increase—or decrease—that amount. Courts may consider these factors: (i) the risk taken by the plaintiff's attorney of not prevailing, (ii) the achievement of exceptional success by the attorney; (iii) the level of skill exhibited by the prevailing attorney; (iv) the attorney's preclusion from other employment because of the demands of the case; (v) the complexity of the case; (vi) the unsettled legal issues in the case; (vii) the encouragement to other attorneys to accept cases; (viii) compensation for the dely in payment of fees; and (ix) the unreasonable refusal of the opponent to settle.[26]

4. Administrative Hearings Included within Fee Award

Lawyer's fees are recoverable for time spent handling mandatory state or federal administrative proceedings.[27] The plaintiff can recover for private lawyer's fees even when the plaintiff is not required to have representation by a lawyer or where a representative is available from the state. The only restriction is that the administrative proceeding be mandatory.

5. Petition for Fees Included in Fee Award

The attorney should include in the fee petition the time spent preparing the lawyer's fees petition, and the time spent defending a challenged request for fees. As a practical matter, the lawyer should separately designate the time spent recovering lawyer's fees.

6. Expert Fees Awarded as Part of Lawyer's Fees

Title VII was amended in 1991 to allow courts the discretion to award expert fees as part of the lawyer's fees.[28] This amendment was in response to several court decisions that denied, or strictly limited, expert fee recovery. Under the Age Discrimination in Employment Act, the recovery of fees for experts is unsettled.[29]

B. Costs

Title VII and the Age Discrimination in Employment Act also provide that costs may be awarded to the prevailing party.[30] Local rules or practices often affect costs petitions. There is a form for your bill of costs for federal court. Awardable costs are those that are traditionally passed on to the client. This may include computer-assisted research, filing fees, witness fees, travel expenses, deposition expenses, and copying charges.

The costs sought must be reasonable. To increase the chance that a court will find the costs reasonable, the lawyer should attempt to break down the costs and identify the purpose of the charge. For example, rather than submitting a large figure for computer research expense, the total should be broken down to identify the time spent researching particular issues and also the time spent checking the validity of citations.

V. Motion for Remittitur (or Additur)

A losing defendant in an employment case may have a basis for a reduction in damages if the court finds the verdict was unreasonably high—so exorbitant as to shock the judicial conscience, when it is clearly unsupported by the evidence or when it exceeds the amount needed to make the plaintiff whole.[31] Some courts will also grant a motion for reduction if the verdict reflects bias, passion, prejudice or the improper motive on the part of the jury; other courts will grant a motion for a new trial on this issue, as described earlier in this chapter.

Remittitur gives the plaintiff the choice of submitting to a new trial on accepting a reduced amount of damages as determined by the court.

Additur is theoretically possible when a verdict is unreasonable low. Research, however, has not disclosed such an order for employment cases.[33]

VI. Motion to Mold the Verdict

Following a successful jury verdict awarding damages, plaintiffs typically file motions to mold the verdict in order to recover an award of pre-trial and and post-trial interest on the verdict. Some plaintiffs also seek an additional amount as compensation for the negative tax consequences of the jury's damages verdict, *i.e.* for the various taxes plaintiffs owe that result in a higher-tax bracket. In response, defendents can make a structural settlement rather than a lump sum payment.

A. Motions for Sanctions under Rule 11*

Rule 11 allows for the imposition of sanctions for groundless pleadings, motions, or other papers filed with the court. Rule 11 places certain minimum obligations on all lawyers before signing and submitting papers to the court.

---

* See also chapter 13, "Professionalism and Ethics," regarding Rule 11 motions.

Rule 11 contains two grounds for sanctions: (1) where there is no basis in law or in fact for the pleading and (2) where the pleading is brought for an improper purpose, such as to harass, cause unnecessary delay, or increase the cost of litigation.[34]

A lawyer's signature signifies that the lawyer has satisfied three duties:

1. that the lawyer has read the documents;
2. that the lawyer has made a reasonable inquiry as to the facts and law therein; and
3. that the lawyer is not acting in bad faith.[35]

Each duty is independent, and the violation of any one duty triggers a Rule 11 violation.

In 1993, Rule 11 was amended. This amendment was in recognition of the fact that Rule 11, a rule designed to reduce federal court litigation, had itself generated extensive litigation. Significantly, the amendment made the award of Rule 11 sanctions discretionary, and it added a safe harbor.

Rule 11 was amended to provide that sanctions for a Rule 11 violation are no longer mandatory. The imposition of sanctions in the case of a Rule 11 violation is totally within the discretion of the trial judge, and the decisions of the judge on all aspects of the Rule 11 motion will be reviewed under an abuse-of-discretion standard. The Advisory Committee Notes to the Rule detail the factors a judge should consider in deciding to impose sanctions:

> Whether the improper conduct was willful, or negligent; whether it was part of a pattern of activity, or an isolated event; whether it infected the entire pleadings, or only one particular count or defense; whether the person has engaged in similar conduct in other litigation; whether it was intended to injure; what effect it had on the litigation process in time or expense; whether the responsible person is trained in the law; what amount, given the financial resources of the responsible person, is needed to deter that person from repetition in the same case; what amount is needed to deter similar activity by other litigants.

Rule 11 dictates that the district court judge determine the sanction with an eye toward the purpose of Rule 11—the deterrence of similar conduct in the future. Thus, the rule now specifically provides for and encourages the court to require the violator to pay a fine into the court. However, the court may instead exercise its discretion to award the movant reasonable lawyer's fees and costs. The determination turns on which remedy is likely to discourage the conduct in the future.

Rule 11 was also amended to provide a safe harbor—a 21-day waiting period during which a party charged with a Rule 11 violation can withdraw the pleading that allegedly violates Rule 11. As a result of the amendment, the procedure for filing a Rule 11 motion has been altered.

The moving party must first serve the Rule 11 motion on the opposing party pursuant to Rule 5. If after 21 days, the opposing party has not corrected or withdrawn the paper, then the motion may be filed with the court. The Advisory Committee Notes also speak of a required informal notice prior to the service of the motion on the opposing party:

> [C]ounsel should be expected to give informal notice to the other party, whether in person or by telephone call or letter, of a potential violation before proceeding to prepare and serve a Rule 11 motion.

Failure to comply with this informal notice may result in the rejection of the Rule 11 motion.

VII. Appendix: Posttrial Checklists for the Practitioner

1. **Postverdict Motion for Judgment as a Matter of Law**
   A postverdict motion for judgment as a matter of law (formerly known as JNOV) filed in federal district court should contain the following:
   A. Proposed order
   B. Motion for judgment as a matter of law (with supporting affidavits or exhibits as applicable)
   C. Memorandum of law in support of motion
   D. Certificate of service

2. **Motion for a New Trial**
   A motion for a new trial filed in federal district court should contain the following:
   A. Proposed order
   B. Motion for a new trial (with supporting affidavits or exhibits as applicable)
   C. Memorandum of law in support of motion
   D. Certificate of service

3. **Motion for Lawyer's Fees and Costs**
   A motion for fees and costs filed in federal district court should contain the following:
   A. Proposed order
   B. Motion for lawyer's fees and costs
   C. Memorandum of law in support of motion
   D. Certificate or affidavit of service
   E. Affidavit of lawyer's fees (This should be an affidavit from the lead billing lawyer stating the fees of all lawyers on the case and stating that the time billed was reasonably incurred in bringing the action.)
   F. A brief biography of lawyers and legal assistants whose time is billed to the case
   G. A detailed breakdown of lawyer's fees and costs

4. **Rule 11 Motion**
   A Rule 11 motion filed in federal district court should contain the following:
   A. Proposed order
   B. Motion for sanctions pursuant to rule 11
   C. Memorandum of law in support of motion
   D. Certificate of service
   E. A second certificate of service when the motion is actually filed with the court 21 days after the first Certificate of Service

Notes

1. *See, e.g.,* 9A CHARLES A. WRIGHT & ARTHUR R. MILLER, FEDERAL PRACTICE AND PROCEDURE, § 2357, at 335–36 (1995).

2. Boyce v. Board of County Comm's, 857 F. Supp. 794, 796 (D. Kan. 1994) (citing McDonough Power Equip., Inc. v. Greenwood, 464 U.S. 548, 556 (1984)).

3. Valenti v. Int'l Mill Serv. Inc., 634 F. Supp. 57, 60 (E.D. Pa. 1985) (citing Fireman's Fund Ins. Co. v. Videfreeze Corp., 540 F.2d 1171 (3d Cir. 1976), *cert. denied,* 429 U.S. 1053 (1977)).

4. *Id.* at 60.

5. *Id.* at 61 (citations omitted).

6. FED. R. CIV. P. 59(b).

7. Fed. R. App. P. 4(a)(4).

8. Grace Lines, Inc. v. Motley, 439 F.2d 1028, 1031 n.2 (2d Cir. 1971).

9. *See, e.g.,* Freeman v. Package Mach. Co., 865 F.2d 1331, 1333 (lst Cir. 1988).

10. *Id.* at 1333–34; *see, e.g.,* Abrams v. Lightolier, Inc., 841 F. Supp. 584, 592 (D.N.J. 1994), *aff'd in relevant part,* 50 F.3d 1204 (3d Cir. 1995).

11. Dombeck v. Milwaukee Valve Co., 823 F. Supp. 1475, 1479 (W.D. Wis. 1993) (citations omitted), *vacated on other grounds,* 40 F.3d 230 (7th Cir. 1994).

12. *See e.g.,* Dombeck, 823 F. Supp. at 1479.

13. *See, e.g.,* Morgan v. Kansas City Area Transp. Auth., 720 F. Supp. 758 (W.D. Mo. 1989).

14. J.H. FRIEDENTHAL ET AL., CIVIL PROCEDURE § 12.4, at 555 (1993); *see also* 11 CHARLES A. WRIGHT & ARTHUR R. MILLER, FEDERAL PRACTICE AND PROCEDURE § 2806, at 44–45 (1995).

15. *See, e.g.,* Courtney v. Safelite Glass Corp., 811 F. Supp. 1466, 1471 (D. Kan. 1992) (*citing* Joyce v. Davis, 539 F.2d 1262 (10th Cir. 1976)) ("[i]n reviewing a motion for a new trial, the court must view the evidence in the light most favorable to the prevailing party").

16. Christiansburg Garment Co. v. EEOC, 434 U.S. 412, 417 (1978).

17. New York Gaslight Club v. Carey, 447 U.S. 54 (1980).

18. Christiansburg Garment Co. v. EEOC, 434 U.S. 412 (1978).

19. Ford v. Temple Hosp., 790 F.2d 342 (3d Cir. 1986).

20. Cote v. James River Corp., 761 F.2d 61 (1st Cir. 1985).

21. *See, e.g.,* Malarkey v. Texaco, Inc., 794 F. Supp. 1237, 1246 (S.D.N.Y. 1992) (awarding $175 per hour for partners and $100 per hour for associates despite lawyers' inexperience in civil rights litigation), *aff'd,* 983 F.2d 1204 (2d Cir. 1993).

22. Hensley v. Eckerhart, 461 U.S. 424 (1983).

23. *Id.* at 434.

24. Muvree v. Local 41, Int'l Bhd. of Elec. Workers, 847 F. Supp. 1059 (W.D.N.Y.) , *aff'd,* 29 F.3d 620 (2d Cir. 1994).

25. Farrar v. Hobby, 113 S.Ct. 566 at 572–73 (1992).

26. *See, e.g.,* Hensley v. Eckerhard, 461 U.S. 424, 429–430, 103 S.CT. 1933, 1937–1938 (1983), *referring to,* Johnson v. Georgia Highway Express, Inc., 488 F.2D 714 (5th Cir. 1974).

27. New York Gaslight Club, Inc. v. Carey, 447 U.S. 54 (1980).

28. 42 U.S.C.A. § 2000e-5(k).

29. *See, e.g.,* Downes v. Volkswagen of America, Inc., 41 F.3d 1132, 1144 (7th Cir. 1993) (expert fees recoverable as costs under Civil Rights Attorney Fees Award Act); Pinkham v. Camex, 894 F.3d 292, 295 (8th cir. 1996) (expert fees not recoverable).

30. 42 U.S.C. § 2000 e-5(k); 29 U.S.C. §§ 216(b), 626(b).

31. *See, e.g.,* Starceski v. Westinghouse Elec. Corp., 54 F.3d 1089 (3rd Cir. 1995); Brunneman v. Terra Int'l, Inc., 975 F.2d 175, 178 (5th Cir. 1992).

32. Gasperini v. Center for Humanities, Inc., 518 U.S. 415, 433 (1996).

33. *See, e.g.,* Dimick v. Schiedt, 293 U.S. 474, 486–488, 55 S.Ct. 296, 301 (1935); Taylor v. Green, 868 F.2d 162, 164–165 (5th Cir. 1989), *cert. denied,* 110 S.Ct. 761 (1990) (added nominal damages in prisoner civil rights case).

34. Total Tele. Ent. Corp. v. Chestnut Hill Village Assoc., 14 5 F.R.D. 375, 382 (E.D.

Pa. 1993) (granting sanctions where court dismissed plaintiff's complaint for lack of jurisdiction and plaintiff frivolously attempted to reassert jurisdiction on previously unasserted grounds in subsequent filing).

35. CTC Imports & Exports v. Nigerian Petroleum Corp., 951 F.2d 573, 578 (3d Cir. 1991), *cert. denied,* 504 U.S. 914 (1992).

CHAPTER 12

Appeals

BLESS STRITAR YOUNG*
CALVIN HOUSE†

---

* Formerly of Fulbright & Jaworski L.L.P.; Los Angeles, California; Currently Park City, Utah.

† Gutierrez & Preciado; Pasadena, California.

I. Introduction

Neither the jury's verdict nor the disposition of the last pretrial motion necessarily concludes the case. The loser normally has the right to appeal. This chapter focuses upon federal appellate procedure, the Federal Rules of Civil Procedure, and the Federal Rules of Appellate Procedure and identifies several important issues that an employment lawyer might encounter in the appellate process. Each circuit court of appeals may have its own "local" rules that vary or supplement those provisions. A lawyer involved in an appeal should review those rules carefully at the outset. For example, local rules vary regarding briefs and appendices.

II. Appealability

The district judge has just issued a ruling, and the losing lawyer is certain that the ruling is erroneous. Before rushing off to the court of appeals, the lawyer must first determine whether the court of appeals may review the ruling. Generally, the court of appeals will only entertain an appeal at the conclusion of the entire case.

A. Final Decision Rule

The jurisdiction of the U.S. courts of appeals is generally limited to review of "final" decisions of the district courts.[1] A decision is final if it "ends the litigation on the merits and leaves nothing for the court to do but execute the judgment."[2] For example, the entry of judgment on a jury verdict for plaintiff in the amount of $500,000 is a final decision that is immediately appealable. The denial of a defendant's motion to dismiss for failure to state a claim does not end the litigation and is *not* immediately appealable. The following sections explain the application of the final judgment rule to particular situations, and some exceptions to the rule.

1. Removed Cases

Because many employment cases make their way into federal court through removal, it is particularly important that employment lawyers understand the rules governing appealability of decisions that determine the propriety of removal. A refusal to remand a removed case does not end the case, is not a final decision, and therefore is not appealable.[3]

Moreover, by statute, "[a]n order remanding a case to the State court from which it was removed is not reviewable on appeal or otherwise."[4]

2. Collateral Orders

A "collateral order" is immediately appealable, even if it does not end the entire case. To be "collateral," the order "must conclusively determine the disputed question, resolve an important issue completely separate from the merits of the action, and be effectively unreviewable on appeal from a final judgment."[5]

Some examples of orders held to be collateral, and therefore immediately appealable, are denial of a claim of immunity, refusal to require posting of a bond in a shareholder derivative action, and an order imposing the costs of notice to class members on the defendant.

The collateral order doctrine poses a potential problem for litigants who forego an opportunity to appeal from what might later turn out to be an appealable collateral order. Under 28 U.S.C. § 2107 and Fed. R. App. P. 4(a), an appeal from a final order must be filed within 30 days of entry of the order.

One might argue that the ability to obtain review of a collateral order is lost if a notice of appeal is not filed within those 30 days.[6] The better view, however, is that an immediate appeal from a collateral order is optional and that review is available on appeal from a final judgment if the party does not exercise the option.[7]

3. Injunctions

By statute, appeals from orders "granting, continuing, modifying, refusing or dissolving injunctions, or refusing to dissolve or modify injunctions" are immediately appealable.[8] This includes the dismissal of a claim for a permanent injunction, even though other claims remain.[9] It includes the grant or denial of a preliminary injunction but *not* of a temporary restraining order.[10]

4. Final Judgment, Federal Rule of Civil Procedure 54(b)

Where an action involves multiple claims or multiple parties, the district court has discretion to enter a "final judgment" as to fewer than all the claims or parties. To do so, it must make "an express determination that there is no just reason for delay."[11]

5. Certification, 28 U.S.C. sec. 1292(b)

A party may also ask the district court to certify an otherwise non-appealable decision for appellate review. Such certification is limited, however, to orders involving "a controlling question of law as to which there is substantial ground for difference of opinion" in circumstances where "an immediate appeal from the order may materially advance the ultimate termination of the litigation."[12] The court of appeals is not required to take the appeal, but may, "in its discretion," permit the appeal.

6. Arbitration

The Federal Arbitration Act favors arbitration as a means of resolving disputes. Pursuant to that policy, orders favoring arbitration (such as ones compelling arbitration or staying an action pending arbitration) are generally *not* appealable. Orders disfavoring arbitration (such as ones refusing to compel arbitration or refusing a stay) generally *are* appealable.[13] (See chapter 14, "Arbitration and Mediation.")

7. Postjudgment Orders

Several types of orders may follow entry of a final judgment. They include an award of costs or of lawyer's fees, decisions dealing with enforcement of the judgment, or the disposition of a motion to vacate the judgment. Such decisions are considered "final" under 28 U.S.C. § 1291 and are therefore appealable independently of the final judgment.[14] (See chapter 14, "Arbitration and Mediation.")

B. Separate Document Rule

The district court may generate a number of pieces of paper related to its final decision. For example, an order granting a motion to dismiss is normally merely preliminary to a later judgment of dismissal. To ensure that the parties know when their time to appeal starts to run, the district court must set forth its "judgment" on a "separate document."[15] Even if the trial court's memorandum decision recites that an action is "dismissed," the time to appeal does not start to run until that separate "judgment" is entered.[16] The "separate documents" requirement may be waived. Therefore, an aggrieved party may appeal from a final order even if the court has not entered a separate judgment.[17] Further, if a notice of appeal is filed before a final order is entered, it "is treated as filed on the date of and after the entry."[18]

C. Review by Mandamus

A party may also seek review by the court of appeals of actions through a petition for writ of mandamus, without regard to whether there is a final decision or not. Filing such a petition technically commences a separate proceeding directly against the district court, asking that it be directed to take particular action. The Supreme Court has held, however, that "it is clear that only exceptional circumstances amounting to a judicial 'usurpation of power' will justify the invocation of this extraordinary remedy."[19]

There are two areas where mandamus is more readily available than the foregoing statement of the general standard might suggest—right to a jury trial and transfer of venue.[20]

III. Notice of Appeal

A party takes an appeal by filing a notice of appeal with the district court (not the court of appeals).[21] (A sample notice of appeal is included among the forms at the end of this chapter.) The notice must be filed "within 30 days after the date of entry of the judgment order appealed from."[22] It is important to note that the rule says 30 days from entry, not from service of notice of entry. While the clerk should serve notice of entry by mail, the clerk's failure to do so does not affect the time to appeal.[23] (See below with respect to getting relief from the filing of an untimely notice of appeal.)

Upon the making of any of the following motions the time for appeal runs from entry of the order disposing of the last such motion: for judgment notwithstanding the verdict, to amend or make additional findings of fact, to alter or amend the judgment, for a new trial, or for relief from judgment.[24] In addition, if a notice of appeal has been filed between the entry of a judgment and the filing of one of those motions, it does not become "effective" until after the last motion has been determined.

Recent amendments to the Federal Rules of Civil Procedure affect the timing of an appeal in a case where a party applies for an award of lawyer's fees. Under new Rule 54(d)(2), an application for lawyer's fees must generally be made by motion within 14 days after entry of judgment. Under revised Rule 58, the trial court may (but apparently is not required to) order that the time to appeal from the underlying judgment does not start to run until the lawyer's-fees motion is decided, provided that the motion is filed before the notice of appeal has become effective. (See chapter 11, "Posttrial Motions," regarding lawyer's fees.)

Under Fed. R. of App. P. 4(a)(5) the district court may extend the time for filing a notice of appeal upon a showing of excusable neglect or good cause provided that an appropriate motion is filed not later than 30 days after the deadline. If a party does not receive notice of entry of the judgment within 30 days of the entry, the district court may reopen the time for filing a notice of appeal. A motion for such relief must be filed within 7 days of receipt of the notice of entry or within 180 days of entry of judgment, whichever is earlier.[25]

IV. Effect on Proceedings in the Trial Court

A. Transfer of Jurisdiction

As a rule, the filing of a notice of appeal transfers jurisdiction over the action from the district court to the court of appeals. The district court loses its authority to do anything further that affects the rights of the parties or the condition of the subject matter involved in the decision from which the appeal is taken.[26]

Certain authority is retained, however. The district court may continue to deal with "collateral" matters that do not relate directly to the pending appeal. After a final judgment on the merits, these would include such matters as awarding costs and lawyer's fees, and correcting clerical errors. If the appeal itself deals with a collateral issue, the district court does not lose jurisdiction to continue with the merits of the case.

The district court also retains jurisdiction to rule on motions for a new trial and for judgment notwithstanding the verdict after a notice of appeal has been filed.[27] (See chapter 11, "Posttrial Motions," regarding these motions.)

B. Stays

The filing of an appeal generally does not automatically suspend the prevailing party's ability to enforce the judgment rendered by the district court. The appellant remains obligated to comply with the judgment unless a stay is obtained.

Federal Rule of Civil Procedure 62 and Federal Rule of Appellate Procedure 8 govern stays pending appeal. There is an initial automatic stay for ten days after entry of every judgment except a judgment in an injunction or receivership action or a judgment for an accounting in a patent infringement action.[28]

The district court also has discretion to enter a stay during the pendency of a posttrial motion for a new trial, for judgment, notwithstanding the verdict, for relief from judgment, or for amended or additional findings.[29]

In all cases except those exempted from the ten-day automatic stay provision, the appellant may obtain a stay by giving a "supersedeas bond." Such a stay becomes effective upon the approval of the bond by the district court.[30] The district court also has discretion to stay enforcement of such a judgment without requiring a bond if other considerations demonstrate that the judgment would be paid if the appeal were unsuccessful.[31]

In cases where the bond method is not available (such as where an injunction was granted), applications for stays are decided under the following standards: "(1) whether the stay applicant has made a strong showing that he is likely to succeed on the merits; (2) whether the applicant will be irreparably injured absent a stay; (3) whether issuance of the stay will substantially injure the other parties; and (4) where the public interest lies."[32]

Application for a stay must usually be made to the district court in the first instance.[33] However, the court of appeals also has authority to issue a stay.[34]

V. Record on Appeal

The pleadings and exhibits filed in the trial court, any necessary transcripts of oral proceedings, and the clerk's docket sheet comprise the record on appeal.[35] The court of appeals has access to the entirety of this record when considering an appeal.

However, appellant's lawyer must prepare an appendix that focuses the appellate court's attention on the dispositive portions of the record. The appendix must contain (1) the relevant docket entries in the proceeding; (2) any relevant portions of the pleadings, charge, findings, or opinion; (3) the judgment, order, or decision in question; and (4) any other parts of the record to which the parties wish to direct the particular attention of the court.[36]

VI. Briefs

The key to a successful appeal is an effective appellate brief. This section explains the rules regarding format and filing. It then offers some suggestions for writing an effective brief.

A. Technical Rules

Appellant's brief is due within forty days after the filing of the record of appeal.[37] The maximum length is fifty pages.[38] The font used must be at least 11 point; the cover should be blue.[39] The party must file twenty-five copies, and serve two copies on each opposing counsel.[40]

The brief must contain the following, in the order indicated:

1. Corporate disclosure statement identifying all parent companies, subsidiaries, and affiliates of a party that have issued shares to the public.[41] (A sample disclosure statement is included among the forms at the end of this chapter.)
2. Table of contents and table of authorities.[42]

3. Statement of jurisdiction stating (a) the statutory basis for subject matter jurisdiction in the district court, (b) the basis for claiming appealability and the statutory basis for jurisdiction in the court of appeals, and (c) the date of entry of the order appealed from, the date of filing of the notice of appeal, and the basis for claiming that the appeal is timely.[43] (A sample statement of jurisdiction is included among the forms at the end of this chapter.)

4. Statement of the issues presented for review.[44]

5. Statement of case, indicating the nature of the case, the course of proceedings, and the disposition in the trial court, followed by a statement of the relevant facts with appropriate references to the records.[45]

6. A summary of argument.[46]

7. An argument.[47]

8. A conclusion stating the precise relief sought from the court of appeals.[48]

9. Certificate of Service.[49]

Appellee's brief must be served and filed within 30 days after service of appellant's brief.[50] This is extended by three days if appellant's brief was served by mail.[51] The cover should be red.[52] Appellee's brief must otherwise follow the same format as appellant's brief except that the statement of jurisdiction may simply state appellee's agreement with appellant's statement, and the statements of issues, the case, and the standard of review may be omitted if appellee is satisfied with appellant's recitation.

Appellant may serve and file a reply brief within 14 days after service of appellee's brief, extended by three days for service by mail.[53] The cover should be gray.[54] The maximum length is 25 pages.[55]

B. Effective Brief Writing

To be an effective writer, one must keep the audience in mind. The audience for an appellate brief are the judges and clerks who will determine the outcome of the appeal. That audience is very busy and has a lot of other briefs to read. To get the audience's attention, the presentation must be lucid and to the point.

The principal goal of an appellate-brief writer should be to marshal the evidence in the record into a convincing story. It is also important to make effective use of legal authorities. It is through the factual presentation, however, that the appellate lawyer persuades the court to look favorably on the case.

Of course, to tell an effective story, the writer must first identify the arguments to be made on appeal. It is advisable to limit the number of arguments to a few cogent ones, rather than to make every point that a creative mind can imagine. Appellate judges and their clerks uniformly advise that strong arguments may lose their effectiveness if they are accompanied by a number of weak arguments. As an appellant, pick out two or three critical issues and brief them thoroughly, concisely, and persuasively.

Good organization is also crucial to effective brief writing. Organize your presentation of the facts and your arguments logically, so that someone who is completely unfamiliar with your case can follow easily. Use effective headings that, when placed in the table of contents, will give a synopsis of the story told in the brief.

VII. Oral Argument

Oral argument is the appellate advocate's opportunity to engage the court of appeals in a conversation about the appeal. It is a chance to clear up any confusion that may have arisen from the record or the briefs. Counsel may be able to alleviate any concerns that the court has developed. It is a chance to focus and shape the court's approach to the case, after it has become familiar with the record and the briefs.

As with writing the brief, it is important to focus on the audience. A typical appellate court hears from 18 to 25 oral arguments over a three- or four-day workweek. Most cases are allotted no more than 30 or 40 minutes for argument. That is not a lot of time within which to have an impact on the court's decision-making process. Use the time wisely.

The most important ingredient in a successful oral argument is preparation. It goes almost without saying that the oral advocate must have mastered the record and the important cases and statutes that bear upon the appeal. Once that is done, the lawyer should find some time for what Judge Frank Coffin of the First Circuit calls "isolated pondering"—to develop a sense of what the case is really about, to winnow out the unimportant, and to discern the central point or points on which the appeal hinges.

The final step is rehearsal. The most well thought out presentation may be of little assistance if it does not lend itself to persuasive oral discourse. The only way to know for sure how an argument will actually sound is to try it out. You might try first saying it out loud to yourself. But, you should also round up some colleagues to listen to the argument and to pose questions that might expose areas of weakness.

It is not advisable to appear at the actual oral argument with a prepared speech. Make an outline of your key points so that you will not forget any in the heat of the moment. Talk to the panel in a conversational tone, but forcefully. Keep in mind the following advice from Judge Pregerson of the Ninth Circuit:

Your primary job at oral argument is to answer the judges' questions carefully. Do not view these questions as interruptions, but as indications of the court's interest in a particular area. Pay careful attention to each question—there may be a hook in it or it may be the lifeline that will help you win the appeal. Do not assume that a judge is for you or against you based on the questions asked. If you do not understand the question, ask for clarification.[56]

VIII. Appendixes: Appeals Checklists and Sample Forms for the Practitioner

A. Appeals Checklist

1. *Upon receipt of the decision*
   a. If you are the prevailing party
      1. Assess the probability of appeal.
      2. Review strategy options, including waiver of appeal in full or partial settlement of underlying claims.
   b. If you are not the prevailing party
      1. Review potential procedural and substantive issues for appeal.
      2. Conduct legal research regarding same to evaluate the law of the jurisdiction in which the appeal would be brought.
      3. Evaluate prospects for successful appeal.
      4. Calendar the due date for the notice of appeal.
2. *If the decision has been made to file an appeal or the appeal has been noticed*
   a. Immediately obtain a copy of the local rules of the applicable court.
   b. Carefully review same and note all pleading requirements, filing dates, and other important provisions. If cross-appeals are involved, pay particular attention to correctly identifying when each pleading must be filed.
   c. Have another attorney in your office independently perform that same task and review the results to ensure that they are consistent with one another. (Cases have been lost by unintended waivers resulting from a party's misreading the requirements of the local rules.)
   d. Establish contact with court clerk personnel for purposes of confirming compliance with court rules and in consideration of future needs that your client may have that can be influenced by the dispatch and care with which court personnel respond to your request.
   e. Confirm briefing schedule and record extract provisions with court clerk.
   f. Review record to determine portions desired for appendix.
   g. Double-check to ensure that such evidence/testimony is in fact a part of the record.
   h. Consider carefully how you will frame your statement of the issues on appeal. (The way the question is articulated *may* determine the nature of the court's response.)
   i. Consider carefully all alternative grounds for appeal and the response thereto from the perspective of the like willingness of the court to grant same.
   j. Establish a file system for legal research that will facilitate the updating process during the course of the briefing and preparation for oral argument.
   k. Know your judges and their prejudices or obtain that information from those who possess it.

  l. In your briefs, consider the views of your best possible panel and your worst possible panel.

  m. Determine special printing requirements imposed by local rules and arrange for compliance with any such requirements.

3. *Appellant*

  a. Is there a final decision, or does an exception to the final decision rule apply?

  b. Has the trial court entered a separate document as a final judgment?

  c. Calendar time to file notice of appeal.

  d. Designate the record on appeal.

  e. Calendar due date for opening brief.

  f. Calendar due date for reply brief.

4. *Appellee*

  a. Review designation of record by appellant.

  b. Calendar due date for appellee's brief.

B. Sample Notice of Appeal

UNITED STATES DISTRICT COURT
FOR THE _____ DISTRICT OF _____

A.B., Plaintiff	)	Case No. _____
	)	
v.	)	Notice of Appeal
	)	
C.D., Defendant	)	
	)	
_____	)	

Notice is hereby given that [name all parties taking the appeal], [plaintiffs] [defendants] in the above named case, hereby appeals to the United States Court of Appeals for the _____ Circuit [from the final judgment] [from an order (describing it)], entered in this action on the _____ day of _____ , 19____.

/s/ _____
Attorney for _____
Address: _____

C. Sample Corporate Disclosure Statement

CORPORATE DISCLOSURE STATEMENT

Defendant-Appellant ABC Corp. is a Delaware corporation, with its principal place of business in the State of _____. The following parent companies, subsidiaries, and affiliates have issued shares to the public: ABC Mega-Corp., ABC Leasing Co., ABC Land Co., and XYZ Sales Co.

D. Statement of Jurisdiction

STATEMENT OF JURISDICTION

The District Court had subject matter jurisdiction under 28 U.S.C. § 1332, because plaintiff and defendant were citizens of different states and the matter in controversy exceeded the sum or value of $50,000. [For diversity cases]

[OR]

The District Court had subject matter jurisdiction under 28 U.S.C. § 1331, because the action arose under 42 U.S.C. § 2000e-2. [For Title VII cases]

The basis for appellate jurisdiction in this Court is 28 U.S.C. § 1291, which establishes jurisdiction for appeals from all "final decisions" of the district courts. Defendant-appellant appeals from the ["Judgment on Jury Verdict,"] entered by the District Court on [date]. Defendant-appellant filed its notice of appeal on [a date within thirty days after entry of the final decision]. This appeal is timely pursuant to Federal Rule of Appellate Procedure 4(a).

Notes

1. 28 U.S.C. § 1291.
2. Coopers & Lybrand v. Livesay, 437 U.S. 463, 467 (1978).
3. Estate of Bishop v. Bechtel Power Corp., 905 F.2d 1272 (9th Cir. 1990).
4. 28 U.S.C. § 1447(d). For a discussion of the very limited exceptions to these principles, see 15A CHARLES A. WRIGHT ET AL., FEDERAL PRACTICE AND PROCEDURE § 3914.11 (2d ed. 1992).
5. Coopers & Lybrand v. Livesay, 437 U.S. 463, 468 (1978).
6. *Cf.* Dickinson v. Petroleum Conversion Corp., 338 U.S. 507 (1950).
7. *In re* "Agent Orange" Prod. Liab. Litig., 818 F.2d 179 (2d Cir. 1987); 15 WRIGHT ET AL., *supra* note 4, § 3909, at 305 n.38.
8. 28 U.S.C. § 1292(a)(1).
9. McNally v. Pulitzer Publ'g Co., 532 F.2d 69 (8th Cir.), *cert. denied*, 429 U.S. 855 (1976); Abercrombie & Fitch Co. v. Hunting World, Inc., 461 F.2d 1040 (2nd Cir. 1972); Stewart-Warner Corp. v. Westinghouse Elec. Corp., 325 F.2d 822 (2nd Cir. 1963), *cert. denied*, 376 U.S. 944 (1964).
10. WRIGHT ET AL., *supra* note 4, § 3914.3; *see* FED. R. CIV. P. 65.
11. For Supreme Court interpretations of the rule, see Seatrain Shipbuilding Corp. v. Shell Oil Co., 444 U.S. 572 (1980); Liberty Mutual Ins. Co. v. Wetzel, 424 U.S. 737 (1976); Sears, Roebuck & Co. v. Mackey, 351 U.S. 427 (1956).
12. 28 U.S.C. § 1292(b).
13. *See* 9 U.S.C. § 16.
14. Diaz v. San Jose Unified Sch. Dist., 861 F.2d 591 (9th Cir. 1988).
15. FED. R. CIV. P. 58.
16. *See* McCalden v. California Library Ass'n, 955 F.2d 1214 (9th Cir.), *cert. denied*, 112 S. Ct. 2306 (1992).
17. Bankers Trust Co. v. Mallis, 435 U.S. 381 (1978).
18. FED. R. APP. P. 4(a)(2).
19. Will v. United States, 389 U.S. 90 (1967).
20. Beacon Theaters, Inc., v. Westover, 359 U.S. 500, 511 (1959) ("Whatever differences of opinion there may be in other types of cases, we think the right to grant mandamus to require jury trial where it has been improperly denied is settled."); Van Dusen

v. Barrack, 376 U.S. 612, 615 n.3 (1964) (transfer of venue); Hoffman v. Blaski, 363 U.S. 335, 340 n.9 (1960) (transfer of venue).

21. FED. R. APP. P. 3(a).
22. FED. R. APP. P. 4(a).
23. FED. R. CIV. P. 77(d).
24. FED. R. APP. P. 4(a)(4).
25. FED. R. APP. P. 4(a)(6).
26. Marrese v. American Academy of Orthopaedic Surgeons, 470 U.S. 373 (1985).
27. FED. R. CIV. P. 50(b), 59; FED. R. APP. P. 4(a)(4).
28. FED. R. CIV. P. 62(a).
29. FED. R. CIV. P. 62(b).
30. FED. R. CIV. P. 62(d).
31. *See, e.g.*, Federal Prescription Servs., Inc. v. American Pharm. Ass'n, 636 F.2d 755 (D.C. Cir. 1980) (no bond required to stay $102,000 judgment where judgment debtor had net worth of $4.8 million).
32. Hilton v. Braunskill, 481 U.S. 770, 776 (1987).
33. FED. R. APP. P. 8(a).
34. FED. R. CIV. P. 62(g).
35. FED. R. APP. P. 10(a).
36. FED. R. APP. P. 30(a).
37. FED. R. APP. P. 31(a).
38. FED. R. APP. P. 28(g).
39. FED. R. APP. P. 32(a).
40. FED. R. APP. P. 31(b).
41. FED. R. APP. P. 26.1.
42. FED. R. APP. P. 28(a)(1).
43. FED. R. APP. P. 28(a)(2).
44. FED. R. APP. P. 28(a)(3).
45. FED. R. APP. P. 28(a)(4).
46. FED. R. APP. P. 28(a)(5).
47. FED. R. APP. P. 28(a)(6).
48. FED. R. APP. P. 28(a)(6).
49. FED. R. APP. P. 25(d).
50. FED. R. APP. P. 31(a).
51. FED. R. APP. P. 26(c).
52. FED. R. APP. P. 32(a).
53. FED. R. APP. P. 26(c), 31(a).
54. FED. R. APP. P. 32(a).
55. FED. R. APP. P. 28(g).
56. Harry Pregerson, *The Seven Sins of Appellate Brief Writing and Other Transgressions*, 34 UCLA L. REV. 431 (1986).

CHAPTER 13

Professionalism and Ethics

JOHN W. ROBINSON, IV*

ROBERT J. TRUHLAR[†]

* Fowler, White, Gillen, Boggs, Villareal & Banker, P.A.; Tampa, Florida.

† Truhlar & Truhlar; Littleton, Colorado.

I. Introduction

Successful counsel and our courts recognize that professionalism is a part of advocacy. Ethical and trustworthy practice of law benefits all members of the profession. Our clients benefit when counsel handle matters fairly, competently, and expeditiously. Our society benefits from a well-established system of civilized justice. Finally, our court system grows stronger when our legal profession practices with integrity. As a practical matter, hostility, abuse, delay, and personal attacks are usually counterproductive to every client's interest and the continuing interests of society.

Ethics rules and legal sanctions vary from state to state. An attorney should refer to his or her jurisdiction's ethics code and opinions and case law when facing any ethical questions. For example, most states follow the American Bar Association (ABA) Model Rules of Professional Conduct, but others have rules modeled after the earlier Model Code of Professional Responsibility. Many states modify these model rules. This chapter also discusses concepts of professionalism, which represents a quest for the highest levels of integrity and trustworthiness, beyond codified rules.

II. Plaintiff's Counsel's Responsibilities in Representing Current and Former Employees as Clients

A primary ethical responsibility that plaintiff's counsel owes to a potential new client in an employment matter is to provide the basic information the client needs to make an informed decision concerning his or her rights and how to proceed with protecting them. However, this is only one aspect of the initial contact with a lawyer.

A. Analysis of Claims Includes Other Responsibilities

If the client is interested in pursuing a demand, claim, or legal action to protect employment rights, it is most important to present the client with a realistic picture of how the legal system works and the efforts necessary to obtain any remedy. This must include a very frank discussion of cost analysis in both the investigative and evaluation phases, and also the litigation of the case. Counsel should discuss both incidental out-of-pocket costs and lawyer's fees. In developing an understanding of what is involved, the attorney should advise the client about the client's rights and responsibilities, the employer's rights and responsibilities, society's perspective on the employment relationship, and legal requirements, including those overlaid upon the law by court rules. Counsel should understand and explain the facts from the view of both the employee and the employer, the legal claims available, and the probability of obtaining a remedy. Anything less than a full discussion of each of these aspects of a potential client's matter does not fulfill the professional responsibility of the employment attorney.

Since the employee's counsel is likely to be the first lawyer to give legal advice regarding potential litigation of a claim, it is extremely important that the advice be concise, fair, competent, realistic, and never exaggerated, yet complete enough to give the client an ability to decide whether to proceed further. The initial contact of the potential client with the employment lawyer should also set the tone for the professional and ethical standards of the entire attorney-client relationship.

B. Conflicts

A current or former employee's first contact with a lawyer or law office on an employment matter is most often a telephone call. At first this call appears to be informal and preliminary, but ethical considerations immediately apply. It is important for any counsel to have a conflict system, to quickly spot a potential conflict of interest in the first conversation with a potential client. Educating each person who may have the first conversation with a potential client to identify conflicts in the office is imperative. (A sample conflict form to assist with this task follows at the end of this chapter. Other formats, of course, are acceptable if they determine a conflict situation early in the conversation.) Some firms on networking systems may require an immediate data entry into a computer system to check for conflicts on a continuing instantaneous basis.

You can recognize a conflict as early as learning the name of the potential client, the type of matter, or the name of the current or former employer. Even the name of opposing counsel or the opposing firm can alert one to a potential conflict. Anyone in counsel's office talking to a potential client must take a moment after learning this initial information to consider the conflict issue, make a determination, and act if necessary.

Nonlawyers who may speak to potential clients should not give legal advice. Plus, you should not give legal advice until after an agreed upon attorney-client relationship. So, the intake process should concentrate on obtaining the facts of a situation without giving out any legal advice or analysis. (A sample telephone inquiry form, which obtains the minimal but necessary facts to set up an appointment, or to decide whether to schedule an appointment, follows at the end of this chapter.) Each lawyer must determine whether more information is necessary for that lawyer to decide whether or not he or she is competent and ready, without a conflict, to meet face-to-face with a new client.[1] (More follows on this topic in a later substantive section in this chapter, Conflicts of Interest.)

C. Confirmation of Appointment and Parameters of Consultation

Counsel should confirm every initial appointment, date, and time by letter, when possible. That letter can serve to list needed documentation from the client at the first meeting. The letter should reiterate the exact agreed-upon fee arrangement up to this time. It is uncommon to send potential new clients a fee agreement prior to the first meeting, but counsel should confirm a complete understanding as to the cost of the first meeting before it happens. (A sample initial consultation confirmation letter follows at the end of this chapter.) Each lawyer should draft the letter according to the lawyer's style and preference. The purpose of the letter is to give information to the client regarding the first steps in the attorney-client relationship.

D. The First Meeting

By the end of the first meeting with a new client, the client should have an understanding of his or her legal rights, how to preserve these rights, what is at stake, and how counsel will proceed with representing the client. In order to present this information in a professional and ethical manner, it is necessary for the lawyer to spend an adequate amount of time discussing each subject with the client.

Usually a lawyer needs no less than one hour, and sometimes as much as three hours, to give a complete and competent description of rights and responsibilities to a new client. A shorter time is likely to inhibit client understanding or questions.[2] Lawyers should be very careful not to shortchange the initial meeting. Clients often believe the lawyer already has made a decision about their matter at the end of the first meeting. Counsel must be very clear as to what counsel has determined about the case and what counsel still needs to investigate.

E. Preliminary Investigation*

A reasonable investigation is extensive. It includes background checks to determine if a problem, such as the after-acquired evidence doctrine, will come into effect.[3] (See chapter 6, "Pretrial Motions," and chapter 7, "Special Evidentiary Concerns," regarding this topic.) Check on medical expenses in cases where your client may claim emotional distress and determine subrogation rights. Identify witnesses with addresses and telephone numbers. Investigate the "other side's" view of things. For example, you should review documents in the possession of the client, review administrative agency files, which include the position of the employer, talk to witnesses, or actually contact a representative of the employer to discuss the situation at an early stage. Of course, if a lawyer knows that an employer has counsel relating to this particular matter, employee contact should be through the employer's counsel. If you are not aware that the employer is represented concerning the matter, consider that many corporations have their house counsel responsible for all matters.

F. Fee Agreements

Fee arrangements are replete with ethical considerations that cause many of the problems between lawyers and clients. The initial consultation must allow time to discuss lawyer fee arrangements, costs, and the possibility of paying lawyer's fees to the other side where appli-

---

* See also Case Evaluation: "To Take or Not to Take," chapter 1, "Commencing the Lawsuit."

cable. It is a very good practice to explain fee arrangements to the client and to give the client a blank copy of the fee agreements. The lawyer should allow the client additional time outside of counsel's presence to review the fee agreement and follow-up time to ask any questions before signing the fee contract. If time is of the essence, this can involve overnight consideration or even having a client return several hours later.

Contingency fee agreements are especially complex in employment litigation. A wrongful termination may include any of the following as a remedy: reinstatement, injunctive relief, promotion, payment of wages with tax consequences, and settlements with a variety of terms and waivers. The availability of multiple remedies raises questions about computing fees. As a result, a lawyer cannot realistically expect to cover a fee arrangement with a potential new client in five or ten minutes. As a matter of professionalism, the lawyer should not charge for time spent with the client related to fee arrangements.

Some states require certain elements in every contingent fee agreement. (A sample disclosure statement based on the requirements of Colorado follows at the end of this chapter.) The client must read and sign this type of contingent fee agreement, which must be in writing. It is most important to check your local rules and ethics code for each and every requirement of written fee agreements. (A sample of a contingency fee agreement that raises some of the issues unique to employment litigation follows at the end of this chapter. See also chapter 1 and its sample forms for commencing the lawsuit.)[4]

G. Time Limits

Another extremely important issue requiring a clear understanding in the initial consultation is relevant time limits. Employment litigation often involves very short time limits, for examples, the filing of a grievance in a collective bargaining context, protection of a wage claim under a state statute, filing of a charge of discrimination under state or federal law, or notification to a governmental employer under a state immunity statute. Usually these time limits are shorter than general personal injury or contract statutes of limitations. Often the client has already let some of this time run before contacting a lawyer. Also, employment clients often contact a lawyer just before having to make a decision on a severance program proposed by the employer, which might include a release of all claims, or just before signing a new contract with extensive noncompete sections.

Allow enough time to discuss time limits and take action to ensure that the client understands them. If the lawyer agrees to represent the client, the representation will entail meeting all pending time limits. Even if representation does *not* continue past the first meeting, the lawyer should advise the potential client of all pending time limits. This confirmation should be in writing.

H. Settlement

Finally, allocate time during the initial consultation to discuss settlement. Most cases settle. Therefore, settlement is very important. It is critical to bring your client's expectations into line with reality. Differentiate real settlement values from newspaper jury verdicts and national news story verdicts, which skew many clients' expectations. In fact, many state ethic codes require a discussion of alternative dispute resolution in any case where there is a potential for litigation. Explanation of settlement and alternative dispute resolution has become standard in attorney-client relationships. (More follows on this topic in a later substantive section in this chapter, Negotiating Settlements.)

I. Listening to the Client

Throughout the entire initial consultation with the client and during subsequent representation, especially throughout litigation, the lawyer will get to know the client more and more as time passes. This process starts at the very first meeting. Make sure that in your effort to impart all of the necessary information, you do not end up doing all of the talking. A lawyer can best serve the client, the profession, and the system of justice by *listening* carefully to the client's needs. The lawyer has an ethical obligation to attempt to meet the client's needs, and you will not know what these needs really are unless your meeting with your client involves true dialogue.

Other areas that raise special ethical considerations follow in later sections of this chapter.

III. Defense Responsibilities

Recent suggestions from legal groups, such as the American Inns of Court, stress the twin ideals of legal excellence and legal professionalism. Recurring professionalism themes are civility, courtroom competence, and a spirit of mutual cooperation among officers of court. For example, local federal court rules, state rules, and local practice now encourage, and sometimes require, good faith resolution efforts among counsel before filing motions, especially motions on routine and discovery matters. Defense counsel are wise to consider how their practices measure up to these aspirational goals.

Defense counsel have special ethical responsibilities. Employer's counsel should prevent and oppose any improper interviews of managers where employer's counsel represents management. (More follows on this topic in a later substantive section in this chapter, Witness Interviews/Ex Parte Contacts.) Employer's counsel should ensure that managers know of their legal representation and instruct them not to discuss any potential claims with outsiders, especially counsel for potential claimants.

A defense counsel should evaluate and resolve, in writing, potential conflicts of interest, especially when there are multiple potential respondents or insurance coverage. For example, defense counsel often represents the employer and individual managers. (More follows on this topic in a later substantive section in this chapter, Conflicts of Interest.) A defense counsel should draft engagement letters confirming the scope of work and fee arrangements. A defense counsel should, likewise, draft written joint defense agreements to guard against any waiver of work product when counsel for different defendants work together. Also, a counsel needs a client's written consent if someone other than the client pays the client's legal fees. (Sample forms follow at the end of this chapter.)

When investigating claims, consider whether counsel (as opposed to other employer officials) should conduct the interviews with witnesses to preserve the work product doctrine. To successfully defend the claim, however, counsel may ultimately need to waive this work product doctrine. Counsel may also consider the "critical self-analysis" privilege for any internal investigation, as described under substantive topics later in this chapter.

IV. Other Responsibilities for Representing Entities (Corporations, Unions, and Associations)

Special considerations come into play when representing a corporation, association, union, or any group operating under a collective bargaining agreement. In each of these situations the lawyer must very carefully identify who the client is. The client may be the organization or entity, not an individual.

The ABA Model Rules of Professional Conduct are very specific about conflicts in this area.[5] A lawyer at all times must be alert to determine the interests of the organization, as opposed to interests of the representative with whom the lawyer is working. This is a very delicate matter, but the lawyer must protect the organization in giving legal advice to the individual representative. (More follows on this topic in a later substantive section in this chapter, Conflicts of Interest.)

When first agreeing to represent such an organization, the lawyer should discuss the organization's principles, agreements, letters of understanding, and general method of handling individual member matters. Counsel should establish a system of checking on the association's mission statement and discuss the scope of the authority of the association's representative.

V. Substantive Topics

This section gives an overview of recurrent professionalism and ethical problems in employment litigation.

A. Abusive Discovery

Rule 26(c), of the Federal Rules of Civil Procedure limits discovery "to protect a party from annoyance, embarrassment, oppression. . . ." Likewise, Fed. R. Civ. P. Rule 30(d), condemns depositions conducted "in such manner as unreasonably to annoy, embarrass, or oppress the deponent or party. . . ."[6]

B. Attorney-Client Privilege

The attorney-client privilege protects confidential communications between a lawyer and a client regarding legal advice. The privilege protects the contents of the communications. The burden of establishing the privilege lies with the party asserting it. Lawyers' communications to clients are not uniformly privileged. Instead, courts examine each communication independently. For the privilege to apply to a document, the document must disclose or rely upon confidential communications from the client.[7]

Several factors affect this privilege, such as whether corporate supervisors directed the communication to obtain legal advice, whether the communications concerned matters in the scope of corporate duties, whether the information was unavailable from higher managers, whether employees knew the corporation was seeking legal advice, and whether the communications were confidential.[8]

C. Class Actions

Class action counsel must fairly and adequately protect the interests of the class.[9] Counsel should communicate with their class representatives. For defense counsel, communication with potential class members can be a problem under Fed. R. Civ. P. 23 and local federal court rules.[10]

D. Conflicts of Interest

Rule 1.7 of the ABA Model Rules of Professional Conduct provides that a lawyer shall not represent a client if the representation will be "directly adverse to another client" unless the attorney reasonably believes there is no adversarial relationship and "each client consents after consultation."

Examples of some practical problems are an alleged wrongdoer or harasser who acts outside the scope of employment, a case in which the employer or alleged wrongdoer or harasser seeks indemnification from the other, and a situtation where the employer takes prompt remedial action by disciplining or even discharging the alleged wrongdoer or harasser. (An employer can avoid liability where there is prompt remedial action against the sexual harasser.)[11] All of these potential conflicts suggest that before undertaking joint representation, counsel should inform the parties in writing of the potential conflicts and the fact that later developing conflicts may require one or all parties to obtain new counsel. Substitute counsel are both expensive and time consuming. Clients need to understand this risk.

E. Insurance*

Another concern is a conflict or potential conflict between an insurer and the insured respondent in an employment case. For example, an insurer may escape liability for damages if a jury decides against the insured employer on a particular noncovered claim. This frequently occurs where a complaint alleges that the insured employer committed both intentional and negligent misconduct, and the policy does not cover intentional misconduct. Likewise, an insurer may have little economic incentive to defend claims where the only obligation is to defend rather than to pay any claims. Other problems may arise from disputes about whether a workplace tort comes under a general liability insurance policy or not.

For example in *NPS Corp. v. Insurance Co. of N. Am.*, 213 N.J. Super. 547, 517 A.2d. 1211, 2 IER Cases (BNA) 471 (N.J. Super. A.D. 1986), an insurer declined to defend or indemnify an employer in a lawsuit for battery arising out of allegations of sexual harassment. A female plaintiff claimed that a male coworker repeatedly touched her in an offensive manner causing serious emotional distress. The general liability policy only covered "bodily harm," and the carrier concluded emotional distress was not "bodily harm." The employer settled the case without the participation, consent, or approval of the insurance company. The em-

---

* See also chapter 2, "Responding to the Lawsuit," regarding insurance.

ployer then sued the insurance company seeking to recover its costs of settlement and legal fees. The state court held that because emotional distress can and often does have a direct effect on other bodily functions, the term "bodily harm" included emotional distress from sexual harassment.

F. Internal Investigations/"Critical Self-Analysis" Privilege

Counsel should consider investigating claims under the protection of the attorney-client privilege and the work product doctrine. Also, some courts have protected internal materials under a "critical self-analysis" privilege. This privilege stems from the public policy recognizing that voluntary compliance by employers with federal equal employment opportunity laws is essential. Voluntary compliance should encourage employers to be candid and forthright in assessing employment practices. Disclosure of "critical self-analysis" may chill voluntary compliance.[12]

Still, a privileged investigation makes it difficult for the client, such as an employer in a sexual harassment claim, to show that it promptly corrected any impropriety. An employer could later waive these privileges, if the employer raises the investigation or corrective action as a defense at trial.[13]

G. Joint Defense Agreements

A joint defense agreement between or among parties protects the attorney-client privilege as long as the parties share a common interest. *United States v. Melvin*, 650 F.2d 641 (5th Cir. 1981) recognized "a respectable body of law ... that the attorney-client privilege applies to confidential communications among attorneys and their clients for purposes of a common defense."[14] (A sample joint defense agreement is at the end of this chapter.)

H. Joint Representation*

Employment claims, particularly sexual harassment cases, frequently accuse employers and the individual alleged wrongdoers or harassers. Often the employer (or insurer) will recommend or attempt a joint legal defense to minimize litigation costs. Such a joint defense creates potential conflicts of interest and issues of attorney-client privilege and work product. One approach is to draft a joint defense agree-

---

* See also Conflicts of Interest, in chapter 2, "Responding to the Lawsuit."

ment for separate counsel (see sample forms) or a specific consent to joint representation.

I. Negotiating Settlements

The primary rule to remember in negotiations is to be honest. Professionalism demands a commitment to the highest levels of integrity and truthfulness in the important area of settlements. Although concepts of bluffing tactics, leverage, threats to go to trial, and unrealistic bottom lines arise in obtaining the "best" settlements, they cannot justify misrepresentations, dishonesty, or hostility. Nothing is more harmful towards serving the client's needs, society, the court system, or the profession as unethical tactics during settlement discussions.

Ethical considerations may affect a simultaneous negotiation of lawyer's fees and damages, such as requiring each party to bear her or his own lawyer's fees and costs or including plaintiff's statutory lawyer's fees in the total settlement amount.[15]

J. Payment of Fees by Nonclient

ABA Model Rules of Professional Conduct, Rule 1.8(f) requires that a party consent to payment of legal fees by any other person. For example, a manager should consent, in writing, to his employer's payment of her or his defense legal fees and costs. (Sample language at the end of this chapter covers this consent.) (Also see sample engagement letter at the end of chapter 2, "Responding to the Lawsuit.")

K. Publicity

A lawyer's communication with the press or a third party can violate rules of professional responsibility. A lawyer has a general duty to refrain from inflicting needless injury on an opposing party.[16] Likewise, ABA Model Rules of Professional Conduct Rule 3.6 provides, in part: "A lawyer shall not make an extrajudicial statement that a reasonable person could expect to be disseminated by means of public communication if the lawyer knows or should have known that it would have a substantial likelihood of materially prejudicing the administrative proceeding." Local rules of several U. S. district courts and bar associations restrict comments that could interfere with a fair trial.[17]

L. Rule 11*

Rule 11 of the Federal Rules of Civil Procedure provides that the signature of a lawyer or party reflects that the facts and claims in a pleading are "formed after an inquiry reasonable under the circum-

---

* See chapter 11, "Posttrial Motions," regarding Rule 11 motions.

stances." Many states have patterned court rules or statutes after Rule 11.[18]

Many plaintiffs' lawyers ask their clients or prospective clients to provide a detailed, written account of the events supporting their allegations. It is wise when seeking such a written account to ensure that the client or potential client addresses the document to the lawyer and shows it to no one else. Plaintiffs' and defense counsel should review germane documents prior to filing any pleadings concerning facts or claims contained in the documents.

M. Soliciting

ABA Model Rules of Professional Conduct Rule 7.2 limits solicitation of prospective clients where there is no family or prior professional relationship. But states cannot prohibit truthful advertising by lawyers concerning the availability and price of legal services.[19] States may ban in-person solicitation.[20]

N. Threatening Criminal Charges

Under Disciplinary Rule 7.105 of the ABA Model Code of Professional Responsibility, a lawyer "shall not present, participate in, or threaten to present criminal charges solely to obtain an advantage in a civil matter." Of course, this does not prevent you from making a pre-lawsuit demand for relief, in which you vow to file a civil suit or pursue "all available legal remedies." But, a lawyer must avoid threatening to press criminal charges if the opponent will not satisfy the civil demands.

O. Witness Interviews/Ex Parte Contacts

Rule 4.2 of the ABA Model Rules of Professional Conduct provides:

> In representing a client, a lawyer shall not communicate about the subject of the representation with a party the lawyer knows to be represented by another lawyer in the matter, unless the lawyer has the consent of the other lawyer or is authorized by law to do so.

This rule is a particular problem in employment litigation where almost all witnesses are employees or former employees. As one court observed, "We are a nation of employees."[21]

Claimants' counsel should consider contacting corporate counsel before contacting any corporation employees, especially managers. Likewise, counsel for the organization and individual respondent need to consider this rule before interviewing each other or the claimant if counsel represent any of these persons or entities. A frequent question is which employees of a defendant corporation or organization enjoy representation of corporate or organizational counsel. In order to adequately investigate the factual and legal basis for a case, claimant's counsel needs to obtain basic facts from witnesses who are likely to be employees or former employees. This is a delicate balance. (See also Ex Parte Witness Contact, chapter 3, "Discovery.") You should evaluate some of the following factors:

1. Current Employees

The comment to the ABA Model Rules of Professional Conduct Rule 4.2 highlights certain organizational employees where ex parte contact presents a problem. These include contacts with managers with responsibilities on behalf of the organization, persons whose acts or omissions may impute civil or criminal liability to the organization, and persons whose statements may constitute admission by the organization.

Some courts or bar association opinions broadly condemn ex parte interviews with any current corporate employee.[22]

Other courts permit contact with some employees.[23] For example, in *B.H. by Monahan v. Johnson*, 128 F.R.D. 659 (N.D. Ill. 1989), plaintiff's counsel could interview low-level corporate employees but could not use this informal evidence as admissions by the corporation. Likewise, in *Bouge v. Smith's Management Corp.*, 132 F.R.D. 560 (D. Utah 1990), plaintiffs could communicate with employees who were mere witnesses in a wage dispute.

In general, the lower the level of the employee's responsibility, the more likely the counsel may properly interview the employee outside the presence of company counsel. But generalizations in this area are of limited use. Different courts apply different standards to determine which are off-limits. You need to research the law of the relevant jurisdiction in *each* case.

2. Former Employees

Courts and bar associations generally allow greater latitude in interviewing former employees. ABA Committee on Ethics and Professional Responsibility Formal Opinion 91–359 (1991) concludes that this ethical rule does not specifically cover contacts with former employees of a corporation.[24]

3. Sanctions

Sanctions for improper communications include disqualification of the lawyer or law firm.[25] Other courts may exclude the interview information,[26] or compel the disclosure of the interview information to opposing counsel.[27]

4. Suggestions for Witness Communications

Counsel cannot induce a current or former employee to violate the employer's attorney-client privilege.[28] Also, counsel must honor his or her duty to unrepresented persons to be truthful, to disclose his or her client's identity and interest, and to respect the rights of others, including their own attorney-client privilege.[29]

One basic way to avoid problems with witness communications is to simply conduct regular discovery under the federal or state civil rules. Some courts believe it is improper for counsel to make a unilateral determination that there is no witness communication problem.[30]

P. Work Product Doctrine

This doctrine protects from disclosure a lawyer's mental impressions, conclusions, opinions, and legal theories.[31] The purpose of the rule is to safeguard the lawyer's trial preparation from discovery.[32] Ordinarily, the doctrine protects the preparation of documents for trial or in anticipation of litigation. An adverse party may argue for disclosure based on a showing of substantial need and inability to obtain the equivalent information by other means without undue hardship.

Unlike the attorney-client privilege, mere disclosure to a third party may not waive the work product doctrine.[33]

VI. Appendixes: Professionalism and Ethics Checklist and Sample Forms

A. Professionalism and Ethics Checklist

1. Plaintiff's Counsel Engagement*

- Check potential conflicts.
- Prepare a written agreement to represent an understanding of the scope of the provided services.
- Clarify financial terms, especially relationship of any statutory legal fees and contingency.
- Plan a system to fairly investigate facts before agreeing to make a claim or to commence litigation.
- Perform a realistic analysis of damages, if any; explain mitigation of damages, and remedies available, even if preliminary.
- Discuss in detail potential costs and lawyer's fee awards.
- Discuss the potential for alternative dispute resolution and settlement.
- Put initial expectations of the representation into final form.

2. Defense Counsel Engagement†

- Check conflicts.
- Reveal and obtain written waiver of any potential conflicts.
- Prepare written agreement.
- Clarify financial terms, especially if there may be insurance defense coverage.
- Obtain client's consent, if payment of legal fees by another.

3. Insurance

- Does coverage exist?
- Has carrier been placed on notice of claim?
- Does coverage extend to all claims, defense costs, and damages?
- Insured has duty to cooperate with insurance carrier.

4. Witness Contacts

- Does organization or person have counsel?
- Are witnesses managers or low-level employees?
- Are witnesses current or former employees?

---

* See also chapter 1, "Commencing the Lawsuit."

† See also chapter 2, "Responding to the Lawsuit."

- Do interviews attempt to impute liability or violate attorney-client privilege?
- Counsel cannot mislead third parties.
- Is regular discovery an option?

5. Joint Defense

- What are potential conflicts?
- Prepare written joint defense agreement.

B. Sample Forms

1. Potential Client Cover Sheet (for Telephone Inquiry)

Date_____

Caller's Name _____

Issue _____
_____
_____
_____

Who do you believe you have a claim against? _____
5 _____
_____
_____
_____

Does opposing side have counsel? _____
If so, who? _____
_____

CONFLICT??

_____
_____

If so, indicate to caller a potential conflict and terminate call.
If not, proceed with gathering information.

2. Telephone Inquiry Form*

Address _____
City/Zip _____
Telephone (H) _____ (W) _____

---

* See also Employment Discrimination Questionnaire, chapter 1, "Commencing the Lawsuit," and Possible Case Intake Questionnaire, chapter 3, "Discovery."

Advised of Rates: Yes   No _____ (fill in rate quoted)

Initial Consult?   Yes   No _____

Appointment set: Date: _____   Time: _____
Can you be called at work? _____   Leave Message at _____
Referred by _____   Letter of confirmation sent _____

****

POTENTIAL DEFENDANT EMPLOYER: _____ Public   _____ Private
Name _____   Type of Business _____
Address _____   Approx. # of employees _____
City/Zip _____   Job Title _____
Duties _____
Union Member?   Yes   No   Length of Service _____
Salary _____ Benefits _____
Summary of facts _____
_____
_____

Employment contract?   Yes   No   Employee Policy Manual?   Yes   No
Dated Terminated _____   Replacement: Yes   No
Reasons given by Employer _____
_____

****

TYPE(S) OF CLAIM:

Age _____ (d/o/b) _____   Denied Equal Pay _____
Failure to Hire _____   Failure to Promote _____
Sexual Harassment _____   Wrongful Termination _____
Race/National Origin _____   Other _____
              Class _____   _____
Sex Discrimination _____   _____

OTHER INFORMATION:

What would you like this office to do for you? _____
_____

Have you minimized your damages? _____
_____

Any witnesses? _____
If termination case: Ever terminated by any other company?   Yes   No
      Name of person who made termination decision _____
      Name of immediate supervisor _____
Damages _____
Other lawyers consulted _____

****

OTHER NOTES/COMMENTS FROM CALLER _____
_____
_____

****

ADMINISTRATIVE REMEDIES:

Grievance Procedure? _____ filed? _____ findings _____
Charges filed: EEOC _____ local or state agency _____
_____ when? _____
Right to sue: EEOC _____ local or state agency _____
_____ notice rec'd when? _____

CHECK FOR DEADLINES

****

Do you have:

Performance appraisals _____
Letters re termination _____
Other documents   _____
Personnel File   _____
Copy of handbook   _____

****

INTERVIEWER COMMENTS TO CALLER:

1. Will review preliminary information with lawyer and confirm appointment.
2. Are there any deadlines in the next 30 days of which you have been made aware?

3. Initial Consultation Confirmation Letter

[DATE]

[CLIENT NAME AND ADDRESS]

Re: **Initial Consultation**
     [Day of Week, Date, Time]

Dear _____:

Thank you for contacting us about your employment matter. I often meet with people to discuss potential claims and give them advice as to their specific employment rights.

I would like to evaluate your matter at the above-referenced date and time and specifically discuss your employment rights.

I would charge an initial consultation fee of $ _____ *per hour*. Payment is due at the time of the initial consultation. For this fee, we can discuss your potential claim, speak about your complaints, review your rights, and provide you with a preliminary assessment of the merits of your claim and how to proceed. Please bring the following materials to your initial consultation, if they are in your possession or you can obtain them:

1. A written chronology of events which you prepare in advance of our meeting;
2. Your recent job resume and/or job description;
3. Your personnel file, including any performance appraisals, relevant memoranda, or correspondence;
4. Employee Handbook or policy manual;
5. Copies of any relevant information already in your possession;
6. Payment.

I look forward to meeting with you on _____ at _____.

If a problem arises and you are unable to keep your appointment, please contact us immediately.

Sincerely,

4. Consultation Follow-up Letter with Fee Agreement

[DATE]

[CLIENT NAME AND ADDRESS]
Re: **[Hourly Rate] [Contingent] Fee Agreement and Retainer for Representation to Make Claim Against [   ]**

Dear _____:

I am enclosing for your review a [Hourly Rate] [Contingent] Fee Agreement, and an initial copy for your records. If this Fee Agreement meets with your approval, please sign the original and return it to me, in the self-addressed stamped envelope provided. Also, send me a retainer of $_____ per the agreement.

Upon receipt of your signed fee agreement I shall complete the signatures on the fee agreement and return a fully executed copy to you. Then I will begin my detailed investigation of your case and prepare a demand letter on your behalf for you to review if we mutually agree to do this.

Sincerely,

5. Disclosure Statement

Type of Attorney Fee Agreements. I have been informed and understand that there are several types of attorney fee arrangements: (1) time based, (2) fixed, or (3) contingent. "Time based" means a fee that is determined by the amount of time involved such as so much per hour, day or week. "Fixed" means a fee that is based on an agreed amount regardless of the time or effort involved or the result obtained. "Contingent" means a certain agreed percentage or amount that is payable only upon attaining a recovery regardless of the time or effort involved. I understand I have the right to choose the type of attorney fee arrangement.

Specially Awarded Attorney Fees. I have been informed and understand that the court or an arbitrator may sometimes award attorney fees in addition to

311

amount of recovery being claimed. I understand that the fee agreement I enter into with my attorney should contain a provision as to how any specially awarded attorney fees will be accounted for and handled.

Expenses. I have been informed and understand that there may be expenses (aside from any attorney fee) in pursuing my claim. Examples of such expenses are: fees payable to the court, the cost of serving process, fees charged by expert witnesses, fees of investigators, fees of court reporters to take and prepare transcripts of depositions, routine expenses such as for copying, mailing, telephone charges, research costs and deliveries and expenses involved in preparing exhibits. I understand that an attorney is required to provide me with an estimate of such expenses before I enter into an attorney fee agreement and that my attorney fee agreement should include a provision as to how and when such expenses will be paid. I understand that the fee agreement should tell me whether a fee payable from the proceeds of the amount collected on my behalf will be based on the "net" or "gross" recovery. "Net recovery" means the amount remaining after expenses and deductions. "Gross recovery" means the total amount of the recovery before any deductions. The estimated amount of expenses to handle my case will be set forth in the contingent fee agreement.

The Potential of Costs and Attorney's Fees Being Awarded to the Opposing Party. I have been informed and understand that a Court or arbitrator sometimes awards costs and attorney fees to the opposing party. I have been informed and understand that should that happen in my case, I will be responsible to pay such award. I understand that the fee agreement I enter into with my attorney should provide whether an award against me will be paid out of the proceeds of any amount collected on my behalf. I also understand that the agreement should provide whether the fee I am obligated to pay my attorney will be based on the amount of recovery before or after payment of the awarded costs and attorney fees to an opposing party.

Associated Counsel. I have been informed and understand that my attorney may sometimes hire another attorney to assist in the handling of a case. That other attorney is called an "associated counsel." I understand that the attorney fee agreement should tell me how the fees of associated counsel will be handled.

Subrogation. I have been informed and understand that other persons or entities may have a subrogation right in what I recover in pursuing my claim. "Subrogation" means the right to be paid back. I understand that the subrogation right may arise in various ways such as when an insurer or a federal or state agency pays money to or on behalf of a claiming party like me in situations such as medicare, medicaid, workers' compensation, medical/health insurance, no-fault insurance, uninsured/underinsured motorist insurance, and property insurance situations. I understand that sometimes a hospital, physician or an attorney will assert a "lien" (a priority right) on a claim such as the one I am pursuing. Subrogation rights and liens need to be considered and provided for in the fee agreement I reach with my attorney. The fee agreement should tell me whether the subrogation right or lien is being paid by my attorney out of the proceeds of the recovery made on my behalf and whether the fee I am obligated to pay my attorney will be based on the amount of recovery before or after payment of the subrogation right or lien.

I acknowledge that I received a complete copy of this disclosure statement and read it this _____ day of _____, 199___.

_____
CLIENT

6. Contingent Fee Agreement

The Client, _____ (the "Client"), whose address is _____, retains the law firm of _____ (the "Attorneys"), at _____ (law firm address) _____

to perform the legal services described in paragraph (1) below. The Attorneys agree to perform the services with due diligence.

The Client acknowledges that the Attorneys have discussed with the Client fee arrangements, specifically a contingent fee arrangement, a fixed fee arrangement, and an hourly rate fee arrangement. Attorney's standard hourly rate is $ _____ per hour for partners, $ _____ for associates, $ _____ for paralegals and $ _____ for law clerks and is subject to change as a matter of business policy provided that it will be consistent with prevailing rates. The Client has decided to accept the contingent fee arrangement provided for by this Agreement.

(1) The claim, controversy and other matters with reference to which the services are to be performed are (a) making a demand upon the _____.

(2) The contingency upon which compensation is to be paid is based on the gross recovery of any money, including attorney's fees, in settlement, collection of a judgment, or otherwise, arising out of the claims described in paragraph (1) above. Pursuant to the statutes under which some of the Client's claims will be brought, attorneys' fees may be recovered. It is agreed by the parties that the gross recovery or judgment out of which the attorneys' fees are paid shall include any attorneys' fees recovered. These attorney fees paid, if any, will be based on the amount of gross recovery before the payment of any costs, or payment of attorney fees to an opposing party. If, however, attorney fees are awarded in pretrial motions or hearings for time spent on procedural aspects of the case, these fees, if recovered, shall be paid 100% to the Attorneys for their efforts upon which the fees are based.

(3) It is agreed by the parties that the contingency fee due to the Attorneys shall be the amount of:

(a) _____ percent (_____%) of all money recovered less costs (net recovery), including a judgment, settlement and attorneys' fees or _____ percent (_____%) if an appeal is pursued, or

(b) Attorneys' fees as awarded by the Court, whichever of (a) or (b) is greater.

(4) *In addition*, should Client obtain relief by way of reinstatement to Client's position with _____, Client agrees that Attorneys shall receive as an *additional* fee on that remedy:

(c) A contingency fee of _____ percent (_____%) of anticipated salary income for one year, or _____ percent (_____%) of the increase in Client's annual salary over Client's previous year's salary, regardless of whether Client works a full year or not, or

(d) Attorneys' fees as awarded by the Court, whichever of (c) or (d) is greater. This amount shall be paid at the time the case is settled or judgment collected.

(5) Any claim for injunctive or declaratory relief will be negotiated on the merits before attorneys' fees are claimed or negotiated.

(6) Any structured settlement entered into by the Client as a result of the claim described in paragraph (1) shall contain a provision for the immediate payment of the attorneys' fees described herein, and for the payment of any outstanding costs advanced by the Attorneys. In the event that there is a structured settlement, the calculation of the attorneys' fees shall be based on the then-present value of such structured settlement.

(7) Termination of this Agreement may be at any time by written notice by or to the Client. If permission for withdrawal is required by the Court, the Attorneys shall promptly apply for such permission and termination shall coincide with a Court Order for withdrawal. The Attorneys reserve the right to terminate this Agreement in the event that the Client misrepresents or fails to disclose material facts, fails to pay expenses, makes it unreasonably difficult for Attorneys to represent the Client, or for any other just cause.

(8) The Client is not liable to pay compensation for time spent by Attorneys for the Client otherwise than from amounts collected for client by the Attorneys, except that, if the client terminates this Agreement, or the Attorneys terminate this Agreement pursuant to paragraph (7), then the Client shall be liable to the Attorneys to pay the Attorneys for a time based fee for time expended in pursuing the Client's claims, with the rates of the Attorneys to be $ _____ per hour, for partners, $ _____ for associates, $ _____ for paralegals, and $ _____ for law clerks.

(9) Collection of any amounts due to the Attorneys from the Client shall be at the Client's expense. The Attorneys may enforce a lien against documents in their possession acquired by their services, in accordance with [state] law. The Attorneys shall be entitled to their attorneys' fees incurred for collection, whether or not a lawsuit is brought.

(10) The Client agrees to cooperate with the Attorneys in the pursuit of the claim, including attending consultations with expert witnesses, such as economists, or meetings with the Attorneys. The Client understands that failure to cooperate with the Attorneys may constitute grounds for the Attorneys to withdraw from the case and that such would constitute a discharge of the Attorneys pursuant to paragraph (7) of this Contingent Fee Agreement.

(11) The Client is in any event to be liable to the Attorneys for expenses and disbursements, such as fees charged by economists, for expert testimony or consultation, investigator's charges, copying costs, mileage, postage, long-distance telephone charges, and charges for taking and transcribing depositions with a written breakdown of itemized costs. The costs are estimated to be $ _____ to $ _____ in the event that a lawsuit is pursued to trial. This does not include any costs of an appeal. The Client understands this is only an estimate and the actual costs are unknown at this time. Attorneys' right to incur individual expenses and make disbursements must be approved by consulting the Client. Client agrees to establish a cost account by giving _____

PROFESSIONALISM AND ETHICS

_____ (law firm) _____ $ _____ upon signing this Agreement, and agrees to pay $ _____ or more each month as client's finances permit.

(12) Subrogated rights have been identified in this case as follows: _____

(13) The Attorneys are authorized to dispose of the Client's files two years after the legal matter described herein has been resolved or two years after the last work on the matter described herein has been performed by the Attorneys, whichever comes first. The Attorneys shall not be required to give notice to the Client prior to disposing of the Client's file. If the Client wishes to obtain such file, rather than having the Attorneys dispose of the file, the Client shall be required to notify the Attorneys of the Client's desire to obtain the file from the Attorneys. Such notification must be made to the Attorneys within two years of the time that the legal matter described herein has been resolved or within two years after the last work has been performed on such matter by the Attorneys, whichever comes first.

(14) The Client understands that a Court may order the losing party in any case to pay some or all of the attorneys' fees and costs to the winning party. Depending on the outcome of this matter, Client may be obligated to pay costs and fees of the opposing party. Also, even if the Court orders the opposing party to pay Client's fees, Client remains responsible for Attorneys' fees and costs pursuant to the terms of this Agreement.

(15) Any controversy or claim of attorneys' fees and cost reimbursement arising out of or relating to this Agreement or breach thereof, including the reasonableness of the fee shall be settled by arbitration in accordance with applicable rules of the American Arbitration Association or another arbitration service to which Client and Attorneys mutually agree. This agreement to arbitrate shall be specifically enforceable. The award rendered by the arbitrator(s) shall be final, and judgment may be entered upon it upon filing of the award in any Court having jurisdiction thereof. Said award shall be considered a basis for a judgment thereof.

(16) This Agreement shall be binding upon the Client, Attorneys, heirs, executors, legal representatives, successors and assigns of both parties. READ THIS AGREEMENT CAREFULLY BEFORE SIGNING AND RETAIN A COPY. YOUR SIGNATURE ACKNOWLEDGES THAT YOU UNDERSTAND THE AGREEMENT AND AGREE TO ITS TERMS.

I RECEIVED THIS AGREEMENT ON _____, HAD ADEQUATE TIME TO REVIEW IT AND CONSULT WITH OTHERS, INCLUDING OTHER COUNSEL, AND HAVE READ THE ABOVE AGREEMENT BEFORE SIGNING, and I acknowledge that I understand and agree to its terms. I have received a copy of this Agreement.

DATED this _____ day of _____, 199___.

BY THE CLIENT:

_____

LAW FIRM

_____
By: Attorney

7. Hourly Rate Fee Agreement

THIS AGREEMENT is made between _____ whose address is _____, referred to as the "Client," and the law firm of _____, of _____, subsequently referred to as the "Attorney."

The Client hereby retains Attorney to represent Client in connection with matters relating to his/her employment at _____. No litigation shall be commenced by Attorney except by mutual agreement of Client and Attorney.

The Client shall pay for legal services at the rate of $ _____ per hour for the services of _____, or other partners of the firm, $ _____ an hour for any associate work, and at the rate of $ _____ per hour for paralegal, and $ _____ per hour for law clerk services. **Client has provided a $ _____ retainer with the signing of this fee agreement.** The first _____ hours of work will be credited against that retainer.

The Client shall be obligated to pay for all court costs, investigation costs, deposition expenses, copying costs, fees charged for extraordinary copying costs, postage, and long-distance telephone charges, if any, with itemization of these costs. Expenses related to providing services shall be included in the monthly bills as additional costs. Billing shall be monthly.

The Client authorizes the Attorney to pay all bills associated with the case, whether incurred by the Attorney or the Client.

Termination of this contract may be at any time by written notice by or to the Client. If permission for withdrawal is required by the court, the Attorney shall promptly apply for such permission and termination shall coincide with a court order for withdrawal. The Attorney reserves the right to terminate this contract if Client misrepresents or fails to disclose material facts, fails to pay fees and expenses upon his receipt of billing or for conduct making it unreasonably difficult to represent the Client or for any other just cause.

Collection of the amounts due to the Attorney by the Client shall be at the Client's expense. The Attorney may enforce a lien against documents in their possession acquired by their services, in accordance with [state] law. The Attorney shall be entitled to their attorney's fees incurred for collection, whether or not a lawsuit is brought.

[Optional][The Client agrees that a service charge of 12 percent per annum may be added to any unpaid balance owed to the Attorney and more than 30 days past due. Outstanding balances shall be due at the time of receipt by the Client of the Attorney's monthly statements.] [NOTE: Counsel should consider implications of Truth in Lending Act, 15 U.S.C. §1601 et seq.]

The Attorney is authorized to dispose of Client's file two years after the legal matter described herein has been resolved or two years after the last work on the matter described herein has been performed by the Attorney, whichever comes first. The Attorney shall not be required to give notice to Client prior to disposing of Client's file. If the Client wishes to obtain such file, rather than having the Attorney dispose of Client's file, the Client shall be required to notify Attorney of the Client's desire to obtain the file from Attorney. Such notification must be made to Attorney within two years of the time that the legal matter described herein has been resolved or within two years after the last work has been performed on such matter by Attorney, whichever comes first.

In the event Attorney dies and Client files still are in the possession of Attorney, Client hereby authorizes Attorney's Personal Representative(s) to decide what to do with Client files. The Personal Representative(s) shall be authorized to destroy Client's file according to the preceding paragraph, and shall be authorized to review such file for the purpose of determining what to do with the file. Client documents shall be returned by first class mail, and communication shall be sent by first class mail to the Client at the address set forth above or such other address as Client shall specify by delivery of a written notice to Attorney.

This contract shall be binding upon Client, Attorney, heirs, executors, legal representatives, successors and assigns of both parties. Read this contract carefully before signing and retain a copy. Your signature acknowledges that you understand the contract and agree to pay.

Read and approved by the Client on (date) _____.

_____
Client

LAW FIRM

_____
by: Attorney

8. Defense Counsel Engagement Letter*

Date

Addressee

RE: Engagement for Labor and Employment Law
Representation (Describe Matter)

Dear

Our firm is honored that you have hired us for handling and defending this matter. We look forward to working with you.

I want to confirm the scope of our representation. Our professional services are limited to (describe matter). If this is incorrect, please advise immediately.

Our firm bills by the hour. My hourly rate, as department head, is _____ per hour. Associates in our Labor Department range from _____ to ____

---

* See also Sample Individual Defendant Engagement Letters, chapter 2, "Responding to the Lawsuit."

per hour, and our paralegals charge _____ per hour. We adjust these rates yearly. Any costs and expenses are extra. Our firm bills monthly with payment due upon receipt.

You may eventually obtain insurance coverage for employment claims. If so, remember that our firm undertakes your representation at our standard hourly rates. Some insurance companies retain counsel for their insureds at lower defense rates. While we will gladly continue your representation, if an insurance company extends coverage, we want to confirm that you will make up the difference between any reduced insurance company fees and our standard hourly rates. If you have any questions or disagreements about these billing arrangements, please let me know right away. If this agreement is acceptable to you, please sign below.

I hope this answers any questions about hiring our firm. If you have any questions, please feel free to call me. I am happy to discuss these matters with you in greater detail.

Again, we look forward to working with you. We really appreciate you entrusting this important matter to our firm.

Sincerely,

Accepted:

_____
(Client signature)

_____
(Title)

_____
(Client name)

Date: _____

9. Consent to Payment of Legal Fees by Another

I _____ consent to the payment of the legal fees of my counsel _____ by _____.

_____
(Signature)

_____
(Name)

_____
(Date)

_____
(Counsel)

_____
[optional] (Payor)

10. Joint Defense Agreement*

THIS JOINT DEFENSE AGREEMENT ("this Agreement") is made and entered into, effective the _____day of _____, 199 ___, by and (between/among) _____ (collectively referred to herein as "the Defendants").

RECITALS

A. The Defendants are named defendants in the following claims in the _____ Court _____ Case No. _____.

B. The Defendants agree and acknowledge that they share common or mutual interests in defending against the claims asserted in these claims and expect to assert many common defenses in those actions.

C. The Defendants further acknowledge that their common or mutual interests in facilitating the disclosure to one another of documents, factual materials, mental impressions, memoranda, witness interviews, and other information, including confidential communications (hereinafter referred to as "defense materials") relevant to matters of common concern, while safeguarding any privilege for these defense materials.

AGREEMENT

In consideration of the mutual obligations under this Agreement, the parties hereto agree as follows:

1. The Defendants agree to exchange or disclose defense materials to one another, and each authorizes its, his, or her counsel to disclose said defense materials to the other defendants' counsel, where relevant and necessary in the pursuit of the Defendants' common or mutual interests.

2. The Defendants agree that such exchanges or disclosures are not intended to diminish the confidentiality of any exchanged or disclosed defense materials or to waive any privilege applicable to such defense materials.

3. The Defendants agree to maintain at all times the confidentiality of any exchanged or disclosed defense materials. They shall only disclose such defense materials to the Defendants, their undersigned counsel, and those individuals under their direct supervision or control who are involved in the defense of these claims. Defendants further agree not to disclose any defense materials received from one another to any other counsel retained by any of the Defendants, if any, until such time as those attorneys also have signed an agreement identical or substantially similar to this one.

4. Defendants' counsel will solely use exchanged or disclosed defense materials and the information contained therein in the preparation of defenses of these claims and for no other purpose. If another person or entity requests or demands any defense materials by discovery request, subpoena, or other-

---

* See also Sample Individual Defendant Engagement Letter, chapter 2, "Responding to the Lawsuit."

wise, Defendants' counsel will take all steps necessary to assert and protect any privilege for such defense materials.

5. The Defendants agree that neither they nor their counsel shall make any claim that the exchange or disclosure of any defense materials pursuant to this Agreement constitutes a waiver of any privilege applicable to such defense materials.

6. Should anyone claim waiver of any otherwise applicable privilege as a result of any exchange or disclosure under this Agreement, the Defendants and their counsel agree to join in defending against such claim.

7. The Defendants agree that they will not use any of the exchanged or disclosed information or materials pursuant to this Agreement for the purposes of impeaching any party to this Agreement in any hearing, trial, or other proceeding involving these claims.

8. In the event any of the Defendants determines that his or her or its interests may be adverse to the interests of any other defendant, or becomes aware of any other circumstances inconsistent with the maintenance of a joint defense privilege, such Defendant shall immediately notify the other Defendants, return to them all previously received defense materials and withdraw from this Agreement. Such withdrawal shall not affect the privileged nature of any exchanged or disclosed defense materials prior to the date of withdrawal, and the withdrawing Defendant and his or her or its counsel shall continue to honor the obligations of confidentiality in this Agreement.

9. The Defendants waive any conflicts of interest for themselves or counsel that may arise due to this joint defense agreement.

10. The parties hereto acknowledge and agree that they may execute this Agreement in counterparts.
(Optional)

11. Notwithstanding anything herein to the contrary, the parties recognize that _____ is providing a defense [on all/some claims and issues to] _____ [under a reservation of rights] [under an indemnification policy]. The parties further recognize and agree that _____ do not waive any of their rights or limitations on such rights or the obligations of the other parties under this [insurance] [indemnification] policy by entering into this Agreement.

("Individual")   ("Corporation")

_____   By _____
        (Signature)   (Signature)

                                            Its _____
                                                    (Title)

_____   _____
        (Date)   (Date)

_____   _____
Attorneys for _____   Attorneys for _____

Notes

1. *See* MODEL RULES OF PROFESSIONAL CONDUCT Rules 1.7 through 1.10.
2. *See* MODEL RULES OF PROFESSIONAL CONDUCT Rule 1.4(b).
3. McKennon v. Nashville Banner Publ'g Co., 513 U.S. 352, 115 S. Ct. 879 (1995).
4. *See* MODEL RULES OF PROFESSIONAL CONDUCT Rule 1.5 on Fees.
5. *See* MODEL RULES OF PROFESSIONAL CONDUCT Rule 1.13.
6. Sanders v. Circle K Corp., 137 F.R.D. 292 (D. Ariz. 1991) (sanctioned plaintiff for compelling corporation to designate harasser as corporate representative); Eggleston v. Chicago Journeymen Plumbers Local Union No. 130, 657 F.2d 890, 903 (7th Cir. 1981), *cert. denied*, 455 U.S. 1017, 102 S. Ct. 1710 (1982) (detailed questioning about racial heritage of a plaintiff in a racial discrimination suit may be abusive and have limited relevance).
7. Potts v. Allis-Chalmers Corp., 118 F.R.D. 597, 44 Fair Empl. Prac. Cas. (BNA) 1484 (N.D. Ind. 1987).
8. Upjohn Co. v. United States, 449 U.S. 383, 394–96, 101 S. Ct. 677, 685–86 (1981).
9. FED. R. CIV. P. 23(a).
10. *See* Kleiner v. First Nat'l Bank of Atlanta, 751 F.2d 1193, 1207 (11th Cir. 1985) (counsel have ethical duty to refrain from discussing litigation with members of class; fining and disqualifying defense counsel); Jackson v. Motel 6 Multipurpose, Inc., 130 F.3d 999 (11th Cir. 1997) (abuse of discretion to allow nationwide advertising and mass mailings before class certification).
11. Steele v. Offshore Shipbuilding, Inc., 867 F.2d 1311, 1316–17 (11th Cir. 1989).
12. *See* Reynolds Metals Co. v. Rumsfeld, 564 F.2d 663, 667 (4th Cir. 1977), *cert. denied*, 435 U.S. 995, 98 S. Ct. 1646 (1978) (reports were not solely internal); *In re* Burlington N., Inc., 679 F.2d 762 (8th Cir. 1982); O'Connor v. Chrysler Corp., 86 F.R.D. 211, 26 Fair Empl. Cas. (BNA) 459 (D. Mass. 1980) (analysis privilege does not extend to facts and data); Webb v. Westinghouse Elec. Corp., 81 F.R.D. 431 (E.D. Pa. 1978) (privilege for subjective evaluations under mandatory government reports); Banks v. Lockheed-Georgia Co., 53 F.R.D. 283, 4 Fair Empl. Cas. (BNA) 117 (N.D. Ga. 1971) (privilege protects candid evaluations of equal opportunity compliance); Etienne v. Mitre Corp., 146 F.R.D. 145 (E.D. Va. 1993) (public policy supported disclosure in discrimination case).
13. Brooms v. Regal Tube Co., 881 F.2d 412, 421–22 (7th Cir. 1989) (corporation protected sexual harassment report by lawyer's investigation, but waived privilege at trial by asserting investigation by "impartial outsider").
14. *See* United States v. Zolin, 809 F.2d 1411, 1417 (9th Cir. 1987), *op. withdrawn in part*, 842 F.2d 1135 (9th Cir. 1988), *aff'd in part*, 491 U.S. 554, 109 S. Ct. 2619 (1989); Eisenberg v. Gagnon, 766 F.2d 770, 778 (3rd Cir.), *cert. denied*, 474 U.S. 946, 106 S. Ct. 342 (1985) (privilege protects communications as "part of an ongoing effort to set up a common defense strategy"); Kevlik v. Goldstein, 724 F.2d 844 (1st Cir. 1984).
15. *See* Evans v. Jeff D., 475 U.S. 717, 106 S. Ct. 1531 (1986) (district court can approve consent decree with fee waiver provision subject to state and local ethics consideration where class action settlement was conditional on waiver of fees).
16. MODEL CODE OF PROFESSIONAL RESPONSIBILITY, EC 7–10 (reproduced in LAWYERS' MANUAL ON PROFESSIONAL CONDUCT (ABA/BNA 1990)).
17. *See* Chicago Council of Lawyers v. Bauer, 522 F.2d 242 (7th Cir. 1975), *cert. denied*, 427 U.S. 912, 96 S. Ct. 3201 (1976) (local federal rule held overly broad and unconstitutional). *See* Gentile v. State Bar of Nev., 501 U.S. 1030, 111 S. Ct. 2720 (1991) ("an attorney may take reasonable steps to defend a client's reputation and reduce the adverse consequences of indictment . . . including an attempt to demonstrate in the court of public opinion that the client does not deserve to be tried.").
18. LAWYERS' MANUAL ON PROFESSIONAL CONDUCT § 61:178 (1994); Willy v. Coastal Corp., 855 F.2d 1160 (5th Cir. 1988), *aff'd after remand*, 915 F.2d 965 (5th Cir. 1990), *aff'd*, 503 U.S. 131, 112 S. Ct. 1076 (1992) ($19,000 fine for filing a wrongful discharge case that lacked legal merit).
19. Bates v. State Bar of Ariz., 433 U.S. 350, 384, 97 S. Ct. 2691, 2709 (1977).
20. Ohralik v. Ohio State Bar Ass'n, 436 U.S. 447, 464–68, 98 S. Ct. 1912, 1923–25 (1978). *See* Florida Bar v. Went For It, Inc., 515 U.S. 618, 115 S. Ct. 2371 (1995) (ban on direct mail solicitation for thirty days after personal injury).

21. Pierce v. Ortho Pharm. Corp., 84 N.J. 58, 66–67, 417 A.2d 505 (1980).

22. Cagguila v. Wyeth Labs., Inc., 127 F.R.D. 653 (E.D. Pa. 1989); *Nassau County Bar Association Commission on Professional Ethics*, Op. 89–2 (1989) (summarized in Laws. Man. on Prof. Conduct at 901:6267 (1990)).

23. Porter v. Arco Metals Co., 642 F. Supp. 1116 (D. Mont. 1986) (counsel can contact nonmanagerial corporate employees directly); Frey v. Dept. of Health and Human Servs., 106 F.R.D. 32 (E.D. N.Y. 1985) (corporate "party" cannot include all employees, or ethical rule would bar civil rights plaintiff from inexpensive access to witnesses and would frustrate plaintiff's claim).

24. *Accord* Polycast Technology Corp. v. Uniroyal, Inc., 129 F.R.D. 621, 628 (S.D. N.Y. 1990) (disciplinary rules did not cover contacts with former employee of defendant corporation, but protective order prohibited disclosure of any privileged information); Florida State Bar Opinion 88–14 (1988) (summarized in Laws. Man. on Prof. Conduct at 901:2507 (1990)). *See* New Jersey Rule on Professional Conduct 4.2 (1996) for a narrower view of insulating former employees from lawyer contacts.

25. *Rentclub*, Inc. v. Transamerica Rental Finance Corp., 811 F. Supp. 651 (M.D. Fla. 1992), *affirmed*, 43 F.3d 1439 (11th Cir. 1995).

26. University Patents Inc. v. Kligman, 737 F. Supp. 325, 329 (E.D. Pa. 1990).

27. Resnick v. American Dental Ass'n, 95 F.R.D. 372 (N.D. Ill. 1982).

28. MODEL RULES OF PROFESSIONAL CONDUCT Rule 4.2 Cmt. (1994).

29. MODEL RULES OF PROFESSIONAL CONDUCT Rules 4.1, 4.3, and 4.4 (1994).

30. Cagguila v. Wyeth Lab., Inc., 127 F.R.D. 653, 654 (E.D. Pa. 1989) ("in such an uncertain area of ethical conduct, we believe that a prudent attorney would have given notice to opposing counsel of the intent to take such a statement").

31. FED. R. CIV. P. 26(b)(3); Hickman v. Taylor, 329 U.S. 495 (1947).

32. Shields v. Sturm, Ruger & Co., 864 F.2d 379, 382 (5th Cir. 1989).

33. Castle v. Sangamo Weston, Inc., 744 F.2d 1464, 1466–67 (11th Cir. 1984) (disclosure to Equal Employment Opportunity Commission, while preparing for joint trial, is not a waiver).

CHAPTER 14

Arbitration and Mediation

First Part: Arbitration and Mediation of Employment Disputes: The Employer's Perspective

JODY E. FORCHHEIMER[*]

---

[*] *Bingham, Dana & Gould; Boston, Massachusetts.*

I. Introduction

If you practice employment law, you will arbitrate and mediate some disputes. You will have clients who are required to arbitrate or mediate by contract. You will have cases that are ordered to mediation by the courts. More importantly, you will encounter many situations in which it is in your client's best interest to propose and utilize a form of alternative dispute resolution. This chapter addresses the questions of when you must arbitrate or mediate, when it is in your best interest to do so, and how to maximize the value of alternative dispute resolution for your client.

Arbitration is an adjudicatory substitute for litigation and is, in most instances, binding on all parties who participate. Arbitrators decide both the extent of discovery allowed and the merits of the claims, and their decisions are, except in extremely limited circumstances, non-appealable. Mediation, by contrast, is a settlement mechanism. Since mediation is a settlement process in which the mediator attempts to bring the parties to a mutually agreeable settlement, the mediation process is nonbinding.

II. Arbitration

A. What Is Arbitration?

Arbitration is usually a creature of contract. Parties may provide by contract for any form of alternative dispute resolution. Thus, in a real sense, arbitration is what the parties decide it shall be. This chapter will discuss the usual forms of arbitration created by most predispute and postdispute agreements.

The purpose of arbitration is to reach a decision as to whether the defendant (typically called a respondent in arbitration) is liable, and, if so, how much it must pay to the plaintiff (who is typically referred to as the claimant in arbitration). Arbitration is a decision-making mechanism, not a settlement mechanism. Arbitrators hear witnesses, take evidence, and render decisions.

In general, arbitration is also binding. Contractual provisions requiring arbitration usually provide that the parties are bound by the decision of the arbitrators. In the alternative, the contract may provide that the arbitration shall be in accordance with the rules of a particular forum (for example, the American Arbitration Association), and the rules of most forums provide that the results of arbitration are binding. The federal and state statutes governing arbitration, discussed at greater length below, provide only restricted grounds for review of arbitration decisions, which also have the effect of making those decisions final.

Procedurally arbitration may be characterized as "semiformal." Most arbitration forums have some rules of procedures, and arbitration panels are generally empowered to issue orders to effectuate the purposes of efficient and just dispute resolution. However, the formal rules of evidence, procedure, discovery, and motion practice applicable in state and federal courts are rarely applicable to arbitration proceedings.

The governing rules of most arbitration panels leave room for the parties to negotiate procedural and discovery disputes. In the absence of successful negotiation, most forums provide for the parties to have access to a member of the panel or the forum's staff to resolve those disputes prior to the arbitration. During the arbitration, broad discretion is generally vested in the arbitrator. Given the flexibility of most arbitration standards, the resolution of evidentiary and other procedural issues will typically depend more on a sense of efficiency and equity than on an appeal to court rules and precedents.

B. Under What Circumstances Must My Client Arbitrate?

Generally, your client must arbitrate if your client has entered into a contract requiring arbitration.[1] In isolated cases a corporation must arbitrate where the corporation's alter ego signed the agreement. Also, a nonsignatory may be bound to arbitrate when stepping into the shoes of a party who did enter into the arbitration agreement (for example, an estate prosecuting a claim held by the deceased must arbitrate if the deceased had agreed to do so.) An agreement entered into prior to the existence of a dispute (for example, at the outset of the employment relationship) is called a predispute arbitration agreement.

In some industries and at some firms, agreements to arbitrate are mandatory. For example, in the securities industry, all persons who wish to become registered with an exchange (a prerequisite to selling securities) must agree to arbitrate any disputes they may have with the broker-dealer.[2] (As of this writing, the securities industry's mandatory arbitration rule is in flux. The National Association of Securities Dealers (NASD) Board of Governors has recommended that it be eliminated; that recommendation is under consideration by the Securities and Exchange Commission.) Similarly, some companies require employees, as a condition of employment, to agree that any disputes with the employer will be submitted to arbitration. Despite the efforts of the plaintiffs' bar, the majority of judicial decisions have held that these agreements are enforceable and that an employer may condition employment on an agreement to arbitrate disputes.[3]

There was some uncertainty in earlier years about whether predispute arbitration agreements were enforceable with respect to employment discrimination claims. In 1991, the Supreme Court clarified the law in the case of *Gilmer v. Interstate/Johnson Lane Corp.*, 500 U.S. 20 (1991). *Gilmer* held that claims under the Age Discrimination in Employment Act could be compelled into arbitration. *Gilmer* distinguished and criticized its earlier decision in *Alexander v. Gardner-Denver Co.*, 415 U.S. 36 (1974), which had held that an employee who had arbitrated a claim pursuant to a collective bargaining agreement was not foreclosed from later bringing a Title VII action.[4] *Gilmer* also criticized *Gardner-Denver's* hostility to the arbitration of employment disputes:

> The Court in [*Gardner-Denver*] also expressed the view that arbitration was inferior to the judicial process for resolving statutory claims. That 'mistrust of the arbitration process,' however, has been undermined by our recent arbitration decisions. 'We are well past the time when judicial suspicion of the desirability of arbitration and of the competence of arbitral tribunals inhibited the development of arbitration as an alternative means of dispute resolution.'[5]

Gilmer further noted, "generalized attacks on arbitration 'rest on suspicion of arbitration as a method of weakening the protections afforded in the substantive law to would-be complainants' and as such, they are 'far out of step with our current strong endorsement of the federal statutes favoring this method of resolving disputes.'"[6]

Since *Gilmer*, the courts have applied the reasoning in that case to compel virtually all forms of employment disputes into arbitration, where the employee has entered into a contract agreeing to arbitrate.[7]* Employees may be compelled to arbitrate their common law and federal statutory discrimination claims when their employment handbook provides for arbitration of employment disputes.[10]

Employees who do not wish to arbitrate disputes may raise the same defenses to a motion to compel arbitration that apply to any contractual agreement. (See "The Plaintiff's Perspective: How Plaintiffs Can Avoid Mandatory Arbitration," later in this chapter.) An employee may avoid arbitration if he or she can prove that the arbitration clause was itself fraudulently induced. However, if the employee's claim is that the entire contract was the product of fraud or duress, that contention will not be adequate to defeat the contractual right to arbitration, but rather must be considered in the arbitration itself.[11]

Employees wishing to avoid arbitration have argued that predispute arbitration agreements that the employees are required to sign as a condition of employment are unenforceable as contracts of adhesion. Alternatively, they argue their contracts are unenforceable because they were not agreed to "voluntarily and knowingly." These arguments have frequently failed on the basis of *Gilmer*.[12] Furthermore, "mere inequality in bargaining power . . . is not sufficient reason to hold that arbitration agreements are never enforceable in the employment context."[13] Absent a showing of affirmative fraud or genuine duress, an argument that the agreement was not knowingly or voluntarily entered into will fail.[14]

Arguments that arbitration deprives the employee of substantive rights are also frequently subject to failure. The arbitral procedures afforded by the generally available forums have been recognized by numerous courts as affording the same substantive rights as litigation, albeit in a different forum. "By agreeing to arbitrate a statutory claim, a party does not forgo the substantive rights afforded by the statute, it only submits to their resolution in an arbitral, rather than a judicial, forum."[15]

Contractual defenses to arbitration are rarely successful, as they are assessed in light of the Supreme Court's holding that there is a strong public policy in favor of enforcing arbitration agreements. Doubts as to the enforceability of arbitration agreements usually will be resolved in favor of arbitration.[16] Accordingly, where a contract expressly provides for arbitration, and the contract may reasonably be read to cover the dispute, experienced practitioners rarely view a challenge to arbitration as cost-effective.

---

* Editors' Note: However, as this book goes to press, a Massachusetts federal district court[8] and the Ninth Circuit[9] have just ruled that the 1991 Civil Rights Act prohibits employers from compelling employee(s) to arbitrate Title VII claims as a condition of employment.

C. Under What Circumstances Should My Client Voluntarily Choose to Arbitrate?

The following is a list of factors to consider in evaluating whether to voluntarily submit a claim to arbitration.

1. Cost

Arbitration is usually less expensive than litigation in employment cases because discovery and motion practice are far more limited. In arbitrations, there are typically no depositions, and highly burdensome "whole company" document productions are infrequent. Moreover, there is usually little motion practice in arbitration other than discovery skirmishes.

The other factor that tends to reduce the cost of arbitrations is that, in arbitration, a hearing date is usually a real date. The costs incurred in court in preparing for trial on numerous occasions, only to learn that the case will not be reached, are unlikely to be incurred in arbitration. In short, if the case settles before the first witness is called, arbitration is likely to be substantially less expensive than litigation.

There may, however, be significant costs incurred in employment arbitrations that do go to hearing and in which the hearings last more than a day or two. Arbitrations tend to be tried a few days at a time, with lengthy cases often extending over a period of months. Thus, a lengthy hearing in an employment arbitration may well be as expensive or more expensive than a lengthy court trial because significant costs are associated with repeated preparation of counsel and witnesses.

Another factor influencing the relative costliness of arbitration versus litigation is that cases in arbitration tend to be less likely to settle than cases in litigation. Respondents may feel less compulsion to settle absent the possibility of a runaway jury. Also, it is rare for arbitrators to "bang the parties' heads together" to force each side to be reasonable.

Management concerns about whether or not to require mandatory arbitration agreements from employees center on the likelihood that, with the availability of arbitration, more claims will be filed in the hopes of extracting a quick settlement at little cost. On the other hand, for a company that faces a considerable volume of costly lawsuits anyway, of which the vast majority are settled, arbitration may be a cost-effective alternative.

2. Availability of Substantive Motions

Arbitration usually provides very limited mechanisms for pre-hearing substantive motions such as summary judgment, including motions directed to the statute of limitations and related defenses. Such motions are typically heard at the outset of the arbitration hearing and are considered by the panel in the course of its overall deliberations.

Since an arbitration is unlikely to be dismissed on prehearing motion, counsel may have an opportunity to present the witnesses to the panel before the panel considers whether to dismiss the case on legal grounds. Moreover, intensive analysis of legal arguments is sometimes lacking in arbitration. Thus, an employee whose claim is vulnerable to dismissal in court may choose to propose arbitration.

3. Jury Awards versus Arbitrator's Decisions

The general view of both employee and management counsel is that employees secure more base hits, but hit fewer home runs, in arbitration. That is, the employee is more likely to prevail in arbitration, but less likely to obtain a million-dollar award (although very large, even multimillion-dollar awards have been granted in arbitrations of employment disputes). This phenomenon is due in part to the reluctance of arbitrators to grant prehearing dispositive motions, meaning that the employee's chances of being dismissed altogether are much lower in arbitration. This does not mean that the employee is always better off in court: most cases do not have serious potential of yielding a million-dollar verdict.

4. Speed and Finality

Generally, arbitrations are faster and more final than trials. Arbitrations are typically resolved, by hearing or settlement, within a year of filing. Since appellate rights are severely limited, the arbitration case is usually over when the arbitrator rules. By contrast, in many jurisdictions, it takes years to get to trial, and adverse judgments are often appealed by the losing party.

5. Publicity

Arbitrations are generally private proceedings. Although a lawyer may choose to disclose the results to the press, there will be no reporters at an arbitration hearing, making it less likely that the case will be the subject of a high-profile news story.

6. Fairness

The fairness of an arbitration proceeding, like the fairness of any proceeding, depends upon the fairness of the decision maker. Arbitration panels are usually composed of lawyers, academics, and, in some circumstances, individuals in disciplines related to the subject matter of the dispute. A practitioner considering arbitration should call the forums that provide arbitration in his locality and ask for a list of the available panelists and for the rules about how panelists are appointed. If counsel's research reveals that the available panels include arbitrators who would be viewed as unacceptable, one option is to include in the arbitration agreement a designation of an arbitrator or another selection mechanism that would exclude panelists unacceptable to either side.

D. What Laws and Rules of Procedure Govern Arbitration Proceedings?

1. The Federal Arbitration Act

The Federal Arbitration Act, 9 U.S.C. § 1-16 (1997), (FAA) governs any contract "evidencing a transaction involving commerce."[17] "Commerce" is defined as interstate or foreign commerce.[18] The statute contains an exception that has been the subject of some confusion, exempting "contracts of employment of seamen, railroad employees, or any other class of workers engaged in foreign or interstate commerce." This exception has been read narrowly to exclude from the coverage of the FAA only workers employed in transportation industries.[19] (The only exception to the overwhelming consensus that this exclusion should be narrowly construed was a 1954 Fourth Circuit decision limited to collective bargaining agreements: *United Electrical, Radio & Machine Workers v. Miller Metal Products, Inc.*, 215 F.2d 221 (4th Cir. 1954). It has been questioned and criticized many times, and "there is some question whether the Fourth Circuit's rejection of *Tenney* 40 years ago still constitutes good law."[20] Accordingly, unless the scope of the employer's operations is clearly and exclusively local, employment disputes will generally be subject to the FAA.)

The FAA does not create an independent basis of federal jurisdiction. In other words, the fact that an agreement is subject to the FAA does not create subject matter jurisdiction in federal court to enforce that agreement. However, under the Supremacy Clause, the FAA is applicable in state court to the same extent that it would be in federal court.[21] A party wishing to enforce a provision of the FAA in state court who also has available a complementary state court statute may be well advised to cite both the state and the federal law.

The key provisions of the FAA are as follows:

a. Availability of Proceedings to Compel Arbitration

If a lawsuit is filed on a claim that is referable to arbitration under the FAA, either party may obtain a stay from the court of all proceedings pending arbitration.[22] Once the court determines that the dispute falls within the scope of a valid arbitration agreement, the court must compel the case to arbitration.[23] Similarly, if either party refuses to arbitrate a claim that is subject to arbitration under a valid arbitration agreement, a proceeding may be brought to compel the resisting party to arbitrate.[24]

    b. Compulsory Process The FAA provides that the arbitrators have the power to subpoena parties to testify and to produce documents.[25] The procedures governing the rights and obligations between the parties with respect to discovery are generally provided for by the rules of the forum, discussed below. This provision, however, is generally viewed as giving the arbitral forum the power to impose duties on third parties.

    c. Confirmation of Award Either party may move to confirm the award within one year of the entry of the award.[26] Confirmation must be awarded unless the very narrow grounds for vacating or modifying the award, discussed below, are found.[27] As a matter of general practice, parties do not routinely file petitions to confirm. Such petitions tend to be filed where the prevailing party believes that he will need to utilize the judicial process to enforce the award.

    d. Vacating the Award Arbitration awards may be vacated on only very narrow grounds, including (1) the award was procured by corruption or fraud, (2) there was evident partiality or corruption in the arbitrators, (3) the arbitrators were guilty of misconduct, or (4) the arbitrators exceeded their powers.[28] Some courts have also held that an arbitration award can be vacated for "manifest disregard of the law."[29] Generally, if there is any evidence supporting the arbitrator's award, it will be upheld.[30] Arbitration awards are entitled to a strong presumption of validity.[31] As a matter of practice, arbitrators typically do not state the reasons for their awards. Accordingly, it is exceedingly difficult in most cases to prove that the arbitrators exceeded their powers or manifestly disregarded the law.

2. State Arbitration Acts

    The Uniform Arbitration Act (UAA) has been adopted (in some cases with amendments) by twenty-five states and the District of Columbia. The states that have adopted the UAA are Alaska, Arizona, Arkansas, Colorado, Delaware, Idaho, Illinois, Indiana, Kansas, Maine, Maryland, Massachusetts, Michigan, Minnesota, Missouri, Nevada, New Mexico, North Carolina, Oklahoma, Pennsylvania, South Carolina, South Dakota, Tennessee, Texas, Wyoming, and the District of Columbia. In addition, sixteen other states, including New York, have arbitration acts that contain provisions similar in many respects to the UAA.[32] The provisions of the UAA are, in large part, similar to those of the FAA.

3. The Rules of the Forum

Each arbitral forum has its own rules of practice and procedure.[33] These rules generally govern the nature of the claims that the forum will hear, the procedures for filing pleadings, discovery procedures, procedures for motion practice (if any), the procedures for the selection of arbitrators, and hearing procedures.

III. Practical Advice for Arbitrating Employment Disputes

For counsel accustomed to litigating employment disputes, arbitration requires some adjustments in strategy and practice:

A. Learn the Rules of the Arbitral Forum

Although there are fewer rules and fewer traps for the unwary, most forums do have deadlines and other requirements that one overlooks at one's peril, such as short time limits for exercising peremptory challenges.

B. Do Not Expect as Much out of Discovery

Arbitration generally affords fewer discovery devices. Most forums require document production, and some permit limited interrogatories, but most do not permit depositions except where a witness will truly be unavailable. The power to subpoena third parties usually exists but may require an order from the arbitration panel. In addition, arbitrators are less inclined than courts to order very extensive and broad-ranging discovery. The upshot is that greater effort must be taken to obtain information outside the discovery process. For the employee, this means you may not be able to find out what happens in the executive offices by deposing the officers; for the company, you may not be able to obtain information about the employee by deposing him or her. Extensive and comprehensive interviews of the witnesses who are at your disposal, computerized database research, courthouse searches, records of unemployment and workers' compensation filings, and private investigators can compensate for some of what is lost by not taking depositions.

C. Focus on the Facts and the Equities

For practitioners accustomed to litigating discrimination claims, the legal requirements as to who has the burden of proof and what quantum of evidence is necessary to meet or shift it are of overwhelming significance. In court, the case will live or die at the summary judgment stage based on these factors.

In arbitration, with very rare exceptions, there will not be any summary judgment hearing. The panel may or may not consider whether the requisite level of proof has been proffered by each side, but that consideration will, with rare exceptions, take place at the close of the case, after all of the evidence has been submitted. There is nothing inappropriate about arguing legal rules, but it is critical to do so without appearing to be "hiding behind technicalities."

D. Make Your Record "User Friendly"

Arbitrators generally are not paid—or are paid less than their ordinary hourly rates—for time spent in deliberations. When selecting exhibits, confine yourself to the documents that you need to establish your case and that you really want the panel to read, and put those documents in a tabbed index. In all but the most complex cases, a single notebook of exhibits should suffice. Where possible, summarize a large volume of exhibits in a single chart or charts. If the underlying documents must be introduced, do so in an "appendix" volume of exhibits so that the volume of documents does not appear overwhelming.

The same rule applies to legal authorities. Take care to select the handful of authorities that you really want the panel to read and give the panel copies of those. Long string cites and volumes of cases are of questionable value in many courtrooms; they are worth very little in arbitration.

E. Do Not Expect the Arbitrators to Play Any Role in Settlement

In discrimination cases, settlement can be particularly difficult because emotions often run high and because the major element of damages is typically of the emotional distress variety, and thus not quantifiable. In these cases, the settlement process often benefits from the involvement of a neutral third party. You cannot expect the arbitrators to play this role: arbitrators rarely become involved in settlement discussions. Counsel whose practice it is to wait to discuss settlement until the "courthouse steps" on the assumption that the arbitrators will raise the subject may find that the subject never gets raised.

IV. Mediation

A. What Is Mediation?

The term mediation generally refers to a nonbinding settlement mechanism, not an adjudicatory mechanism. A mediation usually involves retention of a neutral third party to help the parties reach a settlement. There are as many forms of mediation as there are styles of settlement negotiations. In a typical mediation, the parties make a presentation of some sort to the mediator, who then confers with the parties to help them find common ground for settlement.

B. Under What Circumstances Must My Client Mediate?

Compulsory mediation is typically a creature of a "step" grievance procedure or other company-generated dispute resolution mechanisms. If an employee is required to use some form of mediation procedure prior to filing a lawsuit or arbitration, that requirement will usually be found in an employee handbook or similar document. Some courts also require mediation as a condition for proceeding with a lawsuit or appeal.

C. When Should My Client Voluntarily Mediate?

Mediation should be considered when (1) you want to settle the case for an amount that the other side would conceivably accept and (2) you cannot do so by more conventional means. Mediators are generally looking for a middle ground: If compromise is unacceptable to your client, mediation is a waste of time. Mediation can work where more conventional forms of negotiation do not because it allows the neutral to talk directly to the parties. The mediator may be able to say things that counsel cannot tell his own client. In addition, mediation can allow an opportunity for the emotional side of employment litigation to be vented.

Second Part:
Arbitration of Employment Disputes:
The Employee's Perspective

CHRISTOPHER P. LENZO[*]
NANCY ERIKA SMITH[†]

V. The Pitfalls of Mandatory Arbitration for Plaintiffs

Increasingly employers require employees to sign predispute mandatory arbitration agreements as a condition of employment. These agreements may eviscerate the civil rights guaranteed to employees by federal and state employment statutes, as well as employees' federal and state constitutional rights to jury trials and access to the courts. Employees may lose crucial rights in arbitration such as the rights to jury trials, discovery, lawyers' fees awards, punitive damages, reasonable statutes of limitations, and appeals. In essence, employers are trying to exempt themselves from government regulation through these predispute mandatory arbitration agreements. If plaintiffs' counsel do not vigorously oppose this movement by employers, the legal protections that employees currently have will effectively be repealed without any legislative debate, executive approval, or judicial review.

Mandatory arbitration is inherently skewed to the disadvantage of employment litigation plaintiffs. In arbitration, plaintiffs lose the advantage of a jury of their peers. Instead, employees submit their claims to arbitrators who are usually paid by the employer and rely on the employer's repeat business for their livelihood. Thus, there is a serious question about whether arbitration is inherently biased against plaintiffs. In addition, current arbitrator lists supplied by the largest arbitration associations indicate that the arbitrators (often retired judges) are predominantly white men. Thus, arbitrators are not nearly as representative a cross-section of the community as jurors. Furthermore, arbitrators in some sectors of business, such as the securities industry, are not necessarily lawyers. Arbitrators often have no experience with or

---

[*] *Francis, Lenzo & Manshel; Millburn, New Jersey.*

[†] *Smith Mullin; Montclair, New Jersey.*

knowledge of employment law. Thus, the quality of arbitration decisions is often dubious.

Mandatory arbitration is also detrimental to employment litigation plaintiffs in very practical ways. First, the severely limited scope of discovery in arbitration (and in some cases the complete unavailability of discovery) essentially cripples employment litigation plaintiffs. The employers are likely to have access to all of the witnesses and documents. Second, most plaintiffs cannot afford to pay a lawyer to represent them. Many arbitration agreements force plaintiffs to forfeit the right to lawyer's fee awards after a decision in their favor has been rendered. So mandatory arbitration agreements seriously hamper the ability of plaintiffs to find lawyers to represent them. Third, the fact that arbitration agreements (and some states' law) often strip plaintiffs of their right to seek punitive damages is particularly disturbing. Such agreements undermine the deterrent and remedial effects of the laws that regulate employers. Fourth, in a further effort to limit their exposure, employers are now using arbitration agreements to shorten the applicable limitations period, thus precluding otherwise viable claims. Finally, because arbitration awards can be appealed only under very limited circumstances, plaintiffs are left with no remedy for an erroneous adverse decision, even if the arbitrators blatantly misapplied the law.

In short, if every employer eventually requires arbitration of employment disputes as a condition of employment, the hard-won legal protections for employees that we presently have will cease to exist. A presidential commission has recognized as much, as have the Equal Employment Opportunity Commission (EEOC) and the National Labor Relations Board (NLRB).

In 1994, the President's Commission on the Future of Worker-Management Relations (the Dunlop Commission) issued a report under the auspices of the U.S. Department of Labor and the U.S. Department of Commerce recommending that the courts and/or Congress construe the Federal Arbitration Act (FAA) to prohibit employers from requiring employees to sign predispute mandatory arbitration agreements as a condition of employment. The Dunlop Commission noted that "[e]mployees required to accept binding arbitration of [employment] disputes would face what for many would be an inappropriate choice: give up your right to go to court, or give up your job."

Similarly, the EEOC has issued an Alternative Dispute Resolution Policy Statement that requires that alternative dispute resolution mechanisms be voluntary and provide employees the opportunity to opt out of alternative dispute resolution at any point prior to the issuance of a decision. In fact, in at least one case, the EEOC has successfully obtained an injunction enjoining an employer from requiring its employees to submit employment disputes to alternative dispute resolution as a condition of employment.[34]

The NLRB sought a similar injunction that would require an employer to rescind its nationwide policy of requiring employees to submit all employment disputes to arbitration as a condition of employment.[35]

VI. How Plaintiffs Can Avoid Mandatory Arbitration

There are several grounds on which employment litigation plaintiffs can avoid mandatory arbitration based on predispute arbitration agreements that were signed as a condition of employment. Most of these arguments against mandatory arbitration are merely basic defenses to the enforceability of any contract drawn from the common law of contracts. The Supreme Court has held that under the Federal Arbitration Act, state law governing the validity, revocability, and enforceability of contracts should generally be used to determine whether the parties entered into a valid and enforceable agreement to arbitrate.[36]

A. Predispute Mandatory Arbitration Agreements That Force Employees to Forfeit Statutory Rights and Remedies Are Void as a Matter of Public Policy*

Plaintiffs' counsel should challenge the enforceability of any predispute mandatory arbitration agreement that was signed by the plaintiff as a condition of employment if the agreement strips the plaintiff of statutory rights and remedies, such as discovery, lawyer's fee awards, punitive damages, and a reasonable statute of limitations. Such agreements are generally void as a matter of public policy under the general contract law principles of most states.

Although it is not an employment law case, *Graham Oil Co. v. Arco Products Co.*, 43 F.3d 1244 (9th Cir.), *cert. denied*, 116 S. Ct. 275 (1995), is extremely helpful to employment litigation plaintiffs seeking to challenge mandatory arbitration agreements that deprive them of statutory rights and remedies. In *Graham*, a small franchisee was required by a powerful franchisor to sign an arbitration agreement that deprived the franchisee of important statutory protections under the Petroleum Marketing Practices Act (PMPA). In particular, the arbitration clause prohibited an award of punitive damages or recovery of lawyer's fees and

---

* See Editor's Note on page 323.

reduced the statute of limitations from one year to 90 days.[37] The U.S. Court of Appeals for the Ninth Circuit held that the arbitration clause violated the purpose and terms of the PMPA, declared the clause void as a matter of public policy, and remanded the matter for trial.[38] Significantly, the *Graham* court struck down the *entire* arbitration clause, rather than just the provisions prohibiting punitive damages and lawyer's fee awards and shortening the statute of limitations, because (1) the arbitration clause was "a highly integrated unit containing three different illegal provisions"; (2) "the offensive provisions clearly represent[ed] an attempt . . . to achieve through arbitration what Congress has expressly forbidden"; and (3) "[s]uch a blatant misuse of the arbitration procedure serves to taint the entire clause."[39]

In striking down the arbitration clause, the Ninth Circuit reasoned as follows:

> [T]he fact that franchisees may agree to an arbitral forum for the resolution of statutory disputes in no way suggests that they may be forced by those with dominant economic power to surrender the statutorily-mandated rights and benefits that Congress intended them to possess. This is certainly true in cases arising under the PMPA, which was enacted to shield franchisees from the gross "disparity of bargaining power" that exists between them and franchisors. If franchisees could be compelled to surrender their statutorily-mandated protections as a condition of obtaining franchise agreements, then franchisors could use their superior bargaining power to deprive franchisees of the PMPA's protections. In effect, the franchisors could simply continue their earlier practice of presenting prospective franchisees with contracts of adhesion that deny them the rights and benefits afforded by Congress. In that way, the PMPA would quickly be nullified.[40]

Similarly, if employers are allowed to use their superior economic power to exact so-called "arbitration agreements" that eviscerate substantial statutory rights, the laws that protect employees will become a nullity. Eventually, all employers will require the forfeiture of statutory rights and remedies as a condition of employment, thus effectively repealing the laws that protect employees.[41]

The Ninth Circuit's decision in *Graham* is really nothing more than a logical application of the principle that "[b]y agreeing to arbitrate a statutory claim, a party does not forgo the substantive rights afforded by the statute; it only submits to their resolution in an arbitral, rather than a judicial, forum."[42] The Supreme Court cases that have upheld arbitration agreements have all started from the basic premise that the arbitral forum preserves all substantive rights and remedies. There has been no indication that the Supreme Court would uphold an arbitration agreement that strips plaintiffs of substantive statutory rights or remedies. Indeed, quite to the contrary, the Court noted in *Mitsubishi* (which concerned the arbitration of federal antitrust claims) that "in the event the choice-of-forum and choice-of-law clauses [in an arbitration agreement] operated in tandem as a prospective waiver of a party's right to pursue statutory remedies for antitrust violations, we would have little hesitation in condemning the agreement as against public policy."[43] The Court is essentially bound to use that logic to strike down any predispute mandatory arbitration agreement as applied to discrimination claims because it has already held that "there can be no prospective waiver of an employee's rights under Title VII."[44]

Recently, however, the Third Circuit ruled in *Great W. Mortgage Corp. v. Peacock*, 110 F.3d 222 (3d Cir. 1977), *cert. denied*, 118 S. Ct. 299 (1997), that a mandatory agreement to arbitrate was enforceable despite provisions shortening the statute of limitations from two years to one year, and waiving the employee's rights to lawyer's fees and to punitive damages. In addition, the court upheld the implicit waiver of the right to a jury trial and to discovery under the federal and/or state rules of procedure. The Third Circuit held that federal courts only have the jurisdiction to determine arbitrability under the FAA; the waiver of substantative rights, such as the statute of limitations and punitive damages, is for the arbitrator to decide.[45]

B. Predispute Mandatory Arbitration Agreements Are Unconscionable Contracts of Adhesion

It is a black letter principle of contract law in virtually every state that unconscionable contracts are unenforceable. Consequently, when the arbitration agreement that an employee has signed is a company-wide, nonnegotiable, predispute form contract, plaintiffs' counsel should always assert the defense of unconscionability as basis for avoiding enforcement of the agreement.

Such an argument succeeded recently in *Stirlen v. Supercuts, Inc.*, 51 Cal. App. 4th 1519 (Cal. App. 1997). In that case, the California Court of Appeal struck down an executive's predispute mandatory arbitration agreement, holding that the agreement was unenforceable under California contract law because it was both procedurally and substantively unconscionable. The court held that the agreement was a procedurally unconscionable contract of adhesion because the terms of the agreement were nonnegotiable, and every corporate officer was required to sign the same agreement. The court also held that the agreement was substantively unconscionable because (1) it required the employee to arbitrate all employment disputes, but allowed the employer to take certain employment disputes to court; (2) it stripped the employee of all statutory remedies except actual contract damages; (3) it permitted the employer to discharge the employee pending resolution of the arbitration; and (4) its one-year limitations period shortened the applicable statutes of limitations for many employment claims that employees may bring under the law.[46]

C. Predispute Mandatory Arbitration Agreements Do Not Constitute a Knowing and Voluntary Waiver of the Plaintiff's Statutory and Constitutional Rights

That any waiver of rights must be knowing and voluntary is a fundamental principle of the common law of contracts. In the context of arbitration agreements, that principle takes on special significance because the right to a jury trial is guaranteed by the U.S. Constitution and most state constitutions. As a result, plaintiffs' counsel should always analyze any predispute mandatory arbitration agreement and the circumstances under which it arose to determine whether the plaintiff knowingly and voluntarily waived any rights and remedies that the arbitration agreement takes away.

The starting point for an evaluation of whether an arbitration agreement is a knowing and voluntary waiver of rights is the statute under which the plaintiff is bringing the cause of action. If the statute or its legislative history indicates that the rights and remedies provided by the statute are nonwaivable or that waiver of those rights and remedies is disfavored, the plaintiff has a strong argument against enforcement of the arbitration agreement.

If the statute at issue does not have any provisions regarding the waivability of claims, counsel should focus on the circumstances under which the plaintiff entered into the arbitration agreement. Those circumstances will determine whether the arbitration agreement constitutes a valid waiver (that is, a knowing and voluntary waiver).

Several factors should be considered in analyzing whether an employee knowingly waived his or her rights by entering into an arbitration agreement. First, if the agreement was signed by the employee before any dispute arose, one can argue that the waiver of rights is not knowing because it is prospective.

The waiver of rights is also not knowing if the employee was never advised in the agreement, or by any other means, of the rights that applicable laws provide to employment litigation plaintiffs. This argument has particular appeal if the type of claim at issue must be waived explicitly and specifically. For example, the federal Older Workers Benefit Protection Act requires that a waiver of any rights under the federal Age Discrimination in Employment Act (which, as amended by the Civil Rights Act of 1991, guarantees plaintiffs the right to a jury trial) specifically mentions the Age Discrimination in Employment Act.[47]

In evaluating whether an arbitration agreement constitutes a knowing waiver of rights, the employee's opportunity to consult counsel is also extremely important. For example, the Older Workers Benefit Protection Act requires employers to provide employees with twenty-one days to consider the waiver of any rights guaranteed by the Age Discrimination in Employment Act so that employees have the opportunity to consult counsel.[48]

Whether an employment arbitration agreement is a voluntary waiver of rights is determined primarily by considering two factors: (1) whether the agreement was signed by the employee as a condition of employment or under threat of termination and (2) whether the terms of the agreement were subject to negotiation by the employee. If the employee entered into the agreement as a condition of employment or under threat of termination, the agreement is certainly not a voluntary waiver of rights. The same is true if the terms of the agreement were completely nonnegotiable.[49]

Finally, plaintiffs' counsel should keep in mind that the Federal Arbitration Act (FAA) *requires* both federal and state courts to hold a jury trial regarding the issue of whether there was a valid agreement to arbitrate the dispute at issue if the party opposing arbitration requests such a trial on or before the return date of the other party's motion to compel arbitration.[50] Thus, in cases in which the employer is moving to compel arbitration pursuant to the FAA, plaintiffs' counsel should demand a jury trial on the issue of whether there is a valid agreement to arbitrate if there is any evidence that the arbitration agreement was not knowing and voluntary.

The Ninth Circuit has adopted a strict standard governing the determination of whether agreements for mandatory arbitration are knowing and voluntary. In *Prudential Insurance Co. of America v. Lai*, 42 F.3d 1299 (9th Cir. 1994), plaintiffs, who were suing under Title VII, had signed a form providing that the employees agreed "to arbitrate any dispute, claim or controversy that may arise between me or my firm . . . that is required to be arbitrated under the rules, constitutions, or bylaws of the organizations with which I register." The court found no knowing waiver because the provision did not specify "employment" or "discrimination" disputes.[51] The California state courts have also carefully scrutinized purported agreements to arbitrate.[52]

D. Arbitration Policies Contained in Nonbinding Employment Handbooks Are Not Enforceable

In states where employment handbooks and employer policy manuals can be contractually binding, employers may try to include an arbitration policy in such documents. Plaintiffs' counsel should always examine such documents carefully to determine whether there is a disclaimer indicating that the document does not constitute a contract. If there is such a disclaimer, the arbitration provision is not enforceable.[53]

E. Arbitration Clauses in Employment Contracts May Not Be Enforceable under the Federal Arbitration Act

The FAA provides that "nothing herein contained shall apply to contracts of employment of seamen, railroad employees, or any other class of workers engaged in foreign or interstate commerce."[54] The same sentence defines "commerce" for purposes of the FAA as embracing the fullest extent of Congress's Commerce Clause power.[55] Thus, whenever an employer moves to compel arbitration of an employment dispute under the FAA, the employee's counsel should argue that the FAA does not apply if (1) the arbitration provision is part of a broader employment contract and (2) the employee's job involved some element of interstate commerce.

However, counsel should be aware that the Supreme Court has not yet decided the scope of the FAA employment-contract exclusion, having explicitly left the issue open in *Gilmer v. Interstate/Johnson Lane Corp.*, 500 U.S. 20, 25 n.2 (1991). Currently there is a split in the circuits on the issue. Some courts have held that the employment-contract exclusion applies to any employee involved in interstate commerce.[56] Other courts have held that the exclusion only applies to workers who are directly involved in the transport of goods across state lines.[57]

F. The Rules of the Arbitration Organization Involved May Preclude Arbitration of Certain Disputes

In seeking to avoid mandatory arbitration, plaintiffs' counsel should carefully read the rules of the arbitration organization in which the employer seeks to compel arbitration to determine whether the dispute at hand is arbitrable under those rules. For example, several courts have ruled that employment disputes were not arbitrable in the NASD until the NASD revised its rules in October 1993 to refer explicitly and specifically to arbitration of employment disputes.[58] Similarly, at least one court has construed the insurance-industry exception to arbitration under the NASD rules to preclude arbitration of a whistle-blower claim where the whistle-blowing concerned "churning" in the sales of insurance policies.[59]

Notes

1. *See e.g.* Local 285, Serv. Employees Int'l Union, AFL-CIO v. Nonotuck Resource Assocs., Inc., 64 F.3d 735, 738 (1st Cir. 1995).

2. *See* New York Stock Exchange Rule 347; NASD Uniform Application for Securities Registration or Transfer (Form U-4) ¶ 5, at 4.

3. Gilmer v. Interstate/Johnson Lane Corp., 500 U.S. 20 (1991).

4. 415 U.S. at 49–50.

5. 500 U.S. at 34, n.5 (quoting Mitsubishi Motors Corp. v. Soler Chrysler-Plymouth, Inc., 473 U.S. 614 (1985)).

6. 500 U.S. at 30.

7. *See, e.g.*, Armijo v. Prudential Ins. Co. of Am., 72 F.3d 793 (10th Cir. 1995) (employment discrimination claims arbitrable); Alford v. Dean Witter Reynolds, Inc., 939 F.2d 229 (5th Cir. 1991); Willis v. Dean Witter Reynolds, Inc., 948 F.2d 305 (6th Cir. 1991); Mago v. Shearson Lehman Hutton, Inc., 956 F.2d 932 (9th Cir. 1992); Bender v. A.G. Edwards & Sons, Inc., 971 F.2d 698 (11th Cir. 1992); Maye v. Smith Barney Inc., 897 F. Supp. 100 (S.D.N.Y. 1995); Solomon v. Duke Univ., 850 F. Supp. 372 (M.D.N.C. 1993) (Americans with Disabilities Act claims arbitrable); DiCrisci v. Lyndon Guar. Bank of New York, 807 F. Supp. 947 (W.D.N.Y. 1992); Kramer v. Smith Barney, 80 F.3d 1080 (5th Cir. 1996) (ERISA claims arbitrable); Pritzker v. Merrill Lynch, Pierce, Fenner & Smith, Inc., 7 F.3d 1110 (3rd Cir. 1993) (employee benefits claims arbitrable).

8. *See* Rosenberg v. Merrill Lynch, _____ F. Supp. _____ (D. Mass 1998).

9. *See* Duffield v. Robertson Stephens & Co., _____ F. 3rd _____ 1998 U.S. App. LEXIS 9284 (9th Cir. 1998).

10. *See* Nghiem v. NEC Elec., Inc., 25 F.3d 1437 (9th Cir. 1994).

11. Prima Paint Corp. v. Flood & Conklin Mfg. Co., 388 U.S. 395 (1967); Meyer v. Dans un Jardin, S.A., 816 F.2d 533 (10th Cir. 1987) (claim of fraud in inducement of entire contract is referred to arbitration).

12. *See* Sheller v. Frank's Nursery & Crafts, 957 F. Supp. 150 (N.D. Ill. 1997) (holding that even though employees were minors when they signed the arbitration agreement, it was enforceable and employer could condition employment on employee's acceptance of arbitration agreement); Durkin v. CIGNA Property & Casualty Corp. 942 F. Supp. 431 (D. Kan. 1996) (rejecting plaintiff's argument that arbitration agreement was contract of adhesion because she was forced to sign it to keep her job); Beauchamp v. Great W. Life Assurance Co., 918 F. Supp. 1091 (E.D. Mich. 1996) (stating that the "conclusion that an arbitration clause is only binding when the claimant has actual knowledge that his particular employment . . . claims will be covered by the agreement . . . flies in the face of the language of the Civil Rights Act of 1991, the Supreme Court's opinion in *Gilmer*, and the fundamental principles of contract law"); Maye v. Smith Barney, Inc., 897 F. Supp. 100 (S.D.N.Y. 1995) (holding that an arbitration agreement was not a contract of adhesion nor was it entered into involuntarily or unknowingly: "[g]iving the required healthy regard to the strong federal policy favoring arbitration, an argument . . . that one did not have the time to read an agreement before signing it must fail or else almost every arbitration agreement would be subject to an effective court challenge").

13. *Gilmer*, 500 U.S. at 33.

14. *Id. But see*, Rosenberg v. Merrill Lynch, Pierce, Fenner & Smith, Inc., No. 96-12267, 1998 U.S. Dist. LEXIS 877; 76 Fair Empl. Prac. Cas. (BNA) 681 (1998) (denying arbitration due to lack of free market presumptions).

15. Mitsubishi, 473 U.S. at 628. *But see*, Rosenberg v. Merrill Lynch, Pierce, Fenner & Smith, Inc., _____ F. Supp. _____ (D. Mass. 1998) (rejecting arbitration due to loss of substantative rights to damages and jury trial).

16. Moses H. Cone Mem'l Hosp. v. Mercury Const. Co., 460 U.S. 1, 24 (1983); Peerless Pressed Metal Corp. v. Int'l Union of Elec., Radio and Mach. Workers, AFL-CIO, 451 F.2d 19, 20 (1st Cir. 1971), *cert. denied*, 414 U.S. 1022 (1973). *See also* Beauchamps Great W. Life Assurance Co., 918 F. Supp. 1091, 1095 (E.D. Mich. 1996).

17. 9 U.S.C. § 2.

18. *See* Medical Dev. Corp. v. Indus. Molding Corp., 479 F.2d 345 (10th Cir. 1973); Varley v. Tarrytown Assocs., Inc., 477 F.2d 208 (2d Cir. 1973).

19. Asplundh Tree Expert Co. v. Bates, 71 F.3d 592 (6th Cir. 1995) (overruling dicta in Willis v. Dean Witter Reynolds, Inc., 948 F.2d 305 (6th Cir. 1991), which broadly construed the exclusion); Miller Brewing Co. v. Brewery Workers Local Union No. 9, AFL-CIO, 739 F.2d 1159 (7th Cir. 1984), cert. denied, 469 U.S. 1160 (1985); Erving v. Virginia Squires Basketball Club, 468 F.2d 1064 (2d Cir. 1972); Dickstein v. DuPont, 443 F.2d 783 (1st. Cir. 1971); Tenney Eng'g, Inc. v. United Elec. Radio & Mach. Workers of Am., 207 F.2d 450 (3d Cir. 1953); Albert v. Nat'l Cash Register Co., 874 F. Supp. 1324 (S.D. Fla. 1994); Malison v. Prudential-Bache Sec., Inc., 654 F. Supp. 101 (W.D.N.C. 1987).

20. Durkin, 942 F. Supp. at 486.

21. See, e.g., Three Valleys Mun. Water Dist. v. E.F. Hutton & Co., Inc., 925 F.2d 1136 (9th Cir. 1991).

22. 9 U.S.C. § 3.

23. Houlihan v. Offerman & Co., Inc., 31 F.3d 692 (8th Cir. 1994).

24. 9 U.S.C. § 4.

25. 9 U.S.C. § 7.

26. 9 U.S.C. § 9.

27. Id.

28. 9 U.S.C. § 10.

29. See, e.g., Siegel v. Titan Indus. Corp., 779 F.2d 891, 892 (2d Cir. 1985) ("an arbitrator's award, although subject to limited judicial scrutiny, will not be confirmed if it is demonstrated that the arbitrator acted in manifest disregard of the law."); Madison v. Fire Fighters Local 311, 124 LRRM 2131, 2133 (Wis. Ct. App. 1986); DeGaetano v. Smith Barney, Inc., 1997 U.S. Dist. LEXIS 17350 (S.D.N.Y. Nov. 5, 1997).

30. Glennon v. Dean Witter Reynolds, Inc., 83 F.3d 132 (6th Cir. 1996).

31. City of Parkersburg, W. Va. v. Turner Const. Co., 612 F.2d 155 (4th Cir. 1980).

32. See N.Y. CIV. PRACT. LAW & RULES § 7501, et seq.

33. See, e.g, American Arbitration Association's National Rules for the Resolution of Employment Disputes, Arbitration and Mediation Rules; National Association of Securities Dealers Regulation, Inc. Code of Arbitration Procedure; New York Stock Exchange, Inc. Arbitration Rules, New York Stock Exchange Guide, Rule 600-637.

34. EEOC Notice No. 915.002; EEOC v. River Oaks Imaging and Diagnostic, 1995 WL 264003, 63 U.S.L.W. 2733 (S.D. Tex. June 23, 1995).

35. Great Western Bank, Case 12-CA-16886 (NLRB, Region 12, Jan. 26, 1996).

36. See, e.g., Doctor's Assocs., Inc. v. Casarotto, 116 S. Ct. 1652, 1656 (1996); First Options of Chicago, Inc. v. Kaplan, 115 S. Ct. 1920, 1924 (1995); Perry v. Thomas, 482 U.S. 483, 492 n.9 (1987).

37. Id. at 1247–48.

38. Id. at 1248–49.

39. Id.

40. Id. at 1247.

41. See also, Rosenberg v. Merrill Lynch, Pierce, Fenner & Smith, Inc., No. 96-12267, 1998 U.S. Dist. LEXIS 877; 76 Fair Empl. Prac. Cas. (BNA) 681 (1998) (rejecting arbitration of age and gender discrimination and sexual harassment due to substantive statutory rights).

42. Mitsubishi Motors Corp. v. Soler Chrysler-Plymouth, Inc., 473 U.S. 614, 628 (1985).

43. Id. at 637 n.19.

44. Alexander v. Gardner-Denver Co., 415 U.S. 36, 51 (1974).

45. Id. at 16.

46. Rosenberg v. Merrill Lynch, Pierce, Fenner & Smith, Inc., No. 96-12267, 1998 U.S. Dist. LEXIS 877; 76 Fair Empl. Prac. Cas. (BNA) 681 (1998) (rejecting arbitration due to lack of freedom to bargain about arbitration). But see, Great W. Mortgage Corp. v. Peacock, 110 F.3d 22 (3rd Cir. 1977), cert. denied, 118 S. Ct. 299 (1997) (mandatory agreement to arbitrate employment disputes not unconscionable despite unequal bargaining power).

47. 29 U.S.C. § 626(f) (1998). See also Keelan v. Bell Communications Research, 289 N.J. Super. 531, 543–45 (App. Div. 1996) (noting that "although employers are not absolutely obligated to mention a specific statute in order to validly bar claims under that statute, the failure to make such specific mention is detrimental to the employer's case that the release is valid" and holding that "[c]ertainly, a release executed by an employee who is unaware of his rights is not a knowing or voluntary release").

48. 29 U.S.C. § 626(f) (1998).

49. *See, e.g.,* Fairfield Leasing Corp. v. Technigraphics, Inc., 256 N.J. Super. 538, 543 (Law Div. 1992) (holding that "where . . . a non-negotiated jury waiver clause appears inconspicuously in a standardized form contract entered into without the assistance of counsel, the waiver should not be enforced").

50. 9 U.S.C. § 4.

51. *Id.* at 1305. *See also* Renteria v. Prudential Ins. Co. of Am., 113 F.3d 1104, 1106 (9th Cir. 1997) (where the court also refused to force a plaintiff to arbitrate although the waiver provision added the phase "all disputes listed in the NASD Code as 'may be amended from time to time' "); Nelson v. Cypress Bagdad Copper Corp., 119 F.3d 756, 761 (9th Cir. 1997) (no agreement to arbitrate where employee signed form acknowledging that he had received employee handbook containing mandatory arbitration provision); and Rosenberg v. Merrill Lynch, Pierce, Fenner & Smith, Inc., No. 96-12267, 1998 U.S. Dist. LEXIS 877; 76 Fair Empl. Prac. Cas. (BNA) 681 (1998) (critizing structural bias due to securities industry domination of arbitration).

52. *See* Cheng-Caminchin v. Renaissance Hotel Assocs., 50 Cal. App. 4th 676, 57 Cal. Rptr. 2d 867 (Cal. App. 1996) (plaintiff's agreement to appear before "review committee" of coworkers and officers was not binding for Title VII dispute because the term "arbitration" was not used, there was no third-party decision maker, and no provision for assuming minimum level of impartiality and finality of decisions).

53. *See, e.g.,* Heurtebise v. Reliable Bus. Computers, Inc., 550 N.W.2d 243 (Mich. 1996) (holding that arbitration provision in employee handbook that included disclaimer stating that handbook was not a contract was not enforceable), *cert. denied,* 117 S. Ct. 1311 (1997). *See also,* Nelson v. Badgad Copper Corp., 119 F.3d 756 (9th Cir. 1997).

54. 9 U.S.C. § 1.

55. *Id.*

56. *See, e.g.,* Willis v. Dean Witter Reynolds, Inc., 948 F.2d 305 (6th Cir. 1991).

57. *See, e.g.,* Great W. Mortgage Corp. v. Peacock, 110 F.3d 222 (3d Cir. 1997) *cert. denied,* 118 S. Ct. 299 (1997); *see also*: Nelson v. Bagdad Copper Corp., 119 F.3d 756 (9th Cir. 1997).

58. *See, e.g.,* Renteria v. Prudential Ins. Co. of Am., 113 F.3d 1104 (9th Cir. 1997); Prudential Ins. Co. of Am. v. Lai, 42 F.3d 1299 (9th Cir. 1994), *cert. denied,* 116 S. Ct. 61 (1995); Kresock v. Bankers Trust Co., 21 F.3d 176 (7th Cir. 1994); Farrand v. Lutheran Brotherhood, 993 F.2d 1253 (7th Cir. 1993).

59. Young v. Prudential Ins. Co. of Am., Inc., 297 N.J. Super. 605 (App. Div. 1997).